CHIEF JUSTICE

John Jay

John Rutledge

Oliver Ellsworth

John Marshall

Roger Brooke Taney

Salmon Portland Chase

Morrison Remick Waite

Melville Weston Fuller

Edward Douglass White

William Howard Taft

Charles Evans Hughes

Harlan Fiske Stone

Fred M. Vinson

Earl Warren

Warren Earl Burger

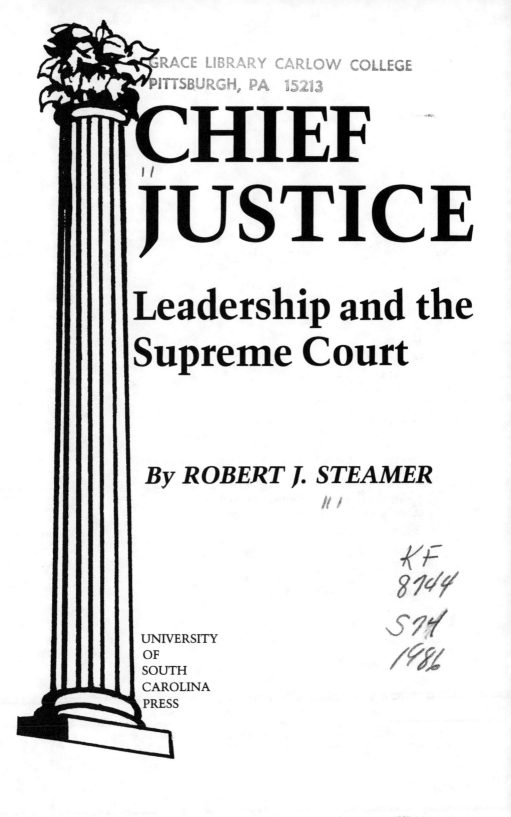

CHIEF JUSTICE

Leadership and the Supreme Court

By ROBERT J. STEAMER

UNIVERSITY
OF
SOUTH
CAROLINA
PRESS

Published in Columbia, South Carolina, by the
University of South Carolina Press, 1986

FIRST EDITION

Manufactured in the United States of America

Library of Congress Cataloging-in-Publication Data

Steamer, Robert J.
    Chief justice.

    Includes bibliographies and index.
    1. Judges—United States—Biography. 2. United
States. Supreme Court—History. I. Title.
KF8744.S74 1968   347.73'2634'09   86-4331
ISBN 0-87249-482-9   347.30353409

To my sons,
Gregg and James

CONTENTS

PREFACE

THIS BOOK IS ABOUT the fifteen men who occupied the highly coveted office of Chief Justice of the United States. It is about leadership of a peculiar kind, partly political in nature but with dimensions and qualities that differ markedly from those associated with the American presidency.

Over the years the ways in which chief justices have expended their energies have depended upon each incumbent's perception of the office and of the duties he wished to emphasize. In a conference on the office of chief justice at the University of Virginia in 1982 Peter Fish detailed the duties of the chief justices under five headings: "Jurist/Presiding Officer," "Court Manager," "Court Defender," "Third Branch Chieftain," and "Statesman."[1] Jeffrey Morris, formerly a staff member in the Office of the Administrative Assistant to the Chief Justice divided the duties somewhat differently, suggesting the following: "Chairman of the Court," "Circuit Justice," "building manager," "Chief Justice of the United States," "titular head of the American Bar," "minor league diplomat," and "ceremonial symbol of justice or law."[2]

Regardless of how one outlines the duties of the chief justice there is complete agreement among Court observers that the job is one of relentless pressures and overwhelming demands. Although a chief justice today has numerous tasks to perform on a daily basis, he is expected to assume leadership in four areas. In each he exerts a special, personalized influence on public policy, but much of his work is done within a judicial framework with all the limits of custom and esoteric trappings that surround the Anglo-American legal tradition. Unlike the president whose power horizons are infinitely broad, the chief justice is confined to a relatively narrow path. His most important and obvious role is leader of the Supreme Court, but additionally he is: (1) head of the federal judicial system which consists of scores of trial and intermediate appellate courts staffed by hundreds of judges; (2) political lobbyist for legislation which will aid or improve the American judiciary; and (3) chief judicial officer of the United States, a ceremonial component which requires that he maintain the prestige of the office and foster continued public support for the Supreme Court.

In the latter posture the chief justice establishes a special relationship with bar associations, law schools, state judiciaries and the American public, each of which demands a commitment of valuable time to writing and delivering speeches at meetings, conferences and seminars. Since the end of the Civil War this has been an expanding role and it emphasizes the changing nature of the chief justiceship. John Marshall and Roger Brooke Taney, unlike Warren Burger, were not burdened with the task of presiding over the annual Judicial Conference of the United States or addressing law school faculties on the need for curricular improvement. Nor were they involved in sponsoring and defending legislation which would alter the Supreme Court's jurisdiction, increase the number of lower courts or add more judges to the federal judiciary. Activities in this latter role have continued to expand since the late nineteenth century.

The chief's duties as head of the federal judicial system and leader of the Supreme Court have been an integral part of the office from the beginning. Keeping the judicial establishment running efficiently and smoothly is accomplished by giving it a sense of direction and purpose, a task which the chief handles by personal contact, formal and informal, with the circuit and district judges. Always, of course, the lower courts are guided by the Supreme Court's decisions over which the chief has only modest control. In his primary role as leader of the Supreme Court a chief's success depends upon his ability to minimize friction among the justices and to maximize harmony and cohe-

sion by creating an atmosphere of collegiality and friendliness
while dispelling any doubts about who is in charge.

With the advent of research on the psychology of leadership,[3]
students of judicial behavior have suggested that the chief justice exercises different types of leadership, each possessing special characteristics and functions. He is first, a social leader
which essentially translates into personality and the ways in
which a chief relates to his colleagues, how he reacts to criticism, to tense situations, how his presence is perceived by the
group. Affability, warmth, friendliness, empathy, and humor are
the keys to successful social leadership.

Second is task leadership which D. Grier Stephenson has
wisely subdivided into managerial and intellectual. In addition
to keeping the docket up to date managerial leadership requires
that the chief use political acumen in guiding the conference,
assigning opinions and in knowing when to write the opinion of
the Court—for example, the strategic Hughes opinions in *Jones
and Laughlin* and *Blaisdell*, the Warren opinion in *Brown*—and
also that he have a sense of timing and a perspicacious assessment of the political and legal factors that must be taken into
account prior to the final deciding of a case.

Intellectual leadership is provided in two ways, at the conference and in the display of talent in writing opinions. David Danelski characterized the chief's performance at the conference as
"the matrix of leadership in the Court" for it is at this point that
the chief attempts to persuade his colleagues that his views of
the case and his doctrinal ideas ought to prevail. The extent to
which he is successful is, of course, a measure of his ability. His
stature is also enhanced if those opinions he chooses to write
have been carefully researched, are sharply reasoned, fluently
written and manifest an inner integrity that result in plausible
conclusions even if one disagrees with them.

My purpose in this study is to analyze the style and substance
of the chief justices who have managed the Supreme Court's
business and directed the judicial machinery of the nation. My
approach has been comparative rather than chronological, a
methodology which entailed the grouping of chiefs according to
the type of leadership that they provided, in each instance an
uneven amalgam of managerial dexterity, social adroitness, and
intellectual powers. In judging performance ranging from

"great" to "moderately successful" to "adequate," I have not taken
political persuasion—liberal, conservative, Republican, Democrat, etc.—into account, but I have tried to make assessments
based on the criteria I have outlined above and to give proxi-
mate answers to the following: How significant has each chief
justice been in determining the direction the American Constitution has taken? What are the qualities that have made some
chief justices great leaders? Why have some been mediocre in
spite of prior political success or demonstrated legal talent?
What is the relationship, if any, between judicial statesmanship
and legal craftsmanship? What has been the influence of chief
justices on constitutional interpretation and on the Supreme
Court as an institution?

Anyone familiar with the history of the Supreme Court is
quite aware that the greatest lawyers and the sharpest intellects
who have graced the high bench have generally not been chief
justices, that chiefs were frequently overshadowed by associates. Nevertheless, the chief justiceship is a constitutional office second in national authority and prestige only to the
president and is deserving of respect, deference, and attention.
Since the duties of the chief justice are undefined in the Constitution and only partially so in statutes, the incumbent of the office has been given carte blanche to use his personal talents,
whatever they may be, to add to the warp and woof of America's
never quite completed constitutional tapestry. "While the chief
justice has only one vote," wrote Charles Evans Hughes, "the
way in which the Court does its work gives him a special opportunity for leadership." I have attempted to provide a tentative answer to the question implied in Hughes' observation: How have
the occupants of the office taken advantage of that "special opportunity"?

NOTES

1. Peter Fish, *The Office of Chief Justice*, Charlottesville: White Burkett Miller
   Center, University of Virginia, 1984.
2. Ibid., pp. 168–69.
3. Particularly influential have been: R. Bales, *Interaction Process Analysis:
   A Method For the Study of Small Groups*, Cambridge, Mass.: Addison-
   Wesley (1950); Fred Fiedler, "A Contingency Model of Leadership

Preface

Effectiveness," 1 *Advances in Experimental Social Psychology* 149 (1964); David Danelski, "The Influence of the Chief Justice in the Decisional Process of the Supreme Court" in W. Murphy and C. H. Pritchett, *Courts, Judges and Politics*, New York: Random House (1979); Walter Murphy, "Courts As Small Groups," 79 *Harvard Law Review* 1556 (1966); and Walter Murphy, "Marshalling the Court: Leadership Bargaining and the Judicial Process", 29 *University of Chicago Law Review* 640 (1962).

ACKNOWLEDGMENTS

I WISH TO EXPRESS my appreciation to the Board of Project 87 for a major grant which enabled me to be free of university duties in order to devote full time to research and writing for a few months and to the Research Council of the University of Massachusetts at Boston, to former Dean Michael Riccards and Associate Dean Midori Hayashi, for underwriting travel for the purpose of reviewing the papers of some of the chief justices and associate justices of the Supreme Court. Paul Heffron, Acting Director of the Manuscript Division of Research Services at the Library of Congress was very helpful in directing me to the appropriate sources. I also wish to thank those students in American Constitutional Law who compiled the statistics on opinion assignments of some of the chief justices, particularly Carl Will, John Murray, and Tamami Ushiki.

I owe a considerable debt to Professor Glenn Abernathy of the University of South Carolina, to Professor David O'Brien of the University of Virginia, and to Louis Fisher of the Congressional Research Service at the Library of Congress, all of whom read the manuscript and made exceptionally valuable suggestions. I also wish to thank J. Lawrence Kelly who assisted in the final checking of the documentation, Mary Thornton of the University of Massachusetts, and Faye Burgoyne of the University of Exeter for transforming difficult handwriting into a typescript. To my wife, Jean, I owe the greatest debt of all for her patience, encouragement and sharply critical reading of the manuscript in various stages of its development.

Chief Justices Of The United States

John Jay	1789–1795
John Rutledge	1795
Oliver Ellsworth	1796–1800
John Marshall	1801–1835
Roger Brooke Taney	1836–1864
Salmon Portland Chase	1864–1873
Morrison Remick Waite	1874–1888
Melville Weston Fuller	1888–1910
Edward Douglass White	1910–1921
William Howard Taft	1921–1930
Charles Evans Hughes	1930–1941
Harlan Fiske Stone	1941–1946
Fred M. Vinson	1946–1953
Earl Warren	1953–1969
Warren Earl Burger	1969–

Chapter 1

THE OFFICE
OF CHIEF JUSTICE

IF A NOTICE WERE to appear in the help wanted section of *The New York Times* announcing a vacancy in the chief justiceship of the Supreme Court, the job description would read something like the following:

The primary duty will be to preside over an appellate tribunal which must scrutinize over 4,000 cases annually, and discreetly choose 150 from that number to hear on their merits and to dispose of by written opinion. Although the Chief Justice will be responsible for assigning the writing of opinions among eight associate justices, he will have no legal authority to discharge or take minimal disciplinary action against any of the associates for any reason whatsoever. If any of them is slothful, senile, abrasive or downright impossible, the Chief's ability to cope with such an exigency must depend solely on his powers of persuasion.

Other duties include: (1) chairman of the Judicial Conference of the United States, the governing body for the federal judicial system consisting of judges who represent the various federal courts; (2) chairman of the Federal Judicial Center, a research, training and planning arm of the federal judiciary whose seven-member board meets four times annually; (3) supervisor of the Administrative Office of U.S. Courts, the housekeeping agency which employs over 500 people; (4) chairman of the board of the Supreme Court Historical Society; and (5) membership on the Boards of Trustees of the National Gallery of Art, of the Hirshhorn Museum and Sculpture Garden, and of the Smithsonian Institution. In addition, some twenty congressional statutes authorize specific duties of the Chief as head of the Supreme Court and over thirty acts of Congress define duties related to the administration of the federal judiciary. The Chief also may be asked to perform extraordinary tasks either at home or abroad by the President of the United States.

4

Chief Justice

If a President of the United States is elected during the Chief's tenure, he will administer the oath of office, and if the President should be impeached, the Chief will preside over the trial.

Qualifications: Law degree desirable.
Experience in public office, any branch, state or federal desirable.

Salary: $104,700 per annum.

Perquisites: A staff of over a dozen including an administrative assistant, four law clerks, four secretaries, a chauffeur-driven limousine, and a messenger.

Under the regulation of the Department of Health and Human Services the announcement would end with the declaration, *An Equal Opportunity Employer,* but an applicant should be aware that the office has never been held by a woman, a black, an Asian, an Hispanic, a Slavic-American, an Italian-American, an Indian or an Eskimo. As a matter of fact, all but three of the previous occupants of the office had antecedents in the British Isles, with one of the three, John Jay, being of French derivation and the remaining two, Earl Warren and Warren Burger, having their origins in northern Europe.

If a similar announcement had appeared in the *New York Daily Advertiser* in 1789, it would have said simply:

Person wanted to preside over the newly created federal supreme court. Duties: traditional judicial; Qualifications: experience in legal matters. Salary: $4,000 per year. Perquisites: None.

For an office that today carries such overwhelming authority, responsibility, influence and prestige, it is worth noting that its beginnings were indeed humble. The Constitution mentions the title, Chief Justice, only once, and then not in Article III but in the impeachment clause of Article I, Section 3, with respect to the chief's presiding over the trial of a miscreant president. In the debates at the Convention, in *The Federalist* essays, and in the debates in the first Congress prior to the passage of the Judiciary Act of 1789, there is not so much as an allusion to the office of chief justice, let alone a discussion of its conceptual framework or a suggestion of its powers. In the Judiciary Act it-

self the only reference to the chief justice is in the specification
that the Supreme Court should consist of a "chief justice and
five associate justices." So what did the framers of the Constitution and of the Judiciary Act have in mind when they made reference to the "chief justice"? Apparently the general perception
was English with famous jurists like Coke, Holt, Hale, and
Mansfield being the obvious models. When President Washington was considering the appointment of the first chief, correspondence indicates that the head of the judiciary was referred
to variously as "Lord Chief Justice," "Chief Justice of the United
States," and "Chief Justice of the Supreme Court." In the milieu
of a rapidly developing democracy, the prefix "Lord" soon disappeared from the national vocabulary, but the current designation of the office, "Chief Justice of the United States," did not
appear officially until 1866 when the radical Congress petulantly
reduced the size of the Supreme Court from ten to seven.[1]

In 1869, when Congress increased the size of the Court to
nine, the language of the statute again referred to the "Chief Justice of the United States."[2] It was Salmon P. Chase who first
insisted on the broader title when he presided over the impeachment trial of President Andrew Johnson. The record reads: "The
court was organized on Thursday, the 5th day of March, the oath
being administered to the Chief Justice of the United States by
Associate Justice Nelson," and on each succeeding day of the
trial the record begins: "The Chief Justice of the United States
entered the Senate Chamber and took the chair."[3] However, it
was not until 1888 that a person was nominated, confirmed,
and commissioned as "Chief Justice of the United States."
Upon his selection of a successor to Morrison R. Waite, President Cleveland declared: "I nominate Melville W. Fuller, of Illinois, to be Chief Justice of the United States." The Senate
confirmed, and the commission was drawn in that form.[4]

What the office has become in terms of its prestige, its authority and its influence has depended in the main upon the innate
abilities and personal traits of the incumbents, although not to
be underestimated is the impact of the associate justices who by
a turn of fate happen to hold office during the tenure of the
chief, a matter over which most chiefs have minimal or no control. Unlike the presidency or the Congress the office of chief
justice has never been won by announcing one's candidacy and

Chief Justice

rarely by surreptitious self-seeking. With the exception of William Howard Taft those who have coveted the honor have not been successful; historically the office has sought the man. Even in the beginning when only the most prescient among our forebears could have predicted the powerful role the Supreme Court would assume in the American system, there were those who unsuccessfully pleaded their own cause. James Wilson wrote President Washington that he would not decline if the President saw fit to nominate him—a polite way of asking for the job—but Washington turned instead to his trusted friend and confidante, John Jay.[5] And always eager to accept the mantle of leadership if offered have been sitting associate justices, most of whom were left waiting in the wings—Story, McLean, Miller, Field, and in the modern day, Robert Jackson—to mention the more obvious contenders.

In the beginning the workload of the Supreme Court was meager, and whatever talents the pre-Marshall chiefs may have had were displayed for the most part in circuit duty. From 1789 to the opening of the Marshall regime in 1801, a total of eighty-six cases were entered on the docket of the Supreme Court, fifty-three of which were adjudicated on their merits. On the average, the justices wrote about one opinion per year. During his five years as chief, John Jay wrote only three opinions, whereas Oliver Ellsworth in his four years wrote eleven. Jay was absent for a year and a half on a diplomatic mission to England for the president and twice ran for governor of New York—the second time successfully, at which point he resigned from the chief justiceship. President Washington assumed that federal judges, like their English counterparts, were to be consulted on matters of state, and Chief Justice Jay was not only used in an advisory capacity, but also served officially on two administrative bodies with the secretaries of state and the treasury and the attorney general.[6] For Jay the office of the chief justice was neither estimable nor interesting and he forthrightly declined when he was asked to resume the post by President John Adams.

George Washington has the distinction of being the only president to see a chief justice resign (I distinguish here between resigning in order to undertake new duties and retiring because of one's age or physical infirmities). When Jay left the Court, the

The Office

president first appointed John Rutledge of South Carolina whom the Senate refused to confirm because of an intemperate speech he had delivered against the Jay Treaty. He served in an interim capacity for a few months but wrote only one opinion and left no mark on the office. Charles Warren suggests that the rejection of Rutledge was extremely important for the future of American constitutional law since, had he been confirmed, it is most unlikely that Adams would have appointed John Marshall upon Rutledge's death in 1800.[7] The nation's third chief justice was not the president's first choice. After the Rutledge rebuff in the Senate, Washington offered the position successively to Patrick Henry and to Associate Justice William Cushing, before naming Oliver Ellsworth of Connecticut. Ellsworth had been at the Convention of 1787 and had served in the first United States Senate where he had not only drafted the Judiciary Act of 1789 but had also been instrumental in shepherding it through Congress. But Ellsworth, like Jay, did not contribute the kind of leadership that would enhance the Supreme Court's authority and prestige, in part at least because of his poor health which was the cause of his missing several sessions. Nevertheless, to Ellsworth's everlasting credit he began to promote the writing of shorter opinions, and the trend toward eliminating *seriatim* opinions had set in as the number of decisions rendered *seriatim* declined while opinions by a single justice increased.

The Supreme Court's workload changed radically during the Marshall years with a concomitant increase in the output of the chief justice. There has been a considerable disparity, however, in the number of opinions the chiefs have authored since John Marshall was appointed in 1801. During his 34 years on the bench John Marshall wrote 539 opinions—only 6 of which were in dissent—for an average of 16 per year. This is particularly amazing since the Court met for only 3 months annually until 1827 and never for more than 5 months a year after that. Thus, John Marshall had ample time to spend with his wife Polly, to counsel with his ten children and to improve his quoits game with his Richmond friends and neighbors. Morrison Waite, however, holds the record for hard work. In 14 years he authored 908 opinions—23 in dissent—for a yearly average of 65. Of all the chiefs only Melville Fuller comes close to Waite's prodigious output with an average of 42 per year. No associate justice, including the energetic and prolific William O. Douglas in our own time, ever averaged more than 40 opinions annually. Comparing the chief justices of the post-World War II period, we note that Fred Vinson averaged only 13 opinions per year, the second lowest since 1801, Roger Brooke Taney holding that record with 10. What stands out, however, is Earl Warren's record of only 14 per term compared to Warren Burger's present average of 33.

If dissents by the chief justice tell us something about the chief's leadership, Stone's record is the worst, he having been in disagreement with his own Court almost half the time. Marshall comes out the best in this respect with only 6 dissents, and Taft a close second with 2 written dissents and 17 without opinion. It is also surprising that Earl Warren dissented either with or without opinion about a quarter of the time and Warren Burger, up until now at least, about 20 percent of the time. The fact that the chief cannot "mass the Court," in Taft's phrase, may suggest an inability to lead intellectually. However, the chief is always a prisoner of the times in the sense that some issues are so controversial—affirmative action, abortion, integration of the schools through busing, capital punishment—that the most charismatic leader in the nation could not persuade eight independent colleagues to adopt a single view. In recent years, in fact, it has become increasingly difficult to produce a maximum of two statements of the law, a majority grouping and a dissent, let alone one. From the time that John Marshall regularized the practice of writing a single opinion of the Court in 1801 to 1956 the justices produced only 45 plurality opinions. But from 1956 to 1980 the Court rendered 101 such opinions in which there was no precise statement of the law.[8] The salient fact remains that if an associate justice chooses not to follow the chief's lead, the chief has no power to coerce. Persuasion is all, and with some people it will not work.

In viewing the appointment and tenure of the fifteen chiefs one is struck by the role that fate and accident play in history and by the brevity and continuity of the American experience. With respect to the latter we note that Taney was twelve-years-old when George Washington was inaugurated; Hughes had already been born when Taney died; and the present chief was in his thirties when Hughes died. Thus, the lives of three chiefs

span the entire period under the Constitution, a period unsurpassed in human history for technological and social change.
With respect to fate and accident, we note with certainty that
one-third of the chiefs were not the president's first choice. Marshall and Fuller were second choices, Ellsworth a third, and
Waite the seventh. Chase was Lincoln's first nominee, chosen
with little enthusiasm, for Lincoln was reputed to have said
that he "would rather have swallowed his buckhorn chair than
to have nominated Chase." All were in consideration with others prior to being chosen. As we pointed out earlier, had Rutledge been confirmed by the Senate, it is doubtful that Marshall
would have had the opportunity to serve, and had circumstances not forced President Lyndon Johnson to withdraw the
nomination of Abe Fortas, the present chief might still be sitting on the Court of Appeals for the District of Columbia.

LEADERSHIP ROLES OF THE CHIEF JUSTICE

Of all the powerful offices designated in the Constitution
that of the chief justice is the least explicit in its grant of powers, and unlike the articles dealing with the presidency, the Senate and the House, the clauses are totally silent on the matter of
qualifications for appointment to the office. Once a nominee
has been confirmed and has taken the oath of office (two oaths
actually)[9] that broad constitutional phrase "good behavior" is
the only qualification for remaining chief justice for life. Since
John Marshall's day only three chiefs, Taft, Hughes and Warren,
chose to live for a few years in retirement rather than die in office. Taft maintained that he preferred being chief justice to being president, said in fact that he would rather have been John
Marshall than George Washington.[10] Felix Frankfurter, in his
witty, whimsical and wise informal talk at the University of
Virginia in 1953 declared in discussing John Jay that today "only
a madman, a certified madman would resign the chief justiceship to become governor,"[11] and he might have added "or president." Depending upon the grace of God, the term of office is
much longer than any other in the government and that in itself
is the source of some of its power and authority. Of the fifteen
chiefs only five served fewer years than those presidents elected
to two terms, and that group includes Jay, Rutledge and Ells-

Chief Justice

worth. Since 1801 only two, Stone and Vinson, served less than eight years, but even they presided over the Court beyond a single presidential term.[12] Long tenure is not in itself enough to establish a reputation for leadership or legal craftsmanship nor does a brief tenure necessarily preclude it. Adequate but undistinguished was the twenty-two-year chief justiceship of Melville Fuller, whereas the eleven-year reign of Charles Evans Hughes was one of the high points of the Supreme Court's history. Nevertheless, the fact that a chief has no specified time limit on his service is an important, albeit not the most important, factor in his ability to exert leadership.

It has been almost routinely accepted protocol among the scholarly fraternity of Court watchers to refer to the chief justice as *primus inter pares*,[13] first among equals, but is this really so? The chief justice has always had certain prerogatives not available to the associates, but the *primus inter pares* concept more nearly approximates the truth prior to the incumbency of William Howard Taft, and it has become totally inappropriate since the time of Charles Evans Hughes. There is considerably more than a mere technical distinction between the titles "Chief Justice of the Supreme Court" and "Chief Justice of the United States." Although a subtle and almost imperceptible transition from the former to the latter was underway from the beginning, the chief justices from Jay to White were primarily, almost exclusively, engaged in deciding cases and administering the peripheral processes surrounding the making of decisions. John Jay, perhaps lacking in vision after having served as chief, was nevertheless convinced as he wrote President Adams declining the second offer of the chief justiceship, "that under a system so defective [the Supreme Court] would not obtain the energy, weight and dignity which was essential to its affording due support to the national government."[14] And the *Aurora* commenting upon the office in 1801 declared: "That the Chief Justiceship is a sinecure need no other evidence than that in one case the duties were discharged by one person who resided at the same time in England and by another during a year's residence in France."[15] From 1789 to 1801 the chief was little more than a part-time judge with a very imposing title.

After more than three score years of superb leadership under Marshall and Taney, Chief Justice Chase would still say that the chief "is but one of eight judges, each of whom has the same powers as himself. His judgement has no more weight, and his vote no more importance, than those of any of his brethren. He presides, and a good deal of extra labor is thrown upon him. That's all."[16] Chase was the first and only chief to exercise the constitutional duty of presiding over the impeachment trial of a president, a task which alone gives credence to the proposition that the chief is not simply one of nine, and yet, in spite of the initial statutory designation in 1866, the office had not yet become that of the national judicial leader, of "Chief Justice of the United States." Nor did it become so under Chase's immediate successors, Waite, Fuller and White, all of whom presided over the Court efficiently and with dignity. Waite and White lacked the political interest in expanding the role of the chief, in part because that role as it existed was already more than a full-time job. Fuller, however, saw the need to pressure congressional leadership if the Court were to obtain relief from an overcrowded docket.

Judicial business increased markedly after the Civil War, and it became more and more difficult for the Supreme Court to keep up with the case load. During the first sixty years of the Court's history the output in majority opinions ranged from zero during some of the pre-Marshall years when business was minimal and no discernible majority opinion existed, to a high of 94 in 1851. When Marshall died in 1835 the Court had decided an average of 31 cases per term. Between 1835 and 1868, the rate went to 64 per term and from 1868 to 1900 the number almost quadrupled to 232 decisions per term.[17] Under Chief Justices Chase and Waite the Court was extremely hard-working, increasing the number of cases decided each term to almost 200 under Chase and to slightly less than 300 under Waite's direction.[18] But the sad fact is that when Fuller was appointed in 1888 the Court was in arrears by 1571 cases, a three-year backlog, and by 1890 the Court was facing no less than 1816 cases.

Something more was needed from a chief justice than simply acting as presiding officer of the Supreme Court, namely, the taking on of a political role in order to persuade Congress to authorize a streamlining of the caseload. Fuller began to assume such a role when, in January 1890, he gave a dinner in honor of David J. Brewer to celebrate his appointment to the Court; and along with his fellow justices, he invited several prominent Senators: Edmunds, Evans, Hoar, George, Ingalls, Vest and Pugh. Within a few weeks the Judiciary Committee of the Senate, of which Fuller's senatorial guests were members, sent the chief justice a compendium of all the previously proposed measures dealing with the Supreme Court and suggested that the committee would be willing to entertain the views of the justices. For better than a decade various proposals had been offered in Congress to relieve the Supreme Court's congested docket,[19] and eventually the entire Fuller bench concurred in a report prepared by Justice Horace Gray which urged the establishment of a court of patent appeals and the creation of intermediate courts of appeals between the federal trial courts and the Supreme Court.

As a result of Fuller's careful planning, Congress enacted the Circuit Court of Appeals Act of 1891 the centerpiece of which was the creation of new courts of appeals for each of the existing nine judicial circuits covering the United States, and temporarily at least, the Act did what it was supposed to do. In 1890 just prior to the Act's passage the Court received 623 new cases, but by 1892 the number of new appeals had diminished to 290.

Additional action was needed, however, to stem the tide of appeals to the Supreme Court. Chief Justice White whose special province lay in legal procedure simply tried to refuse to hear cases that were only marginally within the Court's jurisdiction rather than engage in political activities which might bring statutory relief. White's skill in finding reasons why the Court should not hear a case became famous, and the brethren gratefully accepted his sometimes tortured reasoning as a legitimate means of lightening the workload. Nevertheless, when Taft took over the Court in 1921 it was still far behind in its calendar. When the Supreme Court adjourned prior to Taft's appointment in June 1921, there were 343 undisposed cases.

Seven months later the number had increased to 516, and when the Court opened the October term in 1925 the backlog had increased to 533. In spite of Taft's constant pressure on his colleagues, they were unable to decongest the docket, and it was under these conditions that the leadership role of the chief took on a much broader posture. As a direct result of Taft's efforts Congress enacted two major pieces of legislation dealing with the federal judicial system, one in 1922, the other in 1925. The first, in addition to creating more judges for the lower courts, gave the federal judicial system a sense of direction and a much needed administrative unity by creating the Conference of Senior Circuit Judges to advise Congress on legislation governing the judiciary and to promote effective standards of judicial administration in the lower federal courts. The second, the Judiciary Act of 1925, streamlined the entire method of appeals. Under its terms most decisions of the federal courts of appeals and of the state appellate courts were now reviewable in the Supreme Court only by a writ of *certiorari*, a writ by which the Court would have broad discretion to decide which cases should have a full hearing. The Court was now able to conserve its time for handling cases of national significance.

More important for our purposes, however, is the effect of the two laws on the chief justiceship. By giving the Court almost complete control over its own docket, the 1925 law added a dimension of internal strength to the chief that he might, depending upon his personal powers of persuasion, provide that margin of leadership that would determine which controversies were to receive a full hearing and be decided by full opinion. But to return to our main point, the expansion of the chief's role from a presiding officer over the Supreme Court to a true head of the judiciary came with the Act of 1922. Although the establishment of the Conference of Senior Circuit Judges "constituted only a first step toward a more integrated administrative system," it "created an institutional framework with administrative leadership and informal responsibility lodged in the Chief Justice and the presiding officers of the intermediate appellate courts."[20] But if William Howard Taft became the first *Chief Justice of the United States* in substance, his duties in comparison to the modern-day chief were minimal.

Since 1922 Congress has authorized creation of the Judicial Conference of the United States, the outgrowth of Taft's original brainchild, which is essentially a board of directors for the federal judicial system with the chief justice as its "chairman of the board";[21] the Administrative Office of U.S. Courts (1939), the housekeeping agency for the federal court system; and the Federal Judicial Center, a research, training and planning arm of the federal judiciary, of which the chief justice is chairman. The

Chief Justice

most recent innovation is the Supreme Court Historical Society, a nonprofit organization conceived by Chief Justice Burger to enhance public knowledge of and interest in the Supreme Court. The chief is designated honorary chairman of the board of the latter organization, but the title adds one more dimension to his national stature as does his membership on the Board of Regents of the Smithsonian Institution and on the Board of Trustees of the National Gallery and Hirshhorn Museum.

As the duties of the chief justice have expanded in the past three-quarters of a century they have become almost overwhelming. The office is manageable, of course, with help; and like the rest of Washington, the Court has built its own bureaucracy. In part at least the changes in the Court's professional housing have been responsible for the necessity of additional staff support. It was not until 1810 that the Court had any permanent home, and even then the chief had virtually no responsibilities for maintaining the quarters.

The first Supreme Court met in the Royal Exchange Building at the intersection of Broad and Water streets in New York City in what is now the nation's leading financial district. When the capital was moved to Philadelphia in 1791, the Court, along with the state and municipal courts, met in the newly constructed city hall, and with the final location of the central government in Washington in 1800 it occupied temporary quarters first in the east basement of the Capitol, then in the library formerly occupied by the House of Representatives. The latter became so inconvenient and so cold that at one point the Court sat in Long's Tavern on First Street, S.E., where the Library of Congress now stands. Beginning in 1810, it sat for forty years in a room especially designed for it in the basement below the new Senate chamber, although it had to move to temporary quarters between 1814 and 1819 after the British burned the Capitol, allegedly having started the fire with Supreme Court documents.

In 1860 the Court for the first time occupied quarters in the old Senate chamber which, while still inadequate, seemed commodious compared to what it had been allocated in the past. In addition to the courtroom the justices now had a robing room, a conference room (also serving as a library) and a dozen odd anterooms for office space and storage, although none of the brethren had individual offices. Nevertheless, they remained in the

The Office

old Senate chamber until October 7, 1935, when the Court held its first session in the present "Marble Palace." It was at that point that the chief justice had an entire building to worry about but with the expansion of quarters came an increase in supporting personnel.

Chief Justices Marshall and Taney were responsible for the caliber of the work of only two people: the clerk of the Court and the reporter of decisions, and partially responsible for a third, the marshal of the Court. The latter two offices began informally. Alexander J. Dallas, the first reporter, undertook to report Supreme Court decisions as a public service; the second, William Cranch reported the decisions while sitting on the circuit court in Washington. In 1816 Congress formally recognized the position of court reporter by providing for the publication of court decisions and, in 1817, by fixing the reporter's salary. Henry Wheaton was the first occupant officially appointed by the Supreme Court itself. The post of marshal of the Court was not formally established by law until 1867, although beginning in 1794 the marshal for the District of Columbia also served in that capacity for the Supreme Court.

Established by a rule of the Court in 1790, the office of clerk has from the beginning been the Court's leading administrative arm, and through the years the clerk's duties have increased in tandem with the chief's. The clerk's office, now consisting of more than thirty people, has a computerized information service to help it perform its myriad duties. A new post, Supreme Court librarian, was created in 1887, initially as a part of the marshal's department. It became a separate office in 1948. That now indispensable adjunct of every justice, the law clerk, did not become institutionalized until 1886 when Congress provided $1,600 per year for a stenographic clerk for each justice. Actually the first law clerk was hired in 1882 by Justice Horace Gray who paid the clerk's salary out of his own pocket. The present chief justice has four clerks, an administrative assistant, four secretaries, a messenger and a chauffeur.

In this day of the mass media and insistence on speedy communication of governmental activities to the public, it was inevitable and desirable that the Court have its own public spokesman. Congress authorized the creation of the office of public information officer in 1935 and the way in which such an

Chief Justice

office is handled is very much the concern of any chief justice who knows the value of public relations. In 1972, 1973, and 1974 three new offices, the administrative assistant to the chief justice, the legal office, and the curator's office were added to the Court staff. The legal office is composed of two attorneys who assist the Court with procedural questions arising out of petitions for *certiorari* and applications for extraordinary relief; the curator maintains the Court's historical collection, develops exhibits which brighten the decor in the building as well as highlight the historical significance of the Court, and answers questions from the public concerning the Court's history.

In his role as chief executive of one of the three coequal branches of the government the modern chief justice must inevitably deal with a budget and with the general procedural efficiency of the federal court system. In fiscal 1986 the Supreme Court requested upwards of $17 million, the bulk of which will pay the salaries of over 300 employees as well as those of the nine justices. The remainder takes care of the building and grounds, printing and miscellaneous expenses such as books for the Supreme Court library. It is, incidentally, a relatively small sum compared to the $115 million requested by the executive office of the president and the excess of one billion dollars appropriated annually for the congressional bureaucracy since 1980.

Chief Justice Taft's incumbency marks the point at which the office made the transition from presiding officer of the Court to substantive head of the third branch of government, and yet if we view Taft's schedule, it would appear that even the most energetic of men could not absorb any additional duties. Taft once said: "I am never free from the burden of feeling that whenever I attempt to do anything else I am taking time from my judicial work. The exhausting character of it everyone testifies to."[22] Taft rose daily at 5:15 A.M. and began work promptly at 6:00 o'clock. He breakfasted at 8:00 and then worked for just under two hours before walking to the Capitol. After the Court closed at 4:30 P.M. he worked until 10:00 with an hour out for dinner at 7:00. And this schedule was devoted almost exclusively to presiding over the Court and writing his share of opinions.

In his memoirs Earl Warren gives us some insight into the demanding schedule of the modern day chief. Warren wrote:

The Office

We accepted practically no invitations to private homes because that called for reciprocation, and that would crowd our evenings and so could not be accommodated to my work. I worked almost every night to some extent, even on nights when we attended a White House or embassy dinner. Even at that pace, I never felt that I was abreast of my reading. I am not a fast reader of important materials, and the amount of such reading at the Court is colossal. When I first came to Washington I wondered how I would ever get through it. At that time the Court met at noon, recessed for lunch for thirty minutes at 2:00 P.M. and then sat until 4:30. This was the procedure Monday through Friday while hearing the cases argued. Then on Saturday morning at ten o'clock, we would convene in conference and, with the exception of thirty minutes for lunch, would continue until our work was completed—until five, six, or even seven o'clock.[23]

Warren went on to say that the schedule was "backbreaking" since his morning hours were occupied with administrative tasks—management of the Court, coordinator of the Judicial Conference, the incidental activities connected with his duties on the Smithsonian and National Gallery boards. The time that was left was used to confer with his law clerks, write his opinions and prepare for the oncoming cases. His practice was to take home briefs and memoranda every night and he generally read until midnight. He awakened at 7:00 A.M., read until 8:30 and left for the Court at 9:30. Leaving later in the morning made sense since the drive at 9:30 took fifteen minutes whereas between 7:00 and 9:00 the intolerable urban traffic in Pierre L'Enfant's beautifully designed city for anything but automobiles took a minimum of forty-five minutes.[24] In his sixteen years as chief, Warren missed only one business day at the Court, and on that day he was too sick with the flu to get out of bed. He did eliminate the Saturday conference by persuading the brethren to move it to Friday afternoon, but he was a confirmed Saturday morning worker and he appeared at his office regularly on Saturdays in order to tie up loose ends and to reflect upon the momentous issues before the Court.[25]

To be a successful chief justice today, successful in the sense of managing the Court's business with some degree of efficiency, one must adhere to Hughes' dictum that "Life is only work, then more work, and then more work." It has been said of Hughes that he "early became an exponent of the theory that the Lord created Sunday so that there would be one day in the week when a man could work with relatively little interruption from telephone calls."[26]

And Chief Justice Burger, in spite of his expanded staff, adheres to a schedule to which the ghost of Hughes must be giving smiling approval. When working on the famous Nixon tapes case he appeared at the Court forty-two consecutive days without a break, and one of his weeks was clocked at ninety-two hours.[27] No chief has had more energy nor labored more intensely than Warren Burger. There is unanimous agreement among all who observe him closely on a day-to-day basis that no one in the Supreme Court building from janitor to justice surpasses him in sheer energy. One may question the way in which he allocates his time but never the fact of his thorough dedication to the performance of his duties as he sees them.

SOCIAL AND POLITICAL LEADERSHIP

As late as 1930 Justice Stone could quip: "being Chief Justice of the Supreme Court is a good deal like being Dean of the law school—he has to do the things that the janitor will not do."[28] There is, of course, a sardonic element of truth in Stone's humorous lament, and it also reveals a weakness in Stone's chief justiceship that prevented him from being a successful leader in the political and social roles that a chief must assume both internally and externally. Whether the chief is dealing with his colleagues on the bench, foreign dignitaries, congressional leaders, the president, lower court judges, or the American Bar Association, he must do so with political acumen and social grace if he is to retain the respect of the groups and individuals with whom he has professional and personal relations.

Decision making by the Court aside for the moment, the ways in which the chief conducts himself with the brethren is a crucial factor in establishing and retaining his authority. Under John Marshall the Court was as socially cohesive as it would ever be, due in no small part to the Chief's engaging personality, but due as well to size—only six instead of nine—and probably

The Office

most important, to the practice of living together in a rooming-house while the Court was in session. The latter practice would hardly have fitted the second half of the nineteenth century, let alone the twentieth. It is difficult to imagine the brethren living in close proximity under one roof and taking their meals together for nine or ten months rather than six to ten weeks. During the turbulent years when Vinson was chief, a law clerk once characterized the Court as "nine scorpions in a bottle" and then as now, they saw each other almost exclusively during business hours and at ceremonial functions. Actually the practice of the justices living together during the term disappeared with the accession of Taney to the office of chief and was therefore a peculiar feature of the Marshall era.

Chief justices, like all leaders, lead through "instinct, knowledge, persuasion, intelligence, craft, example, patience, inspiration and compromise,"[29] but given the intimacy and size of the group which they are presumed to lead, in order to be successful they must always be alert to the necessity of maintaining the highest possible degree of social affability among the justices. And being a "nice guy" is not enough although it helps. The chief must have a constant concern for the well-being of his colleagues and he must show it in his every act.

Earl Warren instinctively watched over the Court like a shepherd his flock, and his natural decency in human relationships was a major factor in his ability to retain the goodwill of the brethren throughout his tenure as chief justice. For example, he tried for several years to persuade Congress to appropriate money for cars and drivers for each of the justices since he believed the pressures on the Court were so great that Frankfurter at seventy and Reed, Black, Burton, Minton, and Jackson in their sixties should not, as drivers, be subjected to the traffic congestion of Washington. He was aware that Murphy and Rutledge had died of heart attacks in their fifties, and he saw Jackson succumb to the same malady during his first years in office. Warren failed to obtain the cars, but his efforts were appreciated. In Warren's words: "The Subcommittee of the House, at the insistence of its dictatorial and revengeful chairman, John J. Rooney of Brooklyn, each time rejected the request with a cutting jibe until the Justices finally suggested that I save the Court embarrassment by forgetting it."[30]

Chief Justice

There are always what we tend to call the "little things" which every chief must handle with care if he is to retain a rapport with his colleagues. What does the chief do when a justice is in the hospital and yet seems willing to do his share of the work? When Justice Douglas was ill for a period in 1947 the recently appointed Vinson reacted with an appropriate letter:[31]

Dear Bill:

Received your note relative to No. 715, State of Oklahoma vs. the United States.

I also have your note of the 11th, insisting on some more work. I am saving some cases without assignment, but with the understanding that they will be ready for you if you are ready for them. Actually, old-timer, I hesitate to assign any cases to you for a week or so until you are dead certain that you can do it without the slightest danger from it. So, hold your horses and get well. That bug innervates, and not a one of the Brethren wants to retard your speedy recovery.

Missed you at Tom Clark's party, and Mildred didn't act like she was having a good time at all.

Harold [Burton] did a good job for you on the rate case.

Felix [Frankfurter] has a re-arrangement of his dissent in Craig v. Harney, and it ought to be ready shortly.

The Island of Palmyra has been the center of a lot of good natured raillery towards Stanley [Reed]. We would say that he needs you to back-stand him as his other adherents are pretty quiet.

So, again, hold your horses, and get back in trim. If you are in fit form, we will enter you for the home stretch; otherwise, you will not even get to the paddock.

Affectionately,

Fred

An even-handed approach by the chief to whatever perquisites the justices are entitled is essential if he is to avoid the charge of arbitrariness or favoritism. Any rupture in personal relationships with the justices simply produces an irritant that unnecessarily complicates the main task of deciding cases. When Justice Reed retired in 1957 Justice Frankfurter advised Warren that he would prefer Reed's office to his own. Warren agreed but not before consulting Justice Black who was senior to Frankfurter. He then wrote the remaining justices indicating that he had assigned Reed's quarters to Frankfurter, adding: "Unless one of you wishes to move into the rooms vacated by Justice Frankfurter, that suite will be assigned to the new Justice."[32] This concern for fairness and an understanding of the universal human desire to be consulted and informed by the person in charge was typical of Earl Warren's style. His sensitive use of power was a significant factor in preserving his authority.

Internally, there are the professional and official functions for which the chief is responsible, and again, the manner in which he handles such matters as visiting dignitaries, permits the use of the Court's facilities for social affairs or how he makes certain that the justices are in attendance at ceremonial rituals such as presidential inaugurations or funerals of public figures, all of these "little things" are in various ways determinants of the effectiveness of his role as leader. When Charles Evans Hughes was chief, the justices were informed of a meeting with President Roosevelt on September 30, 1939, by a memorandum from the marshal's office which read:

> By direction of the Chief Justice, the Marshal circulates the following memorandum:
>
> The President will receive the Court at the White House at 5:00 o'clock, Monday afternoon, October 2nd.
> The Court will assemble in the Blue Room of the White House at 4:55.
> By direction of the Chief Justice, the Attorney-General and the Solicitor-General have been invited to accompany the Court.[33]

Under the austere and authoritative Hughes the memorandum read "by direction of the Chief Justice," language which seems in keeping with Hughes' general demeanor and which the brethren found no cause to resent. Vinson or Warren would more likely have "requested" rather than "directed." But even Hughes, with all his radiation of authority, could not control the irascible McReynolds who, in the oft-told story, once said to a messenger sent by Hughes: "Tell the Chief Justice that I don't work for him." He was right, of course, the justices do not work for the chief. On the other hand, they are not precisely his equal either as the foregoing makes clear.

How the chiefs react to external pressures depends in part upon the political climate of their times, in part upon the institutional needs of the judiciary, in part upon the chief's personal predilections. We have pointed out that Fuller and Taft were responsible lobbyists for congressional action which ultimately resulted in the Court's acquiring greater control over its docket, and every chief since Taft to a greater or lesser degree has had some influence in persuading Congress to modernize and reform the judicial branch. Such activities have embraced everything from increasing the number of judges in the district and appellate courts—a periodic necessity if the federal courts are to handle with dispatch the increasing number of cases resulting from population growth and emerging novel areas of litigation—to major procedural reforms. The Judiciary Acts of 1891 and 1925 are the most notable examples of the latter and of successful political pressures being applied by chiefs on the legislative branch.

For several years Chief Justice Burger has been urging Congress to create a new "National Court of Appeals" as an intermediate tribunal between the circuit courts of appeals and the Supreme Court.[34] Unlike earlier landmark reforms the chief's proposal does not have the full support either of the supreme bench or of the bar. It has, in fact, engendered somewhat bitter controversy and it is by no means certain that it will ever attract enough legislative support to ensure its passage.

Taking his cue from executive reorganization, Burger has also proposed that Congress authorize the Judicial Conference to create judgeships as they are needed, subject to a congressional veto. Less emotion-laden than the idea of a national court of appeals, this proposal would be similar although not identical to what presidents may already do in the executive branch. However, in 1983 Burger spoke for the Court in *Chadha* v. *United States* in an opinion which, while technically invalidating a permissive veto by one house of Congress over an executive act, cast doubt on the constitutionality of any congressional veto. This is a contradiction, perhaps even a repudiation, of his earlier stand.

The Office

When the Court comes under attack from external forces, the chief's reaction may be the determining factor in protecting the independence and integrity of the institution whether the onslaught comes from the president, members of Congress or private groups who are disenchanted with the work of one or more of the justices. Chief Justice Hughes played this role to perfection when, with dignity and decorum, he made certain that Franklin Roosevelt's plan to increase the size of the Court from nine to fifteen would never become law. It was common knowledge that the president wished to appoint additional justices who would not frustrate his social and economic reforms, but the president's justification for altering the Court's size was that the superannuated justices who would not retire were unable to keep up with the docket. In a masterful letter which Senator Burton K. Wheeler of Montana read to the Senate Judiciary Committee, Hughes refuted Roosevelt point by point. He outmaneuvered the president and thus checked the most aggressive and crassly political attack ever made on the Supreme Court by a president.

During the immediate post-Civil War years when Chase was chief, Congress was reasonably successful in its manipulation of the Court, and Chief Justice Chase acquiesced in silence as the Congress first reduced its size from ten to seven, then increased it to nine solely for political reasons. Similarly, in the famous *McCardle Case*[35] Chase wrote for a unanimous Court upholding the power of Congress to withdraw jurisdiction of a case on which oral arguments had been heard. Admittedly, it would have been suicidal for Chase to take on the radical Congress frontally, but pleading *nolo contendere* hardly added lustre to Chase's reputation or authority to the office of chief justice. In all fairness it should be noted that even the great Marshall in his one chance to make a public defense of an independent judiciary failed miserably. When he appeared as a witness in the impeachment trial of Associate Justice Samuel Chase in February 1805 he seemed to be frightened.[36] A Federalist senator, hardly sympathetic to the Jeffersonian attempts to control the judiciary, said that the "Chief Justice really discovered too much caution—too much fear—too much cunning. He ought to have been more bold—frank [and] explicit than he was."[37] The

acquittal of Chase was essential to the maintenance of the independence of the Supreme Court, and yet, as Justice Rehnquist
suggests, "the chief justice of the Supreme Court decided to
hunker down before the political storm that appeared to be
brewing."[38] Perhaps wisely so, given the times; nevertheless, a
chief's conduct in public when the Court is under siege is an important ingredient of the final mix that determines the quality
of the chief's leadership. Not every chief has been tested in this
respect but the record of those who have is not one of untar-
nished valor.

JUDICIAL LEADERSHIP

Up until now we have been discussing what are basically ancillary roles to the chief's main function which is to lead the
Court in deciding cases. Since cases are decided by a vote of the
justices, the chief's role in the process of arriving at the final decision is the crucial factor in determining whether he leads the
Court, whether he is pulled into a majoritarian mainstream by
others, or whether he votes against a majority which he cannot
command. Clearly the office of chief justice "contains an internal political dimension with which each occupant is forced to
come to terms,"[39] internal politics being defined as knowing
when to press one's advantage, when to compromise, and how
to maximize administrative authority while minimizing the
elation that comes with success. While forced to deal with all
the personal antagonisms, petty differences, human frailties,
egos and conceits of his colleagues, the chief attempts to present a face to the public that conveys a collective image of harmony, statesmanship and wisdom. Moreover the chief expects
to convince not only the litigants but the American people that
what the Court collectively decides is ethically and morally
sound and legally correct, that the Court is not only conforming
to the Constitution but is in tune with transcendent justice.
Only unanimity can convey this perfectly, and while unanimity
is not unusual, it is not the norm. Thus, a chief is performing
reasonably well if he can persuade a majority to join him most
of the time and particularly in those cases which have strong
implications for national public policies.

John Marshall and, to a lesser extent, William Howard Taft were able to approximate the ideal, partly through fortuitous circumstances and partly through the influence of their own personalities, but no other has been able to carry the entire Court with him more than a small fraction of the time in the major cases. Recent examples of brilliant successes were the unanimous decisions in the desegregation cases under Warren and in the Nixon tapes case under Burger, both of which were politically explosive. The decisions would have lost much of their authority had there been dissenting opinions around which the opposition might have rallied. Such was the case, incidentally, in the reapportionment and abortion decisions in which strong dissents detracted from the binding force of the majority opinions. In most instances, a case does not involve a question of absolute justice or absolute injustice; nevertheless, there are times when the moral rightness of a decision is at issue and it is always left in doubt when the members of the Court of last resort cannot agree on the result.

As we all know, however, many difficult and complex issues confronting the nation reach the Supreme Court because strong differences of opinion have prevented them from being settled elsewhere, and opinion among the justices usually reflects public division. Thus, a chief will obtain unanimity at a cost, and for some the political gain is not worth the judicial loss. If the final opinion is the result of a negotiated settlement, it is bound to be somewhat opaque and lacking in clarity and precision.[40] Often to obtain unanimity or even near unanimity the chief must spend much precious time and energy in cajoling his colleagues as some chiefs have or, like Hughes, join the majority even when in disagreement with it.[41] But for those occasional crucial policy-reversing or politically oriented cases, the attainment of unanimity may be worth the loss of a fine-tuned legal opinion and of legal and linguistic clarity. Although some cases come to the Supreme Court on automatic appeal[42] and a few others by statutorily permissive routes,[43] over 90 percent of the Court's business arrives on writs of *certiorari*, or "certs" in the language of the inner fraternity of lawyers and judges.

The petitions for *certiorari* are of two types: those for which the costs of lawyers and filing fees have been paid by the litigants and those which are filed *in forma pauperis,* a procedure by which indigent persons, by taking an oath of poverty, may come into the Court without paying expenses. In the latter instance, the cost is born by Congress, but originally expenses were met from the fees paid by lawyers for the privilege of practicing before the Supreme Court. Until 1970 *certiorari* petitions were divided into the Miscellaneous docket, essentially for *in forma pauperis* requests and the Appellate docket for those who were paying the bills. In 1970 the Miscellaneous docket was abolished and the clerk's office began to report the number of *in forma pauperis* cases filed as a separate category now called the 5000 series. Both among those who pay and more generally among those who do not, there are many frivolous requests, and equally important with deciding the some 150 cases each year by written opinion is winnowing out the chaff from the 4000 to 5000 cases filed. Many are dismissed, some are affirmed or reversed without opinion, and the remainder are accepted for oral argument.

Until the appointment of Associate Justice Powell to the Court the cases on the Appellate (paid) docket were circulated among the justices for their consideration, and those on the Miscellaneous (unpaid) docket were sent to the chief justice's office where copies were made and sent to each individual justice. After studying the cases and reading at least some of the memoranda written by their law clerks, each justice informed the chief justice which of the 80 to 90 petitions merited extended consideration, and the chief then set the agenda for the conference. If no justice suggested a case for further discussion, it was placed on the "dead list" which meant that the chief would read the title of the case at the conference in order to make certain that no justice wished to reconsider his original decision, and if there were no response, the case would be set for dismissal.

Under Justice Powell's system the chief's role remains unchanged, but at Powell's suggestion a pool has been established to sift through *certiorari* petitions, and although only five justices—Blackmun, White, Rehnquist, Burger and O'Connor—have joined Powell's arrangement, the system has lightened the workload, not so much of the justices who still must look at the materials in each case, but of the law clerks who have more time for research.[44]

The Office

Unquestionably the fate of an individual hangs in the balance in each of the cases reaching the Court, and in the minds of some observers no cases should be regarded as trivial.[45] But as more than one chief has pointed out, litigants have already had their rights protected by one appellate review on the state level, and the Supreme Court must continue to decide those cases in which broad questions of national policy and constitutional law are at stake, cases which will have an impact far beyond the immediate facts of a specific dispute.[46]

Central to the decision making of the Supreme Court is the conference, a weekly meeting normally lasting from two to four hours in which the justices meet, discuss and decide cases, and it is in the conference that the chief has a notable advantage over his colleagues. The conference is the "matrix of leadership of the Court," and only if the chief can exert personal and intellectual leadership can he minimize conflict, increase social cohesion and move the work to completion.[47] Justice Rehnquist has suggested that the chief's advantage lies in the fact that he states the case first, including an analysis of the governing legal principles. "If he cannot, with this advantage, maximize the impact of his views, subsequent interruptions of colleagues or digressions on his part or by others will not succeed either."[48] What the chief does initially then may be the determining factor in convincing an uncommitted justice to join a nucleus in forming a majority and ideally it will produce a unanimous Court. Generally the conference is not an occasion for conversions since each justice has already heard oral arguments and has studied the briefs and memoranda from his law clerks and his colleagues. Nevertheless, there are always those few marginal or "hard" cases, usually the most politically sensitive in that they will trigger congressional or presidential opposition and anger or will arouse public indignation. In such cases, the chief's ability to lead will be crucial to the outcome of the decision.

Only two chiefs, Marshall and Hughes, approximate the ideal in the simultaneous exertion of personal and intellectual leadership. We do not know the precise ways in which John Marshall dealt with his Court, but we do know of his warmth, his magnetism, the respect, affection and esteem in which he was held by his colleagues, and, of course, the brilliant results of his labors. The Hughes record is well documented. At one time or another, virtually all of the brethren paid tribute to Hughes' leadership generally and to his conduct of the conference specifically. Hughes' penchant for order and his photographic memory brought him to each conference almost formidably prepared. After summarizing a case accurately and comprehensively, he would then suggest how the case ought to be decided, and in some instances that was the only discussion the case received as the justices proceeded to vote for the disposition suggested by the chief. When a justice did wish to speak, he did so in order of seniority and without interruption, which meant that interchange of views was with the chief and not with the other justices.

Most of the chiefs have been extremely able personal leaders but more often than not they have been deferential to the intellects of others. Waite, Fuller, Taft, Vinson, and Warren were warm, decent human beings who possessed an ability to command, yet each could recognize and accept the intellectual leadership of men like Field, Miller, Van Devanter, Holmes, Black, or Frankfurter. White and Stone, on the other hand, while intellectually the equals of any of the brethren of their day, were incapable of running an orderly conference or orchestrating a cohesive Court. Chaos is the only word to describe the Court after Stone succeeded Hughes. The conference became a debating society with tempers out of control and tensions running high as the justices bickered almost endlessly, with honest intellectual differences escalating into personal antagonisms. Rather than concluding the conference in a few hours, Stone permitted it to go on for days. White, a genial, well-liked man did not, could not give the conference firm leadership. Encountering a difficult case he was known to say: "Here's a baffling case. I don't know what to do with it. God help us!"[49] Clearly such prefatory remarks to the discussion of a case give wide berth to the brethren to debate *ad infinitum* until one of them assumes the leadership role abandoned by the chief.

However long it takes and by whatever route arrived at, the conference does terminate with the justices deciding to decide, and if the chief is in the majority, which all chiefs have been most of the time, he then must assign the writing of opinions. For the most part this involves an equitable division of labor. Once again, though, there are a few cases in which the justice's name on the opinion has important public overtones and/or political significance. It needs to be emphasized, however, that the final opinion is a collegial affair. It has been worked and reworked after being read and commented on by those justices in dissent as well as those who concur, and some of the most pungent and eloquent phrases may have been integrated into the opinion at the insistence of a justice as the price to be paid for the supporting vote. Nevertheless, the author's identity may affect the "decision's acceptability, its value as precedent or future guideline, and the support of other judges."[50]

Throughout history the chiefs have tended to assign the politically and constitutionally significant cases to themselves. John Marshall, as we know, wrote virtually all the important opinions of the Court. With the inexorable escalation of litigation, however, no chief since Marshall has attempted to emulate his practice, even if it were desirable, which it is not. We can note, however, examples of every chief's self-assignments since Marshall in dealing with crucial constitutional issues: Taney on slavery;[51] Chase on the nature of the Union;[52] Waite on state regulation of the economy;[53] Fuller on the federal income tax;[54] White on the military draft;[55] Taft on presidential removal power;[56] Hughes on collective bargaining and interstate commerce;[57] Stone on the prosecution of Nazi saboteurs during World War II;[58] Vinson on the conviction of officials of the Communist Party;[59] Warren on racial desegregation;[60] Burger on the limits of executive privilege.[61]

In addition to equalizing the work load the chief's reasons for matching the justice to the case include: holding him in the majority; attracting dissenters to the majority; maximizing the desired content of the opinion; rewarding a justice who has a particular interest in writing the opinion or conversely, preventing a colleague from placing his imprimatur on the decision; and finally, giving the opinion a public relations or political advantage.[62] Chief justices, like all humans, have their likes and dislikes, preferences for some colleagues over others. Showing an obvious bias or favoritism in opinion assignment is, however, a sure way to engender disaffection, disrespect and ultimately a loss in stature and authority. And history will not be kind to the chief whom the brethren hold in contempt.

Unlike the private nature of the chief's role in the conference which we learn about indirectly, there are two areas of official performance which the public observes directly. First, the chief

Chief Justice

presides over the Court's open hearings and his behavior is observed by all, including the press, an ever-present critic and not always a friendly one. During Marshall's time opposing counsel argued their cases for days, but with the gradual increase in litigation oral argument came to be limited to one hour for each side. Eventually the summary calendar came to be used for some cases, an arrangement whereby each side was permitted only one half hour. This has now become the norm under Warren Burger, and only in cases of special importance are the litigants allotted a full hour.

As is true of the presiding judge in any Anglo-American courtroom, the chief justice has absolute control over the proceedings. How the chief conducts his Court is an individual matter but variations in style have been more a matter of degree than kind. Hughes was a tough taskmaster, sticking rigidly to a timetable to the point of halting counsel's presentation in the middle of a sentence and insisting upon impeccable decorum on both sides of the bench. All the chiefs since Hughes have been aware of the need to conserve time within the limits of fairness to both sides in the dispute and with allowances for questions from the bench. Warren, less Jehovah-like than Hughes but equally imposing in his own way, created a more relaxed atmosphere and was known to give a flustered lawyer some help under the relentless interrogation of Frankfurter or Black. Chief Justice Burger certainly looks the way a chief ought to look, and his sonorous voice has an authoritative ring regardless of what he says.

Under the chief's direction the marshal keeps track of the allotted time since the Court simply cannot, in this day of litigation almost out of control, afford to tarry overly long on a single case. No chief has failed to perform satisfactorily in holding court, and it is unlikely that any will in the future since the preparatory road to the chief justiceship, whether it be through the bench, the bar or elective office is such that the appointee will have had more experience than most in presiding over open meetings in which self-control, timing and evenhandedness are prerequisites to success.

There is, of course, the ultimate public performance of the chief, the writing of the opinions which he assigns to himself. There for all to see, for the constitutional lawyers to scrutinize intensely, is the competence with which he handles his craft. In one sense, as one of the nine judges who write opinions, the chief has no greater authority than any of his colleagues. Yet, even in this respect there is a subtle distinction between writing an opinion as chief and writing one as an associate justice, for in part at least the chief's ability to dominate the Court depends upon the intellectual powers that unfold as he defends a constitutional position or technical points of law. What kind of a balance does he strike between precedent and creativity? What sort of rhetoric does he employ to make his points? Does he write coherently and imaginatively? What are his literary allusions? Who are his heroes? What is his view of the role of the judiciary, of the role of government, his perception of the American system?

These questions are appropriately asked of any justice, but they have special significance for the chief for whom respect— both from his own court and from literate critics in the universities and the press—will depend upon his ability to use the language with authority and with grace. Legal craftsmanship will not, in and of itself, produce judicial statesmanship as the career of Harlan Fiske Stone amply demonstrates. His excellence as a judge is firmly established in history, but as chief he must be rated as barely adequate. Earl Warren, on the other hand, while meeting the requisite desideratum in his opinions, including the use of permanently quotable aphorisms, cannot be ranked among America's outstanding judges. He was, however, because of other personal characteristics, a great, powerful leader. John Marshall, as we know, was able to combine all the essentials of leadership during his tenure, but contributing much to his greatness are those ringing phrases from his opinions in *Marbury, McCulloch, Gibbons, Dartmouth College* and others that have had eternal staying power partly because of their exciting rhetorical style.

Always elusive to biographers, even in this day of advanced behavioral studies, is the answer to the question: What characteristics and phenomena combine to produce exceptional leadership, to create that special quality in a human being that entitles him to be called a great leader? It is a simple matter to make a list of those qualities that a great leader should possess, but it is a meaningless exercise, for in the final analysis leader-

Chief Justice

ship is intrinsic—a matter of "intrinsic authority" in Felix Frankfurter's phrase—and no amount of "leadership training" or "success" courses will make a leader of a follower. Not even observation of a great leader in action will help; nor will reading about great leaders in one's chosen field. The essence of leadership is, in short, enigmatic and it can be appraised only after the fact and then not by perfectly defined objective standards but by the application of intelligent common sense. Always, of course, there are the times, periods in history in which crises will provide opportunities that make the difference between passive and dynamic leadership. This is certainly true of the American presidency and to a lesser degree it is true of the chief justiceship.

NOTES

1. Act of Congress of July 13, 1866, Ch. 210 (14 Stat.L, p. 209).
2. Act of Congress of April 10, 1869, Ch. 22. The language in the statute was slightly different in that it spoke of *the* chief justice instead of *a* chief justice. Section 673 of the Revised Statutes uses the language of the 1866 statute. It states: "The Supreme Court of the United States shall consist of a Chief Justice of the United States and eight associate justices, any six of whom shall constitute a quorum."
3. This information was obtained from a reprint of an article in the Fuller papers in the Library of Congress: "Chief Justice of the United States or Chief Justice of the Supreme Court of the United States," by William A. Richardson, then Chief Justice of the Court of Claims, originally published in the *N.E. Historical and Genealogical Register* July 1895.
4. Ibid., p. 6.
5. See Charles Warren, *The Supreme Court in United States History,* Boston: Little, Brown (1923) I, p. 36.
6. John Jay served on the Sinking Fund Commission, an agency created by Congress under Alexander Hamilton's plan to reconsolidate and fund the national war debt. Jay also served on a cabinet level committee which was responsible for inspecting the operation of the U.S. Mint. George Washington clearly saw the chief justice as one of his official advisers. See Russell Wheeler, "Extrajudicial Activities of the Early Supreme Court," *The Supreme Court Review,* 1979, 123–58.
7. Charles Warren, op. cit., p. 139.
8. See Linda Novak, "The Precedential Value of Supreme Court Plurality Decisions," 80 *Columbia Law Review* 756 (May 1980) for a balanced discussion of the issues.
9. Every newly appointed chief takes two oaths: (1) an oath of fealty administered privately by the senior associate justice in the judges' robing

room; and (2) the oath of office administered publicly by the clerk of the Court in which he swears to do justice alike to rich and poor without fear, favor or affection.

10. Alpheus Thomas Mason, "The Chief Justice of the United States: Primus Inter Pares," 17 *Journal of Public Law* 23 (1968).

11. Felix Frankfurter, "Chief Justices I Have Known," 39 *Virginia Law Review* 884 (Nov. 1953).

12. Number of years served by chief justices: John Jay, 6; John Rutledge, ½; Oliver Ellsworth, 4; John Marshall, 34; Roger B. Taney, 28; Salmon P. Chase, 9; Morrison R. Waite, 14; Melville W. Fuller, 22; Edward D. White, 11; William H. Taft, 9; Charles E. Hughes, 11; Harlan F. Stone, 5; Fred M. Vinson, 7; Earl Warren, 16; Warren E. Burger, 16 (as of 1986).

13. See for example Alpheus Thomas Mason, "The Chief Justice of the United States: Primus Inter Pares," op. cit.; John P. Frank, *Marble Palace*, New York: Knopf (1968); Henry Abraham, *The Judicial Process*, New York: Oxford Univ. Press (1980) (4th ed.), p. 206; and Walter Murphy, *Elements of Judicial Strategy*, Chicago: Univ. of Chicago Press (1964), p. 82.

14. Letter from John Jay to John Adams as quoted in Mason, op. cit., p. 22.

15. Quoted in Charles Warren, op. cit., pp. 173–74.

16. Letter from Salmon P. Chase to John D. Van Buren, March 25, 1868, as quoted in Mason, op. cit., p. 22.

17. Albert P. Blaustein and Roy M. Mersky, *The First Hundred Justices*, Hamden, Conn.: Archon Books (1978), p. 94.

18. Ibid., pp. 138–39.

19. See Willard L. King, *Melville Weston Fuller*, New York: Macmillan (1950), pp. 148–51 and Felix Frankfurter and James Landis, *The Business of the Supreme Court*, New York: Macmillan (1928) pp. 93–102 for a discussion of the proposals.

20. Peter Graham Fish, *The Politics of Federal Judicial Administration*, Princeton: Princeton Univ. Press (1973), p. 39.

21. The Judicial Conference of the United States consists of the chief justice, the presiding judges of the thirteen circuits, twelve district judges elected by the regionally defined circuits and permissively after April 1, 1984, two bankruptcy judges.

22. Letter from Taft to Moses Strauss: June 5, 1927, as quoted in H. F. Pringle, *The Life and Times of William Howard Taft*, 2 vols. New York: Farrar and Rinehart, Inc. (1939), p. 963.

23. Earl Warren, *The Memoirs of Earl Warren*, New York: Doubleday & Co., Inc. (1977), p. 345.

24. Ibid., p. 346.

25. Ibid., p. 347.

26. Kenneth B. Umbreit, *Our Eleven Chief Justices*, New York: Harper & Bros. (1938), p. 459.

27. Interview with Barrett McGurn, public information officer of the Supreme Court; subsequently confirmed in letter of December 16, 1980.

28. Letter from Harlan Fiske Stone to F. C. Hicks, February 5, 1930, as quoted in Mason, op. cit., p. 21.

29. Lance Morrow, "A Cry for Leadership," *Time*, August 6, 1979, p. 28.

34

Chief Justice

30. Warren, *Memoirs*, op. cit., p. 348.
31. Letter from Chief Justice Vinson to Justice Douglas, May 13, 1947, William O. Douglas Papers, Library of Congress.
32. Memorandum from Chief Justice Warren to Justices Black, Douglas, Burton, Clark, Harlan and Brennan, Feb. 8, 1957, Harold H. Burton Papers, Library of Congress.
33. Memorandum of September 30, 1939, from the marshal's office to Justice Douglas, William O. Douglas Papers, Library of Congress.
34. As a result of Chief Justice Burger's initiatives the Federal Judicial Center appointed a committee of seven under the chairmanship of Paul Freund to prepare a report with recommendation on the caseload of the Supreme Court. The committee made four recommendations, the most controversial of which was that a national court of appeals be established to screen all petitions for *certiorari* and appeal and pass about 400 of the most "review-worthy" to the Supreme Court and retain for their own decision cases involving a conflict between circuit courts of appeal.
35. *Ex parte McCardle*, 7 Wallace 506 (1869).
36. Albert Beveridge, *The Life of John Marshall*, v. 3, Boston: Houghton, Mifflin Co. (1916–19), p. 192.
37. Beveridge, op. cit., p. 196.
38. William Rehnquist, "Chief Justices I Never Knew," 3 *Hastings Law Quarterly* (Summer, 1976), p. 650.
39. G. Edward White, *The American Judicial Tradition*, New York: Oxford Univ. Press (1976), p. 228.
40. Richard Hodder-Williams, "The Workload of the Supreme Court: A Comment on the Freund Report," 10 *American Studies* 215, 229.
41. Edwin McElwain, "The Business of the Supreme Court as Conducted by Chief Justice Hughes," 63 *Harvard Law Review* 5 (1949), p. 19.
42. Under a writ of appeal the aggrieved party has a statutory right to take his case to the Supreme Court although the court has discretion to dismiss on the ground that: (1) the federal question is insubstantial; (2) the federal question was not validly raised in a state court; or (3) the state court's judgment might be sustained upon an independent basis of state law. Automatic appeal is available: (1) if a state court has declared a federal law or treaty unconstitutional; (2) if a state court has upheld a state law or state constitutional provision against a challenge that it conflicts with a federal law, treaty or the U.S. Constitution; (3) if in a suit in which the U.S. is a party, a federal court declares a federal law or treaty unconstitutional; or (4) if a federal court of appeal invalidates a state law as contrary to the Constitution.
43. For example, when a special three-judge federal district court has granted or denied an injunction, an automatic appeal may be taken to the Supreme Court.
44. Under the scheme *certiorari* petitions are divided each week into groups of 25 to 30 and are sent to the offices of three of the justices in the pool in alternate weeks. The justices must still read the law clerk's memoranda on each petition, but the clerk's work is cut back since he reads only 9 or 10 petitions every two weeks instead of the 25 or 30 which every clerk used to read.

35

The Office

45. See, for example, Alexander M. Bickel, "The Overworked Court," *New Republic*, February 10, 1973, p. 17.
46. See Hodder-Williams, op. cit., p. 223.
47. David J. Danelski, "The Influence of the Chief Justice in the Decisional Process," in W. F. Murphy and C. H. Pritchett (eds.), *Courts, Judges and Politics*, New York: Random House (1979), pp. 497–508. Danelski uses the terms "task" and "social" leadership as the twin hooks upon which the chief's ability to lead depends. He borrowed these terms from Robert F. Bales, particularly his article "Task Roles and Social Roles in Problem Solving Groups," in Maccoby, Newcomb and Harley, *Readings in Social Psychology*, New York: Henry Holt & Co., (1958), pp. 437–47.
48. Rehnquist, op. cit., p. 647.
49. Quoted in Merlo J. Pusey, "Chief Justice Hughes," in Allison Dunham and Philip Kurland, *Mr. Justice*, Chicago: Univ. of Chicago Press (1956), p. 154.
50. S. Sidney Ulmer, "The Use of Power in the Supreme Court: The Opinion Assignments of Earl Warren, 1953–1960," 19 *Journal of Public Law* 49 (1970) at 52.
51. *Dred Scott v. Sandford*, 19 Howard 393 (1857).
52. *Texas v. White*, 7 Wallace 700 (1869).
53. *Munn v. Illinois*, 94 U.S. 113 (1877).
54. *Pollock v. Farmers' Loan and Trust Co.*, 157 U.S. 429 (1895).
55. *Selective Draft Law Cases*, 245 U.S. 366 (1918).
56. *Myers v. U.S.*, 272 U.S. 52 (1926).
57. *N.L.R.B. v. Jones & Laughlin Steel Corp.*, 301 U.S. 1 (1937).
58. *Ex parte Quirin*, 317 U.S. 1 (1942).
59. *Dennis v. United States*, 341 U.S. 494 (1951).
60. *Brown v. Board of Education*, 347 U.S. 483 (1954).
61. *U.S. v. Nixon*, 418 U.S. 683 (1974).
62. Ulmer, op. cit., Note 10.

Chapter 2

LEADERSHIP
THROUGH
INSPIRATION
AND CONVICTION

As ONLY A HANDFUL of presidents may be singled out for greatness, only three of the fifteen chief justices are entitled to that lofty accolade, "great leader". As one views the lives, the times and the legacies of John Marshall, Charles Evans Hughes, and Earl Warren, it is not at all certain that each would have been as successful at another time, that any of them was "a man for all seasons." As we suggest above, the times have much to do with the way a public figure is remembered, and each of these chiefs served during periods which were conducive to constructive leadership. But so did John Jay and Oliver Ellsworth who did not seize the opportunity to define and anchor the crucial and necessary principles of American constitutional law as did Marshall. So did Vinson who would not take the opportunity to extend civil liberties in the manner of Warren. And Stone was by nature incapable of administering the Court with the efficient, statesmanlike methods of Hughes. Always the intrinsic qualities must be taken into account, the individualized style that intermingles with the extrinsic forces to fashion a kind of exceptional, judicial leadership, leadership that bequeathes an enduring and dynamic legacy to the American Republic.

BACKGROUND, TEMPERAMENT, AND TRAINING

So much has been written about John Marshall, Charles Evans Hughes, and—to a lesser extent—Earl Warren that it is im-

Leadership Through Inspiration and Conviction

possible to distill the essence of each without some repetition, but perhaps we can rely on the advice of Justice Holmes who counseled that "we frequently need better understanding of the obvious rather than further investigation of the obscure."

While outwardly unalike in temperament, and bred in backgrounds so dissimilar that attitudes formed early in life would tend toward very different adult behavior, Marshall, Hughes, and Warren nevertheless shared some similar traits and held significant views and habits in common. All had a commanding physical appearance; all had robust health and all were capable of hard work, Hughes by nature, Warren and Marshall by necessity, the latter only in spurts. All were exemplary patriots with a deep respect for the American system and a mission to preserve it. They were basically conservative in outlook, but all were willing to stretch judging—in different degrees—to accommodate their own convictions, a not uncommon trait in American appellate judges generally. All had a certain natural dignity. Marshall and Warren liked most people and were liked in return, but each had a reserve which only the most intimate might penetrate. Hughes' reserve was closer to the surface, very much so in fact, and he was generally characterized as personally aloof, a human icicle, but many of those close to him found him charming and warm and not at all like the public image he projected.

All were strong self-disciplinarians, Hughes sternly so, Marshall and Warren, less rigid than Hughes but concerned with regulating their lives in order to accomplish the tasks at hand. All had an ability to see the irony and fate in life; they were serious men who did not take themselves seriously, men who were never impressed with any self-importance, a trait that enabled them to discern the superficial and the shallow among them. John Randolph wrote that John Marshall was the "most unpretending and unassuming of men" and the same can be said of Earl Warren and Charles Evans Hughes. Perhaps most important, all were straightforward, moral men, personally, professionally and publicly uncorruptible. Justice Story said of Marshall that he could never be an "intriguer," and again the same may be said of Hughes and Warren. None of them was a scheming, petty politician; none was an aggressive office seeker. Although there is a difference in degree from the reluctant participation of Marshall in public affairs to the seeking of a governorship and the presidency by both Hughes and Warren, neither of the latter was an enthusiastic political self-starter but was borne on the winds of circumstance in pursuing elective office.

John Marshall received very little formal education, there being no formal schools on the western frontier of Virginia. He was tutored initially by his father who used the Bible and the writings of Alexander Pope from whom he derived an enduring love of poetry, particularly the writers of the old English school, of Milton, Shakespeare, Dryden and, of course, Pope.[1] Later he was tutored for two years, one away from home, in the classics, and except for the brief two-month study of law with George Wythe at the College of William and Mary, he never received instruction in any public institution. In the words of Joseph Story, "his attainments in learning, such as they were, were nourished by the solitary vigils of his own genius."[2] Or to put it more succinctly, he was, after brief orientation and direction, self-educated, and he came to maturity during very exciting and challenging times.

He was not yet twenty in the summer of 1775 when he became a first lieutenant in a company of Virginia minute-men, was a youthful twenty-six when Cornwallis surrendered at Yorktown and thirty-four when the Constitution went into effect in 1789. Although not a member of the Constitutional Convention he was a participant in the founding of the Republic in various ways throughout his early adult life, first as a soldier in the Continental Army, then as a member of the Virginia legislature, and finally as a delegate to Virginia's ratifying convention. Describing his feelings about this "new" country many years later, he wrote in a letter to a friend:

> When I recollect the wild and enthusiastic notions with which my political opinions of that day were tinctured, I am disposed to ascribe my devotion to the Union, and to a government competent to its preservation, at least as much to casual circumstances, as to judgment. I had grown up at a time, when the love of the Union, and the resistance to the claims of Great Britain, were the inseparable inmates of the same bosom; when patriotism and a strong fellow feeling with our suffering fellow-citizens of Boston were identical; when the maxim, "United we stand, divided we fall"

Leadership Through Inspiration and Conviction

was the maxim of every orthodox American. And I had im-
bibed those sentiments so thoroughly, that they constituted a
part of my being. I carried them with me into the army,
where I found myself associated with brave men from
different States, who were risking life and everything valuable, in a common cause, believed by all to be most precious, and where I was confirmed in the habit of considering
America as my country, and congress as my government.[3]

During most of the 1790s, John Marshall refused George
Washington's entreaties to join his administration—first declining the offer of attorney general, then the ambassadorship to
France—preferring instead to remain in Virginia defending Federalist principles in public forums and to advance his private
law practice. From all accounts once the Constitution was
adopted, Marshall had expected to relinquish public life and to
pursue a professional career as an advocate, as much out of necessity as interest since he had a growing family to support. Always, however, he seemed to yield to the pressures of his friends
and associates who convinced him that his talents and his
views were needed to secure the principles of the new Constitution. Thus he reluctantly served as a member of the Virginia legislature from 1788 to 1792 and again from 1795 to 1797. He
entered national service only at the urgings of John Adams and
George Washington, the former insisting that he join Charles
Cotesworth Pinckney and Elbridge Gerry in an attempt to conciliate the intractable problems with France (the notorious XYZ
Affair), the latter convincing him that he was needed to assist in
counteracting the growing Jeffersonian particularism in the
House of Representatives to which he was elected in 1799. The
last was his most fateful decision, for he never again returned to
private life, although national service in the early years was not
the demanding full-time effort that it is today. His official career
was, in fact, "a somewhat leisurely one,"[4] as he "was on view before his contemporaries as a private citizen rather more of the
time, perhaps, than as Chief Justice."[5]

John Adams' presidency was something less than a great success partly because of the lack of rapport with his cabinet, some
of whom remained closely aligned with Alexander Hamilton.
In desperation, he finally fired both James McHenry, his secretary of war and Timothy Pickering, his secretary of state in May

1800. Without any consultation with John Marshall, he sent his name to the Senate on May 7 as secretary of war which the Senate confirmed on May 9. Three days later, having changed his mind, Adams nominated Marshall to be secretary of state and in the same message named Samuel Dexter of Massachusetts to be secretary of war. The Senate confirmed the nominees and on May 13 President Adams announced Marshall's appointment as secretary of state.

Meanwhile Marshall had returned to Richmond and had no idea that he had legally been secretary of war for a few days and that he was now secretary of state. He served in the office for ten months and in the detailed memorandum he left for his successor—James Madison as it turned out—it appeared that he left the office as he found it. England was still impressing American seamen; the Barbary pirates were still demanding and receiving tribute; Spain was still attacking American shipping; and France still considered the United States her enemy. Perhaps these affairs of state were beyond the capacity of the infant, not very powerful United States to deal with, and Marshall's recent biographer, Leonard Baker, suggests that his service as secretary of state should not be underrated.[6] Marshall had avoided war with France; he had helped shape negotiations that would settle the question of British debts; and he had articulated a policy toward Europe—live and let live—that was appropriate for the time, and once firmly executed by the end of the War of 1812 and the Monroe Doctrine, would permit the United States to grow and prosper.[7]

In 1826 John Adams wrote: "My gift of John Marshall to the people of the United States was the proudest act of my life. . . . I have given to my country a Judge, equal to a Hale, a Holt, or a Mansfield."[8] But John Marshall had not been Adams' first choice for the post. After John Jay had turned down the nomination, Marshall recommended the appointment of Associate Justice William Paterson of whom Adams approved but finally decided against because he did not wish to offend Associate Justice Cushing who was senior to Paterson, and more important, because Paterson had been a Hamilton supporter in the Federalist Party rift that had denied John Adams a second term.[9] Also urged upon Adams were Samuel Sitgreaves of Pennsylvania, Charles Pinckney of South Carolina who had once declined an appointment offered by Washington,[10] and finally, Adams himself. To the latter suggestion Adams replied that the "office of Chief Justice is too important for any man to hold of sixty-five years of age, who has wholly neglected the study of law for six and twenty years."[11]

John Marshall was forty-five years old and in perfect health when President Adams decided that he was the man who might hold the Federalist principles intact in the judiciary against the Jeffersonian onslaught from the presidency and Congress. He knew not then how well he had chosen. Marshall had attained some stature as a prominent Federalist in both state and national office and as a leader of the Virginia bar, although some observers have always questioned his legal talents.[12] Nevertheless, he was opposed in the Senate, partly for the reason that the Federalist leadership had preferred William Paterson, in part because of some doubts about his temperament and resolve. Senator Jonathan Dayton, who led the opposition initially, voted finally to confirm—as did the entire Senate—but not with great enthusiasm for Marshall. In a letter to Paterson, Dayton indicated that with only one exception the senators would have preferred him to Marshall but since Adams was inflexible on Paterson's appointment they "thought it advisable to confirm Mr. Marshall, lest another not so well qualified, and more disgusting to the bench, should be substituted. . . ."[13] But it was Speaker of the House Theodore Sedgwick who stated the case against Marshall, a view held by fellow Federalists who knew him well. Sedgwick wrote: "He is a man of very affectionate disposition, of great simplicity of manners, and honest and honorable in all his conduct. He is attached to pleasures, with convivial habits strongly fixed. He is indolent therefore. He has a strong attachment to popularity but is indisposed to sacrifice it to his integrity; hence he is disposed on all popular subjects to feel the public pulse, and hence results indecision and *an expression* of doubt."[14]

Whatever may have been Marshall's idiosyncratic faults as legislator, diplomat and member of the president's cabinet, they seemed not to hinder his leadership of the judiciary. Like George Washington and the presidency, John Marshall was a perfect fit for the chief justiceship. As John Randolph said in 1805, Marshall's "real worth was never known until he was appointed Chief Justice," but his appointment was an accident, the choice of a desperate, rejected but strong-willed president who was determined to maintain some semblance of his own political philosophy after his departure from office and through someone who had demonstrated personal loyalty as well as adherence to Federalist principles.

If we search for those traits that were instrumental in forming the nucleus of Marshall's greatness, we are totally mystified. Throughout his career his general coarseness of appearance seems to have left an unfavorable first impression. He was not a colonial aristocrat in the mold of Jefferson or Washington or his predecessors, Jay and Ellsworth, but was more the frontiersman, a precursor of Jackson or Lincoln.[15] At the time of his appointment he was described as "tall, meagre, emaciated; his muscles relaxed, and his joints so loosely connected, as not only to disqualify him, apparently, for any vigorous exertion of the body, but to destroy everything like harmony in his air and movements. Indeed, in his whole appearance and demeanor; dress, attitudes, gesture, sitting, standing or walking; he is as far removed from the idolized graces of Lord Chesterfield, as any other gentleman on earth."[16]

Throughout his life he was careless in his dress, almost oblivious to it. He usually wore a black suit of ordinary quality, "but his body was so ill compacted, that it balked and marred the utmost skill of the shears."[17] This casualness in dress extended to everything he did, including the misplacing or losing of important papers,[18] so that those who knew him were undoubtedly not surprised when as outgoing secretary of state he failed to deliver Marbury's (and others') commissions for the reason of sheer administrative confusion.

The famous attorney, William Wirt, wrote that Marshall's voice was "dry and hard," his attitude when speaking "extremely awkward," and yet, said Wirt, this "extraordinary man without the aid of fancy, without the advantages of person, voice, attitude, gesture, or any of the ornaments of an orator, deserves to be considered one of the most eloquent men in the world." Why then? Because, continues Wirt, he possesses "the faculty of developing a subject by a single glance of his mind, and detecting at once the very point on which every controversy depends."[19] Two very important faculties may account for his judicial success: first, his ability to acquire information from conversations and attorneys' arguments—he was a good listener; and second, his incomparable facility to digest and analyze information.[20] He could grasp the principles of a case quickly and accurately, clear it of its "accidental encumbrances" (Story's phrase) and re-state it in proper form for final decision.

Edward S. Corwin, in his engaging book on John Marshall, de-scribes him from his portraits which "with all their diversity, are in accord on that stubborn chin, that firm placid mouth, that steady, benignant gaze, so capable of putting attorneys out of countenance when they had to face it overlong. Here are the lineaments of self-confidence unmarred by vanity, of dignity without condescension, of tenacity untouched by fanaticism, and above all, of an easy conscience and unruffled serenity."[21] Self-confident, dignified, tenacious, serene—these words reli-ably describe the chief justice, although these without more would not have made him a great leader. They certainly form, however, a propitious desideratum and would not inaccurately be attributed to Chief Justices Hughes and Warren, also inciden-tally, from viewing their portraits.

Charles Evans Hughes was the first chief justice whose father was not a native-born American, the first in fact whose family had not come to the United States before the Revolution.[22] Hughes had no illustrious ancestors, something that could be said only of Ellsworth before him, although it has been true of every chief since Hughes; he needed no family name to support his talents, however, for he is the only chief who at the time of his appointment was generally recognized as the leader of the American bar.

Hughes was born on April 11, 1862, when Roger Brooke Ta-ney was nearing the end of his career and when the United States Supreme Court's reputation was still at a low ebb almost exclusively because of Taney's infamous opinion in Dred Scott's case. The Court would not, in fact, become as controversial again until Hughes himself became its head. Hughes' parents, strict, Baptist, God-fearing people, took care of his education until he reached the age of nine, and the environment is best de-scribed as disciplined and God-centered. He was an only child and he received undivided parental attention, all of it designed to produce a virtuous, learned, self-disciplined being with a highly developed sense of morality. When Hughes was five years old, his mother gave him copies of the New Testament and Psalms in order that he could take his turn reading verses at family prayer, and when he reached the advanced age of eight his father presented him with a Greek New Testament with lexicon.

Always his educational watchword was thoroughness—absolute, unerring thoroughness. At thirteen he was writing essays with such titles as "The Limitations of the Human Mind" and "The Evils of Light Literature" and at fourteen he entered Colgate University (then Madison College) intending to follow the ministry, the occupation of his father. Within two years, however, the study of law became more appealing, and he moved to Brown University where he graduated fourth in his class of forty-three, a standing that earned him a Phi Beta Kappa key. He also graduated with highest honors from Columbia Law School, and except for two years (1891–93) during which he taught at the Cornell Law School, he remained in private practice until 1905. In that year Hughes began his public career as counsel to the Stevens Committee established by the New York legislature to investigate gas rates. Thereafter he remained a public figure until he retired as chief justice in 1941 at the age of seventy-nine, thus dividing his adult life almost evenly between private business and public service.

Unlike John Marshall but similar to Earl Warren, Hughes had a long and distinguished life of public service prior to his appointment as chief at the age of sixty-eight. He had been an outstanding governor of New York, had served as secretary of state under President Harding and was responsible for shaping American foreign policy and directing it toward a path that the nation would follow up to the eve of World War II.[23] He had served as a member of the Permanent Court of Arbitration at The Hague and as a judge of the Permanent Court of International Justice, and for six years had been a distinguished associate justice of the Supreme Court. Historians would have treated him with respect had he never been chief justice.

Hughes' record was such that when President Hoover submitted his name to the Senate for confirmation on February 3, 1930, one would have expected approval without objection. The appointment, however, occasioned the bitterest debate over the confirmation of a chief justice since the Taney appointment.[24] Although the opposition, chiefly Republican progressives and southern Democrats, knew from the beginning that they did not have the votes to block the appointment, they took the opportunity to canvass every aspect of Hughes' public life. They highlighted his association with and presumed approval of great wealth and emphasized the fact that since he had once resigned from the Supreme Court to run for the presidency (he was defeated by Woodrow Wilson in 1916), it would set a dangerous precedent to return him to the bench. It was argued that it would encourage political activity by other Justices.[25] The final vote for confirmation was 52 to 26 and Hughes became the nation's eleventh chief justice.

No chief before or since has surpassed Hughes in the combining of superb intellectual equipment with exceptional energy. Everyone who knew him gave evidence of his towering intellect, the speed at which he worked, the disciplined schedule to which he adhered, and his outward calm and composure, rarely giving the impression of frenzy or hurried effort.[26] On the darker side he had difficulty in overcoming a reputation for coldness which, it has been suggested, was based on an innate shyness that had caused him to develop an "almost impenetrably hard shell of reserve."[27] Herbert Hoover called him "the most self-contained man I ever knew" and said that Hughes "had no instinct for personal friendship" that he "could ever discover." Yet William Howard Taft, while believing him "rigid and . . . metallic in matters in which perhaps wiser men would yield a bit" nevertheless characterized him as "genial, a good fellow, will sit up late into the night drinking Scotch whiskey and soda, has a keen sense of humor and is the best campaigner for votes I have ever met."[28] Holmes described him as "a good fellow, experienced and wise, but funny, and with doubts that open vistas through the wall of a nonconformist conscience."[29] And Felix Frankfurter wrote that Hughes was "genial though not promiscuous, full of fun and whimsey, a delightful tease and sparkling storyteller, a responsive listener and stimulating talker . . . self-critical rather than self-righteous, extremely tolerant towards views he did not share and even deemed mischievous. . . ."[30]

Beneath the calm, self-possessed exterior of Hughes the public man, was Hughes the imperfect, sensitive and at times frightened and uncertain human being. When he was directing the insurance investigation in New York, then in his forties, he said that at times he found the responsibility "almost too heavy to bear and the work too exacting to be continued," that he was "worn out" and "depressed," that he would say to his wife, "I simply can't go on."[31] At one point he even took to bedtime drink in order to relax. Just two years prior to his appointment as chief, having returned to his law practice, he confesses that he "almost suffered a breakdown" and had difficulty arguing his cases,[32] but as chief, with the exception of a few weeks in the Spring of 1939 when such tensions within him may have been the cause of a bleeding ulcer, he never missed a "single hour of the work of the Court" from the time he took his seat in February 1930 until he retired in June 1941.[33] In spite of those internal conflicts Hughes' exemplary standard of excellence in everything he did was maintained through frequent vacations which appeared to re-energize him and fit him even at an advanced age for the toughest of mentally and psychologically debilitating tasks. As chief he seemed to have an even greater vitality than he had had as an associate, to have a younger mind in an older body,[34] and whatever went on in the inner recesses of that mind, outwardly his performance remains a model for American public leadership.

On March 19, 1891, Earl Warren was born of parents who had both come to the United States from Norway as infants, and his father Mathias Varran had anglicized the family name. Earl Warren had no middle name—not even a single unidentified initial like President Harry S. Truman—and at one point when he asked why this was the case, his father replied, "My boy, when you were born I was too poor to give you a middle name."[35] Although born in Los Angeles, a county then populated by only 100,000 people, Warren grew up in Bakersfield where his father worked as a car repairman and inspector for the Southern Pacific Railroad. The temperature could reach 110°F in Bakersfield which boasted few cultural facilities or activities—the main place for social gatherings was the railroad station. The local high school had barely one hundred students at the time that Earl Warren was in attendance and when the young men graduated they went to work for the railroad. Warren was among the first to be graduated from college.[36]

Bakersfield was a poor community in hard times—the land hard, dry, unyielding—a place to get away from, and when War-

Leadership Through Inspiration and Conviction

ren left for the university at Berkeley, he never returned.[37] Many years later, however, he compared Bakersfield to a Chautauqua speaker's story of the man who was told in a vision that he was to discover acres of diamonds of untold wealth, but who returned home at the end of his life ragged and destitute. Only after his death did someone discover a treasure of diamonds in the garden behind his house. As Warren related it: "The boys and girls I went to school with, whose families worked so hard to scratch a living from the dusty, dry dirt, thought that only by getting away would they find what they sought. But those dirt farms now are irrigated and with water are some of the richest farm land in the world. And the acres of diamonds were there too—those farms all sat on top of tremendous petroleum pools and nobody guessed it."[38]

In temperament Warren was nothing like Hughes, and only in the sense of his easy-going, friendly demeanor can he be said to resemble Marshall. His background until the time he entered college would not have been familiar to either Hughes or Marshall, and although like Hughes he completed a curriculum successfully at a major law school and served as governor of one of the nation's largest states, he did not, as did Hughes and Marshall, serve in any official national capacity. Moreover, by his own admission, he had little knowledge of either the activities or the membership of the Supreme Court at the time of his appointment. He had had professional contacts with Justice Tom Clark over the years and had a slight acquaintance with Justices Jackson and Douglas; he knew the remaining five justices not at all. He had not engaged in legal practice—had not even been in a courtroom—for several years. After graduating from law school Warren was employed in private practice for three years, served in the Army during World War I (not in a legal capacity), was clerk of the judiciary committee of the California legislature— his entry into public service—and went on to serve as district attorney in the San Francisco Bay area (1925–1939), attorney general of California (1939–1943) and governor from 1944 until he was appointed chief justice. He said of the moment he assumed office: "The day of my induction as Chief Justice of the United States was for me at once the most awesome and the loneliest day of my public career."[39]

Earl Warren, however, was not to be lonely for very long, for the Supreme Court very soon became his court—the Warren

Chief Justice

Court—in every sense of the word, but most of the public law which his court fashioned was not to the liking of the president who appointed him. When Chief Justice Vinson died suddenly on September 8, 1953, President Eisenhower had an opportunity not available to most presidents, a chance to appoint a chief justice, and although he had spoken to Earl Warren about a seat on the Court, he had not thought of him initially in the role of chief. Eisenhower discussed the appointment with John Foster Dulles, his secretary of state, who had no interest in changing jobs, and he apparently considered Thomas E. Dewey of New York, two-time Republican presidential candidate and deserving loyal party politician, as well as the distinguished chief justice of New Jersey, Arthur T. Vanderbilt.[40] But Earl Warren, the three-term popular governor of California and vice-presidential running mate with Dewey in 1948, was also a Republican of stature who deserved national recognition. Furthermore, his demonstrated executive abilities appeared to qualify him at a time when the Court was projecting a public image of divisiveness and personal rancor, and his political views, as far as Ike could ascertain, were generally in accord with his own.

Just three weeks after Vinson's death Warren was given a recess appointment on the assumption that when Congress, then out of session, returned to Washington he would be routinely confirmed. It took some two months, however, after Senator William Langer of North Dakota, a member of the judiciary committee, began his campaign of opposing all nominees to the Court until the president appointed someone to the high bench from his state—to this day none has—but the confirmation finally came on March 1, 1954—unanimously.

It has been suggested that had the Senate been able to look into the future, the Warren appointment might have been rejected,[41] but had the president been clairvoyant, he never would have named Warren in the first place, having later denounced the act as the "biggest damn fool" mistake he had made as president. In his memoirs Warren writes of the coolness of the president toward him, of his being invited to the White House during Ike's presidency only for official occasions and he tells of a conversation between them—Eisenhower had then retired to private life—when flying in *Air Force One* to Winston Churchill's funeral. The former president had expressed disappointment in

Leadership Through Inspiration and Conviction

him and in Justice Brennan because he thought they were "moderate" when he appointed them but had concluded otherwise. Warren then asked what decisions had brought him to that conclusion. Ike replied: "Oh, those Communist cases." Warren asked which ones, to which the former president responded: "All of them." When asked by Warren if he had read them, Eisenhower said that he had not, but that he knew what was in them. Warren then explained that in the courts Communists had to be judged by the same rules as everyone else and asked Ike what he would do with Communists in America? To which the President replied: "I would kill the S.O.B.'s." Ending the conversation, the chief justice said: "Perhaps that could be done in the Army, but it could not be done through civilian courts."[42] After ten years of Warren's service as chief, Anthony Lewis was to write in the New York Times: "It is a delicious irony that the appointment of Chief Justice Warren may go down in history as the single most important act of Eisenhower's presidency."[43]

In 1947 in his chronicle of state politics in America, Inside U.S.A., John Gunther wrote of then Governor Earl Warren of California that "he will never set the world on fire or even make it smoke; he has the limitations of all Americans of his type with little intellectual background, little genuine depth or coherent political philosophy; a man who probably never bothered with abstract thought twice in his life. . . ."[44] One of Warren's biographers suggests that at the time of his appointment he was "regarded as a man of good will, a healer of quarrels, a balance wheel," a man who would do a quiet and effective job on a Court torn by personal quarrels. He "was not too liberal for the conservatives and not too conservative for the liberals," a sort of competent but colorless manager who might restrain and moderate among the brilliant prima donnas, Black, Frankfurter, Jackson and Douglas. It was not long, however, before Warren became "a peacock among sparrows,"[45] unquestionably the man in charge.

By no means the intellectual equal of Hughes or Marshall, Warren had above all a presence, an ability to communicate his authority in such a way that it would elicit respect and loyalty from his colleagues. What came through to all who knew him was his uncompromising spirit of fairness, his instinctive impartiality and a warmth that one could feel from a single encounter. Like Marshall and like Hughes, he was a good listener, an attribute that enabled him to learn quickly. Warren was neither scholar nor lawyer preeminent, but no matter, he created an ambiance that was to give the Court a unique and exciting character at a time when presidential leadership, at least during the first half of Warren's tenure, was passive and tended to ignore the surfacing of issues like racial discrimination, malapportionment of political bodies, and injustices in the courts. Under Earl Warren's leadership the Supreme Court became the refuge for those who had been ignored by the president, the Congress, and by governors and state legislatures, with mixed consequences both for the future of constitutional law and for the future of the nation.

RUNNING THE COURT

With the appointment of John Marshall the Supreme Court stepped out of swaddling clothes[46] and the office of chief justice would never again be referred to as a sinecure. By force of personality, conviction, energy and will, Marshall invested the office with a power and prestige second only to those of the presidency. An English writer after observing Marshall in action suggested that the chief justiceship was in fact the most important position an American could enjoy because first, it was less subject to the arbitrary will of the people than elective office and second, the court over which the chief presides can decide "what is and what is not the Constitution of the United States."[47]

Whether or not the Court moves in the direction of the chief's preferences is dependent not only upon the chief, but also upon the associate justices. Marshall, for example, could dominate some of the fourteen justices who served with him but certainly not all, and as the years went on and the original Federalists were replaced by Jeffersonians, his influence began to wane. In the beginning, in addition to his own intellectual powers and his amiable and unassuming nature, he was fortunate in that his persuasiveness fell upon cooperative colleagues. He was "sufficiently likable and admirable as a human being to make palatable, in his own person, the judicial power he asserted."[48] According to Thomas Jefferson's first appointee, Justice William Johnson who served during thirty of Marshall's thirty-four years, "I was not a little surprised to find [Marshall], delivering

all the opinions in which he sat, even in instances when contrary to his own judgement and vote. . . . I soon found out, however, the real cause, Cushing was incompetent, Chase could not
be got to think or write, Paterson was a slow man and willingly
declined the trouble, and the other two judges [Marshall and
Bushrod Washington] you know are commonly estimated as
one judge. . . ."[49]

It is amusing that Justice Johnson thought most of his associates indolent, for Marshall himself was regarded as "far fonder
of leisure than of work." His working year—between Supreme
Court and circuit duty—consisted of at most twenty weeks.[50]
What is important is that when he worked, he worked with an
intensity that could produce a prodigious quantity of high quality material in a short time. For example, he wrote the decision
in the Aaron Burr trial—some 25,000 words—with a quill pen
over a weekend, having no more time than Saturday evening,
Sunday and possibly a brief period on Monday morning.[51] He
has been accurately characterized as giving the impression of "a
man with a peculiarly quick, penetrating, and facile mind, able
to take a variety of intellectual short cuts."[52]

Whatever may have been his operational methods, he was
able to shape the chief justiceship into a mode and the Court
into a routine that has been followed ever since his day. First
and foremost he established the custom of the chief speaking
for the Court or deciding which justice would so speak in those
cases in which the chief was in the majority. It was in the case of
the *Amelia*[53] during his first term as chief that he initiated the
practice of a single spokesman for the Court as opposed to the
seriatim tradition of his predecessors, and he did so by delivering a comprehensive opinion rather than by adhering to the previous custom of writing a simple, brief statement of the law. For
the first seven years of his tenure he spoke for the Court in every
case in which he participated, although as the Court's personnel
began to change with the appointment of anti-Federalist judges
by Presidents Jefferson, Madison and Monroe, he began to assign opinions to senior and then even to junior associate justices. Marshall continued, however, until his death in 1835 to
deliver the Court's opinions in most of its cases.[54]

By calmly disregarding past practice Marshall assumed power
boldly and "took the first step in impressing the country with

the unity of the highest court in the Nation."[55] Second, he "fed the law's myth of certainty by presenting a united front"[56] to the public, and even in dissent, which was rare, he acquiesced silently or sometimes wrote the Court's opinion. For the first two decades and occasionally thereafter he was able to produce compromise opinions acceptable to his colleagues, and the Court's prestige as well as his own remained high in spite of some bitter personal criticism from political adversaries like Thomas Jefferson and from the states rights advocates in Georgia, Kentucky and his own Virginia when they lost their cases in the Supreme Court. Third, he asserted a public and private leadership by firmly establishing the role of presiding officer, both in open court and in the discussion of cases at the conference. In the former his demeanor was a significant factor in presenting the Court's public face as learned, tranquil and constitutionally authoritative; in the latter it was a matter of maintaining internal harmony while persuading the brethren to his point of view. Justice Story described Marshall in both roles: "You heard him pronounce the opinion of the Court in a low but modulated voice, unfolding in luminous order every topic of argument, trying its strength and measuring its value, until you felt yourself in the presence of the very oracle of the law. . . . follow him into the conference room, a scene of not less difficult or delicate duties, and you would observe the same presiding genius, the same kindness, attentiveness, and deference; and yet, when occasion required, the same power of illustration, the same minuteness of research, the same severity of logic, and the same untiring accuracy in facts and principles."[57]

John Marshall fixed the practice of the chief opening the Court's private deliberations of the cases by giving his views first and then calling on his associates for comments. According to Joseph Story, "he excelled in the statement of a case; so much so, that it was almost itself an argument" and he was often able to persuade an associate that his view of the law was the correct one "however repugnant it might be to [the associate's] preconceived notions."[58]

Historians have tended to emphasize the importance of the Court's cohesion under Marshall, of the unique practice of the judges living together in the same boardinghouse where they were able to discuss the cases informally in their rooms or while dining. Marshall himself believed the practice essential to the smooth and relatively quick determination of the issues, having written to both his wife and to Story about his inabilities to conduct the Court's business with dispatch if the judges were to "scatter ad libetum."[59] As important as the practice may have been to Marshall's leadership, it was not in itself the crucial factor in his success. More important was the establishment of the principle of informal consultation among the justices, a principle that has been carried out in practice under every chief. If anything, the physical surroundings today are such that informal contacts among the brethren may be more frequent than they were in the early nineteenth century. What is greatly different after almost two hundred years is the expansion of the chief's roles and duties. Whether a chief will take the time to stroll down the hall and drop in on an associate, whether he insists that they lunch or dine together on occasion is a matter of individual temperament and priorities.

Finally, Marshall impressed upon the American system not simply a judicial independence but a judicial aloofness, a refusal of the chief and his Court to be dragged into public controversy over the Court's work, thus creating an institutional character that placed the Court in theory—and permitted it to appear to be so in fact—above the partisan political battle. Marshall was able to do this by insisting that the Court did not make law but simply followed the Constitution, or a higher fundamental law when the Constitution lacked clarity. Only the people could make law. This is, of course, a myth, but a necessary one if the judiciary is to have equivalent powers with Congress and the president. It has protected the Court in times of crisis from being shorn of its powers because of its unpopular decisions. The justices can remain silent as the controversies rage around them for they have not "made" the law; they have simply "found" it in the Constitution. Even in the modern day when intellectuals appear to take great satisfaction in demythologizing all of the traditions of Western civilization, those of American consitutional law among them, the myth that politics is incompatible with judging may have saved the Supreme Court from neutralization and possibly from destruction under both Hughes and Warren, not to speak of Taney or Chase.

Like John Marshall, Charles Evans Hughes was rarely in dissent for he conceived the role of chief as one of fostering cohesiveness, of presenting the nation with a picture of judicial nonpartisanship and unanimity, of a Court committed to justice above all else. It was his misfortune, however, to have presided over one of the most divided Courts in history, at least from the day of his confirmation in 1931 until the resignation of Justice Van Devanter in 1937. It was his good fortune, nevertheless, to have come to the Court with superb intellectual baggage, with an incorruptible character, with a sense of duty second to none, and with a thorough knowledge of and commitment to the American system. Hughes also came to the chief justiceship with a special kind of knowledge that could only have been obtained by sitting on the Court as an associate justice and observing the faults of another chief. As Hughes in retirement modestly put it in a conversation with Felix Frankfurter: "Whatever little success I may have achieved when I became Chief Justice, I think was largely due to the lessons I learning in watching [Chief Justice] White during the years when I was an Associate Justice and seeing how it ought not to be done. I am fond of saying that perhaps parents help their children most through their faults, because children hate the faults and failings of their parents and are helped thereby. And so if I had any virtues as Chief Justice they were due to my determination to avoid White's faults. . . . White did not take hold the way a Chief Justice should in guiding the discussion and taking a position in expounding the matters before the Court."[60]

Hughes was referrring to White's ineffectiveness in leading the conference and in that respect Hughes is without peer, but his conduct was equally superb in the other aspects of the chief's functions: holding open court, assigning opinions, maintaining social cohesion in spite of bitter intellectual differences, and overseeing the federal judicial system. The word used to describe the atmosphere of the Court under Hughes by close observers at the time was "taut."[61] His very presence kept everyone around him—his associate justices, opposing counsel, the clerk's office, the marshal's office, the law clerks—alert. He created "an air of discipline which moved the details of the Court's business at a hitherto unheard-of speed."[62] Frankfurter referred to Hughes as "Toscanini Hughes," the maestro, the man with the remarkable gift of bringing things out of people if they are "evoked, sufficiently stimulated, sufficiently directed."[63]

Leadership Through Inspiration and Conviction

Preparations for the Saturday conference which convened at noon began a week in advance when the clerk would circulate the petitions for *certiorari* and other memoranda comprising a stack of papers that often reached a height of four feet in the chief's office.[64] Hughes, who could absorb an entire paragraph almost at a glance, read a treatise in an evening and a roomful of papers in a week,[65] would devour the briefs and records in order to ready himself for the conference. With a thoroughness that few can match, Hughes sat at the conference table and "exuded complete preparation and conveyed the impression that anyone who disagreed with him had better know *all* the facts and know them well."[66] As a consequence he was rarely challenged, and his own detailed knowledge of the cases elevated the Court's deliberations to an extraordinarily high level.

During the five and one-half hour conference the Court would normally dispose of some thirty cases as Hughes would review each one and listen to the comments of any justice who wished to speak prior to taking a vote. At the annual conference immediately following the summer recess Hughes would guide the Court through some two hundred and fifty petitions for *certiorari* and other motions and memoranda, clearly stating the issues and the law "at a speed and with a spirit which kept the entire Court on its toes."[67] He could, however, shift gears very easily, and when the justices broke for lunch, Hughes, according to Justice Roberts, would become "the center of a delightful half-hour talk which ranged from the merest local happening to world events. The current business of the Court was completely forgotten in the sociability of the group."[68]

There was near unanimity of view among the justices—both on the early 1930s Court and among the later Roosevelt appointees—that Hughes' conduct of the conference was effective, fair and appropriate. Only Stone expressed some dissatisfaction, suggesting that he was not always given an opportunity to state his views and that Hughes overelaborated the unimportant and then disposed of the vital questions almost summarily.[69] Frankfurter appeared to be answering Stone when he wrote in 1953 that it simply was not true that "there wasn't free and easy talk in Hughes' day. . . . There was less wasteful talk. There was less repetitious talk. There was less foolish talk. You just didn't like to talk unless you were dead sure of your ground, because that gimlet mind was there ahead of you."[70]

Eugene Gerhart, Robert Jackson's biographer, tells of a conversation between President Roosevelt and then Solicitor General Jackson at the time of Frankfurter's appointment to the Court in which they agreed that someone was needed who had the learning and self-assurance to "hold his own" with Hughes in the conference discussions. They were certain that Felix Frankfurter filled the bill.[71] Once on the Court, however, Frankfurter became one of Hughes' strongest supporters and he developed in the manner of Story to Marshall, an almost reverential respect for and devotion to the "great man"; he spoke of him only in superlatives. But so did all the other justices who served with him, including the testy McReynolds, and in his later years, even Stone. Moreover, Hughes had the ability to keep personal animosities in check with the result that the brethren remained socially friendly, even when constitutionally locked in mortal combat.

Paradoxically, with one glaring exception—McReynolds' outrageous mistreatment of Brandeis—the Court was socially harmonious while presenting a face to the nation of irreconcilable differences between uncompromising factions, the latter state of affairs being precisely opposed to the wishes and intentions of the chief. He was very careful to avoid all internal politicking among the justices, studiously remaining aloof from the informal meetings of both the "Four Horsemen" (Sutherland, Van Devanter, Butler and McReynolds) and the "Three Musketeers" (Brandeis, Cardozo and Stone). Given the nature of the division and the rigidity of the antagonists, Hughes saw his role as primarily that of moderator. Thus he attempted to secure support for moderate opinions, to assign opinions in such a way as to soften identification of the justices with consistently hardline positions, and to fashion a jurisprudence that would conserve the principles of the past and yet permit a modicum of reform.[72]

As presiding officer Hughes has never been equaled. In Paul Freund's words: "His Jovian figure seemed to occupy the central seat by natural right. His powers of concentration were total; he transfixed counsel with a piercing stare, at intervals betraying his purpose to intervene by a quickening movement of the eyelids. When he did intervene, he showed a remarkable capacity to bring an argument into focus, to go for the jugular. Not infrequently he rescued counsel as they suffered repetitive assaults from vantage points along the bench."[73] Hughes had the knack of sizing up counsel, very quickly assessing his limitations, and then keeping him on track, knowing at least as much and usually more about the case than anyone else in the courtroom.[74] He was always gracious, genial, good mannered, but exacting and firm. Under Hughes the Court opened at noon, not 11:59 A.M. or 12:01 P.M., and the chief's gold pocket watch clocked the proceedings with finite exactitude until the docket was completed. It was a masterful public performance, and it gave his leadership a charismatic glow that enhanced his reputation not only with the press but with the public generally.

Completely in character was Hughes' careful assigning of opinions, a responsibility which he ranked first among the various duties of the chief justice.[75] In addition to making certain that each associate justice was given a fair share of the work, Hughes attempted to balance three factors.[76] First, he viewed the Supreme Court as a bench of generalists who could understand and justify in a legal opinion any decision growing out of legislation which the Court might encounter. Thus, every justice, instead of being consigned to one or two areas of expertise, was expected to write on all subjects. Second, when the Court was strongly divided, he tried to avoid the extremes of right and left by choosing a justice whose views were likely to produce a moderate opinion. Within this framework of "moderating" the result, he often assigned liberal justices the writing of opinions in which the decision had been conservative and vice versa. This practice had the additional effect of possibly converting some of the judges and moving the decision closer to unanimity. Third, in the final phase, the writing and circulating of the opinion, he discouraged pride of authorship in order to eliminate dissents and concurrences by adding or deleting phrases or words and making the opinion acceptable to a larger majority. He was, of course, successful only to a degree, for the Four Horsemen and the Three Musketeers were so far apart on many crucial issues that their differences could not be mitigated, and ironically, in spite of Hughes' Herculean efforts to maintain the institutional integrity of the Supreme Court—always his central concern—it came closest to being mortally wounded during his stewardship.

Chief Justice

The story of President Roosevelt's battle with the Court has been told and retold, and there is no need to recount it here in detail. What is significant is the reaction of the chief justice when his Court is under political attack, and the Hughes record in this respect is one of dignity, decorum, and effectiveness. Between January 1935 and June 1936 the Court decided twelve cases[77] which, taken together, persuaded the president that the Court would not look favorably on such coming measures as the Social Security Act, the National Labor Relations Act, and the Public Utility Holding Company Act. Three of the twelve were unanimous against the government, and in the remaining nine Cardozo supported the government in all, Brandeis and Stone in eight each, Hughes in five, Roberts in three, Van Devanter, Butler and Sutherland in one each, and McReynolds in none.[78]

Clearly, four of the justices were irrevocably committed to an economic and constitutional philosophy that would permit little, if any, compromise with the president's New Deal, and much of the time they were joined in their opinions by a fifth, and some of the time by a sixth, the chief.

The president's reaction was a proposal to Congress, the main feature of which would have permitted him to appoint an additional judge to the Court when any member with at least ten years' service had served six months after reaching the age of seventy and failed to resign or retire. The size of the Court would be limited to fifteen, and this measure, had it become law, would have permitted counter appointments for Hughes and the Four Horsemen, all of whom were over seventy. Although several factors combined to insure the defeat of the "Court packing" bill, the action taken by Hughes must be counted as one of the most significant. The president's defense of the measure alluded to old men not being in tune with the times, but its main theme was the need for more judges to handle the workload, a charge which Hughes in his systematic way was to refute point by point.

Relying on the advice of Justice Brandeis, Hughes correctly refused to appear before the Senate Judiciary Committee but instead sent a letter to the leader of the opposition, Senator Burton Wheeler of Montana who read the text in an open committee hearing. Hughes contended that about 60 percent of the

Leadership Through Inspiration and Conviction

petitions for *certiorari* were wholly without merit and that the Court had, if anything, been overgenerous in granting hearings. Increasing the size of the Court, wrote Hughes, would only impair its efficiency since there would be "more judges to hear, more judges to confer, more judges to be convinced and to decide." As to dividing up the work in such a way that all of the judges would not participate in every case, Hughes maintained that any such practice would contravene the Constitution which vests judicial power "in one Supreme Court," not in two or more, or parts of one functioning as separate courts.

An action of this kind could not be taken without stimulating criticism, and the chief had not closed all avenues of vulnerability. By suggesting that the plan was unconstitutional he was giving an advisory opinion on an issue not before the Court in a proper case which, his critics argued, was equally unconstitutional. Moreover, he had not consulted the entire Court on the contents of his letter but had obtained the concurrence only of Brandeis and Van Devanter, the senior leaders of the Court's two opposing factions. The critics were justified on both counts but there are times when a chief, in defending the institutional integrity of the Supreme Court must press his advantage to the outer limits, and this was one of those times.

Just prior to the adverse report on the Court-packing bill issued by the Senate Judiciary Committee in June 1937, the Court handed down opinions in which a majority of five voted to uphold liberal state and federal legislation, giving rise to speculation that the Court had been intimidated and that the president had already accomplished his purpose. The legislation upheld included the state of Washington's minimum wage law for women,[79] the National Labor Relations Act,[80] and the Social Security Act,[81] the latter two being major components of the president's New Deal construct. In retirement Hughes vehemently denied that the Court had "changed front" in order to defeat the president's bill, maintaining that the notion that "these cases, or any others, were influenced in the slightest degree by the President's attitude, or his proposal to reorganize the Court, is utterly baseless."[82] He pointed out that the minimum wage case had been argued and discussed in conference before the attack on the Court or before anyone knew that it was coming, and he observed that the decision in the National Labor Relations Act case "would have been the same if the President's bill had never been proposed."[83]

It is a tribute to Hughes' leadership—and to that of President Roosevelt as well—that neither displayed any personal rancor during or after the crisis, a factor that may be crucial to the vitality of the American system, or any free system for that matter. Hughes wrote of his "agreeable" personal relations with President Roosevelt, of FDR's "utmost cordiality and friendliness," of his personal call to Mrs. Hughes in 1939 telling her that he was going to seat her next to King George VI at a state dinner which he did. Not very long after the Court battle the chief justice administered the oath of office to Roosevelt for the third time, after which he told the president: "I had an impish desire to break the solemnity of that occasion by remarking: 'Franklin, don't you think this is getting to be a trifle monotonous?'"[84]

Unquestionably Hughes was a near-perfect fit for the chief justiceship, and the way in which he filled the various leadership roles of the office remains a model for his successors. Nevertheless, there is an irony in the office, according to G. Edward White who, while not disputing the fact of Hughes' seemingly ideal qualifications for the office, suggests that "under Hughes the Court first isolated itself from the mood of the nation, then painfully and embarrassingly embraced it, revealed itself as being polarized and rancorous, saw its autonomy and even its composition threatened, and lost its aloofness from politics. Hughes himself was not responsible for most of these difficulties, but he was powerless to alleviate them and may even have exacerbated them."[85] In a perceptive and succinct summary of this major constitutional crisis, Roosevelt's attorney general, Robert Jackson—soon to join the Court himself—wrote: "In politics the black-robed reactionary justices had won over the master liberal politican of our day. In law the President defeated the recalcitrant justices in their own Court."[86] Nothing had altered the Court's structure or impaired its functions but during the remaining four years that Hughes served as chief, no act of Congress was declared unconstitutional and during the eighteen years immediately following the presidential assault, only two minor federal laws were invalidated.[87]

If the atmosphere of the Court under Hughes has been aptly characterized as "taut," the single most descriptive word for the

Leadership Through Inspiration and Conviction

Warren ambiance must be the opposite—"relaxed." And if there is general agreement that Hughes' background, talents, and temperament tailored him perfectly for the office of chief justice, it appears that Warren's qualifications at the time of his appointment were barely adequate. He came to the Court "with no judicial experience, limited exposure to the world of ideas, no easily characterizable social attributes, and no evidence of literary talent."[88] On the day that he entered the chambers of the chief justice he violated a cardinal rule of leadership. Instead of firmly taking charge he modestly deferred to others until he could learn the ropes. He asked the then senior associate justice, Hugo Black, to chair the conferences until he, Warren, could familarize himself with the internal procedures. Warren writes amusingly of his first days in office when he attempted to learn from official records just what the duties were of the clerk, the marshal, the librarian and the reporter of decisions. There was nothing in writing; it was simply a matter of incumbents explaining to their successors how things were done.[89]

Nor did the new chief confront a happy, harmonious group of associates on that first day. Although the times of the Four Horsemen versus the Three Musketeers were long gone, five strong and intellectually assertive Roosevelt appointees, Black, Reed, Frankfurter, Jackson and Douglas, were the senior associates. They had been joined by three Truman appointees, Burton, Clark and Minton, all less aggressive than FDR's men and none disposed to the flamboyance and effusiveness of Frankfurter, the cutting wit and sarcasm of Jackson, the literalism and intensity of Black, or the doctrinaire liberalism of Douglas. Jackson had had an open rupture with Black in 1946, and Frankfurter was to write a note to Black in 1955 which was hardly calculated to improve personal relations. It read: "I'm going to say something that you won't like to hear but it's true even if unpleasant. I've never known anyone who more steadily reads for confirmation of his views and less for intellectual enlightenment."[90]

Within two years of his inauspicious beginning, Earl Warren was able to bring this group to unanimous agreement in one of the most momentous decisions in the Court's history, the declaring of racial segregation unconstitutional in the public schools. Had he done nothing else, this alone would have entitled him to a permanent seat of honor in the national constellation of great statesmen. Before Earl Warren retired in 1969 that famous desegregation Court of 1954 had been almost totally replaced as resignation and death necessitated the appointment of eight new justices, four by President Eisenhower (Harlan, Brennan, Whittaker, and Stewart), one by President Kennedy (White), and three by President Johnson (Goldberg, Fortas, and Thurgood Marshall). Only Justices Black and Douglas were to serve the full sixteen years of Warren's tenure, the three usually forming a nucleus and often a key part of the majority in civil liberties cases.

Like John Marshall in his early years Earl Warren fortuitously had a core of associate justices whose views were congenial to his own, but unlike the latter Marshall years, this remained true throughout his entire term as chief.[91] In addition to Justices Black and Douglas, the group consisted of Justice Brennan who joined the Court in 1956, Justice Clark who tended to move back and forth between the liberal and conservative wings, and Justices Fortas, Goldberg, and Marshall who served with Earl Warren for relatively brief periods, four, three and two years respectively. Also joining a Warren majority on occasion in important constitutional cases were Justices Stewart and Frankfurter. As Justice Fortas has written, it was an expanding and contracting core depending upon resignations, retirements and particular issues which might attract justices normally opposed to Warren's views.[92] For a chief to be recognized as a particularly effective leader, however, it is not enough that a majority of the Court shares his constitutional and personal values. Nor is it a matter of the overwhelming erudition and administrative deftness that characterized Hughes. Justice Fortas called Warren "a great and powerful leader," declaring: "We know this; we feel it,"[93] but he could not say why. He finally took refuge in the phrase: "By some process short of the occult,"[94] no more descriptive perhaps than Frankfurter's "intrinsic authority" or as others would say, an x-factor, an unknown quality.

Earl Warren initiated several changes in the Court's procedures, all of which seem to have attained a permanency. Probably most important was the changing of the meeting times of the conference and of the Court's open hearings. He believed that starting the Court's sessions at noon was an anachronism,

Leadership Through Inspiration and Conviction

having originated in the days of unpaved streets and primitive modes of travel, and at a time when the pace of judicial business was leisurely. Taking due care to avoid a conflict among the brethren through any precipitous action, he suggested that the Court ought to meet at 10:00 A.M. in conformance with judicial practice throughout the nation, but the response was less than enthusiastic. He then kept it, in his words "on a back burner," referring to it periodically until the justices agreed to the new meeting times. He had less of a problem in changing the conference from Saturday morning to Friday, a move made possible by adding a week of argument in the fall and two weeks in the spring.

After the alterations in the schedule the chief continued to be in his office on Saturdays when he spent a good deal of time with his law clerks, including the well-known two-hour lunches at which the conversation ran from current litigation before the Court to contemporary politics to professional sports, the chief having had a healthy American addiction to the latter.

Other innovations of Warren's include a change in the method of releasing opinions to the press and the elimination of a single day for the public announcement of decisions. Traditionally Monday had been "opinion day" but in 1965 the Court announced that opinions would henceforth be handed down on any day of the week, a practice which gave reporters a chance to improve their own analyses with the spread of releases over several days rather than by concentrating them all in one.

For many years it had been the practice not to give copies of opinions to the press until after they had been delivered in open court, a system that could be open to abuse in that an astute court-watcher might guess the outcome of a case as soon as he knew who authored the opinion, and in financial cases he might buy or sell stocks before the public had received official notice of the results. Warren in his memoirs tells a story of a lawyer who did just that, although an editorial note indicates that on opinion days the courtroom doors were locked and only after they were unlocked could reporters get to a telephone.[95] In any event Earl Warren believed that fairness required the release of every opinion to the press the moment a justice commenced his delivery, an arrangement that quickly found public acceptance.

Chief Justice

In general Earl Warren's relations with the press, while never strained, were nevertheless formal and distant, and he insisted that his clerks and other personnel not conduct interviews with the media nor gossip with reporters. As a result the Court spoke almost exclusively through its opinions, a practice that insulated the Court and permitted it to retain an indispensable aura of majesty, mystery, and impersonality. It also helped it to preserve that judicial dignity so essential to its effectiveness and authority, especially in controversial cases or in times of crisis.

It has been suggested that Warren was astoundingly weak on names and faces and seemed to want to confine the Court to its own environment,[96] but whatever his motives, the placing of some distance between the Court and the public contributed to the respect in which he and the Court were held. Too great a familiarity would have spawned disrespect and might well have bred contempt. Warren, not sympathetic with those critics who believed the Court's processes to be overly secretive, insisted that the judiciary was the most open of the three branches.[97] As he correctly observed, all of the records of the cases before the Court are open to public inspection, as are the briefs and transcripts of arguments made in open court. Only the route taken by the justices to arrive at a final decision is confidential. On the other hand, decision making in the executive branch, as well as in much of the legislative process, is carried on in secret.[98]

Like Vinson, Stone, Hughes, and Taft, his four immediate predecessors, Earl Warren voted with the majority on his court in over 75 percent of the cases and therefore was responsible for assigning opinions most of the time.[99] Polished and practiced politician that he was, Warren used the assignment power to his and the Court's best advantage, always within the framework of an equitable division of labor. First, he tended to take on the significant cases himself, a not uncommon practice among chiefs but more clearly pronounced in some than in others. Second, by strategic assignments he shrewdly attempted to mold majorities and to use the talents of individual justices in a way that would accommodate both personal preferences and the best possible internal relationships. For example, in significant cases his preferred opinion assignees were the Court's leading intellectual adversaries, Black and Frankfurter.[100] In close cases (5 to 4) Frankfurter was assigned the opinion at a higher rate than anyone else, probably to hold him in a majority, although statistically Frankfurter received fewer assignments than his colleagues.[101] If a justice is to have any lasting influence, if his work is to acquire distinction, he must write the opinion of the Court in constitutional cases which have a major impact on the public[102] and the record indicates that Warren made certain that all who served with him had the opportunity to speak for the Court in some significant cases.[103]

Although always prepared, Warren never ran the conference in the didactic, Zeus-like manner of Hughes. His style, while firm, was more in the nature of a moderator who knew when to let the discussion take its course and when to call a halt and synthesize what could become a majority view. Abe Fortas, who observed Warren closely as chief, gives us this portrait: "He made no apparent effort to impress his views on his brethren. He was no more emphatic than some of them in stating his conclusions. He did not attempt to persuade by one-to-one off the record sessions. He did not convert his fellow Justices by the kind of penetrating, irresistible, jugular stroke which is so often the contribution of Mr. Justice Douglas. He did not press his brethren against a stone wall of logic and stern assurance in a manner that characterized the formidable Hugo Black. His effectiveness did not stem from the kind of calm and impressive scholarship that was the contribution of John Harlan."[104]

Where, then, lay Warren's abilities? For Fortas it was a matter of setting a standard, of impressing upon his colleagues the "simple view that the imperatives of truth and justice and fairness could not, and should not be avoided."[105] Unquestionably this courageous stand in behalf of what is fair comes through in the Warren Court's decisions on desegregation, criminal justice, reapportionment, on fundamental civil liberties issues, and it is the main theme of the law clerks who worked so closely with him. As one recalled, "Above all, Earl Warren was moved by an uncompromising spirit of fairness."[106] This spirit apparently was infectious as was his dedication to his work, his devotion to the Court and "the unmistakable purity of his motives."[107]

In spite of Justice Douglas' flattering term, "Superchief," Warren was not a superman and it is doubtful, for example, that he alone was responsible for orchestrating a unanimous decision in the desegregation cases, *Brown I* and *Brown II*.[108] After a trilogy of unanimous antisegregation cases in 1950 under Chief

Justice Vinson[109] the old "separate but equal" support for segregation stood on very shaky legal props, and a majority of the Warren Court—Black, Douglas, Burton, Minton and Warren—were agreed that segregation should be held unconstitutional. However, the fact that the decisions in *Brown* et al. were ultimately unanimous is almost as important as the decisions themselves[110] in that it gave them a sense of legitimacy—at least to the lay public—that they would not have had in a split decision.

Despite flimsy and inconclusive evidence, the attainment of unanimity is a tribute to Earl Warren's patience, diplomacy, and good humor. Justice Frankfurter wrote in a letter to Judge Learned Hand shortly after the announcement of the decisions that unanimity "could not possibly have come to pass with Vinson"[111] but three years later he wrote: "No doubt Warren had a share in the outcome, but the notion that he begot the unanimous Court is nonsense. . . . the ultimate outcome was in a significant way influenced by factors that antedated Warren's being here."[112] Yet in the same letter he said: "I do not mean to minimize the personal influence wisely exerted by a Chief Justice in the work of the Court" and in a telling sentence seems to give Warren more credit than he intended: "[T]he wise use of time in the Court's dealing with the problem raised by segregation under the Fourteenth Amendment was probably the chief factor in the ultimate decision."[113] The "wise use of time" was, in the final analysis, under the direction of the chief, and he carefully pursued a strategy of informal discussions at the end of regularly scheduled conferences and over lunch.[114] In short, Warren kept the pressure on the associates, subtly but firmly, and the results, while not exclusively a product of his leadership, might not have been attained without it. Furthermore, his opinions in both the original *Brown* decision and in the enforcement decree obtained unanimous support only after painstaking negotiations with his colleagues.

Like the Court under John Marshall and under Charles Evans Hughes, the Court led by Earl Warren faced a barrage of criticism, some of which took the form of proposals in Congress designed to neutralize its decisions or to circumscribe its powers. The crisis came in 1957 just twenty years after the Roosevelt attack on the Hughes Court but there were significant differ-

Leadership Through Inspiration and Conviction

ences. In the earlier conflict the Court had been applying brakes to reformist economic policies; conversely the Warren Court, with its emphasis on fairness and equality, had moved ahead of the elected branches by judicially confronting problems like segregation that legislative bodies had ignored and by protecting the rights of unpopular groups, primarily Communists, whose constitutional liberties had been curbed by both state and federal laws. The attack was also not a single, sledgehammer blow like the Court-packing plan but a series of legislative measures, some of which would have diminished the Court's authority while others would have softened the impact of specific decisions. In the Eighty-Fifth Congress some thirty such bills were introduced but only one, the so-called Jencks bill was enacted into law.[115] This was a reaction to the case of *Jencks* v. *United States*,[116] in which the Court had reversed a perjury conviction on the ground that the defendant Jencks, was entitled to see confidential FBI reports to ascertain whether any discrepancies existed between the oral testimony of witnesses in court and what they had told the FBI. Although the bill was originally intended as a rebuke to the Court, in its final form it was virtually a confirmation of what the Court had said. All of the above took place before the precedent-shattering decisions on reapportionment and criminal justice, both of which occasioned the introduction of countermeasures in the Congress.

Throughout the period of congressional assaults on the Court, the chief justice said very little publicly, relying instead on strong allies in Congress to stem the tide of negativism—responsible senators (both Democrats and Republicans) like Hubert Humphrey, Paul Douglas, Thomas Hennings, Wayne Morse, Joseph Clark, Jacob Javits, John Sherman Cooper, and above all, the majority leader, Lyndon Johnson. While not always in agreement with the Court's decisions, these men held the view that the existing rules under which the Court exercised judicial review would be devitalized in some attenuated version. Even in the midst of the legislative incursions, Earl Warren and his Court continued to expand civil liberties and his final months as chief saw no retreat in the areas of reapportionment and the rights of blacks.

Clearly a chief justice is the most vulnerable when the Court, and he as its leader—either real or symbolic—is the target of reproof from either the president or the Congress. He cannot engage in debate with the enemy since the justices, if they are to retain their perceived and appropriate role as above partisan politics, must never be in the center of public controversy. A reasoned defense of the Court's decisions has already been made in its opinions and the unconvinced will not be converted by a public lecture from the chief. The Hughes letter to a Senate committee, solicited by a friendly senator and made possible by a president who had left himself wide open to rebuttal, is probably the outer limit of a chief's response from a Court under siege.

It is more difficult to deal with scores of congressmen and senators whose reasons for criticizing the Court embrace a broad spectrum of complaints, and Earl Warren appropriately found public silence the wisest and most effective posture. Although no chief can impress his views on his often aggressively independent colleagues, he can give the Court a "discernible character, if not necessarily a coherent jurisprudence."[117] Of the three great chiefs only Marshall was able to endow the Court with a coherent jurisprudence and even he could not hold the justices in his desired pattern of national supremacy during the last decade of his service.[118] Under all three, however, the Court generally acted in predictable ways and this "discernible character" was based primarily on the influence of the chief, an influence that was maintained through a public performance and a private life that commanded respect.

CONSTITUTIONAL PHILOSOPHY AND LEGACY

Probably the most telling comment on Marshall's reasoning in his greatest opinions was that of John Randolph of Roanoke: "All wrong, all wrong, but no man in the United States can tell why or wherein."[119] Marshall had the supreme ability to synthesize axioms of republican political theory with syllogistic logic, a combination which created the impression that his conclusions were inevitable.[120] As described by an observer of his advocacy in the courtroom, Marshall's "art consisted in laying his premises so remotely from the point directly at the base, or else in terms so general and so spacious, that the hearer, seeing no consequences which could be drawn from them, was just as willing to admit them as not; but his premises once admitted, the demonstration, however distant, followed as certainly, as cogently, as inevitably, as any demonstration in Euclid."[121]

Justice Story reported a similar characterization by Marshall's great adversary, Thomas Jefferson: "When conversing with Marshall, I never admit anything. So sure as you admit any position to be good, no matter how remotely from the conclusion he seeks to establish, you are gone. . . . Why, if he were to ask if it were daylight or not, I'd reply, 'Sir, I don't know, I can't tell.'"[122]

Despite Marshall's modesty and humility in his personal relationships, the tone of his opinions was imperious, always written in a style, calculated or not, to put the reader off balance. His assumptions were stated as self-evident truths and his conclusions were interspersed with phrases like "an absurdity too gross to be insisted upon,"[123] "too extravagant to be maintained,"[124] "It can require no argument to prove,"[125] "all America understands, and has uniformly understood,"[126] and "That this could not be intended, is . . . too apparent for controversy."[127] The reader is made to feel that if he disagrees with the assertions, he is either ignorant or a fool or both. Coupled with the imperiousness was a mastery of majestic generalities, a rhetoric that has been quoted and requoted by every generation of constitutional lawyers since Marshall's day, even though close scrutiny may reveal little meaning.[128]

None of this suggests, however, that the judicial opinions of John Marshall were shallow or without substance. They were in a mold of great statesmanship based not on *a* theory but on *the* theory of the Constitution and a commitment to cement it to the American people with a permanent adhesive. As Edward Corwin maintains, John Marshall regarded the Court and the chief justiceship as not only a judicial tribunal but a platform from which to promulgate sound constitutional principles— the intentions of the framers—which he insisted must prevail. The Supreme Court as Marshall saw it was the "very cathedra . . . of constitutional orthodoxy."[129]

Equally important, he succeeded in making the foundations of American constitutional law unchallengeable, and he did so by resting his assumptions on self-evident, fundamental principles rather than on precedent alone.[130] As a practical matter he sought to maintain a balance between two overriding objectives: establishing Federalist constitutional theory as the law of the land and insisting that the Court give the appearance of solidarity in order to enhance its authority.[131]

As a substantive thinker John Marshall was a child of the enlightenment, a believer in Lockean liberalism with its key elements of the right to life, the freedom to express one's views, the opportunity to acquire property, and to possess and enjoy the fruits of one's labor. Marshall saw man as an imperfect being whose judgment is controlled more by passion than reason.[132] Thus he needs to be subject to a governmental authority with the ability to compel obedience, but at the same time the government must be based on popular support, albeit filtered through representative, republican institutions. Successful government must be in tune with the natural propensities of man for whom a decent political life includes human liberty in all its ramifications. Within this framework Marshall fashioned his constitutional discourses, using them to mold legal opinion in the country and ultimately to set the direction of the nation itself.[133] In his greatest opinions he defined and confined power, and by insisting that fundamental principles of the Constitution were grounded in moral precepts universally adapted to man's nature, he endowed them with a permanence second in importance only to the Constitution itself.

Judicial review was the essential first step in limiting governmental powers by making the judiciary a referee over the complexities of federalism and the separation of powers and, most important, establishing judicial protection for individual liberties. John Marshall did not invent the principle of judicial review but he gave it practical application. It has stood the test of time because it helped to solve one of the most perplexing problems of democratic government: how to make legislative power tolerable and limited. After having emphasized the necessity of limiting legislative power in *Marbury* v. *Madison*,[134] Marshall nevertheless maintained that the national legislature has broad discretion so long as it confines its lawmaking to the appropriate constitutional sphere. In upholding the power of Congress to create a national bank in *McCulloch* v. *Maryland*,[135] he wrote: "We admit, as all must admit, that the powers of government are limited, and that its limits are not to be transcended. But we think that the sound construction of the Constitution must allow to the national legislature that discretion, with respect to the means by which the powers it confers are to be carried into execution, which will enable that body to perform the high duties assigned to it, in the manner most beneficial to the people."

He thus enunciated the famous principle of implied powers, a doctrine that permitted almost infinite expansion of national power in the twentieth century, power that was, ironically, to make several inroads upon the institution of private property and upon the personal liberty to acquire it. However, in 1819 Marshall's concern was, like Alexander Hamilton's earlier, that the then fledgling nation with a potential for greatness must always possess the constitutional authority to meet the exigencies of the times. As he said in *McCulloch*,[136] the Constitution was "intended to endure for ages to come, and, consequently to be adapted to the various crises of human affairs. To have prescribed the means by which government should, in all future time, execute its powers, . . . would have been an unwise attempt to provide, by immutable rules, for exigencies which, if foreseen at all, must have been seen dimly, and which can be provided for as they occur."

The powers of the states, of course, Marshall viewed differently. Within the total horizon of government in the new union, if the nation were to exercise powers expansively, it followed logically that the states must settle for a diminished role, a fact which the states were to accept reluctantly. Thus circumscribing state powers became the ancillary hallmark of Marshall's constitutional law, although in the twilight of his service he tended to accommodate the increasingly recalcitrant state legislatures. In the inevitable conflicts between state and nation John Marshall insisted that the states recognize and accept a subordinate role in the new federal system. As he said in striking down the state tax in *McCulloch*,[137] "the American people . . . did not design to make their government dependent on the states. . . . the states have no power, by taxation or otherwise, to retard, impede, burden, or in any manner control the operations of the constitutional laws enacted by Congress to carry into execution the powers vested in the general government."

In *Gibbons* v. *Ogden*,[138] "his profoundest, most statesmanlike opinion,"[139] Marshall once again narrowed the states' role and simultaneously endowed the enumerated powers of Congress with exceptional vitality. "This power," Marshall declared, "like all others vested in Congress, is complete in itself, may be exercised to its utmost extent, and acknowledges no limitations, other than are prescribed in the Constitution."[140] By 1820 the Supreme Court had invalidated laws in seven states and by 1825, in ten,[141] as John Marshall continued to combine his idea of judicial sovereignty with the framers' views of national supremacy into a constitutional amalgam which would never be undone.

It is essential to remember that with few exceptions Marshall's great opinions in which the Constitution was construed in favor of nationalism had their origins in economic conflicts, a fact which gave Marshall the opportunity to promote a nationally supported capitalism.[142] Equally significant for the development of corporate enterprise were Marshall's pronouncements on contracts, corporations, and bankruptcy. Broadly construed was the word "contract" in Article I, Section 10 to mean public executed as well as private executory contracts[143] and to embrace corporate charters.[144] Corporations were held to be public in character and subject to legislative authority,[145] and although corporations are not citizens within the law, the citizens who comprise the corporation have legal rights which attach to the aggregate, including the right to sue. Therefore, corporations may sue in the federal courts under the diversity of citizenship clause.[146]

Marshall's views on state bankruptcy laws are clear enough, but in this area of constitutional law—the only one—he was in dissent from his own Court. He had managed to hold a majority in *Sturges* v. *Crowninshield*[147] when he declared that in the absence of congressional legislation, a state may enact a bankruptcy law although such a law might not alter the substance of a contract. The New York law in this instance was invalid since it had applied to contracts made prior to its passage. When a majority later held in *Ogden* v. *Saunders*[148] that a bankruptcy law may be applied to contracts made after the law's passage, Marshall disagreed, maintaining that under no circumstances could a state law interfere with a contract.

During Marshall's chief justiceship civil liberties issues comprised only a minuscule part of the Supreme Court's docket, but his opinion in the Aaron Burr trial evinces a concern for the protection of the rights of the accused that is unsurpassed to this day. His interpretation of the treason clause was so stringent that even a hostile jury had no course but to return a verdict of not guilty, and in the *Swartwout* and *Bollman*[149] cases he carefully defended the Supreme Court's authority to issue writs of *habeas corpus*, the ancient English legal protection against arbitrary imprisonment of a citizen.

As chief justice, Marshall had no occasion to formulate a judicial policy on First Amendment rights, but as a candidate for Congress in 1796 he had publicly opposed his own party's Alien and Sedition Acts and, while in Congress, at the expense of ending his political career, had voted to repeal that part of the Sedition Act punishing seditious speech. His opposition was not, incidentally, based on constitutional scruples but on the belief that such laws were inflammatory and calculated to undermine national unity.[150] Security for the individual and his property were still paramount in Marshall's scheme of values.

Although the American nation was founded with the writing of the Constitution in 1787, it required very special leadership to fix the course that the founders intended, and John Marshall provided that leadership in the judiciary. He did so in giving the Supreme Court an internal strength by establishing a collegiality and often in fact, unanimity, in its constitutional decisions. He was also able to fashion the law of the land through his own opinions which accurately reflected what the framers envisioned: an extended commercial republic in which the citizens would be free to pursue their self-interest, a governmental system which was not only compatible with, in Machiavelli's words, "Man's natural desire to acquire" but actually encouraged acquisitiveness.

Self-interest would not be a vulgar, greedy, selfishness but in Tocqueville's sense, "self-interest rightly understood," a prescription for ordering the passions and subordinating them to reason and, above all, passions would be restrained by a legal order based upon objective moral criteria. Accordingly, Marshall's views of the American system as expressed in his opinions conformed to the grand design of the Constitution. It was not intended to perfect man but to create the government of a nation that would be compatible with man's nature, strong enough to be effective internally and externally, limited enough to avoid the excesses of tyranny, free enough to permit individual development, open enough to accommodate diversity, and flexible enough to cope with the vacillating currents of history. It was John Marshall who took the plans of the architects and directed the construction of a constitutional edifice in which the chief justice would never be simply a judge but a participant in national statecraft at the highest level.

Charles Evans Hughes was very much like John Marshall in the sense that he held strong views of the American system and of the role of judicial power. Like Marshall, he was not a philosopher but a practitioner of first rank, and like Marshall he left a permanent, personal mark on American public law. Most important, in spite of the philosophical currents of the twentieth century—pragmatism, relativism, determinism and positivism—Hughes remained closer to John Marshall in his views of man, of the universe and of the law than to the leading intellectuals of his day. Not a visionary certainly, and conservative in the sense of preferring what he knew to social experimentation with the unknown, Hughes nevertheless had an abiding concern for fairness which, in the final analysis, controlled his judicial responses.

At the base of Hughes' thought was the spirit of orthodox Christianity indelibly impressed upon him by his parents during his early years, but it was both buttressed and modified through his university studies, particularly by the influence of three teachers, Ezekiel Robinson and J. Lewis Diman of Brown University and Theodore Dwight of the Columbia Law School.[151] All three were in the natural law tradition and permanently implanted in Hughes the wisdom and necessity of a public philosophy if the American nation were to continue to prosper in the vision of the founding fathers. Robinson emphasized the existence of an objective moral law backed by divine justice and commanding both nature and man. Since God gave man the power to reason, there is no conflict between God and rationalism, nor between reason and revelation, the latter being a truth beyond, but not in conflict with, nature. Diman assumed a rational, orderly and just universe, a harmonious natural world with a design and a purpose. Dwight maintained that law was discovered, not made, that it had evolved out of the wisdom of the ages and simply needed judicial interpretation. Dwight's concept of law was the traditional one, perfectly in tune with that of John Marshall and the framers of the Constitution. And this was the view of Charles Evans Hughes. In his public speeches one reads recurring themes: the use of reason in human affairs through God's rule, a harmony of interests in a just social order, no class divisions, respect for the rights of property, a supreme common good based on a permanent truth, and justice discoverable by human reason. Hughes saw this harmony of interests, a rational order, in the United States, and although aware of the lack of virtue in some people, both rich and poor, he opposed radical change, opting instead for moderate reforms carried out gradually and patiently.

Real progress for Hughes was possible only through rational, evolutionary change, and he supported movements for efficient and responsible government as well as moderate increases in government control over the economy.[152] Betty Glad in her brilliant book on Hughes, suggests that in equating the positive law with reason and justice, Hughes did not "consider the possibility that law and custom might sometimes codify the interests of the stronger, that there might be irremediable conflicts of interest between the various segments of society, that social rewards may sometimes be distributed on the basis of position, power, or chance rather than virtue."[153] One might reach that conclusion from reading Hughes' public speeches but it would seem to be too harsh a judgment of Hughes, the Supreme Court justice. For it was Hughes more than any other justice of his time who fixed the direction and who set the standard for protecting the rights of minorities and the less fortunate in society. There is a consistent pattern in his insistence on holding the states to a national standard in civil liberty and to scrupulous fairness in criminal procedure beginning with his years as an associate justice between 1910 and 1916. Moreover, as Paul Freund concludes, Hughes was not an enemy of welfare legislation.[154]

Particularly notable for their defense of individual liberty during his early service were his opinions in *Bailey* v. *Alabama*,[155] *Truax* v. *Raich*,[156] and *McCabe* v. *Atchison, Topeka & Santa Fe Ry.*[157] In *Bailey* the issue was the validity of an Alabama statute providing that any person who entered a contract for services and was given an advance of money, but who failed to perform the service or return the money, was to be assumed guilty of theft, his action being regarded as *prima facie* evidence of intent to injure or defraud. In holding the law both in violation of the Thirteenth Amendment and the Federal anti-peonage law Hughes contended that the statute was simply a means of compelling an employee-debtor to work off his debt, and he seemed compelled to observe that such laws would be "peculiarly effected as against the poor and the ignorant, its most likely victims." What he did not say, but certainly must have known, was that the law's "victims" were generally black.

In *Truax* v. *Raich*, Hughes wrote a seminal opinion on equal protection of the laws in which an Arizona law requiring employers of more than five workers within the state to employ not less that 80 percent qualified electors or natural-born American citizens, was held unconstitutional. Aliens were covered by the equal protection clause, said Hughes, and could not be subjected to such an onerous and unfair burden. States may not deny to lawful inhabitants, he declared, "because of their race or nationality, the ordinary means of earning a living. It requires no argument to show that the right to work for a living in the common occupations of the community is of the very essence of the personal freedom and opportunity that it was the purpose of the Amendment to secure." And Hughes' opinion in *McCabe* was the first to insist as a minimum that blacks and whites be accorded equal treatment in fact under the separate but equal doctrine. In this instance a state law permitting intrastate carriers to provide sleeping, dining, and chair cars for whites only was held to deny equal protection of the laws.

Typical of Hughes' position on the use of governmental power to correct or assuage social evils were his opinions in *Sturges & Burn Manufacturing Co.* v. *Beauchamp*,[158] *Price* v. *Illinois*,[159] and *Miller* v. *Wilson*.[160] In the latter he spoke for a unanimous Court in upholding a California law which forbade employment of women in certain occupations for more than eight hours a day or forty-eight hours per week; in *Price* he wrote that a state might prohibit the sale of food preservatives containing boric acid; and in *Beauchamp* he approved a state law that prohibited employment of children under sixteen in specified hazardous occupations. The law made the employer liable for injuries without permitting a defense that the employer had

Leadership Through Inspiration and Conviction

acted in good faith by determining the minor's age through simply asking him the question. In cases such as these Hughes relied heavily on the principle that the statute in question must have a reasonable relation to a valid state purpose and he conceded a broad discretion to the legislative judgment.

In his eleven years as chief, Hughes wrote 264 opinions of which 2 were in concurrence and 11 in dissent. He dissented without opinion, however, in 42 additional cases. On the surface these figures indicate that Hughes as chief led the Court intellectually most of the time, but always one must remember that the chief's views generally prevail only when they encounter sympathetic and receptive minds. Thus how much of a chief's success can be attributed to personal and intellectual persuasion and how much is due to the luck of the draw is never precisely ascertainable.

In the voluminous literature on Hughes there has been a tendency to concentrate on his "New Deal" opinions and on the crisis in which the institutional integrity of the Court was at stake. For Hughes' impact on American constitutional law, however, we must look elsewhere. As significant as his opinions were at the time in the *Gold Clause Cases*,[161] *Ashwander* v. *TVA*,[162] *NLRB* v. *Jones & Laughlin Steel Corp.*,[163] and *Home Building and Loan* v. *Blaisdell*,[164] they were more a legitimation of public policies in constitutional terms than they were initiatives in fixing the future of the Court's direction. It was in his opinions in the areas of criminal procedure, First Amendment guarantees, and the rights of minorities that Hughes laid the groundwork for what was to become, particularly under Chief Justice Warren, the Court's major preoccupation, and it is a role for which it is best fitted.

Although the Supreme Court under Hughes did not take that final step which would have ended segregation of the races, it so battered the old separate but equal structure that it was barely standing by the time Hughes retired in 1941. In slightly more than a dozen years it would collapse. In *Missouri ex rel. Gaines* v. *Canada*,[165] Hughes spoke for the Court in ordering the state of Missouri to provide facilities for a legal education for blacks substantially equal to those of whites. As in his earlier opinion in *McCabe*, Hughes was insisting that equal protection required at a minimum that a state must treat blacks and whites equally if not identically, but now the decision applied not only to transportation as in *McCabe* but to the much more critical, in fact fundamental, area of education. And in *Mitchell* v. *United States*[166] Hughes, writing for a unanimous Court, ruled that racial segregation on Pullman sleeping cars was a violation of the Interstate Commerce Act. Beyond the statutory construction, however, went the dictum that the denial of equality of accommodations because of race "would be an invasion of a fundamental individual right which is guaranteed against state action by the Fourteenth Amendment."

Combining both a concern for fairness in criminal procedure with the particular need to protect indigent blacks from depredations by white officialdom were Hughes' opinions in the notorious "Scottsboro Cases" which grew out of potentially unfair trials of a group of young blacks who were accused of raping white women. In two of the cases, *Norris* v. *Alabama*[167] and *Patterson* v. *Alabama*[168] the Court held that the exclusion of Negroes from jury duty, trial or grand, was a violation of the equal protection clause of the Fourteenth Amendment. In the *Patterson* case Hughes had to cut through a technical procedural matter which normally would have denied jurisdiction to the Supreme Court, but for him, intrinsic justice demanded that he brush it aside in an uncharacteristic manner, which he did with the declaration that "we cannot ignore the exceptional features of the present case."

Similarly in *Brown* v. *Mississippi*[169] he dismissed the state's technical contention that since counsel for the defense had failed to move for the exclusion of a confession, he had waived the defendant's right to a reversal of his conviction. It had been shown, however, that the conviction was based solely on a confession obtained through a brutal, violent beating of the accused, and again Hughes chose substantial justice over procedural exactness. In his words this was "a wrong so fundamental that it made the whole proceeding a mere pretense of a trial and rendered the conviction and sentence wholly void."

Equally significant for their impact on American public law and subsequently on the social fabric of American society were Hughes' creative opinions involving First Amendment issues. One of his most significant rulings is that in *Near* v. *Minnesota*,[170] a precedent-creating case in which the Court for the first time invalidated a state law on the ground that it violated freedom of speech and of the press, those guarantees held to be in Hughes' words "within the liberty safeguarded by the due process clause of the Fourteenth Amendment. . . ." The law under scrutiny permitted the enjoining of a newspaper for printing scandalous, malicious, defamatory or obscene matter. The injunction was enforceable through the process of punishment for contempt of court and could be lifted only if the issuing judge were convinced that the publication would not engage in objectionable practices in the future. In Hughes' view the statute's purpose was not punishment but suppression for it "imposed unconstitutional restraint upon publication." Historically and constitutionally in America, wrote Hughes, liberty of the press "has meant, principally, although not exclusively, immunity from previous restraints or censorship." The Four Horsemen dissented from this expansive and libertarian view of the First and Fourteenth Amendments.

Hughes wrote in defense of First Amendment rights and in behalf of unpopular causes in another half dozen cases, one in dissent, one in concurrence, the remaining four in the majority. He spoke for the Court in reversing the conviction and seven-year prison sentence of a member of the Communist Party who gave a speech at a meeting held under the Party's auspices[171] and, incidentally, brought freedom of peaceable assembly under the protection of the Fourteenth Amendment. Setting aside the conviction of Yetta Stromberg, a nineteen-year-old member of the Young Communist League who had committed a crime under California law by participating in a red flag ceremony at a children's summer camp, Hughes extended free speech to include symbolic expression and continued to evince a strong tolerance for dissent.[172]

This tolerance extended to religious scruples and to one's conscience. Hughes also wrote one of the early opinions defending the rights of Jehovah's Witnesses, including the right to distribute religious literature on the city streets without first obtaining permission from the city,[173] and he concurred in an opinion by Justice Roberts upholding the Witnesses' right to solicit contributions for religious purposes without first obtaining official permission.[174]

The chief justice dissented from Sutherland's interpretation of the naturalization oath one must take in order to secure citizenship, declaring that the language "support and defend the

Constitution and laws of the United States against all enemies, foreign and domestic, and bear true faith and allegiance to the same" did not exact a promise in advance to bear arms in the nation's defense, contrary to one's religious beliefs.[175] Hughes believed there was "abundant room for enforcing the requisite authority of law as it is enacted and requires obedience, and for maintaining the conception of the supremacy of law as essential to orderly government, without demanding that either citizens or applicants for citizenship shall assume by oath or obligation to regard allegiance to God as subordinate to allegiance to civil power."

In a series of cases evaluating freedom of expression for labor unions, Hughes, with only one mild exception, supported union rights. He joined the majority in upholding the prohibition of injunctions against peaceful picketing,[176] in sustaining the Norris-LaGuardia Act's provisions limiting the issuance of injunctions in labor disputes,[177] in invalidating a New Jersey ordinance prohibiting public assemblies without an official permit which had been used to harass the Congress for Industrial Organization,[178] and in permitting the enjoining of peaceful picketing if enmeshed with violence.[179] He dissented only from the Court's position that peaceful picketing could not be enjoined when it attempted to organize a business in which none of the employees wished to join a union and no employer-employee dispute existed over the matter.[180]

Justice Douglas reported that Hughes once remarked to him that at "the constitutional level where we work, ninety percent of any decision is emotional. The rational part of us supplies the reasons for supporting our predilections."[181] Clearly for Hughes the overriding principle of the American system was freedom and his strong preference for it was both emotional and rational. Furthermore, his opinions suggest that he did not believe freedom to be the exclusive possession of the more fortunate in this world; nor did he believe that its limits were fixed once and for all time. His horizon of liberty was a broad one, embracing freedom of enterprise along with intellectual and religious freedom and, like Marshall, he saw the need for curbs on popular democracy if individual liberty were to survive. During Hughes' public career the only institutional check on popular passions was the Supreme Court, the old Hamiltonian and Madisonian concepts of an aristocratic element in the Senate having given way to popular control with the adoption of the Seventeenth Amendment in 1920.

Hughes had total faith in the Court as the guardian of the American republic. Prior to his inital appointment to the Court he said: "In this country progress cannot be made save in harmony with our constitutional system. . . . The people have not only marked out the spheres and limited the powers of their representatives, but the provisions of our Constitution are also checks upon the hasty and inconsiderate action of the people themselves."[182] Later came the oft-quoted phrase: "We are under a Constitution, but the Constitution is what the judges say it is, and the judiciary is the safeguard of our liberty and of our property under the Constitution."[183]

In spite of his remark to Justice Douglas, Hughes fundamentally expected public policy and judicial decisions to be based on reason. As he said in a public speech in 1908, "We must have constant application of reason. That is what free government means. We have come down the course of history winning the victories of democracy, and summed up in a word, they are the victories of public judgments over force."[184] In the Hughes legacy we see a Supreme Court led internally in a disciplined, responsible and responsive manner, a Court first caught in a powerful political maelstrom during a period of national crisis and attacked by a popular, dynamic president, but emerging finally with its institutional integrity intact. Also rooted in his legacy is the doctrinal basis for the protection and extension of individual liberty which the Court utilized to chart its direction for a half century after Hughes' retirement. Hughes bequeathed to the office dignity, strength and authority along with a wealth of creative constitutional doctrine, but not all who followed could use its prerogatives as effectively as perhaps this one-in-a-generation judicial statesman.

Earl Warren is the only chief with whom I have discussed the Supreme Court's work and the chief justiceship and although, unlike Hughes, he did not "radiate" authority, he did convey, in addition to warmth and friendliness, a tempered self-assurance and an avuncular wisdom that, one surmises, had often enabled him to bring his associates around to his point of view, sometimes in spite of themselves. Although he believed that unanimous opinions were always desirable, he saw nothing wrong with a split court and declared that it was "more important to have the work of nine independent minds regardless of outcome." In his 16 years as chief he wrote 47 dissenting opinions and joined dissents an additional 13 times, but he spoke for the majority in 165 cases. It has been suggested that Earl Warren had "no well developed philosophy of judging" but had instead "a well developed philosophy of governing."[185]

Warren was, like Marshall and Hughes, a practical politician, not a deep thinking philosopher, and like the other great chiefs, he had an intrinsic sense of what was right and wrong, a sense that determined how he thought a case ought to be decided. Underlying his approach to a decision was first and foremost a humanitarian impulse coupled with a sensitivity to the plight of the underdog. Differentiating the political from the legal process in his memoirs, Warren contended that the former involved compromise, "taking a half a loaf where a whole loaf could not be obtained," but the basic ingredient of a judicial decision, he maintained, is principle and "it should not be compromised," should not be parceled out a little at a time "until eventually someone receives the full benefit."[186]

Critical of those who thought the Court was going too fast with respect to equal rights, Warren argued that this was simply a way of saying that "moderation calls for doling out rights only a little at a time to the minority groups, the poor, the uneducated, and the otherwise underprivileged."[187] Thus in order to bring about the desired result—constitutionally protected rights for the demeaned and the disadvantaged in society—he skirted around precedents and cut through internal legal forms. As one astute observer concluded, "Pressed to its logical outcome, Warren's jurisprudence appeared to make humanity and integrity of judges themselves the only check on judicial power. It deemphasized the complexity of the process of judging and emphasized the substantive importance of values at stake in the case."[188] Earl Warren's primary value was fairness, and in order to attain it, he pressed beyond mere equality of opportunity to equality of condition.

Toward the end of his tenure and in retirement Warren maintained that the most important decisions rendered during his years as chief were in the areas of reapportionment, desegrega-

Leadership Through Inspiration and Conviction

tion, and the guarantee of the right to counsel in all felony prosecutions, state and federal. However, he wrote the opinion of the Court only in *Brown* v. *Board of Education*[189] invalidating racial segregation in public schools. In *Baker* v. *Carr*[190] and *Gideon* v. *Wainwright*,[191] although Warren joined the majority, it was Justices Brennan and Black respectively who spoke for the Court. As the Court began to deal with additional refinements to reapportionment and fairness in criminal procedure, it was Warren who spoke for the principle of absolute equality in voting power—"one person, one vote"—and for a literal application in criminal cases of that slogan chiseled in stone on the Supreme Court building, "Equal Justice Under Law." His opinions however, faced hostile and brutally frank rebuttal from members of his own bench which at bottom was a disagreement over the appropriate function of the Supreme Court.

These judicial debates also mirrored the difficulty of coping with the insoluble dilemma of constitutional adjudication, namely, whether a case should be decided on the basis of what is best for the country or according to the existing legal standards.[192] Warren generally chose the former, a posture that was anathema to many scholars and lawyers who may have agreed with the chief's political orientation but nevertheless found his constitutional law unconvincing. Moreover, Earl Warren could not fine-tune a judicial opinion. Many of his arguments were not only discursive and lacking in logical sequence, but his style had an *ipse dixit* quality about it that made his supporters uncomfortable and furnished his adversaries with additional ammunition. More often than not, the justices who were in dissent had the better of the constitutional argument.

Leading examples of Warren the political reformer versus the judicial logician, were his opinions in *Reynolds* v. *Sims*[193] and *Miranda* v. *Arizona*.[194] There is no doubt that reforms were badly needed in the reapportionment of state legislatures and in criminal procedure, but where lay the responsibility to effect change? Although the Supreme Court had already entered the "political thicket" of reapportionment of state legislatures with Justice Brennan's opinion in *Baker* v. *Carr*,[195] Warren pressed judicial intervention beyond permissible limits, according to some members of his Court. In declaring that the equal protection clause required that both houses of a bicameral legislature be apportioned on a population basis with election districts being equal, Warren was ordering the destruction of political patterns that had been in existence since, and in some instances before, the Civil War. In basing his "one person, one vote" theory on the Fourteenth Amendment he went beyond any simple constitutional requirement of a qualified right to vote, to a right to cast an undiluted vote. "Diluting the weight of votes because of place of residence," said Warren, "impairs basic constitutional rights . . . just as much as insidious discrimination based upon factors such as race or economic status."

This was a view that was based on a theory of democracy which in its purest form presupposes equality of voting power but which in Justice John Marshall Harlan's view, failed to take into account the practical realities of representative government. Harlan was even more concerned, however, with what he deemed a misreading of the Constitution and the misuse of judicial power. Of the former he observed that the "history of the adoption of the Fourteenth Amendment provides conclusive evidence that neither those who proposed nor those who ratified the Amendment believed the Equal Protection Clause limited the power of the States to apportion their legislatures as they saw fit." Equally pernicious with Warren's twisted interpretation of the Fourteenth Amendment, said Harlan, was the "blanket authority and the constitutional duty" given to courts "to supervise apportionment of State Legislatures. It is difficult to imagine a more intolerable and inappropriate interference by the judiciary with the independent legislatures of the States." In concluding his remarks Harlan was moved to castigate the chief's reformist views of judging. "These decisions," he declared impatiently, "give support to a current mistaken view of the Constitution and the constitutional function of this Court. This view, in a nutshell, is that every major social ill in this country can find its cure in some constitutional 'principle,' and that this Court should 'take the lead' in promoting reform when other branches of government fail to act. The Constitution is not a panacea for every blot upon the public welfare, nor should this Court, ordained as a judicial body, be thought of as a general haven for reform movements."

Again it was Harlan who wrote a critical rebuttal to the Warren opinion in *Miranda* v. *Arizona.* As in *Reynolds,* the chief

Leadership Through Inspiration and Conviction

justice brushed precedent and history aside in order to institute what he believed to be necessary reforms in protecting persons accused of a crime. In reversing the conviction of Miranda for alleged kidnapping and rape, Warren extended two fundamental guarantees of the Bill of Rights—the right to counsel and the protection against self-incrimination—to the police interrogation level. Fashioning new rules for the police, Warren asserted that at a minimum, prior to any questioning, a suspect must be warned that he had a right to remain silent, that any statement he made might be used against him, and that he had a right to the presence of an attorney, appointed or retained, during the police interrogation. Although these rights might be waived, the waiver must be made "voluntarily, knowingly and intelligently." To answer some questions does not constitute a waiver since at any point in the proceeding the suspect may refuse further interrogation until he has consulted with an attorney.

It was again the equality norm and a concern for fair treatment of the underdog that motivated Warren's opinion. It was common knowledge that the intelligent man of means had always been accorded his rights at the moment of contact with the police but the indigent, the unschooled, friendless and frightened, neither knew of their constitutional rights nor had the courage to protest against mistreatment by law enforcement officers. Furthermore, given America's racial history, the legal inequality cut deeper than ever, not only differentiating the rich from the poor but cruelly singling out the poor black for arbitrary treatment.

Strong dissents were registered by Justices Harlan, White, and Clark with Justice Stewart concurring in both the Harlan and White opinions. Harlan believed that the Warren opinion represented "poor constitutional law" and that it entailed "harmful consequences for the country at large." He would have left in place the due process standard for determining whether the police had used "undue pressure" or coercion to obtain a confession. The new rules, said Harlan, will impair, perhaps wholly frustrate "an instrument of law enforcement that has long and quite reasonably been thought worth the price paid for it." Then, as in *Reynolds*, Harlan accused the chief of misusing the judicial function. Harlan agreed that reforms in criminal procedure may be necessary, but he insisted that the legislature, not the judiciary, was the proper vehicle for the task since it would have "the vast advantage of empirical data and comprehensive study" and "would allow experimentation and use solutions not open to the courts. . . ."

Although the Warren Court has the reputation, and deservedly so, for zealously applying and extending the Bill of Rights, the record of Warren, the judge, is not without its flaws. Often cited among Warren's accomplishments is the *Watkins* case[196] in which he wrote the opinion overturning the conviction for contempt of a witness before the Committee on Un-American Activities of the House of Representatives. Actually the final decision turned on a very narrow point—the witness had not been adequately apprised of the pertinency of the questions to the investigation—and the chief justice's lecture to Congress on how not to conduct investigations apparently fell on deaf ears, for the Court continued to be faced with additional allegations of violations of constitutional rights by congressional investigating committees. When the chips were down in cases like *Barenblatt* v. *United States*,[197] the chief could not muster a majority to curb the excesses of legislative investigations.

Unquestionably the Warren Court extended protections for freedom of speech and press well beyond the frontiers of the past but the chief drew lines at times which by any standard must be characterized as illiberal. For example, he wrote the opinion in *United States* v. *O'Brien*[198] upholding an act of Congress prohibiting the public destruction of a draft card, thus supporting the conviction of O'Brien who had torn up his card in front of the South Boston courthouse. The chief's opinion was acceptable, conventional constitutional law in that on its face the law prohibited the destruction of records which Congress might validly require a citizen to keep intact. Everyone knew, however, that the law was punitive against Vietnam war protesters since the original Selective Service Act already required registrants to keep their draft cards in their "personal possession at all times." This attitude reveals a patriotic conservatism in Warren, the same patriotic conservatism that impelled him to defend the Japanese exclusion cases well into his retirement.

If his patriotism influenced his judgment, so did his Puritanism, the latter having been responsible for, in the words of one biographer, his "greatest judicial aberration."[199] The aberration

Leadership Through Inspiration and Conviction

was in his vacillating, muddled position on obscenity which he found abhorrent, yet attempted to square with his open view of free speech. He also had difficulty in protecting the rights of gamblers and was, for example, the lone dissenter in *Marchetti* v. *United States*[200] in which he implied that gamblers ought not to be protected by the Fifth Amendment. In a series of cases beginning with *Mapp* v. *Ohio*[201] and *Gideon* v. *Wainwright*[202] the Warren Court revolutionized American constitutional law by incorporating most of the Bill of Rights pertaining to criminal law into the Fourteenth Amendment, and although the chief justice supported the movement, the major credit belongs not to Warren but to Justice Black whose dogged persistence finally persuaded a majority to join his crusade. None of this denigrates the leadership role of Chief Justice Warren, but it does indicate that the reasons for his greatness go far beyond his abilities as a judge.

WHY GREAT LEADERS?

Justice William Brennan once suggested that highly developed judicial skill is not a requisite for greatness in a chief justice, that great chiefs might not have made very good state or lower federal court judges.[203] What Brennan is saying is that an acute political sense, both on the daily personal level and on the grand scale of governance, is much more important in a chief than a sharply honed legal mind. No doubt this is true but judicial craftsmanship cannot be ignored in assessing a chief's effectiveness since judicial opinions, irrespective of their political implications, must be defensible as nonpolitical, objective reasoning that the public can accept even if disagreeing with the result. Thus, if a chief's opinions tend to ignore the subtleties of legal reasoning and to avoid answering the hard questions of the critics, including those of dissenting justices, the Court's credibility and independence are severely strained, sometimes to the breaking point.

If we compare Marshall, Hughes, and Warren in this sense, Hughes is the least flawed, Warren the most. For Marshall the slowness of communication, the lack of precedent in constitutional law, the early Federalist domination of the Court, and the acceptance of the myth that judges discover but do not make law tended to soften public criticism of his broad assertions. Warren, of course, had none of these protective screens around his work, and his "majestic generalities," while supporting desirable public policy in the eyes of many Americans, did not carry the necessary legal props to answer his critics, a characteristic that not only weakened his leadership but damaged the reputation of the Court. Hughes, on the other hand, was a sound legal scholar and would have been accorded respect had he remained as an associate justice and never become chief. Attacks on the Hughes Court did not involve the charge that the chief's opinions were inadequately reasoned, a fact which reinforced his ability to lead. In sum, judicial craftsmanship, while not essential to leadership, cannot be disregarded. The lack of it was harmful to Warren; the ability to use it was an asset to Hughes; special circumstances made it somewhat less significant for Marshall.

It has been said that the Supreme Court is not the originator of social, economic, or political policy, that it is a moon rather than a sun, reflecting changes already immanent in society.[204] A fair generalization certainly, but the Court under the great chiefs did more than reflect the public mind. To a certain degree it refracted the main currents of the times but it was also creative, and in this process lies in part the greatness of leadership. Marshall, Hughes, and Warren deserve special recognition for their willingness to take bold initiatives at the decision-making level, for their insistence on maintaining the independence and integrity of the Supreme Court in times of national crisis, for their uncanny ability to foster relatively congenial relationships among their associate justices in spite of unyielding intellectual differences, and for their extraordinary capacity to present a public face of a legitimate and wise use of authority lacking in caprice or arbitrariness.

They were, of course, very different men in many ways, but there were significant common threads in their character and in their fundamental beliefs. All were free of cynicism, all were more pragmatic than ideological, and all were without class arrogance, without special pretense of belonging to a governing elite. All believed in a universal sense of justice and all viewed judicial interpretation as depending as much upon the spirit of

Leadership Through Inspiration and Conviction

the law as upon its literal wording. While certain that man's nature inclines him toward a sense of justice, Marshall, Hughes, and Warren were also aware of the darker side of that nature—the selfishness and meanness that would deny justice to others. Thus rules—constitutions, statutes and judicial guidance—were needed to adjust, to balance, to maintain a maximum of harmony in the myriad personal relationships that inevitably exist in highly developed societies.

Most important, Chief Justices Marshall, Hughes, and Warren were supremely fitted to the office, not because they reflected the prevailing views of their times but because they pursued their inner voices, their instincts, that aggregate of the innate and the attitudes acquired over the years from family, teachers, associates and books. The results of their service must accord them a place of honor among the finest practitioners of American statecraft.

NOTES
1. William W. Story, ed., *The Miscellaneous Writings of Joseph Story*, Boston: Charles C. Little and James Brown (1852), pp. 643–44.
2. Ibid., p. 646.
3. Ibid., p. 651.
4. Edward S. Corwin, *John Marshall and the Constitution*, New Haven: Yale University Press (1919), p. 198.
5. Ibid.
6. Leonard Baker, *John Marshall: A Life in Law*, New York: Macmillan (1974), p. 342.
7. Ibid.
8. As quoted in Charles Warren, *The Supreme Court in United States History*, Boston: Little Brown & Co. (1922), Vol. I, p. 178.
9. Baker, op. cit., p. 351.
10. Henry Abraham, *Justices and Presidents*, New York: Oxford University Press (1974), p. 73.
11. Letter from John Adams to E. Boudinot, January 26, 1801, as quoted in Baker, op. cit., p. 353.
12. See Albert J. Beveridge, *The Life of John Marshall*, Boston: Houghton Mifflin (1916–1920) Vol. 2, p. 554, note 3. See also J. A. Garraty, "The Case of the Missing Commissions," *American Heritage*, June 1963, p. 7.
13. Letter from J. Dayton to W. Paterson as quoted in Baker, op. cit., p. 355.
14. Letter from T. Sedgwick to R. King, May 11, 1800, as quoted in Corwin, op. cit., p. 51.

15. Kenneth B. Umbreit, *Our Eleven Chief Justices*, New York: Harper & Bros. (1938), p. 115.
16. As quoted in Henry Flanders, *The Lives and Times of the Chief Justices of the United States*, Philadelphia: J. B. Lippincott & Co. (1858), Vol. 1, pp. 408–9.
17. Ibid., p. 522.
18. Baker, op. cit., p. 222.
19. Flanders, op. cit., p. 305.
20. Umbreit, op. cit., p. 128.
21. Corwin, op. cit., p. 52.
22. Umbreit, op. cit., p. 453.
23. Betty Glad, *Charles Evans Hughes and the Illusion of Innocence*, Urbana: University of Illinois Press (1966), p. 1.
24. Samuel Hendel, *Charles Evans Hughes and the Supreme Court*, New York: Russell (1951), p. 78.
25. Ibid., pp. 78–90.
26. William T. Gossett, "Chief Justice Hughes—A Recollection," *Supreme Court Historical Society Yearbook*, 1981, p. 76.
27. Umbreit, op. cit., p. 470.
28. As quoted in Glad, op. cit., p. 109.
29. Ibid., p. 108.
30. As quoted in Gossett, op. cit., p. 77.
31. David J. Danelski and Joseph S. Tulchin (eds.), *The Autobiographical Notes of Charles Evans Hughes*, Cambridge: Harvard University Press (1973), p. 127.
32. Ibid., pp. 288–89.
33. Ibid., p. 324.
34. Umbreit, op. cit., p. 498.
35. Earl Warren, *The Memoirs of Earl Warren*, New York: Doubleday & Co., (1977), p. 15.
36. Ibid., p. 19.
37. Arthur Rossett in "Chief Justice Earl Warren: A Tribute", 2 *Hastings Constitutional Law Quarterly* (Winter, 1975), p. 2.
38. Ibid., pp. 2–3.
39. Warren, op. cit., p. 275.
40. Henry Abraham, op. cit., pp. 235–36.
41. Ibid., p. 238.
42. Warren, op. cit., pp. 5–6.
43. Anthony Lewis, *New York Times Magazine*, Jan. 19, 1964, p. 65.
44. John Gunther, *Inside U.S.A.*, New York: Harper (1947), p. 18 as quoted in John D. Weaver, *Warren: The Man, the Court, the Era*, Boston: Little, Brown (1967), p. 16.
45. Leo Katcher, *Earl Warren: A Political Biography*, New York: McGraw-Hill (1967), p. 6.
46. Umbreit, op. cit., p. 113.
47. Charles Augustus Murray, *Travels in North America*, London: R. Bentley (1839), Vol. 1., p. 158.

48. G. Edward White, *The American Judicial Tradition*, New York: Oxford University Press (1976), p. 13.
49. Quoted in Donald Morgan, *Justice William Johnson*, Columbia: Univ. of South Carolina Press (1954), pp. 181–82.
50. White, op. cit., p. 12.
51. Baker, op. cit., p. 510.
52. White, op. cit., p. 13.
53. *Talbot* v. *Seeman*, 1 Cranch 1 (1801).
54. See David Danelski, "The Chief Justice and the Supreme Court," doct. dissert., Univ. of Chicago, 1961, pp. 12–17 for a succinct treatment of Marshall's impact on the Court. During his 34 years Marshall wrote about half of the Court's opinions. A fair distribution of the work would have assigned him no more than one-seventh. See Leo Pfeffer, *This Honorable Court*, Boston: Beacon Press (1965), p. 91.
55. Beveridge, op. cit., III, pp. 15–16.
56. Danelski, op. cit., p. 15.
57. Joseph Story, "Life, Character and Service of Chief Justice Marshall", in William W. Story, ed., *The Miscellaneous Writings of Joseph Story*, New York: DaCapo Press (1972), p. 692.
58. Ibid., p. 693.
59. Danelski, op. cit., p. 13.
60. As quoted in Joseph P. Lash, *From the Diaries of Felix Frankfurter*, New York: W. W. Norton (1975), pp. 313–14.
61. Edwin McElwain, "The Business of the Supreme Court as conducted by Chief Justice Hughes," 63 *Harvard Law Review* 5 (1949), p. 12; Felix Frankfurter, "Chief Justices I have Known," 39 *Virginia Law Review* 883 (1953), p. 902.
62. McElwain, Ibid.
63. Frankfurter, op. cit., p. 902.
64. McElwain, op. cit., p. 12.
65. Gossett, op. cit., p. 76.
66. McElwain, op. cit., p. 14.
67. Ibid., p. 15.
68. Owen Roberts, *Proceedings of the Bar and Officers of the Supreme Court of the United States in Memory of Charles Evans Hughes*, Washington, Privately printed, 1950, p. 121.
69. Danelski, op. cit., p. 90.
70. Frankfurter, "Chief Justices," p. 903.
71. Eugene C. Gerhart, *America's Advocate: Robert H. Jackson*, Indianapolis: Bobbs-Merrill Co. (1958), pp. 165–66.
72. See White, op. cit., pp. 213–15. White takes the position that Hughes may have exacerbated the tensions among his colleagues and that he did not lead jurisprudentially but dominated the Court in minor ways. White does say, nevertheless, that another type of person "might have accomplished far less and tarnished his reputation far more" (p. 215).
73. Paul Freund, "Charles Evans Hughes as Chief Justice," 81 *Harvard Law Review* 4 (1967), p. 13.

Chief Justice

74. McElwain, op. cit., p. 17.
75. Charles Evans Hughes, *The Supreme Court of the United States*, New York: Columbia University Press (1928), pp. 58–69.
76. See McElwain, op. cit., pp. 18–20. For a critical view of the motives behind Hughes' opinion assignments to himself see Irving Brant, "How Liberal Is Justice Hughes," *New Republic*, July 21, 1937, and July 28, 1937. Brant's analysis concludes that when the Court was reactionary, and Hughes was in the majority, he rarely wrote the reactionary opinion, but when Hughes was with the liberal majority, he wrote more than his share of the liberal opinions. Analyzing opinions between 1930 and 1937 Brant indicates that of 43 cases in which Hughes was a part of the liberal majority, he wrote the opinion of the Court in 13. In the 51 cases in which he voted with the reactionary majority, he wrote the opinion only once. Brant then suggests that Hughes' deportment in assigning himself opinions was based on the desire for public approbation, the desire to wield power, and the desire to obtain certain objectives. Assessing motives in this fashion is hardly an objective exercise, but even if Brant's allegations are true, they do not detract from the fundamental concepts of balance and moderation in Hughes' opinion assignments.
77. The decisions were: *Gold Clause Cases (Norman v. Baltimore and Ohio R.R.*, 294 U.S. 240 and *Perry v. United States*, 294 U.S. 330, 1935); *Louisville Joint Stock Land Bank v. Radford*, 295 U.S. 555 (1935); *Railroad Retirement Board v. Alton R.R. Co.*, 295 U.S. 330 (1935); *Humphrey's Executor v. United States*, 295 U.S. 602 (1935); *Schechter Poultry Corp. v. United States*, 295 U.S 495 (1935); *Panama Refining Co. v. Ryan*, 293 U.S. 388 (1935); *United States v. Butler* 297 U.S. 1 (1936); *Ashwander v. TVA*, 297 U.S. 288 (1936); *Jones v. Securities & Exchange Comm.*, 298 U.S. 1 (1936); *Carter v. Carter Coal Co.*, 298 U.S. 238 (1936); *Morehead v. New York ex rel. Tipaldo*, 298 U.S. 587 (1936).
78. See Robert J. Steamer, *The Supreme Court in Crisis*, Amherst: Univ. of Massachusetts Press (1971), pp. 199–200 for a discussion of the cases.
79. *West Coast Hotel v. Parrish*, 300 U.S. 379 (1937).
80. *NLRB v. Jones & Laughlin Steel Corp.*, 301 U.S. 1 (1937).
81. *The Social Security Cases (Helvering v. Davis*, 301 U.S. 619 and *Steward Machine Co. v. Davis*, 301 U.S. 548 (1937).
82. Charles Evans Hughes, *Autobiographical Notes*, op. cit., p. 311.
83. Ibid., p. 313.
84. Ibid.
85. White, op. cit., p. 205.
86. Robert H. Jackson, *The Struggle for Judicial Supremacy*, New York: Knopf (1941), p. 196.
87. *Tot v. United States*, 319 U.S. 463 (1943) declared unconstitutional Section 2 (f) of the Federal Firearms Act of 1938 and *United States v. Lovett*, 328 U.S. 303 (1946) invalidated Section 304 of the Urgency Deficiency Appropriation Act of 1943. The first major Act of Congress to be invalidated after 1937 was Article 3 (a) of the Uniform Code of Military Justice, *Toth v. Quarles*, 350 U.S. 11 (1955).

88. White, op. cit., p. 337.
89. Warren, *Memoirs*, p. 277.
90. Handwritten note from Justice Frankfurter to Justice Black, December 7, 1955. Harold Burton Papers, Library of Congress.
91. Abe Fortas, "Chief Justice Warren: The Enigma of Leadership," 84 *Yale Law Journal* 405 (Jan. 1975), p. 407.
92. Ibid.
93. Ibid., p. 406.
94. Ibid.
95. Warren, *Memoirs*, pp. 284–85.
96. *New York Times*, June 22, 1968, p. 16.
97. Warren, *Memoirs*, p. 342.
98. Ibid.
99. S. Sidney Ulmer, "The Uses of Power in the Supreme Court: The Opinion Assignments of Earl Warren, 1953–1960," 19 *Journal of Public Law* 49 (1970), p. 53.
100. Ibid., p. 57.
101. Ibid., pp. 58, 61. In his study of Warren's opinion assignments, Ulmer indicates that the overall low rate of assigned opinions to Frankfurter is due primarily to underassignment in cases involving commercial relations. Frankfurter was not disfavored in civil liberties or significant cases generally.
102. David N. Atkinson, "Minor Supreme Court Justices: Their Characteristics and Importance," 3 *Florida State University Law Review* 348 (1975), p. 352.
103. Ulmer, op. cit., pp. 56–57.
104. Abe Fortas, op. cit., p. 406.
105. Ibid., p. 406.
106. Graham B. Moody, Jr., in "Chief Justice Earl Warren: A Tribute," 2 *Hastings Constitutional Law Quarterly* (Winter 1975), p. 15.
107. John Hart Ely, "The Chief," 88 *Harvard Law Review* 11 (1974).
108. *Brown* v. *Board of Education*, 347 U.S 483 (1954), and *Bolling* v. *Sharpe* 347 U.S. 497 (1954), enforced *sub nom. Brown* v. *Board of Education*, 349 U.S. 294 (1955).
109. *Sweatt* v. *Painter*, 339 U.S. 629 (1950); *McLaurin* v. *Oklahoma State Regents*, 339 U.S. 637 (1950); *Henderson* v. *United States:* 339 U.S. 816 (1950).
110. For a discussion of how the desegregation decisions were arrived at, see Richard Kluger, *Simple Justice*, New York: Knopf (1975) and Dennis J. Hutchinson, "Unanimity and Desegregation: Decisionmaking in the Supreme Court, 1948–1958," 68 *Georgetown Law Journal* 1 (1979).
111. As quoted in Hutchinson, ibid., p. 35.
112. Ibid.
113. Ibid.
114. Warren, *Memoirs*, pp. 285–86. Also related to the author in a talk with Earl Warren in 1973 during his retirement.
115. See R. J. Steamer, op. cit., pp. 245–59 for a discussion of the proposals.

116. 353 U.S. 657 (1957).
117. G. Edward White, op. cit., p. 318. White uses this phrase to describe only the Warren Court.
118. Robert G. Seddig, "John Marshall and the Origins of Supreme Court Leadership," 36 *University of Pittsburgh Law Review* 785 (Summer, 1975), pp. 823–33.
119. Corwin, op. cit., p. 124.
120. White, op. cit., p. 33.
121. As quoted in Ben W. Palmer, *Marshall and Taney: Statesmen of the Law*, New York: Russell and Russell (1966), p. 65.
122. Ibid., p. 66.
123. *Marbury* v. *Madison*, 1 Cranch 137 (1803).
124. Ibid.
125. *Dartmouth College* v. *Woodward*, 4 Wheaton 518 (1819).
126. *Gibbons* v. *Ogden*, 9 Wheaton 1 (1824).
127. *McCulloch* v. *Maryland*, 4 Wheaton 316 (1819).
128. Leo Pfeffer, *This Honorable Court*, Boston: Beacon Press (1965), p. 91.
129. Corwin, op. cit., p. 122.
130. Robert Faulkner, *The Jurisprudence of John Marshall*, Princeton: Princeton Univ. Press (1968), p. 220.
131. Donald Morgan, "Marshall, the Marshall Court and the Constitution" in W. M. Jones, ed., *Chief Justice John Marshall: A Reappraisal*, Ithaca: Cornell Univ. Press, (1971), p. 170.
132. Faulkner, op. cit., p. 45.
133. Ibid., p. 216.
134. 1 Cranch 137 (1803).
135. 4 Wheaton 316 (1819).
136. *McCulloch* v. *Maryland* at 408.
137. Ibid., at 432–36.
138. 9 Wheaton 1 (1824).
139. Corwin, op. cit., p. 137.
140. *Gibbons* v. *Ogden* at 196.
141. Pennsylvania (*United States* v. *Judge Peters*, 5 Cranch 115, 1809); Virginia (*Martin* v. *Hunter's Lessee*, 1 Wheaton 304, 1816); Georgia (*Fletcher* v. *Peck*, 6 Cranch 87, 1810); New Hampshire (*Dartmouth College* v. *Woodward*, 4 Wheaton 518, 1819); New Jersey (*New Jersey* v. *Wilson*, 7 Cranch 164, 1812); New York (*Sturges* v. *Crowninshield*, 4 Wheaton 122, 1819); Maryland (*McCulloch* v. *Maryland*, 4 Wheaton 316, 1819); Vermont (*Society, etc.* v. *New Haven*, 8 Wheaton 464, 1823); Kentucky (*Green* v. *Biddle*, 8 Wheaton 1, 1823); Ohio (*Osborn* v. *Bank of United States*, 9 Wheaton 738, 1824).
142. Kent Newmyer, *The Supreme Court Under Marshall and Taney*, Arlington Heights: AHM Publishing Corp., 1968, p. 61.
143. *Fletcher* v. *Peck*, 6 Cranch 87 (1810).
144. *Dartmouth College* v. *Woodward*, 4 Wheaton 518 (1819).
145. *Head* v. *Providence Insurance Co.*, 2 Cranch 127 (1804).
146. *Bank of United States* v. *Deveaux*, 5 Cranch 61 (1809).
147. 4 Wheaton 122 (1819).

148. 12 Wheaton 213 (1827).
149. *Ex parte Swartwout and Ex parte Bollman,* 4 Cranch 75 (1807).
150. See Faulkner, op. cit., pp. 13–17 for Marshall's views on freedom of speech and religious liberty.
151. See Betty Glad, op. cit., pp. 29–37, 45–47 for a summary of the views of Robinson, Diman and Dwight.
152. Ibid., pp. 88–94.
153. Ibid., pp. 94–95.
154. Freund, op. cit., p. 9.
155. 219 U.S. 219 (1911).
156. 239 U.S. 33 (1915).
157. 235 U.S. 151 (1914).
158. 231 U.S. 320 (1913).
159. 238 U.S. 446 (1915).
160. 236 U.S. 373 (1915).
161. *Norman* v. *Baltimore & Ohio R.R.,* 294 U.S. 240 (1935); *Perry* v. *United States,* 294 U.S. 330 (1935).
162. 297 U.S. 288 (1936).
163. 301 U.S. 1 (1937).
164. 290 U.S. 398 (1934).
165. 305 U.S. 337 (1938).
166. 313 U.S. 80 (1941).
167. 294 U.S. 587 (1935).
168. 294 U.S. 600 (1935).
169. 297 U.S. 278 (1936).
170. 283 U.S. 697 (1931).
171. *DeJonge* v. *Oregon,* 299 U.S. 353 (1937).
172. *Stromberg* v. *California,* 283 U.S. 359 (1931).
173. *Lovell* v. *Griffin,* 303 U.S. 444 (1938).
174. *Cantwell* v. *Connecticut,* 310 U.S. 296 (1940).
175. *United States* v. *Macintosh,* 283 U.S. 605 (1931).
176. *Thornhill* v. *Alabama,* 310 U.S. 588 (1940) and *Carlson* v. *California,* 310 U.S. 106 (1940).
177. *New Negro Alliance* v. *Sanitary Grocery Co.,* 303 U.S. 552 (1938).
178. *Hague* v. *Committee for Industrial Organization,* 307 U.S. 496 (1939).
179. *Milk Wagon Drivers Union* v. *Meadowmoor Dairies, Inc.,* 312 U.S. 287 (1941).
180. *American Federation of Labor* v. *Swing,* 312 U.S. 321 (1941).
181. William O. Douglas, *The Court Years 1939–1975,* New York: Random House (1981), p. 8.
182. Charles Evans Hughes, *Addresses,* 2nd. ed., New York: Harper (1916), pp. 96–97.
183. Ibid., pp. 139–141.
184. Speech of February 22, 1908, *Addresses,* p. 76.
185. White, op. cit., p. 337.
186. Warren, *Memoirs,* p. 6.
187. Ibid.
188. White, op. cit., p. 341.

Chief Justice

189. 347 U.S. 483 (1954).
190. 369 U.S. 186 (1962).
191. 372 U.S. 335 (1963).
192. Archibald Cox, *The Warren Court*, Cambridge: Harvard University Press (1968), pp. 4–5.
193. 377 U.S. 533 (1964).
194. 384 U.S. 436 (1966).
195. *Supra*, note 190.
196. *Watkins* v. *United States*, 354 U.S. 178 (1957).
197. 360 U.S. 109 (1959).
198. 391 U.S. 367 (1968).
199. Jack Harrison Pollock, *Earl Warren: The Judge Who Changed America*, Englewood Cliffs: Prentice-Hall (1979), p. 355.
200. 390 U.S. 39 (1968).
201. 367 U.S. 643 (1961).
202. *Supra*, note 191.
203. Pollock, op. cit., p. 360.
204. Philip Kurland, "The Court Should Decide Less and Explain More" in Leonard W. Levy, *The Supreme Court Under Earl Warren*, New York: N.Y. Times Book Co. (1972), p. 231.

Chapter 3

LEADERSHIP THROUGH PERSUASION AND EXAMPLE

ROGER BROOKE TANEY, Morrison R. Waite, Melville Weston Fuller, and Edward Douglass White were able but, to a degree, flawed chiefs. They were *good* but not *great* leaders. While Taney presided over the Supreme Court during the period of the nation's greatest travail—the time of uncertainty over the nature and future of the American union—Waite, Fuller, and White occupied the head chair during a sustained period of industrial development, western settlement and a general optimism in the nation. Of the four only White came to the Court with a long record of national public service and most of that was as an associate justice of the Supreme Court. Taney's public career in national office prior to his appointment as chief justice amounted to less than four years; Chief Justices Waite and Fuller had never held federal office prior to their being named to the Supreme Court. Of the four only Taney and White were the president's first choices, and in the latter's case it took President Taft more than seven months to decide to appoint White rather than Charles Evans Hughes to whom he had earlier written a letter indicating that he would *probably* name him chief should a vacancy occur during Taft's presidential term.[1]

Although none of the four was welcomed as the perfect choice for the job, only Taney ran into determined and intransigent opposition. He was finally confirmed by a vote of 29 to 15 after three months of bitter debate in which the most powerful leaders in the Senate—Henry Clay, John C. Calhoun and Daniel Webster—used their oratorical and political skills in a vain attempt to block the appointment. White, a sitting associate justice, was confirmed by a voice vote without opposition but without enthusiasm. Relieved that President Grant had finally settled on a respectable nominee, the Senate gave its approval to Waite by a vote of 63 to 6 within two days of receiving his name. Fuller would have received perfunctory approval had not Senator George F. Edmunds of Vermont, the chairman of the Senate Judiciary Committee, held up the nomination, claiming that President Cleveland had promised the job to one of Edmunds' constituents. When the vote was taken, Fuller was confirmed by a vote of 41 to 2.

ROGER BROOKE TANEY: FROM SUCCESS TO TRAGEDY

When Roger Brooke Taney took his oath as chief justice in 1836, three rivalries or divisive forces were discernible in the American nation: that between the rich and the poor, each in possession of a share of political power; the sectional rivalry between North and South, potentially the most explosive because of the slavery issue; and the continuing rivalry between the national government and the states, always a latent cause of conflict in a federal system. After three decades under Taney's leadership, the Supreme Court, while able to moderate successfully the antagonisms growing out of inequalities in property and the power struggle between the nation and the states, failed abjectly when it attempted to resolve the slavery question, and responsibility for that ignoble failure must forever remain with the chief justice.

In most respects John Marshall and his successor as chief could not have differed more markedly. Where Marshall was robust, self-confident and always willing to engage in light and frivolous conversation, Taney was in delicate health, frequently ill, literally trembled with fear when speaking in public, and had no talent for jocular and playful conversation. Taney's vision was so defective that he could not recognize the face of a man or woman unless he had seen it frequently.[2] The word often used to describe his demeanor was "apostolic" which, it has been said, tended to reflect an innate unworldliness, giving the

Leadership Through Persuasion and Example

impression that he was "never quite at home in everyday affairs."[3] The distinguished attorney, William Pinckney, complained: "I can answer his arguments, I am not afraid of his logic, but that infernal apostolic manner of his, there's no replying to." That "infernal apostolic manner" tended to create an air of sincerity, so much so that listeners, including juries, found it difficult to believe he could be wrong.[4] At the same time he was not impressive in physical appearance. His face was "without one good feature, a mouth unusually large, in which were discolored and irregular teeth, the gums of which were visible when he smiled, dressed always in black, his clothes fitting ill upon him, his hands spare with projecting veins, . . . in a word a gaunt, ungainly man."[5] In some respects, however, Taney and Marshall had similar personal characteristics. Both were careless in their dress, both had simple tastes and were most at ease with close friends, both were considerate and generous, and each had an invalid wife to whom he was loyal and completely devoted.[6]

Prior to his appointment as chief, Taney's career was successful but not spectacular. He was educated irregularly in schools in Calvert County, Maryland, where his father Michael owned a landed estate with slaves. He spoke of possessing only two books in one school, a speller and the Bible, the only two he believed his teacher had ever read.[7] Eventually he was tutored privately at home before entering Dickinson College at the age of fifteen. Taney wrote of his studies at Dickinson, indicating that he worked with four faculty members: James McCormick in mathematics, Charles Huston in Greek and Latin, Robert Davidson in history, natural philosophy and geography, and Charles Nisbet in logic, metaphysics and criticism. Nisbet was his favorite, although he did not agree with Nisbet's anti-Republican views. As Taney wrote later: "He had no faith in our institutions, and did not believe in their stability, or in their capacity to protect the rights of persons or property against the impulses of popular passion, which combinations of designing men might continue to excite. These opinions were monstrous heresies in our eyes."[8] Nevertheless, Nisbet's influence on Taney was profound and lasting, and as a result, Taney combined his Roman Catholicism "with the stubborn integrity and idealism of [the] Scotch Presbyterianism" of Nisbet.

Chief Justice

After graduating from Dickinson, having been chosen vale-
dictorian by his fellow students, he read law in Annapolis at the
office of Jeremiah Townley Chase, who, as a member of the
Maryland ratifying convention of 1788, voted against ratifica-
tion of the Constitution on the grounds that it weakened the
power of the states and had no bill of rights.[9] In 1799 at the age
of twenty-two, Taney was admitted to the bar and made his entry into politics as an elected Federalist member of the Maryland legislature but he was defeated after serving only one term.
Still a Federalist in 1816, he was elected to the Maryland senate
where he served for five years. In the moribund days of the old
Federalist Party, Taney joined the ranks of the Jackson men, supporting Andrew Jackson for president in both 1824 and 1828, in
the latter year having been chairman of the Jackson Central
Committee of Maryland and an active campaigner.

He was mentioned as a possible candidate for attorney general
of the United States but seems to have lacked enough interest
to actively seek the office. Meanwhile he had built a lucrative
law practice and in 1827 had been named attorney general of
Maryland, the only office, he was to say later, that he ever really
coveted and which he left reluctantly.[10] As one of his biographers indicates, there was no reason to believe that Taney
would be appointed to national office when Jackson became
president, but fate "dealt her cards unexpectedly" as Taney's future was to be altered radically by the warfare between Vice
President John C. Calhoun and Secretary of State Martin Van
Buren, and by the social ostracism of Secretary of War John H.
Eaton's wife, the former barmaid Peggy O'Neal, by the families
of Jackson's administration.[11] The upshot was a complete reorganization of the cabinet, one result of which was the appointment of Taney as attorney general of the United States in 1831.

He became one of Jackson's most trusted advisers, and when
Secretary of the Treasury William J. Duane, refused to cooper-
ate with the president in his struggle against the Bank of the
United States, it was Taney to whom Jackson turned, appointing him to the treasury after firing Duane. During his recess appointment he issued the famous "removal order" under which
new revenues were to be deposited in state banks and funds
would gradually be withdrawn from the Bank of the United
States as needed. As a result of these actions Taney created en-

emies in the Senate who were strong enough to prevent his confirmation as secretary of the treasury and he returned to private
life in June 1834.

Six months later when Supreme Court Justice Gabriel Duvall
resigned, Jackson sent Taney's name to the Senate for the position of associate justice of the Supreme Court. In spite of strong
support from many quarters, including that of John Marshall,
24 hostile Senators said no to the nomination and Taney once
again was rejected.[12] Within the year, however, John Marshall
was to die, and on December 28, 1835, Jackson sent Taney's
name to the Senate, this time for the position of chief justice.
Confirmation came on March 15, 1836, by a vote of 29 to 15 and
the new chief met with his court in January 1837.

At the first session the Court consisted of seven members,
five of whom including Taney, had been appointed by Andrew
Jackson. Within the year the membership was increased to
nine, and President Jackson was to name one additional judge
before the end of his term, increasing his total appointees to six,
equal to the number to be appointed by President Taft and fewer
only than the eleven appointed by George Washington and the
nine named by Franklin D. Roosevelt. In no sense, however,
was the Taney Court a monolith of Jacksonian persuasion; it
was composed of a group of independent thinkers whose views
were often in conflict. The ninth justice was to be appointed by
Van Buren, and before the end of Taney's service, eleven more
judges were to join him including a second appointee by Van
Buren, two by Polk, one each by Tyler, Fillmore, Pierce, and Buchanan, and four by Lincoln. Essentially Taney presided over
three groups, one in the 1830s, a second in the 1840s and 1850s,
and the final one briefly in the 1860s. By the time of the *Dred
Scott* decision in 1857, just three of the 1830s associate justices,
James M. Wayne, John Catron and John McLean, were still on
the Court, but only Wayne had concurred in the chief's extravagant pronouncement that a Negro could not be a citizen of the
United States under the Constitution.

Sitting with Taney at his first session were Joseph Story
whose views of the Constitution were indistinguishable from
his hero, John Marshall; Smith Thompson of New York who
had served President Monroe as secretary of the navy and had
been later rewarded by Monroe with a place on the Court; and

the Jackson choices, John McLean of Ohio, former postmaster general under John Quincy Adams and onetime judge of the supreme court of Ohio; Henry Baldwin of Pennsylvania, a Yale graduate and former Congressman whose conduct in his latter years led some observers to think him insane; James M. Wayne of Georgia who remained on the Union side and on the Court during the Civil War; and Philip Barbour of Virginia, a states righter of the Spencer Roane school whom John Adams once described as a "shallow-pated wild-cat." Also joining the Court in 1837 when Congress increased its size from seven to nine were John Catron of Tennessee and Van Buren's first appointee, John McKinley of Alabama. This group was to remain unchanged until 1841 when Barbour died, and Van Buren named Peter Daniel of Virginia as his replacement.

There were three changes in the 1840s and three more in the 1850s. Justice Thompson died in 1843, Baldwin in 1844, and Story in 1845. Both the Thompson and Baldwin seats were vacant for many months as President John Tyler ran into difficulties with the Henry Clay faction of the Whig Party in the Senate. Rejecting five of Tyler's nominees, the record for all time,[13] the Senate finally confirmed Samuel Nelson of New York, a friend of James Fenimore Cooper and a competent technician—particularly in admiralty, maritime and international law. A new president, James K. Polk, filled the Story seat with Levi Woodbury of New Hampshire, a puritanical conservative who opposed slavery but believed that the statutes which supported it must be sustained until altered by national policy. Polk finally filled the Baldwin vacancy in 1846 with the appointment of Robert C. Grier of Pennsylvania who is remembered primarily for writing a letter to President Buchanan detailing the attitudes of the justices on the *Dred Scott* decision and predicting the outcome of the case.

Probably the most able jurists to serve with Taney were Benjamin R. Curtis and John A. Campbell, both of whom resigned over a principle and thus served for relatively short periods. Curtis, Fillmore's lone appointee, was chosen to fill the vacancy created by Woodbury's death in 1851. A distinguished lawyer from Massachusetts, Curtis wrote one of the two dissenting opinions in the *Dred Scott* case but his controversial conduct in the case, including a bitter quarrel with the chief, led to his resignation on September 1, 1857. President Franklin Pierce, whose contributions to the presidency were minimal, displayed perceptive judgment in his appointment of John Archibald Campbell of Alabama in 1853 after the death of the undistinguished John McKinley. Campbell was a brilliant advocate and "respected nation-wide as an expert in both civil and common law."[14] Although personally opposed to secession, Campbell, like Robert E. Lee, felt the call to join the Confederacy, and he resigned in 1861. Between 1861 and 1864 in the twilight of Taney's career the Court was to become Abraham Lincoln's, although President Buchanan was to name one justice, Nathan Clifford of Maine, to replace Benjamin Curtis in 1858. Before Taney died in 1864, President Lincoln fell heir to four vacancies, two as the result of deaths—Daniel and McLean—one because of Campbell's resignation, and the final one as the result of the creation of a tenth circuit (California and Oregon) and a concomitant tenth position on the Supreme Court. The latter appointment went to Stephen J. Field of California, the remaining three to Noah H. Swayne of Ohio, Samuel Freeman Miller of Iowa and David Davis of Illinois. Among the Lincoln appointees only Field and Miller were to serve with special distinction.

RUNNING THE COURT

Inevitably, several important internal changes in the Court's social and administrative structure took place during Taney's tenure. The old practice of the justices rooming together and taking their meals in common had begun to give way during John Marshall's final years and by the end of Taney's headship it had ceased to exist. In 1834 Justice McLean had brought his wife to Washington, and Justice Thompson who appeared for Taney's first session in 1837 with a new wife, lived in another roominghouse from that occupied by the brethren who had left their wives at home.[15] Eventually as living conditions improved in Washington which in the 1840s was still a city of "dust in summer and mud holes in winter" with everyone but foreign visitors taking "as a matter of course the cows, geese and swine that roamed loose in the streets,"[16] the justices began to live apart, and even Taney in 1855 took a house for himself and his daughters on Indiana Avenue.[17] This new mode of living, so abhorrent to Marshall who believed the closeness of living fostered professional harmony, seemed not to alter radically either personal relationships or to cause fragmentation in the Court's decisions.

As in the earlier days the justices during the Taney period spent more than half their working year holding circuit court sessions, often traveling great distances and complaining about it. Personal dissatisfaction and inconvenience aside, the system that required the justices to "ride" circuit and be away from Washington for so much of the year, combined with an expanding population and increased litigation, meant that the Court's docket could never be cleared. In 1810 there had been 98 cases on the docket; by 1845 there were 173, by 1850, 253 and by 1860, 310. In addition to the time spent on circuit, the justices suffered from considerable illness and often one or more were not in attendance. Moreover, as vacancies occurred, they sometimes went unfilled for months as presidents dallied over the appointments. In spite of the exigencies beyond the chief's control, there was something he could have done to ameliorate the condition for an ever-expanding and unfinished docket. He could have curtailed the arguments of counsel which often went on for hours. Justice Catron, impatient with irrelevant oratory, suggested to Taney that he cut the lawyers' speeches to an hour, but to no avail. Catron was, argued Taney's biographer Carl Swisher "asking him for an authoritarian type of performance that was out of character with Taney's gentle and courteous if sometimes highly persistent personality."[18] Unable to persuade Taney to take action, Catron lobbied among his colleagues and finally mustered a majority of them—Wayne and Woodbury remained opposed—to adopt Rule No. 53 which ordered two changes. First, no counsel would be permitted to argue any case for more than two hours without obtaining permission from the Court in advance, and second, counsel had to submit prior to argument a printed abstract with citations for cases or other documents to which he could not subsequently add new material.[19]

In spite of the streamlined procedures for argument the cases continued to pile up on the docket, and proposals surfaced both among the justices and in Congress which would provide the Court with more time. Unfortunately the matter of the justices dividing their time between holding circuit courts and deciding cases in Washington appeared to be the cause of much of the congestion, and yet the issue seemed insoluble. In the 1850s the Court began to hold longer terms, sometimes adjourning in May instead of March, but this simply meant less time on circuit duty where litigation was also expanding. It seemed a logical step to abolish circuit duty altogether, a solution for which there had been some sentiment on and off the Court for some time. It was not to come for many years, however, as the argument continued to be made that the justices should be required to go into the country and, in the words of Stephen A. Douglas of Illinois, "hold courts in different localities, and mingle with the local judges and with the bar."[20]

It was believed by many, including some of the justices, that without this continuing experience the Court would become overly powerful and be alienated from the judicial grass roots. At one point Representative Joseph R. Ingersoll of Pennsylvania, after indicating that in January 1848 the Court was hearing No. 39 on a docket consisting of 198 cases and was close to adjournment, proposed that the justices be relieved of circuit duties for two years. The House passed a modified version that gave a one-year exemption but the Senate refused to concur.[21] It is not at all certain that Taney could have been instrumental in moving Congress toward legislation that would have enabled the justices to clear the docket annually, and after the *Dred Scott* case in 1857 his influence with any but the Southern contingent was hopelessly negative. Politicking in that sense, however, was not his style, and he left to others, Catron particularly, the job of pleading with Congress.

Nor was the chief successful in winning over the brethren to his point of view in the selection of the reporter of decisions, one of the two principal supporting arms of the Court. The occupant changed three times under Taney, none of whom was the chief's choice. Unlike the office of clerk which was created in 1790 by the Court's first formal rule, the position of reporter had somewhat obscure beginnings and remained controversial as to precise duties for some years. Although the reporter's job of transposing the Court's decisions from authorship to print in order to make them available to the public seemed straightforward enough, the early reporters, particularly Richard Peters, ran into serious difficulties.[22] In addition to disagreement among those who reviewed the Court's work over what should be included, i.e., full opinion, summary only, arguments of counsel, briefs, etc., there were problems with some of the justices who were never quite satisfied with the final result, noting errors, omissions or deletions.

In any event at the beginning of the 1843 term with Justices Story and McKinley absent because of illness, four justices, who had been unhappy with Peters' work, Wayne, Baldwin, Catron and Daniel, voted to appoint a new reporter, Benjamin C. Howard of Maryland. Taney urged the retention of Peters but had the support only of Thompson and McLean. Had Story and McKinley been present, the result would have been different, but the point is that the chief was unable to prevail or even to postpone a decision until the full Court was present. Twice more the brethren overruled the chief on the appointment of a reporter. In 1861 Howard ran for governor of Maryland, and although his resignation was before the Court, he was defeated and then asked the Court to retain him as reporter. Taney supported Howard but the Court would not accede to the chief's view and named Jeremiah S. Black, former chief justice of Pennsylvania's supreme court. Black resigned in 1863, and once again the Court appointed a reporter, John William Wallace, who was not Taney's choice.

The fact that Taney could not persuade his fellow justices to follow his lead in appointing a reporter or that he did not pursue a political route in Congress designed to reduce the Court's workload is indicative of a lack of leadership of a kind. Taney's conduct in this respect also suggests that he did not perceive these aspects of the chief's role to be as important as those more closely connected to judging itself. Although not a domineering person, he could and often did dominate the Court, not by imposing his views but by moderating the tensions and disagreements between the Court's extremes—at least until that fateful time in 1857 when constitutional moderation gave way to judicial imperiousness and catastrophe.

Despite his frail health and occasional absence from the Court Taney's output was generally greater than most of his colleagues.[23] During his 28 years Taney wrote 281 opinions, speaking for the majority in 260 cases, writing dissents in 14 and concurrences in only 7.[24] Comparing his average number of majority opinions per year with those of his colleagues prior to the appointment of Nathan Clifford in 1858, we note that only Samuel Nelson averaged more per year than the chief (just under 11), although Nelson's service went some 8 years beyond Taney's. Of those justices whose service was more nearly coterminous with Taney's—McLean, Wayne, Catron, Daniel and Grier, only Grier and McLean approached the chief's record, each writing for the Court on an average of 8 times per year. Wayne, Catron and Daniel each spoke for the Court between 4 and 6 times per year, although the latter two were among the Court's most prolific dissenters, Daniel having led the Court with 47 in 19 years and Catron following with 26 in 28 years. McLean was the third great dissenter with 33 in 27 years. The statistics of dissent reflect the ideological extremes of the Taney years which saw McLean, the constitutional nationalist of the Marshall school at one end and Daniel, the Southern-agrarian, anti-corporation, slavery apologist, at the other.

At no time did Taney have an easy, like-minded group of judges on the bench, but his opinion assignments appear to have been evenhanded, at least in simple division of labor. Like Marshall before him he generally wrote the opinions in the most significant cases,[25] although a few of the most memorable of the period he assigned to others. For example, Justice Story spoke for the Court in *Swift* v. *Tyson*[26] which held that in matters of commercial law not regulated by state statutes federal courts might apply general principles of law without regard to the decisions of state courts. Story also wrote the opinion in *Prigg* v. *Pennsylvania*[27] invalidating the state's personal liberty law which prohibited the seizure of free blacks with the intent to return them to slavery. Such laws, wrote Story, were in conflict with the national Fugitive Slave Law of 1793 which permitted owners to recover runaway slaves. Neither of these opinions was to attain any permanence, although the *Swift* doctrine was to last until 1938 when it was overruled.[28] *Prigg*, of course, died a natural death with the abolition of slavery.

Remaining a precedent even today, however, was the opinion by Justice Curtis in *Cooley* v. *Board of Wardens of the Port of Philadelphia*[29] in which the Court adopted his view of the states' role in regulating commerce, the doctrine of selective exclusiveness. Until Curtis joined the Court there had been virtual chaos over the validity of state laws that either directly or indirectly interfered with interstate and foreign commerce, and Taney had not been able to effect a consensus. In one instance, although all nine judges agreed that state laws licensing liquor were valid, six of them wrote opinions, no one of which commanded a majority.[30] In a second group of cases eight opinions were written, but they revealed such a tangled web of confusing arguments that none was listed as the opinion of the Court.[31] Only five justices, including the chief, were able to agree on the Curtis doctrine which held simply that if the commerce to be regulated were local in nature and required local rules, the states might regulate it until Congress entered the field; on the other hand, any commerce which required a national, uniform rule might be regulated only by Congress, and the states could not legislate even in the absence of congressional action.

It was the custom during Taney's time for the justices to spend their early mornings in study, reflection and writing opinions. The Court then met at eleven o'clock to hear arguments and adjourned at four for leisure and dinner, meeting again at seven for the conference which was sometimes long and tedious. According to Justice McLean the conference was one of give and take in which the chief then "requests a particular judge to write, not his opinion, but the opinion of the Court. And after the opinion is read to all the judges, and if it does not embrace the view of the judges, it is modified and corrected."[32] This is especially instructive with respect to Taney's role in the conference and confirms his and the Court's commitment to the concept of a collegial opinion. McLean did not speak of the chief's "assigning" or "directing" the writing of an opinion but of the chief's "request," and the final opinion was a composite, that of "the Court," and not simply the personal view of the author.

Although Justice Curtis had been one of Taney's severest critics and had had a bitter exchange of letters with him over the *Dred Scott* case, he nevertheless had words of high praise for him as the Court's leader. In an address to the Boston bar delivered after Taney's death in 1864 Justice Curtis declared that Taney's "power of subtle analysis exceeded that of any man I ever knew."[33] Curtis revealed that in conference the chief "could, and habitually did, state the facts of a voluminous and complicated case, with every important detail of names and dates, with extraordinary accuracy, and . . . with extraordinary clearness and skill. And his recollection of principles of law and of the decisions of the court over which he presided was as ready as his memory of facts. . . ."[34] Curtis went on to say that "the surpassing ability of the Chief Justice, and all his great qualities of character and mind, were more fully and constantly exhibited in the consultation-room . . . than the public knew, or can ever justly appreciate. There, his dignity, his love of order, his gentleness, his caution, his accuracy, his discrimination, were of incalculable importance. The real intrinsic character of the tribunal was greatly influenced by them, and always for the better."[35]

Excepting that terrible moment in 1857 when the chief irrevocably lost his authority and prestige, Taney's gentle nature, his innate intelligence, and his commitment to fairness and harmony made him a worthy successor to John Marshall. It was the *Dred Scott* case, however, that put on public display a grievous error in judgment and a failure in moral responsibility. Although a man of exceptional judicial competence, he remained a prisoner of his heritage, and in the moment of supreme crisis he would not, perhaps could not, keep the Court outside a national struggle that was not amenable to judicial solution.

For some, Taney cannot be faulted for trying to find a solution to the slavery problem but only for making the wrong moral and political choices.[36] For others, his insensitivity to the need to avoid arousing public resentment gives us "the full measure of the distance by which Taney fell short of his predecessor."[37] Perhaps no chief could have rallied the Court of that day behind an antislavery opinion or even in support of one that would have positioned the Court on the periphery of this all-consuming national struggle. Taney's ultimate handiwork, however, not only helped to widen the then almost unbreachable chasm between the nation's two most powerful sections but also created judicial fragmentation and internal bitterness among his colleagues, all eight of whom expressed separate views, although seven agreed with his declaration that it was up to the courts of a state to decide a slave's status after his return to the state's jurisdiction. Taney's failure, it seems, was not the result of a commitment to slavery as such but to the culture of the South, to Southern life and values which, of necessity, included the slavocracy.[38] Moreover, his attitude was hardened and embittered by Northern sanctimony which drove him to defensive anger, to an outrage that in its reaction became an even greater outrage. Truly great leaders must be able to transcend the parochialism of their own backgrounds, and this Taney could not do.

PHILOSOPHY AND LEGACY

When one attempts to arrive at a fair assessment of Taney as an intellectual leader by reviewing his opinions over the 28-year span as chief justice, one inevitably must come to grips with *Dred Scott* and that appalling phrase that a Negro "had no rights which the white man was bound to respect." It cannot be dismissed as "unfortunate" or "taken out of context" as some apologists for Taney have done, for it tells us something crucial about Taney's view of law and justice. Although one finds in his opinions an occasional reference to "immutable principles of justice,"[39] the preponderant tendency in his writings is to view the Constitution as the final authority, as the point of reference for deciding cases, without support of natural law or natural rights. Even in his discussions of the Declaration of Independence he speaks not of natural rights but of the "rights of Englishmen, as secured by *magna carta* and the principles upon which the British Government was founded."[40] As a devout Catholic he undoubtedly believed in universal laws in a religious sense, but in legal terms the connection he made was tenuous at best. Thus even though he might be personally opposed to slavery—and evidence indicated that he was—if it was protected by positive laws, by the sovereign will of the people embodied in a Constitution, it was his duty as the nation's chief judge to uphold that sovereign will.

In reading Taney's opinions we see a fairly consistent pattern in his thinking which involved a subtle mixture of Federalist principles and the Jacksonian doctrine of special privileges for none. Had it not been for the slavery issue he would have successfully straddled the prevailing theories of the American union: Calhoun's compact theory of state sovereignty and Webster's theory of divided sovereignty and national supremacy.

Leadership Through Persuasion and Example

Taney, in fact, believed in the classic theory of a federal system, of a central and member governments operating independently over the same territory and people, and each sovereign within its own sphere. The Supreme Court was to be the final arbiter of the inevitable conflicts with the Court itself guided and constrained by the Constitution and the common law tradition.[41] This is, of course, a simplified view of an incredibly complex and difficult system of government, but amazingly enough the Supreme Court under Taney's leadership was inordinately successful in charting a course that made federalism appear eminently workable. The chief had a penchant for construing the powers of the states liberally, yet only when not in conflict with federal authority which he upheld and extended in the Marshall tradition.

In his first term and in one of his most famous opinions, that in the *Charles River Bridge* case,[42] Taney set forth what were to be his views on state power throughout his tenure. Conceding that a charter of incorporation is a contract which a state may not impair, he declared nevertheless that a contract must be construed narrowly and carries no implied rights. The fact that Massachusetts had chartered a company to build a bridge across the Charles River and collect tolls did not preclude the state from chartering a second bridge, eventually to be toll-free. Said Taney: "The object and end of all government is to promote the happiness and prosperity of the community by which it is established; and it can never be assumed that the government intended to diminish its power of accomplishing the end for which it was created. . . . A state ought never to be presumed to surrender this power, because, like the taxing power, the whole community have an interest in preserving it undiminished."

In subsequent decisions he tended to construe state statutes liberally and as a result of his reluctance to strike them down, some observers have suggested that he was an early believer in self-restraint, but this hardly seems tenable in light of his political orientation. He remained enough of a Jacksonian democrat to be wary of corporate privilege and to accept as prudent the state regulation of corporate interests in behalf of the people. At the same time he was willing to use judicial authority in the Marshall manner, both in declaring state laws unconstitutional and in preserving and extending national power. He wrote the opinion in *Bronson* v. *Kinzie*[43] holding that state laws interfering with mortgage foreclosures were in violation of the contract clause. These laws were, incidentally, relatively mild compared to that upheld by Chief Justice Hughes in 1934.[44] One provided that property could not be sold on foreclosure unless it brought a certain proportion of the appraised value, and the other permitted the debtor to repurchase the property subject to time and rate limitations. Also in a Federalist mold and indeed as nationalistic as any rendered by Marshall were Taney's pronouncements in *Holmes* v. *Jennison*[45] and *The Genesee Chief* v. *Fitzhugh*.[46] In the former, upholding exclusive national authority in foreign affairs, he wrote: "But where an authority is granted to the Union, to which a similar authority in the states would be absolutely and totally contradictory and repugnant, then the authority to the federal government is necessarily exclusive; and the same power cannot be constitutionally exercised by the states." In the *Genesee Chief* he interpreted admiralty jurisdiction as extending over all navigable waters in the United States whether used for interstate or foreign commerce, overruling a precedent of the Marshall court of only twenty-five years standing.[47]

For the most part Chief Justice Taney was courteous and moderate; then again he exhibited boldness and unnecessary recklessness in order to confront an adversary. His caution is exemplified not only in his general willingness to uphold and to rationalize state and federal laws but also in his ability to keep the Court out of some controversies altogether. He persuaded the Court to adopt the doctrine of "political questions" as a ground for refusing to take jurisdiction of the case involving the legitimate government of Rhode Island during a rebellion, and it is a doctrine that is still used to restrain judicial power today.[48] Needlessly reckless, however, was the opinion in *Dred Scott* and bold certainly was Taney's confrontation with Lincoln in *Ex parte Merryman*[49] in which he held that the president could not suspend the writ of *habeas corpus* and ordered a prisoner released who had been arrested by the military. Lincoln ignored the order but the principle remains intact as a landmark in the history of civil liberty, an ironical paradox when juxtaposed with *Dred Scott*.

Leadership Through Persuasion and Example

Always Chief Justice Taney's record must be appraised in two parts: the twenty-two pre-*Dred Scott* years and the six years following that fateful decision. In 1856 he was held in high esteem by his colleagues on the Court and was respected nationally as a judicious and circumspect head of the judiciary who had appropriately discarded partisan politics upon his appointment to the bench. Even Henry Clay, who vigorously opposed his nomination, was to tell him that after observing his course on the bench he had done him an injustice. "I am now convinced," said Clay, "that a better appointment could not have been made, and the ermine, so long worn and honored by Marshall, has fallen on a successor. . . every way his equal."[50] Had Taney retired or died in the mid 1850s his reputation would have been secured certainly as a great judge and perhaps as a great chief justice. After *Dred Scott* the opprobrium heaped upon him and to a lesser extent on the Court itself was so intense and widespread that it took more than a half century to moderate the verdict of Charles Sumner that Taney's name was "to be hooted down the pages of history."[51]

After he administered the oath of office to Abraham Lincoln in 1861 he "hovered around Washington like an unrespected ghost,"[52] both he and his opinions being ignored by the president and the Republican administration. More important, however, is the fact that neither the administration nor the Congress made any attempt to remove him, and although various measures were introduced in Congress to curb the Court's powers,[53] none was enacted into law. All of which indicates that the office of chief justice and the Supreme Court as an institution under the leadership of Marshall and Taney had attained a permanent integrity that protected their independence even after the commission of an egregious error. In a speech at the unveiling of a monument to Taney in Frederick, Maryland, in 1931 Chief Justice Hughes called Taney a "great Chief Justice" and spoke of his career as "one of the most distinguished . . . in American annals,"[54] and Justice Frankfurter on at least two occasions referred to Taney as comparable to Marshall in greatness, in fact, "second only to Marshall."[55]

Taney's reputation has been reevaluated since his death in 1863,[56] but his opinion in *Dred Scott* is still a leading example of judicial power extended to its outermost limits, of using the Supreme Court to determine national public policy, a principle suggested certainly, but not really at issue, in *Marbury* v. *Madison*. Furthermore those words that proclaimed blacks to be inferior to whites had an impact of immeasurable proportions on the course of American history, and although constitutionally erased in 1954 by the *Brown* decision, the racist ideas still persist in the national vocabulary and have had a devastating effect upon the American polity. Roger Brooke Taney, undoubtedly possessing attributes of greatness, can never quite be forgiven for using those words.

BACKGROUND AND TEMPERAMENT: WAITE, FULLER, AND WHITE

When appointed to the chief justiceship, Morrison Remick Waite, Melville Weston Fuller, and Edward Douglass White had no special qualities to commend them, and as chiefs perhaps had only that lack in common. Each, however, had his strengths and each superintended a productive, if not always harmonious Supreme Court. Although 37 associate justices served during the 47 years during which Waite (14), Fuller (22), and White (11) presided over the high bench, there was considerably more continuity than the raw figures would indicate. Four of the most influential justices ever to sit on the Court—Samuel F. Miller, Steven J. Field, Joseph P. Bradley, and John M. Harlan I—served under both Waite and Fuller, and another of the Court's intellectual leaders, Oliver Wendell Holmes, Jr., served under both Fuller and White. Four of the justices who sat with White— Hughes, Van Devanter, McReynolds, and Brandeis—were still on the Court when it was under siege by Roosevelt in 1936. Among the remaining judges who sat from 1874 when Waite became chief until 1921 when White died, none was distinguished, several served for less than 10 years and a few for less than 5. With very few exceptions those justices who had only brief careers on the Court were the least influential and did not build a lasting reputation. Thus such men as William Strong, Ward Hunt, William Woods, Howell Jackson, Horace Lurton, and Joseph Lamar, all from the Waite-Fuller-White years, remain only in the shadows of history.

Leadership Through Persuasion and Example

Although Fuller and White may have surpassed Waite in some respects, it is Waite who must be ranked the most capable leader. When he took his seat on March 4, 1874, Waite was virtually an unknown quantity outside Ohio. He had never sat on a court of any kind, had never appeared before the Supreme Court, was twice defeated in bids for Congress and held only three elective positions in Ohio. Except for serving as one of three counsel to the American contingent at the Geneva Arbitration which settled claims against England for depredations committed against the Union during the Civil War by vessels equipped and sheltered in British ports, Waite had never held national office. Justice Field expressed the sentiment of the bench in a letter to a friend just after Waite joined the Court. He wrote: "He is a new man that would never have been thought of for the position by any person except President Grant. . . . But how much of a lawyer he is remains to be seen. He may turn out to be a Marshall or Taney, though such a result is hardly to be expected. My objection to the appointment is that it is an experiment whether a man of fair but not great abilities may make a fit Chief Justice of the United States—an experiment which no President has a right to make with our Court."[57] Waite did not turn out to be a Marshall or a Taney, but he was a successful chief justice. To complain about a presidential experiment in choosing a justice is to labor the obvious, since all appointments to the Court have a strong element of the unknowable, irrespective of the appointee's record,[58] and chief justices have infrequently performed precisely as the presidents who appointed them desired or as the Court which they joined presumed they would. Some did not live up to presidential or public expectations; others surprisingly exceeded them. Waite was among the latter.

Morrison Remick Waite was born in Lyme, Connecticut, on November 27, 1816, the year in which Justice Story wrote the controversial opinion in *Martin* v. *Hunter's Lessee*[59] upholding the validity of British land grants against attempts by the states to assert primacy and override them, and three years before John Marshall was to render his notable opinion in *McCulloch* v. *Maryland*.[60] Waite had an illustrious ancestry that went back to the mid-seventeenth century and contained lawyers and judges on both sides including his father who was an associate judge of the supreme court of errors of Connecticut for twenty years. It thus seemed appropriate that he follow the path of the law. His life prior to his admission to the bar was unceremonious and not atypical for an upper middle-class American of his day. He began his early education in a village schoolhouse of a crude sort, then spent a year at Bacon Academy in Colchester, Connecticut, studying Latin and Greek in preparation for admission to Yale College, and having passed the difficult entrance examination, became a member of the class of 1837.

Yale's curriculum of that day centered on the classics and the natural sciences—mathematics, astronomy and natural philosophy—but included an introduction to economics and law, the latter emphasizing the crucial importance of property rights through the reading of Adam Smith and Kent's *Commentaries on American Law*.[61] It seems likely that Waite was better prepared to face the vicissitudes of life and to enter a professional calling than are most university graduates today whose education too often emphasizes the transient and contemporary rather than the permanent in man's heritage.

After graduating with a Phi Beta Kappa key in what was to be known as the "famous class of 1837"—in it were a future presidential candidate (Samuel J. Tilden), a secretary of state and nationally renowned lawyer (William M. Evarts), an attorney general (Edwards Pierrepont), a famous scientist (George Silliman), and, of course, a future chief justice—Waite returned to Lyme for a year to study law in his father's office.[62] Completing the year, Waite at twenty-two might have remained in Connecticut and, with his family's reputation, established a respectable and financially rewarding law practice. He chose, however, to take his chances in the developing West and set out for Maumee, Ohio, where an uncle Horace Waite was a successful merchant.

Settling in Maumee, a frontier town of 800 people, Waite was admitted to the bar in 1838 and within ten years became a "skillful pleader and a learned chancery lawyer, expert in real estate law and the history and status of legal titles,"[63] unquestionably an able and desirable attorney, among the best in northwest Ohio.[64] In 1850 he moved to Toledo where he was able to profit from the spectacular growth of the city which became Ohio's third largest by 1880, boasting thirteen railroads at its

Leadership Through Persuasion and Example

center, hundreds of industries, and a major grain market. Waite's reputation and his bank account began to grow rapidly as his practice saw an unbroken string of successful representations for railroads and other corporations. Although both of Waite's biographers, McGrath and Trimble, pay tribute to his ability as a working lawyer, documenting various aspects of his practice, it seems likely, and McGrath hints at this, that any competent lawyer would have prospered in northwest Ohio under the prevailing conditions of rapid economic growth.

What does come through, however, in Waite's personal and professional letters and in his biographies, is that he was fair-minded, painstaking, conscientious, and possessed of great energy and industry. In his personal relationships he was warm-hearted, generous, likeable—in fact, impossible to dislike. Moreover, he was well-educated and knowledgeable in his chosen field. What then was on the debit side of the ledger? Waite was human in his desire for success, but he was ambitious in a self-effacing manner which resulted in a blandness of sorts, in a lack of brilliance. He seemed to have no desire for power, not a fault certainly, but he lacked even that minimum aggressiveness that is characteristic of those who rise to the top in a society without fixed classes.

This trait is manifested in his political career—or lack of it—prior to his appointment to the Court. Although active in civic affairs including both Whig and later Republican politics when he strongly supported President Lincoln and the Union cause, Waite made no sustained attempts to hold public office. As he wrote in 1875 just after his appointment as chief, "There has been so little of my public life that it is very easy to find dates."[65] Three times he reluctantly accepted a nomination, in 1846 as the Whig candidate for Congress, in 1850 as a delegate to the Ohio constitutional convention, in 1862 for Congress as an independent supporter of Lincoln, and lost all three races. Other than his brief service on the Toledo city council and one term in the Ohio legislature, his only elective success was as a delegate to the Ohio constitutional convention of 1873 where he was chosen presiding officer, but this gave him no national distinction or prestige. Waite's appointment by President Grant to the Geneva Arbitration tribunal came as a fortuitous surprise, his name having been suggested to Grant by Waite's

Chief Justice

friend William Evarts, himself one of the counsel, and by Secretary of the Interior Columbus Delano, a former associate of Waite's but not a close friend, after the president's first choices, former Supreme Court Justice Benjamin Curtis and Philadelphia lawyer William Meredith had declined.

Waite did a creditable job in presenting the American case to the tribunal which awarded the United States 15.5 million dollars just before the November election in 1872, a factor which may have helped the bungling President Grant obtain a second term. And Morrison Waite, while hardly a national figure as a result of his labors, was a known entity to Grant who invited him to dinner the following year on the occasion of his being admitted to practice before the Supreme Court.[66]

When Chief Justice Salmon P. Chase died on May 7, 1873, President Grant began the tortuous process of appointing a new chief, a process that was to take eight months and result ultimately in Waite's nomination and confirmation by the Senate. In a classic case of executive incompetence President Grant chose and, after encountering Senate opposition, withdrew, two nominees, his attorney general, George H. Williams of Oregon, and his closest friend, 74-year-old Caleb Cushing. He purportedly offered the position to four others, Senators Roscoe Conkling of New York, Oliver Morton of Indiana, Timothy O. Howe of Wisconsin, and Secretary of State Hamilton Fish, all of whom declined. In desperation Grant turned to Waite, and the Senate and the nation accepted the obscure lawyer from Toledo with relief. Had he been Grant's first nominee, he certainly would have run into opposition and quite possibly have been rejected by the Senate. Now, although easily confirmed, he faced a hostile bench.

It is to his everlasting credit that he was able to convert that open hostility not only into acceptance but into overwhelming support, for he came to the Court not with one, or two, but with three strikes against him.[67] First, he was appointed by President Grant which in the eyes of close observers predestined any appointment to mediocrity; second, he had no national reputation which also suggested mediocrity at best; and third, he faced a Court several of whose members actively sought the head chair and were convinced that they were superior in every way to the new boss. Waite's temperament was such, however, that he was

Leadership Through Persuasion and Example

quickly able to overcome what seemed to be insuperable handicaps and became chief justice in fact as well as in name. He did so because of his exceptional ability to get along with everyone, even those whose views or temperament were diametrically opposed to his own, but this involved a tradeoff.

The other side of the coin was an unwillingness, an inability probably, to dominate a group, to thrust himself forward in conversation. Waite was always the good listener, a posture that did not impress upon first or casual meeting, but time was always on his side. He wore well. It would be unfair to attribute his success simply to his genial nature. He commanded respect from his associates for his commitment to hard work, for doing every job with painstaking thoroughness, and for his decency, his strength of character. Morrison Waite was not brilliant, not especially talented, not clever; he was solid, sturdy rather than distinguished,[68] and when fate transposed the midwestern attorney into chief justice of the United States, his success would have been predicted by those who knew him well. Only his new associates, both on and off the Court, were surprised.

When Waite died in 1888 his savings were inadequate to support his wife, and friends and bar associations raised the funds to do so. Waite's salary as chief had been $10,500 per year, considerably less than the $25,000 he had been earning prior to his appointment, and the cost of maintaining his position in Washington far outran his salary and his savings.

Such was not the case with his successor, Melville Weston Fuller, who died a wealthy man. Fuller's earnings at the time of his appointment were reputed to be $75,000 annually, much of which had been invested in real estate at a substantial return. In 1903 the chief's salary was increased to $13,000, but without an independent income Fuller would have been in similar straits to Waite. In many respects Fuller resembled Waite in background and temperament and his education, while not identical, was similar. Like Waite, Fuller was a New Englander of distinguished ancestry who settled in the midwest and established a successful, lucrative law practice, and like Waite's, his selection as chief justice came as a total surprise to the nation.

Melville Weston Fuller was born in Augusta, Maine, in 1833, the direct descendant of the first Fuller in the United States who landed on the Mayflower and the first American Weston who

settled in Salem, Massachusetts, in 1644.[69] In 1849 at age sixteen Fuller entered Bowdoin College where his great-grandfather
had been one of the founders and where two of his relatives then
served as trustees. The curriculum was similar to that pursued
by Waite at Yale, classical and theological with no options. All
courses were compulsory as was chapel attendance twice daily.
Fuller was studious, orderly and thrifty, following his mother's
admonitions to avoid liquor, tobacco and debt, and he graduated
Phi Beta Kappa in 1853. In college Fuller gave evidence of political interests and leanings by organizing the Granite Club to
work for the election of Franklin Pierce, a Bowdoin graduate
and a Democrat whose views accorded with Fuller's which were
essentially Jeffersonian. Fuller was opposed to government pa-
ternalism and to concentrating power in Washington, favoring
state autonomy, sound money, free trade and the preservation of
individual freedom. In an almost simplistic sense this was his
creed throughout life.

In 1854 Fuller entered the Harvard Law School, the first chief
to acquire any law school training, but he attended lectures for
only six months and did not consider the experience of any
great significance to his career. He was admitted to the bar in
1855 and clerked for a few months with an uncle in Bangor before moving to Chicago for reasons not precisely ascertainable,
although his biographer suggests that a broken engagement by a
Susan Robinson of Augusta may have been the cause.

Practicing law was not Fuller's whole life. It was an interesting way to make a good living but he clearly enjoyed certain
avocations as much as his chosen profession. His taste for literature and for the theater were lifelong interests along with his
love of politics, the latter being pursued as a pleasant game
rather than as a bitter struggle to obtain power. He wrote poetry
in college, dabbled in newspaper editing in Augusta before leaving for Chicago, and always preferred reading in his study or
attending the theater to producing legal scholarship. His reading
—preferably novels—was extensive. He "loved to be at the
opening of every new play and exchange rather pointless witti-
cisms with his friends,"[70] and for the ten years prior to his leaving for Washington he belonged to the Chicago Literary Club
which entailed the presentation of a paper by a member each
Monday night. His interest in politics, while intense, was al-

ways on the periphery and never at the center of his life. His only elected offices were a single term in the Illinois legislature in 1862 and membership in the state constitutional convention of 1861. Although a member of the Democratic presidential nominating conventions of 1864, 1872, 1876, and 1880, he never sought nor ran for national office. He did, however, use strong political rhetoric in criticizing Abraham Lincoln which later almost denied him the chief justiceship.

During the senatorial contest of 1858 between Stephen Douglas and Abraham Lincoln, Fuller was one of Douglas' staunchest supporters, giving speeches all over Illinois in behalf of the "Little Giant," and when Lincoln was nominated for president in 1860 he wrote that although Lincoln was "a gentlemen of unblemished moral character . . . little can be said in his praise" as a politician.[71] In 1863 while serving in the Illinois legislature he condemned Lincoln's Emancipation Proclamation, declaring that abolitionism was equally the cause of the war with slavery and that the proclamation was "predicated upon the idea that the President may so annul the constitutions and laws of sovereign states, overthrow their domestic relations, deprive loyal men of their property, and disloyal as well, without trial or condemnation."[72] In 1864 he criticized Lincoln for his conduct of the war, for suspending the writ of *habeas corpus*, for unlawful arrests, and for the unconstitutional admission of West Virginia as a state.

Logically, he campaigned for General George B. McClellan in the 1864 election, but when Lincoln was assassinated, Fuller proudly accepted an appointment by the Chicago city council to a group of Chicago's prominent citizens that escorted the remains of the president to Springfield. Although never a defender of slavery as such—he recognized it for the evil it was—Fuller's constitutional creed insisted that the national government had no legitimate power to interfere with it, that the Kansas-Nebraska Act correctly permitted settlers in the new territories to decide the issue which he presumed would be against slavery. In his attitude toward abolitionism, however, he resembled Taney, and had not a Democrat broken the Republican hold on the presidency in 1884, Fuller would almost certainly have spent his entire life as a prosperous but little known Chicago attorney.

Chief Justice

Stories abound concerning President Cleveland's choice of a relatively obscure lawyer for the chief justiceship; e.g., his wife suggested it to Senator Farwell of Illinois, Fuller had successfully campaigned for it, Cleveland searched for an efficient business manager who would decongest the Supreme Court's docket. Fuller's biographer documents a refutation of such stories and points out that Fuller and Cleveland had been close friends long before the nomination was sent to the Senate, and that the president had attempted to bring Fuller into his administration on three different occasions.[73] He had offered him the chairmanship of the Civil Service Commission, the office of solicitor general and membership on the U.S. Pacific Railway Commission (a body created to investigate financial scandals connected with western railroads), all of which Fuller turned down. Moreover Cleveland had consulted Fuller on several appointments, including federal judgeships.

When Waite died, the president received several gratuitous suggestions for his replacement but he rejected most on geographic grounds. The seventh circuit (consisting of Indiana, Illinois and Wisconsin) was without any representation on the Court, and Cleveland decided to remedy the situation by choosing someone from Illinois. His first choice was Judge John Scholfield of the supreme court of Illinois whom Fuller earlier had enthusiastically urged upon the president for a district court vacancy and now recommended for chief. For personal reasons Scholfield declined both appointments and Cleveland decided upon Melville Weston Fuller whose public life and professional attainments hardly suggested a man superbly qualified for the office of chief justice, and the nomination immediately encountered opposition in the Republican-controlled Senate. Although Fuller had the support of Abraham Lincoln's son Robert, and some of Lincoln's closest friends, Senator George F. Edmunds of Vermont, the chairman of the Senate Judiciary Committee dragged up the Fuller statements against Lincoln and the war, concluding that Fuller was a Copperhead, a Confederate sympathizer, disloyal to the Union cause, and thus unfit to be chief justice. Edmunds may have believed the charges, but part of his opposition was based on pique, on anger toward the president for refusing to appoint Edward J. Phelps, then ambassador to Great Britain, a fellow Vermonter and close friend. Although

Leadership Through Persuasion and Example

the Judiciary Committee reported the nomination to the Senate without recommendation, Fuller was confirmed by a vote of 41 to 20, hardly an overwhelming endorsement but a respectable majority.

Cleveland's choice of a chief, another gamble on the basis of Fuller's record, turned out to be an extremely good one, for Fuller, while lacking in legal craftsmanship and intellectual creativity, was the Court's best manager up to that day and second in the Court's history only to Hughes. In physical appearance he was almost the antithesis of Waite, his predecessor, and White, his successor, both of whom were massive in physical stature. Fuller was "a dapper little man," five feet six inches tall and weighing 130 pounds, who needed a hassock to keep his feet from swinging freely.[74] Yet all who knew him testified to his striking appearance, to his flowing silvery hair, his glossy white mustache, his "bright, sensitive and poetic face," all of which gave him a "rugged," "patriarchal" look,[75] a massive in miniature. He looked and was dignified, but he was neither cold nor unapproachable. Overshadowed by some of the greatest minds ever to sit on the Court, Fuller nevertheless exerted an exemplary personal control over the bench that earned him a deserved reputation of competence and popularity both with his colleagues and with the American people.

Edward Douglass White, while similar to Fuller and Waite in that he possessed a "lovable nature" which endeared him to his associates, was in important respects very different from both. Physically, he was a large hulk of a man who towered over the diminutive Fuller and whose girth almost equaled that of the 300-pound President Taft who appointed him. In temperament he also differed markedly from the two chiefs who preceded him. Unlike either he was primarily a scholar who, even when practicing law in New Orleans, spent most of his evenings in his office studying, attempting to discover why, not simply how, the law operated as it did.[76] He was also adroit at languages, speaking French and English with equal fluency and able to converse in Spanish and Italian. He not only read Latin but spoke it as well,[77] but above all he was a master of both the civil law and the common law which enabled him to build a flourishing practice in New Orleans and to grapple with the constitutional problems rooted in the Anglo-American legal tradition. Neither

Fuller nor Waite were near his equal in learning and intellectual power, but both surpassed him in the role of administrative head of the Court.

White was born to comparative wealth, his father being the owner of a 1600-acre sugar plantation in Thibodaux, Louisiana. His great-grandfather, an Irish Roman Catholic, had settled in Philadelphia in the 1740's, but the second generation of his American ancestry migrated south, and his grandfather practiced law in North Carolina, attended the Annapolis Convention of 1786, became the first U.S. superintendent of Indian affairs, and eventually moved to the Louisiana territory where he became the territory's first federal district judge. White's father continued the tradition of political involvement, serving as governor of the state and several terms in Congress. White's formal education was totally Jesuit-directed from his early years in New Orleans, to Mt. St. Mary's in Emmitsburg, Maryland, to Georgetown College, to part-time legal studies at the University of Louisiana (now Tulane). In 1861 at the age of sixteen White joined the Confederate army, but within two years he was to return to the plantation at Thibodaux, broken in body and spirit, after having been caught in General Nathaniel Banks' siege of Port Hudson on the lower Mississippi River. Healed mentally and physically by the end of the war, White joined the law office of Edward Bermudez, a leading New Orleans attorney, while simultaneously attending the school of law at the University of Louisiana. In 1868, the year in which the Fourteenth Amendment was declared ratified, he passed the state bar.

White joined the rough and tumble politics of the postwar era in Louisiana, and although he supported causes and candidates on the basis of principle, he fortuitously backed the right horse and landed in the United States Senate and then on the Supreme Court. He initially joined forces against the Republican carpetbaggers and was elected to the Louisiana senate in 1874. When Francis R. T. Nicholls, a friend of White's father, became governor after the nefarious Hayes-Tilden election and the Republican retreat from the South, he named 33-year-old White an associate justice of the Louisiana supreme court. In the whipsaw politics of the day Nicholls was suddenly ousted and White along with him. For a decade in his thirties and unmarried, White lived a pleasant life in the New Orleans French Quarter,

Leadership Through Persuasion and Example

building a solid law practice and running the sugar plantation in Thibodaux, but the pull of politics was strong enough to draw him to the Nicholls campaign of 1888 which he successfully managed. Governor Nicholls once again rewarded him, this time with an appointment to the United States Senate. December 7, 1891, saw the beginning of a public career in Washington which would continue until White's death in 1921.

Although his service in the Senate was to terminate in three years with his appointment to the Supreme Court, White's political and constitutional views were clearly apparent from the beginning.[78] He was attuned to the prevailing conservative thinking of his time, the major components of which were social Darwinism, minimum government activity, and a federalism that assigned the state and national governments precise spheres of legitimate authority.[79] During the brief period in the Senate, White was not a vigorous participant, but he spoke out against the Hatch anti-option bill which, in order to prevent trading in commodity futures, levied a heavy license tax on dealers in futures. In White's view the tax was not a revenue-raising measure on its face and was, therefore, unconstitutional.[80] At the same time White fought for a tariff on sugar in order to protect his Louisiana sugar-growing constituents and was at odds in this respect with President Cleveland and the Democratic party platform in their pledges for tariff reduction. When the president called him to the White House to offer him the Supreme Court position, he thought that Cleveland was about to dress him down for his opposition to the president's tariff proposal.

Justice Samuel Blatchford died on July 7, 1893, and six months later President Cleveland sent the name of William B. Hornblower of New York to the Senate without consulting New York Senator David B. Hill who proceeded to block the appointment through the prerogative of senatorial courtesy. Hill's opposition, however, went deeper than the presidential slight. At one time Hornblower had been a member of a committee of the New York bar association which investigated charges that Isaac Maynard, an attorney to the state board of canvassers, had falsified election returns in 1891 in favor of the Democratic party. The report concluded that Maynard was indeed guilty of the charge and had acted under the direction of Hill, then governor of New York. Hill had never forgiven Hornblower whose appointment to the committee had been suggested by Maynard's attorney, and Hill persuaded a majority of his colleagues to deny confirmation.

Determined to place a New Yorker on the bench, but in a direct challenge to Senator Hill, Cleveland then nominated Wheeler H. Peckham, a political opponent of Hill's who had publicly criticized the Senate for rejecting Hornblower. Hill called it a "spite appointment" and orchestrated another defeat for the president, after which the senator from New Hampshire, William E. Chandler, reportedly exclaimed that the Senate would not accept any nominee of the president. When told of Chandler's remark, Cleveland's response was: "Tomorrow I'll name a man whom the Senate will unanimously confirm and for whom that little son of a bitch himself will be compelled to vote."[81] Tossing back the senatorial courtesy coin, Cleveland won unanimous confirmation for White, a fellow senator whom Hill, Chandler and the entire Senate were morally bound to support. White was Cleveland's third choice—the president had also made an offer to Frederic Coudert, a New York lawyer, who declined for personal reasons—but he was by no means a thoughtless choice made in a moment of anger.

Although not close friends, White and Cleveland had a cordial relationship and with the exception of the tariff question, generally saw eye-to-eye on crucial public issues. It is possible that motivating the president's choice was the desire to neutralize White's opposition in the tariff struggle then in progress in the Senate. If the latter were the case, Cleveland was disappointed for White remained in the Senate for several weeks after being confirmed, continuing in his role as antagonist to a reduction of the tariff on sugar. As an associate justice for sixteen years White's performance was energetic, judicially creative and, as was to be expected, politically conservative. He wrote the opinion of the Court in 375 cases for an average of over 23 per year, but he also dissented with some regularity, 170 times to be exact, 44 of which were written.[82]

Unlike Waite and Fuller, White was a known quantity at the time President Taft was faced with a vacancy in the chief justiceship. Only once had a sitting associate, William Cushing in 1796, been nominated and confirmed as chief, but he had declined the appointment. No one, therefore, had ever served in both capacities. Militating against promoting from the bench were both tradition and the practical problem of resentment by those associates who coveted the position and believed themselves better qualified than their chosen colleague, a situation that might be a heavy burden for the chief to bear. Assessing President Taft's motives in elevating White to the head position involves considerable conjecture, but we do know that Taft respected White, had confidence in his judgment and had a warm personal relationship with him.

The President had been impressed with White's creative opinions in *United States* v. *Trans-Missouri Freight Association*[83] and the *Insular Cases*,[84] and this no doubt was influential in the appointment. In the former, White dissented but he began to develop the distinction between reasonable and unreasonable restraints on commerce, later to be adopted by the Court as the "rule of reason." In the latter case he formulated the principle of "incorporated" as opposed to "unincorporated" territories as a means of determining which parts of the Constitution applied to newly acquired possessions. In another context Taft had already disavowed any intention of relying on the precedent of never promoting an associate justice. This he had done in a letter to Charles Evans Hughes when offering him the appointment as an associate in 1910. In the same letter Taft suggested that he would *probably* make Hughes chief if the post became vacant during his presidential term, but the letter is a classic study in ambiguities and could not be construed as an ironclad promise.[85]

Justice Holmes in his correspondence with Sir Frederick Pollock wrote of the pending appointment, betting that it would be Hughes and suggesting that White had "little chance," but he praised White as "the ablest man likely to be thought of," a "profound" thinker and "first rate." Taft's choice of White also may have been motivated in the final analysis by his own consuming passion to become chief justice. Hughes was only 48 and in good health while White was 66, and there was always the chance that the seat might become vacant under propitious circumstances in which Taft would be named. As luck would have it, Taft executed a perfect political maneuver that returned to him what he had yearned for his entire adult life. When White died in 1921, not only a Republican but a fellow Ohioan was in the White House, and Taft became one of Warren Harding's best appointments.

White was the third chief in a row who, above all else, was a likable human being, a person whose presence made each day a pleasurable experience for his associates. In legal learning and intellectual power he was superior to both Waite and Fuller, though his prose style was tortuous, consisting of sentence piled upon sentence or sentences running on to paragraph length, resulting in opinions that have been called "models of what judicial opinions ought not to be."[86] His writing has been described as that of "a man with an overdeveloped power of finding verbal distinctions but who had never paid any attention to the art of expressing himself clearly."[87] It has also been suggested that there may be a connection between White's obscure writing and "a nervous affliction which prevented him from writing unless he pressed the first finger of his right hand against the right side of his nose and held his pen between the second finger and thumb. In order to write in this position he would lower his face until his nose almost brushed the paper. If by accident his finger skipped off his nose the pen would fly out of his hand."[88] The fact is, however, that he usually dictated his opinions to a stenographer and later corrected the typescript. Like Hughes, White had an amazingly retentive memory and could deliver an opinion from the bench without consulting his notes,[89] but the listener had equal difficulty with the reader in deciphering the involuted reasoning.

White was promoted to chief under circumstances considerably more favorable than those surrounding the appointments of Waite and Fuller, but it was not in his nature to lead in the manner of either of his predecessors. With the exception of Harlan, who coveted the position himself, all of his colleagues were pleased with his elevation and were ready to give him every advantage. Moreover, within a year he would be able to attract the loyalty of four new justices and four more within six years. And those conversant with the Court's affairs accepted White's appointment with enthusiasm. It was indeed an auspicious beginning for the modest, courteous, decent, knowledgeable, and in many ways, brilliant White, but in the end his record was not that of a great leader.

Leadership Through Persuasion and Example

MANAGING THE COURT

As managers of the Supreme Court's business Waite and Fuller must be rated among the best, whereas administrative techniques and managerial skills were not among White's strong suits. All three assigned opinions fairly and sensibly; all set an example by writing more than their share of opinions, although only White, in spite of his tortured writing, fashioned imaginative and creative concepts in constitutional law. When Waite took his seat in 1874 he faced not only a hostile bench including Miller, Field, Harlan, Bradley, and Gray, who were among the ablest judges the nation has produced, but an explosion in litigation that was to increase the Court's workload exponentially over what it had been thirty years earlier. In 1850 the Taney Court had 253 cases pending; in 1880 the Waite Court faced 1,212 cases, a number that was to increase to 1,563 in 1888, Waite's final year as chief.[90] His task was made even more difficult by the fact that some of the justices were old and infirm and incapable of performing their duties. For a five-year period from 1878 to 1883 Justices Swayne, Clifford, and Hunt were incapacitated, the latter having suffered a stroke. Waite, however, with his natural propensity for hard work and his innate affability, managed to cope successfully with both his independent and strong-willed brethren and with those scores of cases resulting from the post-Civil War economic growth and the new 13th, 14th and 15th Amendments to the Constitution.

With consummate diplomatic skill Waite was able to effect a smoothly running Court although Justice Miller, who never quite accepted his being passed over for chief, remained harshly critical. He wrote in 1875, "I can't make a silk purse out of a sow's ear. I can't make a great Chief Justice out of a small man."[91] And in 1879 he reiterated the judgment: "Of what is due to that court, and what is becoming his character, he has no conception."[92] Yet in 1885 when Waite was recuperating from an illness, Miller joined the brethren in advising Waite to take adequate time to recover and signed his letters, "Your affectionate friend."

Unlike Earl Warren who permitted Justice Black to preside over the conference until he could learn the ropes, Morrison Waite declined the offer of senior associate Nathan Clifford who suggested that he continue to preside over the Court—he had been acting chief in the interim between Salmon Chase's death and Waite's appointment—until Waite could familiarize himself with the Court's internal processes. Waite reportedly told his friends, "I am going to drive and those gentlemen know it."[93]

The new chief apparently realized that given the circumstances surrounding his appointment and the resentment of the sitting justices, a firmness was essential to an acceptance of his leadership. At that, full acceptance took time, and it came only through the firmness combined with tact, affability and a commonsense psychology. That he successfully applied this amalgam is documented by his letters and those of his colleagues.[94] Initially, Waite had virtually no influence over the justices as is illustrated by the choice of a new reporter after John W. Wallace announced his intention to resign in 1875. Supporting his old friend, J. C. Bancroft Davis, who was well qualified for the post, Waite was able to muster only two additional votes, those of Justices Bradley and Hunt, as a majority selected William Todd Otto, a former judge then serving as assistant secretary of the interior. When Otto resigned in 1883, Waite was able to secure the appointment of Davis without difficulty, indicating that his leadership was then more securely established.[95]

In his opinion assignments Waite's primary goal appeared to be the maintenance of Court unity internally and the appearance externally of a harmonious, cooperative group. He achieved the goal first by assigning where possible the writing of liberal opinions to conservative justices and vice versa; second, by assigning the most significant cases to the Court's most able members; third, by keeping public dissent at a minimum; fourth, by retaining an unruffled composure and tactfully dealing with the sensitive egos of his colleagues; and fifth, by doing more than his share of the writing.

He set the tone of impartiality in assigning opinions in one of the first major cases to be heard by the Court after his appointment, *United States* v. *Union Pacific R.R. Co.*,[96] which was decided in favor of the railroad. He assigned the opinion to David Davis, probably the most liberal member of the Court, instead of to a known friend of the railroads like Field or to a former corporation lawyer who had defended the railroads' interests like Bradley. Field, who had expected the assignment, wrote to Waite of his dissatisfaction, challenging the chief's judgment in intemperate language. Waite answered Field, indicating that there was no personal ill will toward him, and in what was to continue to be his dispassionate and genial style, wrote: "If what I have done is not satisfactory to my brethren, I regret it, but I think if they and you would, as you said the other day, 'put your minds alongside of mine' for a little while, it would be seen that my judgment was correct."[97] Field responded, retracting some of his earlier harsh language, although still maintaining his original view that the assignment should have been his. Waite closed the affair permanently and settled relations for the future. After indicating that he thought it wise that the opinion was to be written by a justice who had not been close to the railroad, Waite wrote:

> No one appreciates your vigorous style more than I do, and, but for these considerations, I should have been glad to have had its use in this case—And while I regret that you do not look on the matter as I do, I cannot but think that my judgment was for the best interest of us all. . . . I certainly intend to treat all my brethren fairly in this most delicate and at the same time important part of my work. If I do not, it is the fault of the head and not of the heart.
>
> I am glad to know that I misunderstood some of the expressions in your former note, and that I may hope to retain your friendship and respect if my conduct shall be such as to merit it.[98]

There is no evidence that Field ever again attacked the chief's authority to assign opinions.

Morrison Waite had the good sense to realize that his role as chief superseded his role as judge, and he was therefore rarely in dissent publicly. Such a posture gave him control over opinion assignments but unquestionably it meant a compromise with principle when he joined majorities with whom he disagreed. Such political trade-offs which chiefs have engineered among the justices in an attempt to arrive at a consensus are well known. All chiefs have at one time or another voted with the majority in order to retain control of a case, and most, perhaps all, associate justices have on occasion joined a majority reluctantly in order to present a unified front to the public. According to Waite's personal docket books kept during his fourteen years as chief, dissents in conference ran as high as 44 percent in a given term, but statistics tell us that of the 3,470 cases decided by full opinion during Waite's tenure, public dissents were registered in only 359, or just over 10 percent.[99] Waite himself wrote only 23 dissenting opinions although he dissented without opinion in an additional 28 cases. However, he wrote the Court's opinion in 872 cases for an average of over 62 per term, the highest output of any justice ever.[100]

The antagonism in Waite's initial encounters with Miller, Field, and Clifford over the manner in which he was to exercise his managerial authority eventually subsided as the skillful diplomat in him dominated his style. Furthermore, if all else failed, he was always willing to relieve a justice of an unwanted assignment and to write the opinion himself. Waite was a good judge of quality and this trait is nowhere more evident than in his way of matching justices to cases. In 1881 at the request of historian George Bancroft, Waite compiled a list of the most important cases involving constitutional questions decided since his appointment in 1874. He listed 72, of which he was in the majority in 66 and thus controlled the opinion assignments. He wrote the most, 14, but the remainder were assigned in almost direct relationship to ability with Miller and Field at the top—each receiving 11—and Clifford and Hunt at the bottom with only 1 a piece. The remainder were strung out in the following pattern: 10 to Strong, 7 to Bradley, 5 to Harlan, 4 to Swayne, and 2 to Davis.[101]

In dealing with his colleagues Waite always used a personal touch that helped to enhance his authority. He complimented his associates on the style of their opinions, expressed concern about their health or personal misfortunes, wrote letters of welcome to new judges, and established the practice of permitting new appointees to choose their first opinions.[102] In short, he did everything possible to make his colleagues feel comfortable with him, with each other and with the Court as an institution, and he succeeded admirably in this respect. He did not and could not lead intellectually, but he used what talents he had to harness those eight independent, egotistic and sometimes cantankerous individuals into a unified team.

Justice Oliver Wendell Holmes, Jr., who served under four chiefs (Fuller, White, Taft and Hughes) once remarked: "Fuller was the greatest Chief Justice I have ever known."[103] Since

Holmes served under Hughes for less than two terms, he was essentially comparing Fuller to White and Taft. Of Fuller's executive abilities Holmes wrote that he was "extraordinary," that he "had the business of the Court at his fingers' ends, he was perfectly courageous, prompt, decided. He turned off the matters that daily called for action easily, swiftly, with the least possible friction, with inestimable good humor and with a humor that relieved any tension with a laugh."[104]

During Fuller's 22 years as chief justice between 1888 and 1910, 19 associate justices served on the Court, and from a reading of the correspondence between the chief and the associates, he was loved and respected by all of them. Third in length of service among the 15 chiefs, Fuller, like Marshall and Taney, presided over roughly two groupings or different Supreme Courts. Of the 8 associates who were serving at the time of Waite's death, only John Marshall Harlan served throughout Fuller's tenure. A second, Horace Gray, died in 1902 after having sat with Waite for 7 years and with Fuller for 14, but 5 members (Matthews, Miller, Bradley, Lamar and Blatchford) were gone within Fuller's first 6 years. Field died in 1897 after 34 distinguished years on the bench, 11 of which were with Fuller. Thus, during his first decade Fuller was overshadowed intellectually by Gray, Bradley and Field, and during the latter 12 years by Harlan, White and Holmes. The remaining 9 justices appointed during Fuller's tenure (Jackson, Moody, Burton, Brown, Shiras, Day, McKenna, Peckham and Brewer) did not leave a permanent mark on American constitutional law or on the institutional development of the Court.

Fuller, like Waite, generally assigned more opinions to himself than to any other justice and, like Waite, retained control of opinion writing by dissenting as little as possible, although his record is not quite as good as Waite's in this respect. During his 22 years he wrote only 30 dissents, dissenting without opinion in an additional 112 cases. Although Fuller wrote the opinion of the Court on average more often than any of his colleagues, the record indicates a loss of vigor as he became older. He wrote 45 majority opinions during his first term, 58 in 1890, 65 in 1893, and 69 in 1894, but in his last 5 years one can see the decline from the earlier pattern as he wrote only 16 in 1907, 14 in 1908, and 18 in 1909.[105] Clearly, Fuller set an example by doing the lion's share of the work. The fact of hard work, however, was not enough in itself to assure him the respect needed for leadership. Respect is generated for the head man when he works harder than anyone else, but to preside over a small group—a committee of 9—one must also have the knack of keeping tempers under control and an ability to mediate without engendering bitterness or ill will. This Fuller was able to do through a natural charm and good humor, although in few important cases was he able to induce unanimity. Throughout his stewardship there were hundreds of dissents and hundreds of non-unanimous decisions, but the Court was devoid of personal feuds and fractious factionalism.

Fuller did what a successful manager must do: pay attention to matters large and small. In the latter he cultivated friendship by looking to the welfare of each justice, inviting new appointees to a special dinner, deferring frequently to the opinion of others, and originating the custom of requiring each justice to greet and shake hands with every other justice before they began the day, a tradition which the Court continues to honor. In matters large, in addition to carrying the heavy burden of writing more than his share of opinions, he ran the conference deftly and with attention to detail, and he presided over open court with dignity and patience, always aware of the need for decorum and ceremony as a means of preserving respect for public authority.[106] In the words of Felix Frankfurter who observed Fuller in the courtroom: "He presided with great gentle firmness. You couldn't but catch his own mood of courtesy. Counselors too sometimes lose their tempers, or in the heat of argument, say things, and there was a subduing effect about Fuller. Soon these men who looked at him out of the corner of their eyes, felt that they were in the presence of a Chief whom they could greatly respect."[107]

As we have indicated earlier, Fuller was the first chief to be sworn in formally as "Chief Justice of the United States,"[108] and in keeping with that title, he was the first to lobby vigorously in behalf of congressional legislation for judicial reform. As a result of his efforts Congress enacted the Circuit Court of Appeals Act of 1891 which reduced the load of the Supreme Court substantially by creating nine intermediate federal courts of appeals, with jurisdiction over diversity of citizenship, patent, admiralty and various commercial matters. Within ten years of the Act's passage the backlog of cases in the Supreme Court was reduced from 1,100 to 300, and the justices for the first time in decades were able to handle cases with reasonable dispatch. Although Waite before him was not able to master the docket, he did master the Court's internal affairs. Fuller mastered both. White mastered neither.

Edward Douglass White was the intellectual equal of all who served with him, was in fact superior to most of them, and in the manner of his immediate predecessors, was liked by all who knew him. When he assumed the mantle of leadership, he had the respect of the bench and bar, of the nation generally. Upon his death in 1921 after eleven years as chief, he had retained that respect in spite of the fact that he had lacked managerial skill and had failed "to capitalize upon his many sources of influence."[109] He seemed unwilling to use his personal and professional prestige—his friendship with past and future presidents (Taft, Roosevelt and Wilson), and his popularity with old colleagues in the Senate—to work in behalf of further judicial reforms to ease the pressures on the Supreme Court and on the federal judicial system generally. White's view of the chief justiceship was the traditional one of a judge whose main duty was to lead the Court in deciding cases, and in spite of his lack of firmness in managing the conference, White and the Court presented a face to the nation of competence, tranquillity, and to a degree, ideological unity. During the early years at least, dissent was far less frequent than it had been under Fuller's final decade in office, but with the appointments of McReynolds in 1914, Brandeis in 1915, and Clarke in 1916, the harmony of the earlier Court under White began to dissipate. In the 1919 term just one year before White's death, dissents were registered in almost every third case decided, a new record for the Court.[110]

Productivity under White compared favorably to that under Waite and Fuller, as the White Court wrote more than 2,000 opinions in 10½ years.[111] White also led the Court as he averaged over 30 majority opinions per term. Moreover, there is no evidence that any of the justices was dissatisfied with the opinion assignments. Although White refused to engage in the political maneuvering necessary to persuade Congress to enact measures that would ease the Court's case load, he used judicial methods to accomplish a similar result. First, by adhering to rigid procedural and jurisdictional standards, he was able to dispose of cases expeditiously, thereby saving valuable time by avoiding a full hearing on the substantial merits. Instead of permitting counsel the usual hours for oral argument, he cut the time to thirty minutes per side in certain cases.

He attempted to set an example to the brethren by stating at the beginning of a hearing which questions he wished answered, and he generally avoided interrupting counsel.[112] All such measures enabled the Court to keep its head above water, but the long-term solution—a judiciary act that would give the Court a broad discretionary power over its docket—was left to be dealt with at another time and by a chief with a different view of the office.

It is unfortunate that White's major failure was in the crucial role as manager of the conference. It was in part his easygoing nature that defeated him in this respect, for in allowing extended debate, he merely exacerbated normal personal differences and elevated the level of tension. As we pointed out earlier, Hughes was to say that he learned from White how not to be a chief justice, and Brandeis was to write after White had been replaced by Taft that the "judges go home less tired emotionally and less weary physically than in White's day. . . ."[113] But if White did not excel in all aspects of leadership, he did some things very well, and his genial nature and sincere concern for the welfare of his colleagues gave him a great deal of capital that he dispensed naturally and unaffectedly. As Hughes said to Frankfurter: "White was a very dear man—one of the dearest I have ever known. He was very warm-hearted and most solicitous that the brethren should be as happy as possible."[114] They might have been happier had White been a tougher taskmaster but that was simply not in his nature.

IDEAS AND LEGACY

When we compare the intellectual baggage of the three chiefs with their administrative abilities, their reputations are reversed. White, the least effective as Court manager, persuaded the justices to adopt some original ideas that are valid principles in constitutional law to this day. Waite and Fuller, the able administrators, leave a somewhat barren field, although Waite's

Leadership Through Persuasion and Example

substantive record is better than Fuller's. Neither of the latter was a philosopher at heart, and whatever ideas they expressed were less the universal and more the parochial, confined to the America of their times. Neither was creative nor imaginative in his judicial thinking and their opinions, while competent, have not withstood the test of time. If one were asked to name Waite's significant pronouncements on constitutional questions, it would be stretching the point to go beyond *Munn* v. *Illinois*[115] and *Stone* v. *Mississippi*,[116] even though he wrote 872 majority opinions, many of which involved constitutional issues. Fuller's most famous or infamous opinion was the *Income Tax Case*[117] and that was nullified within two decades by the Sixteenth Amendment. And Fuller, unlike Waite, generally assigned significant cases to others.

Felix Frankfurter suggested that Waite "moves in the spirit of Taney"[118] even though Waite had been a Whig and later a Republican while Taney stood in the center of Jacksonian democracy. Waite, like Taney, believed strongly in a federalism in which the states would share power coequally with the national government; yet within that framework neither was averse to using the central government to promote the nation's development, particularly in areas essential to commerce like railroads, roads and waterways. Always a major component of their thinking was the preservation of the Union. Taney attempted to compromise the slavery issue in order to hold it together, and Waite, in order to reconcile North and South, supported Justice Bradley's opinion devitalizing the Fourteenth Amendment in the *Civil Rights Cases*.[119] In both instances the welfare of black people gave way to the ideal of national unity. Waite also resembled Taney in his belief that property rights are not absolute, that public constraints on the excesses of a laissez-faire economy were legitimate and proper under the Constitution. This translates judicially into a posture of restraint, of confidence in popular government, of permissiveness in regulatory legislation. It is difficult to ascertain how deeply felt Waite's commitments were since his opinions, like the man himself, were bland, commonplace, unadorned, dry, and dull.

Without doubt the language of Waite most often quoted by historians, judges and students of public law is in his opinion for the Court in *Munn* v. *Illinois*[120] and some of that, perhaps most, may be attributable to others. The case involved the constitutionality of an Illinois statute enacted under the pressure of the Granger movement which fixed maximum charges for storage by the grain elevator industry. Before the Court were two challenges to the law: first, that it was an unconstitutional burden on interstate commerce; and second, that it amounted to a taking of property without due process of law. Upholding the statute, the Court through Waite's opinion, dismissed both contentions. The chief justice declared the law a proper exercise of the police power, a power which had been used in England "from time immemorial, and in this country from its first colonization" to regulate certain kinds of business enterprise. Waite's attitude toward judicial intervention in legislative affairs is clearly demonstrated by his language in *Munn:* "For our purposes we must assume that, if a state of facts could exist that would justify such legislation, it actually did exist when the statute now under consideration was passed. . . . Of the propriety of legislative interference within the scope of legislative power, the legislature is the exclusive judge. . . . For protection against abuses by Legislatures the people must resort to the polls, not to the Courts."

The most significant aspect of the opinion is that which analyzes the due process contention. Waite pointed out that "down to the time of the adoption of the 14th Amendment it was not supposed that statutes requesting the use, or even the price of use, of private property necessarily deprived an owner of his property without due process of law. Under some circumstances they may, but not under all. The Amendment does not change the law in this particular; it simply prevents the States from doing that which will operate as a deprivation." Waite then proceeded to cloud the issue by borrowing a phrase from some seventeenth-century remarks of Lord Chief Justice Hale: "[W]hen private property," he observed, "is 'affected with a public interest, it ceases to be *juris privati* only.'" Now, of course, it was possible to argue that some businesses were *not* affected with a public interest and therefore were being deprived of due process when subject to government regulation. Although Waite apparently meant only that a legislative act might not be arbitrary, his "vague and mischievous language . . . was readily adapted to the restriction of governmental powers."[121]

Leadership Through Persuasion and Example

For some fifty years the business interests brought case after case to the Supreme Court alleging that the due process clause was a bar to state policing regulations and, particularly after the replacement of Waite, Miller and Bradley by Fuller, Brewer and Peckham, they were very often successful in their quest for judicial support of laissez-faire economics. Waite himself, and often a majority with him, generally supported public regulation, both state and national. For example, Waite wrote the opinion upholding a Mississippi law creating a railroad commission to fix rates for railroads operating within its borders, although he appeared to placate financial interests by observing that the "power to regulate is not a power to destroy; and limitation is not the equivalent of confiscation."[122] Furthermore, maintained the chief, the state may not require a railroad to operate without reward, nor can it take private property without due process of law. Certainly Waite was accommodating the conservatives on his own Court as well as attempting to sooth the corporate entrepreneurs, but the qualifying language continued to leave the door open for judicial annulment of legislative policy under the umbrella of due process.

Similarly in the *Sinking Fund Cases*[123] Waite wrote the opinion approving the Thurman Act under which the Pacific railroads were to pay 25 percent of their annual net earnings into the federal treasury, but he was moved to warn that the due process clause of the Fifth Amendment was a barrier to federal repossession of its land grants without just compensation. Waite could not hold the Court with him in the famous *Wabash Rate Case*[124] in which the majority, speaking through Justice Miller, decided that a state might not regulate intrastate railroad rates when the transportation involved was a part of an interstate system. Adhering to his *Munn* opinion in his dissent, the chief justice emphasized the local character of the regulations, that Congress had not acted and that an indirect effect on interstate commerce did not bar state control of railroads operating within their borders.

A majority did support Waite in *Stone* v. *Mississippi*[125] in which he sharply modified John Marshall's doctrine on the contract clause by holding that a state may not bargain away its police power and that a state charter permitting acts against the public welfare which a legislature deems harmful may be rescinded. This opinion was very much in the Taney mold, both in its view of the public good and of property rights as limited by the general welfare.

Waite's greatest failure in intellectual leadership was his unwillingness to take an enlightened and forward-looking stand on the Negro question, although with his cautious view of the Fourteenth Amendment, one might have predicted his constitutional posture on the race issue. In 1875 when he first confronted the Fourteenth Amendment in *Minor v. Happersett*[126] he strayed not at all from the grudging construction of its clauses in the *Slaughter House Cases*[127] two years earlier. Mrs. Virginia Minor contended that the right to vote was one of the "privileges and immunities" of federal citizenship and that Missouri's laws denying her access to the ballot box ran afoul of the Fourteenth Amendment. For a unanimous court Waite wrote that the Fourteenth Amendment added no new privileges and immunities to citizenship but simply confirmed those already in existence. Thus Mrs. Minor had not been deprived of any constitutional guarantee. In the same year Waite refused to expand the Amendment to include the guarantee of jury trial in common law suits in the states.[128]

This narrow construction forbode nothing but grief for the newly freed blacks as Waite and his Court continued along the same path when dealing with federal legislation enacted under the Fourteenth Amendment. A test of the first of such laws reached the Court in 1875 in *United States v. Cruikshank*[129] and *United States v. Reese*.[130] The former involved a section of the Enforcement Act of 1870 which made it a federal criminal offense for two or more persons to deprive or conspire to deprive any citizen of rights guaranteed by the Constitution of the United States. The case arose out of a confrontation between whites and blacks in Louisiana during the reemergence of white power toward the end of the Reconstruction period. For attacking and killing scores of blacks at a political meeting of several hundred black citizens, nine whites were convicted of depriving them of the right to peaceably assemble, to bear arms, to vote and of equal protection of their persons and property. In *Reese* two white inspectors of a municipal election were indicted under sections three and four of the Enforcement Act for refusing to count the vote of a black citizen. Waite, writing for the Court, found all of the indictments defective. The rights allegedly denied the defendants, said Waite, preceded the Constitution and were to be enforced by the states, not the federal government.

Relying on the doctrine of the *Slaughter House Cases*, Waite maintained that the Fourteenth Amendment created no new rights, that it did not add anything "to the rights which one citizen has against another. . . . The only obligation resting upon the United States is to see that the states do not deny the right. This the Amendment guarantees, but no more. The power of the national government is limited to the enforcement of this guarantee and no more."[131] As to the Fifteenth Amendment, it granted a new right, but it was not the right of suffrage; it was, said Waite, simply the "right of exemption from discrimination," for the right to vote "comes from the states."[132] In this reading of the amendments that were designed to secure full and free citizenship to blacks, it would be a long time, indeed, before the vestiges of slavery would be excised from American life.

At no time during his tenure did Waite deviate from his original position that the relationship of states to nation remained unchanged as a result of the Civil War amendments to the Constitution. He joined the majority in the *Civil Rights Cases*[133] in which the Civil Rights Act of 1875 was invalidated on the ground that the Fourteenth Amendment gave Congress no direct authority to guarantee blacks equal access with whites to quasi-public facilities such as railroads, inns, theaters, and restaurants. Congress might take corrective action against state abridgment of rights but could not operate directly upon individuals. In *Hall* v. *DeCuir*[134] Waite could have voted, consistent with his view of state police powers and interstate commerce, to uphold a state anti-segregation law, but he did not. Writing for the majority he struck down Louisiana's Reconstruction statute which required all common carriers to provide equal accommodations for blacks and whites, as a direct burden upon interstate commerce. Even when a majority of his Court concluded that a black tried for murder by a jury from which blacks had been excluded, had been denied equal protection of the laws, Waite dissented, lamely contending that the "mere fact" that no person of color had been allowed to serve "did not constitute racial discrimination and grounds for reversal."

Waite's biographers are defensive about his judicial attitude
on the race question and suggest that he should not be held "to
modern standards of what constitutes social justice for the Negro."[135] As they point out, Waite's concern for national unity
took precedence over the rights of blacks. Moreover, he believed
strongly that education was the key to integrating the Negro
into white society and he supported such movements as the
Peabody Fund[136] with his time and his money. The fact remains,
however, that Chief Justice Waite did not steer the Court on a
course that would lead to fair and equitable treatment of blacks
by American institutions, both public and private. The total effect of Waite and his court on racial progress was negative and
its decisions permitted brutal aggressions against blacks and
postponed for generations a coming to terms in America with a
biracial society. It has been said that "Waite might have gained a
greater personal fame if he had ever rendered a decision which
aroused substantial opposition."[137] Had he persuaded the Court
to uphold the early civil rights measures, he undoubtedly would
have had to endure harsh criticism, even vilification, by some
segments of American society, but his reputation as a statesmanlike leader would have been secure.

If Chief Justice Fuller was "extraordinary" as administrative
head of the Court, he was even less influential intellectually
than Waite. In his 22 years he spoke for the Court over 700
times, but infrequently in cases involving the hard issues of
constitutional law. In fact, with a few notable exceptions, the
Income Tax Case being one, Fuller was in dissent in those cases
in which the meaning of the Constitution was paramount.
Most of his opinions were in cases relating to jurisdiction and
federal practice or suits involving intricate commercial transactions,[138] the kinds of cases that are neither long remembered
nor influential in changing the course of constitutional history.

Although overshadowed by colleagues, particularly Field,
Harlan, Gray, White (as an associate), and Holmes, Fuller did
not obsequiously accept the ideas of others. His opinions in
over a score of cases, some for the majority, some in dissent, suggest a man with firmly held ideas about the Constitution, about
the proper relationships of men to their government and of power
centers within the system to each other. Like Waite, however,
he lacked imagination; he relied too much on the past, unable

Leadership Through Persuasion and Example

to perceive the revolutionary changes going on around him, changes that required boldness and creativity by the Supreme Court. He thus continued to oppose new uses of national power and the extension of the state police power at a time when the individual had no other recourse against the abuses arising out of an almost uncontrollable corporate expansion.

In 1895–96 Fuller wrote the opinion in two cases and joined the majority in two others, all of which demonstrate a lack of foresight, an inability to grasp the principle that the Court "would be drawn more and more into resolving difficult questions where the past offered infirm guidance and the future demanded charting."[139] Historically the most significant of the four was *Pollock* v. *Farmers' Loan and Trust Co.*[140] in which the federal income tax law of 1894 was held unconstitutional. The case was a highly political decision in the sense that the justices attempted to justify their political predilections, and they were able to take a position for or against the tax with impunity since neither the Constitution nor precedents gave a clear, unequivocal answer. As a result of ailing Justice Howell Jackson's absence from the Court initially, Fuller delivered two opinions in *Pollock* and only in the second, after a rehearing with Jackson present, did he speak for a majority of five, declaring the entire income tax unconstitutional.

In the first decision the chief spoke for four justices since the Court had divided evenly on all the issues save two, the tax on income from real estate and that on income from state and municipal bonds, and of the eight, six agreed that such taxes are unconstitutional. Fuller had to come to grips with the meaning of a direct tax in Section 9 of Article I of the Constitution which reads: "No capitation, or other direct, tax shall be laid, unless in proportion to the Census or Enumeration herein before directed to be taken." In attempting to find what the framers meant by "direct tax" Fuller alluded to James Madison's notes: "Mr. King asked what was the precise meaning of direct taxation. No one answered." He then concluded that the distinction between direct and indirect taxes was well understood by all present and needed no prolonged discussion. Fuller argued that on the basis of the debates in the convention and in the state ratifying conventions, representation and taxation went hand in hand as a general constitutional principle, and the direct tax provision was a compromise over slavery. As he saw it, the framers contemplated raising revenue normally by duties, excises and import levies (all indirect taxes) and that only in an extreme emergency should the government resort to direct taxes, i.e., taxes on property.

The direct tax limitation, said Fuller, was "one of the bulwarks of private rights and property" and was designed by the framers "to prevent an attack upon accumulated property by mere force of numbers." Sweeping away precedents that had held an income tax not to be a direct tax,[141] Fuller maintained that in none of the previous cases had income from real property been involved, that what was said concerning direct taxes as they affected rents was merely *dicta* and, most important, the income tax upheld as a war time measure involved emergency conditions. He thus avoided overruling any previous pronouncements.

In his second opinion Fuller admitted that a tax on business, on the professions or on employment were not direct taxes, but these could not be separated from the unconstitutional sections and therefore the entire taxing scheme must fall. We see in Fuller's opinion the view that federal power must be contained lest it interfere with private rights in property, a view which favored the rich at the expense of the poor and one that gave free rein to corporate expansion. Within twenty years and just three years after Fuller's death the decision was overruled by the Sixteenth Amendment which permitted taxes on incomes from whatever source derived and without regard to apportionment.

In *United States* v. *E. C. Knight Co.*[142] Fuller spoke in the same mode as he wrote an opinion devitalizing the Sherman Act. The United States government brought suit requesting dissolution of the American Sugar Refining Company on the ground that it had acquired a monopoly of over 90 percent of the sugar refining facilities in the country. While the company might well have a monopoly, said Fuller, it was a monopoly not of commerce but of manufacturing, and although the power over manufacturing might bring the "operation of commerce into play, it does not control it, and it affects it only incidentally and indirectly. Commerce succeeds to manufacture, and is not a part of it." If the people desire protection from manufacturing monopolies, said Fuller, they must take their grievances to the states, not to Congress which can act only on a monopoly in commerce. To permit congressional regulation of manufacturing, the chief concluded, is to weaken the federal system through interference with the reserved powers of the states. The constitutional distinction between manufacturing and commerce, between direct and indirect effect, were to last into the 1930s, somewhat longer than the Fuller views of taxation, but they, too, were not to be permanent fixtures in constitutional law.

During the same period Fuller supported Justice Brewer's opinion upholding the injunction against labor organizer Eugene Debs issued during the Pullman strike of 1890, thus permitting the first successful criminal prosecution under the Sherman Act not, incidentally, against business, but against labor. With Fuller's blessing Brewer wrote that it was not simply a matter of enjoining mob violence but of restraining "forcible obstructions of the highways along which interstate commerce travels and the mails are carried." Fuller apparently saw nothing inconsistent between this view of interstate commerce and the one he had espoused in *E. C. Knight*. Probably one of the worst decisions of the Fuller Court was that in *Plessy* v. *Ferguson*[143] in which the Court gave official sanction to the pernicious "equal but separate" doctrine. Upholding the principal of separation of the races by law, again with Fuller's approval, the Court observed that a statute which implies merely a legal distinction between two races, a distinction based on color which is ineradicable, does not destroy the legal equality of the two races nor imply the inferiority of either race. Only Justice Harlan had it right in his lone dissent in which he predicted that the decision would "stimulate aggressions more or less brutal and irritating" against the rights of blacks and would vitiate the Civil War amendments. Fuller, like Waite before him in the *Civil Right Cases*, lacked the vision to chart the future wisely.

If Fuller would not lead the Court in interpreting the Fourteenth Amendment to vindicate the rights of blacks, he was willing to support its use to curb state regulation of business by joining in Justice Peckham's opinion in *Lochner* v. *New York*[144] in which "liberty of contract" became a part of due process of law and gave the Court a tool with which to condemn state laws that attempted to protect workers from employer exploitation. Similarly he joined in the opinions of Justices Blatchford and

Brewer declaring that the fairness and reasonableness of railroad rates were a matter for final determination by the Supreme Court[145] and not by the legislature or administrative commissions established by state law. The upshot of such a doctrine was, of course, a victory for the railroads whose allegedly sharp practices might have been curtailed by the states.

In several landmark cases decided during the Fuller years that have withstood the test of time, the chief did not lead the Court, did not even join the majority. He dissented in *Champion* v. *Ames*[146] in which the Court for the first time upheld an act of Congress prohibiting the use of the channels of interstate commerce for objects—in this instance, lottery tickets—not harmful intrinsically, nor harmful to the commerce, but harmful in their effects on society in general. This decision set the stage for a series of federal laws regulating various aspects of American life, thus constitutionally permitting the use of the commerce clause as a basis for a national police power.

What Fuller's biographer called "perhaps his worst defeat on the Court" came in the case of *United States* v. *Wong Kim Ark*[147] in which the majority held that a child born in the United States of resident Chinese aliens who, under the acts of Congress known as the Chinese Exclusion Acts could never become citizens, was a "natural born citizen" under the citizenship clause of the Fourteenth Amendment. The Amendment's language seems straightforward enough, reading: "All persons born or naturalized in the United States and subject to the jurisdiction thereof, are citizens of the United States and of the state in which they reside," but Fuller, joined only by Harlan, gave it a tortuous construction. He argued that "subject to the jurisdiction thereof" prevented American-born Chinese from becoming citizens. Their parents cannot renounce allegiance to the emperor of China and are thus barred from the naturalization process. Since citizenship descends from parents, according to Fuller's reasoning the children are always subject to the jurisdiction of the parental country and are incapable of becoming citizens of the United States.

In two previous cases involving congressional harassment of Chinese aliens Fuller had been on the side of protection, but in neither had he led the Court. In 1893 in *Fong Yue Ting* v. *United States*[148] a majority had approved a measure that required Chinese residents to apply to the government for a certificate of residence within one year of the passage of the law. Anyone found without such a certificate was subject to arrest and deportation. Answering the majority which had held that Congress was not limited by the Constitution in exercising control over aliens, Fuller saw the law as inflicting "punishment without a judicial trial" and called it "absolutely void" and an "assertion of an unlimited and arbitrary power . . . incompatible with the immutable principles of justice, inconsistent with the nature of our government, and in conflict with the written Constitution by which that government was created and those principles secured." Fuller had the support of only two justices, Brewer and Field, and they wrote even stronger dissents than he, which suggests that they, not Fuller, were the leaders of the opposition. In *Wong Wing* v. *United States*[149] the Court struck down a provision of the Immigration Act of 1892 providing that Chinese aliens living in the United States illegally would be imprisoned at hard labor for up to one year, again under the theory that the Constitution did not apply to aliens. This the Court denied unanimously, arguing that the due process clause and the requirement of indictment by a grand jury, both guarantees of the Fifth Amendment, had been violated. Although Fuller voted with the majority, he assigned the opinion to Justice Shiras rather than writing it himself.

Another constitutional trouble spot in which Fuller failed to exert leadership was that of the newly acquired American possessions as a result of the Spanish-American War. How noncontiguous territory in which the inhabitants were of a foreign culture and spoke a foreign language was to be accommodated by the existing constitutional structure was a thorny problem, and initially the Court was fragmented and unable to agree on any first principles. In a series of decisions collectively known as the *Insular Cases*[150] the justices struggled with the question whether the Constitution was applicable to the new territories, and if so, in what respects. The key case was *Downes* v. *Bidwell*[151] in which the validity of the tariff on Puerto Rican products entering the United States was at issue. Constitutionally the question was whether the clause in Article I, Section 8 requiring that all "duties, imposts and excises shall be uniform throughout the United States" prevented Congress from collecting any taxes on Puerto Rican goods entering the mainland. Prior to deciding that issue the Court had to determine the status of Puerto Rico. Although the tax was sustained, there was no majority to support the reasoning behind Justice Brown's opinion which held that "uniform throughout the United States" meant uniform only in the states of which Puerto Rico was not one.

It was in this case that Associate Justice White developed his theory—later to become the accepted principle—that the Constitution applied in all respects to territories which Congress had "incorporated" into the United States. "Unincorporated" territories such as Puerto Rico were subject simply to congressional rules governing territories. Fuller dissented from the White position, contending that under the treaty with Spain Congress need not give the inhabitants of the island full citizenship, but that in all other respects Congress was bound by the Constitution's wording. Leaving aside the validity or desirability of the "incorporation" theory, Fuller was unable to forge a majority which might agree on how to assimilate the acquisitions of the new American empire into the constitutional system.

Fuller's failure to have more influence as a judge "was a defect of intellectual power."[152] He was unable "to appreciate the organic nature of constitutional law"[153] and his "confusion of mind was confined to that branch of the law."[154] Like Waite before him he left no permanent intellectual legacy to constitutional law, but his attainments inspire respect if not awe.[155] There is something to be said for his modesty, for his wisdom in recognizing the strengths of others and in using those strengths for the benefit of the Court and the nation. He had the good sense to understand the need for expanding the role of the chief justice to that of lobbyist for the Court and he successfully persuaded the leadership in Congress to support legislation that created a more efficient federal court structure and gave the Court greater flexibility over the caseload. Like Waite, however, he lacked the spark, the brilliance that would have placed him in the ranks of great jurists, but his managerial and diplomatic skills enabled him to maintain a smoothly functioning group internally, and at a time of dramatic changes in the nation's economic and social organization with their inevitable political reverberations, Fuller's style was largely responsible for the high regard in which the Court was held by the American people generally. Not a great chief certainly, but clearly Melville Weston Fuller was a very good one.

Edward Douglass White's influence on the Court and upon constitutional development was almost precisely the reverse of that of Fuller and Waite. While barely adequate as the Court's manager, he was by nature a scholar, a man interested in ideas, and his opinions, while not known for brevity or clarity, contain flashes of brilliance and creativity not found in those of Waite or Fuller. Although he wrote no abstract treatises in which he expressed a coherent legal philosophy, there is a consistency of principle manifest in his opinions during his 28 years on the Court, 12 of them as chief. In those opinions which have left a permanent mark, there is a recurring theme reminiscent of the thinking of John Marshall, namely, that there is an abstract standard of sound government to which the Constitution and Court of the United States must conform, a standard discoverable by human reason.[156] This natural law position is quite in tune with the thinking of the framers and with the views of Marshall, particularly those expressed in the contract clause cases.

White's intellectual leadership is best exemplified by his ability to persuade a majority to accept his theories—now permanently embedded in American constitutional law—of congressional authority over territories and of the "rule of reason" in antitrust legislation. As indicated above White as an associate wrote a concurrence in the *Insular Cases* in which he originated the concept of "incorporated" versus "unincorporated" territories. Arguing that fundamental law applied to *any* territory belonging to the United States White wrote: "While, therefore, there is no express or implied limitation on Congress in exercising its power to create local governments for any and all of the territories, by which that body is restrained from the widest latitude of discretion, it does not follow that there may not be inherent, although unexpressed, principles which are the basis of all free government which cannot be with impunity transcended."[157] At the same time only territories "incorporated" by Congress are subject to the rules of the Constitution in their entirety.

In 1903 White again, in a concurring opinion, expounded the theory he had enunciated two years earlier in a case involving the newly annexed Hawaiian Islands,[158] and in 1905 White's view became that of the Court as he spoke for the majority holding that Alaska was an incorporated territory.[159] Just prior to White's death in 1922 a unanimous Court accepted the "insular doctrine" as the constitutional law governing acquired territories. What White was able to do was to construct a compromise solution to a potentially explosive division in the country arising out of the new American imperialism. The key issues were first, whether territories belonging to the United States could be held permanently as colonies or whether they must eventually become states, and second, whether Congress in legislating for the new territories was subject to all the restraints of the Constitution.

According to Taney in *Dred Scott* all territories must eventually become states and the Constitution applied to them *in toto*. Within this framework Taney concluded that Congress could not prohibit slavery in the territories west of the Mississippi. This, however, was in conflict with John Marshall's declaration in 1828 that in legislating for territories, "Congress exercises the combined powers of the general, and of a State government."[160] Acting as a state, Congress might legislate differently— prohibit slavery, for example—than when acting as the national legislature. White chose the Marshall position but at the same time he insisted that Congress, while retaining some flexibility, was under the constraints of "principles which are the basis of all free governments."

Indicative of White's perseverence was his triumph in attaining acceptance for the "rule of reason" in antitrust cases. In his dissenting opinion in *United States* v. *Trans-Missouri Freight Association*[161] he first enunciated the "rule of reason" then supported only by Justices Field, Gray and Shiras. At issue was the government's use of the Sherman Act to dissolve an agreement of eighteen previously competing railroads to maintain a fixed rate schedule in the Southwest. In dissent from the majority opinion upholding the government White contended that the Sherman Act covered only "unreasonable" restraints of trade, that not all contracts by competitors were illegal. As he contended: "To define, then, the words 'in restraint of trade' as em-

Leadership Through Persuasion and Example

bracing every contract which in any degree produced that effect, would be violative of reason, because it would include all those contracts which are the very essence of trade, and would be equivalent to saying that there should be no trade, and therefore nothing to restrain."[162]

For fourteen years White would continue to argue his point in dissent before the Court would accept then Chief Justice White's "rule of reason." His triumph came in the famous *Standard Oil* and *American Tobacco* cases in which both companies were alleged to have destroyed all competition through monopolistic practices.[163] In both cases White spoke for the majority agreeing with the government that the companies had engaged in unfair and oppressive methods of competition thereby destroying smaller manufacturers, but only after he had made it clear that the "rule of reason" was to be applied in all antitrust cases. These combinations were "unreasonably" restraining trade. While White's views were considered reactionary and oversolicitous of corporate wealth by the reformers of the day, the concept of reasonable versus unreasonable restraints of trade has become a useful tool in Sherman Act cases. Whether for good or ill, however, the early Sherman Act litigation illustrates White's ability to shape the judicial policy of the Court by gaining his colleagues' support, and in this instance, to expand the Court's power over a vital aspect of American life.[164]

With some exceptions White supported state police regulations and a quasi-federal police power and he lived to see his view of the income tax prevail. Had there been no Sixteenth Amendment overruling the Fuller opinion in *Pollock*, it might well have been overruled by White and his Court. As he said in *Brushaber* v. *Union Pacific Railroad Company*[165] when challenges were made to congressional legislation implementing the Income Tax Amendment: "There is no escape from the conclusion that the Amendment was drawn for the purpose of doing away for the future with the principle upon which the *Pollock* case was decided."

Although White's record on civil liberties during and after World War I is not an enlightened one—he voted, for example, to imprison both Schenck and Abrams, the latter over Holmes' dissent—there is a bright star in an otherwise dark constellation. Of three early cases involving the rights of Negroes White wrote the opinion in two and joined the majority in a third, all expanding civil rights for blacks. As chief he spoke for a unanimous Court in declaring the notorious Oklahoma "grandfather clauses" unconstitutional. To prevent blacks from voting Oklahoma had provided for a stringent literacy test and then exempted from it anyone who had been a registered voter in 1866 or 1867 as well as their lineal descendants. Thus illiterate whites could vote but blacks, unless they could pass the extremely difficult test could not. White declared that "the 1866 standard never took life, since it was void from the beginning because of the operation upon it of the prohibitions of the Fifteenth Amendment."[166] In the second case a Maryland law similar to that of Oklahoma was also void "because it amounts to a mere denial of the operative effect of the Fifteenth Amendment, and, based upon that conception, proceeds to re-create and re-establish a condition which the Amendment prohibits."[167] In the third case, *Buchanan* v. *Warley*[168] White joined the majority invalidating an ordinance of Louisville which had set up housing zones based on race.

These were progressive decisions from a Louisiana Democrat who had served in the Confederate army and who had joined in the postwar movement to return the state to native whites during Reconstruction. But they are in character. As one of White's biographers suggests, the language of the Fifteenth Amendment was mandatory and whatever his personal beliefs, White would subordinate them to the law.[169] He was first and foremost a constitutionalist and a believer in those "great principles of government" that rest upon "truth and justice."[170]

Taney, Waite, Fuller, and White were very different in background, temperament and training, but each in his own way was able to lead the Supreme Court through the judicious use of his natural strengths. All were conditioned by their times and by the men with whom they served, and none was able to transcend completely his predilections and prejudices so deeply formed prior to his appointment. Yet each was able to keep that small group of fiercely independent minds functioning harmoniously, Taney and White through intellectual power and personal charm, Fuller and Waite primarily through a psychology of accommodation and persuasion. All were ever cognizant of the powerful office that they held and made special efforts to

Leadership Through Persuasion and Example

sustain its dignity and to preserve its insulation from partisan politics.

Although Fuller served as an arbitrator in 1897 in a boundary dispute between Venezuela and British Guiana, he wisely declined President McKinley's request that he join the peace commission to negotiate the treaty with Spain at the end of the Spanish-American war. In his reply, he wrote: "I think . . . that considering the nature of the office it is far wiser that the Chief Justice should not participate in public affairs. The circumstances of today are not those which existed in the day of Jay and Ellsworth nor of Marshall who was Secretary of State as well as Chief Justice for a few weeks."[171]

It was Waite, however, who set a permanent standard of judicial propriety. When newspapers began to speculate that he would be a splendid Republican nominee for president, Waite wrote to Clark Waggoner, the editor of the *Toledo Commercial:* "Everyday I live, I see more and more evidence of the great impropriety there is in forming political combinations around a Chief Justice. He cannot be a candidate for any political office without damaging the place he holds. Even though he should not let his political aspirations affect his judicial action, it would be said he did, and that would be almost as bad as if he did. My only ambition is to make my name honorable among those who have preceded me in the high office I hold."[172] Such a view of the chief justiceship gives the office itself a special reserve of power that will not be eroded in the worst of times or during the incumbency of lesser men.

NOTES

1. Abraham, op. cit., p. 157.
2. Samuel Tyler, *Memoir of Roger Brooke Taney,* New York: Da Capo Press (1970), p. 86.
3. Umbreit, op. cit., p. 204.
4. Palmer, op. cit., p. 189.
5. As quoted in Palmer, ibid.
6. Walker Lewis, *Without Fear or Favor,* Boston: Houghton Mifflin (1965), p. 275.
7. Memoir of Taney, op. cit., p. 28.
8. Ibid., p. 41.
9. Charles W. Smith, *Roger B. Taney: Jacksonian Jurist,* New York: Da Capo Press (1973), p. 7.

10. Carl Brent Swisher, *Roger B. Taney*, Hamden, Conn.: Archon Books (1961), p. 142.
11. Ibid., p. 131.
12. Technically the vote was on an indefinite postponement of the nomination which was tantamount to rejection.
13. Abraham, op. cit., p. 97.
14. Ibid., p. 103.
15. Carl Brent Swisher, *The Taney Period*, Vol. V. of the Oliver Wendell Holmes Devise History of the Supreme Court of the United States, New York: Macmillan (1974), p. 45.
16. Lewis, op. cit., p. 277.
17. Ibid., p. 279.
18. Swisher, op. cit., p. 278.
19. Ibid., p. 279. The new rules were printed in 7 Howard V (1849).
20. Congressional Globe, 33rd Congress, 2nd session (1855), p. 194.
21. Congressional Globe, 30th Congress, 1st Session (1848). See Swisher, op. cit., for a detailed discussion of the various proposals dealing with circuit riding and the court's congested docket, pp. 279–84.
22. See Swisher, op. cit., pp. 293–318 for an analysis of the problems faced by the reporters during the Taney period.
23. The statistics for opinions written by the Taney justices are taken from Albert P. Blaustein and Roy M. Mersky, *The First One Hundred Justices*, Hamden, Conn.: Archon Books (1978), pp. 142–49.
24. Taney concurred without opinion in an additional three cases and dissented silently in seventeen. He wrote eight *per curiam* opinions.
25. For example, *Charles River Bridge* v. *Warren Bridge*, 11 Peters 420 (1837); *Bank of Augusta* v. *Earle*, 13 Peters 519 (1839); *Bronson* v. *Kinzie*, 1 Howard 311 (1843); *Holmes* v. *Jennison*, 14 Peters 540 (1840); *The Genesee Chief* v. *Fitzhugh*, 12 Howard 443 (1851); *Luther* v. *Borden*, 7 Howard 1 (1849); *Strader* v. *Graham*, 10 Howard 82 (1850); *Dred Scott* v. *Sandford*, 19 Howard 393 (1857).
26. 16 Peters 1 (1842).
27. 16 Peters 539 (1842).
28. *Erie R.R.* v. *Tompkins*, 304 U.S. 64 (1938).
29. 12 Howard 299 (1851).
30. *License Cases*, 5 Howard 504 (1847).
31. *Passenger Cases*, 7 Howard 283 (1849).
32. Letter from McLean to a newspaper as quoted in John P. Frank, *Justice Daniel Dissenting*, Cambridge: Harvard University Press (1964), p. 174.
33. Benjamin R. Curtis, *A Memoir of Benjamin Robbins Curtis*, Vol. 2, Boston: Little Brown (1879), pp. 338–41.
34. Ibid.
35. Ibid.
36. G. Edward White, op. cit., p. 65.
37. Umbreit, op. cit., p. 241.
38. Don E. Fehrenbacher, *The Dred Scott Case*, New York: Oxford University Press (1978), p. 559.
39. *Ohio Life Insurance and Trust Co.* v. *Debolt*, 16 Howard 416 (1853) at 428.
40. Supplement to the *Dred Scott* decision as reprinted in Tyler, op. cit., p. 600.

41. See Smith, op. cit., pp. 82–105 for a detailed discussion of Taney's views on the nature of the union.
42. 11 Peters 420 (1837).
43. 1 Howard 311 (1843).
44. *Home Building and Loan* v. *Blaisdell*, 290 U.S. 398 (1934).
45. 14 Peters 540 (1840).
46. 12 Howard 443 (1852).
47. *The Steamboat Thomas Jefferson*, 10 Wheaton 428 (1825), opinion by Story, limited admiralty jurisdiction to the ebb and flow of the tide.
48. *Luther v. Borden*, 7 Howard 1 (1849).
49. 17 Fed. Cases 144 (1861).
50. Speech by Reverdy Johnson to the Baltimore Bar on October 14, 1864, as quoted in Smith, op. cit., p. 15.
51. Charles Warren, *The Supreme Court in U.S. History, Vol. III*, Boston: Little Brown (1923), p. 115.
52. *Umbreit*, op. cit., p. 244.
53. See Robert J. Steamer, op. cit., pp. 78–92 for a discussion of congressional reaction to the *Dred Scott* decision.
54. Charles Evans Hughes, "Roger Brooke Taney," 17 *American Bar Association Journal* 785–90 (1931).
55. Felix Frankfurter, *The Commerce Clause Under Marshall, Taney and Waite*, Chapel Hill: Univ. of North Carolina Press (1937), p. 73 and Philip Elman, ed., *Of Law and Men: Papers and Addresses of Felix Frankfurter 1939–56*, Hamden, Conn.: Archon Books (1965), p. 113.
56. See Fehrenbacher, pp. 587–93.
57. Letter from Stephen Field to Matthew Deady, March 16, 1874, as quoted in C. Peter Magrath, *Morrison R. Waite: The Triumph of Character*, New York: Macmillan (1963), p. 107.
58. See Robert Scigliano, *The Supreme Court and the Presidency*, New York: The Free Press (1971), pp. 125–60.
59. 1 Wheaton 304 (1816).
60. 4 Wheaton 316 (1819).
61. See Magrath, op. cit. pp. 26–31 for a detailed discussion of Waite's education.
62. Bruce R. Trimble, *Chief Justice Waite: Defender of the Public Interest*, New York: Russell and Russell (1970), pp. 23–24.
63. Magrath, op. cit. p. 39.
64. Trimble, op. cit., p. 39.
65. Magrath, op. cit., p. 55.
66. Ibid., p. 16.
67. D. Grier Stephenson, Jr., "The Chief Justice as Leader: The Case of Morrison Remick Waite, 14 *William and Mary Law Review* 899 (1973), pp. 903–5.
68. Umbreit, op. cit., p. 305.
69. Willard L. King, *Melville Weston Fuller, Chief Justice of the United States, 1888–1910*, New York: Macmillan (1950), p. 1. The factual biographical material is taken primarily from King, pp. 1–121.
70. Umbreit, op. cit., p. 338.
71. Letter to the New York *Herald* as quoted in King, op. cit., p. 47.

72. King, ibid., p. 56.
73. Ibid., pp. 98–99.
74. Jeffrey B. Morris, "The Era of Melville Weston Fuller," *Supreme Court Historical Society Yearbook, 1981,* p. 41.
75. Ibid. See also King, op. cit., p. 329.
76. Umbreit, op. cit., p. 366.
77. Ibid., p. 367.
78. Robert B. Highsaw, *Edward Douglass White: Defender of the Conservative Faith,* Baton Rouge: Louisiana State Univ. Press (1981), p. 44.
79. Ibid., pp. 4–5.
80. See Congressional Record, 52nd Cong. 1st session, 6561–652.
81. Highsaw, op. cit., p. 53. The remark was quoted in Allan Nevins. *Grover Cleveland: A Study in Courage,* New York: Dodd, Mead (1932), p. 571. A similar quote is found in Robert McElroy, *Grover Cleveland: The Man and the Statesman,* 2 vols., New York: Harper (1923), Vol. 2, p. 134.
82. Blaustein and Mersky, op. cit., p. 144.
83. 166 U.S. 290 (1897).
84. *Downes* v. *Bidwell,* 182 U.S. 244 (1901); *DeLima* v. *Bidwell,* 182 U.S. 1 (1901); *Dooley* v. *United States,* 183 U.S. 151 (1901).
85. The letter is quoted in Merlo J. Pusey, *Charles Evans Hughes,* New York: Macmillan Co., (1951), Vol. 1, pp. 271–72.
86. Umbreit, op. cit., p. 376.
87. Ibid.
88. Ibid.
89. James F. Watts, Jr. *Edward Douglas White* in Friedman and Israel, *The Justices of the United States Supreme Court, 1789–1969,* New York: R. R. Bowker (1969), p. 1641.
90. Felix Frankfurter and James M. Landis, *The Business of the Supreme Court,* New York: Macmillan Co., (1928), p. 86.
91. Miller to Ballinger, Dec. 5, 1975, as quoted in Charles Fairman, *Mr. Justice Miller and the Supreme Court, 1802–1890,* New York: Russell and Russell (1939), p. 373.
92. Letter of Oct. 29, 1879, in Fairman, ibid., p. 409.
93. Magrath, op. cit., p. 104.
94. Extensive use of Morrison Waite's papers is made by C. Peter Magrath and Bruce Trimble in their biographies as well as in more recent appraisals by Jeffrey B. Morris and D. Grier Stephenson.
95. See Magrath, op. cit., pp. 253–57 for a detailed discussion of Otto and Bancroft appointments.
96. 91 U.S. 72 (1875).
97. As quoted in Magrath, op. cit., p. 259.
98. Ibid., p. 260.
99. Stephenson, op. cit., p. 918.
100. Blaustein and Mersky, op. cit., table 11, pp. 147–49.
101. Magrath, p. 263.
102. Ibid.
103. King, op. cit., p. 290.
104. Ibid, p. 334.

Leadership Through Persuasion and Example

105. These figures are taken from the statistics compiled by King, ibid., pp. 339–41.
106. Jeffrey B. Morris, op. cit., p. 43.
107. Frankfurter, "Chief Justices I Have Known," 39 *Virginia Law Review* 883 (November 1953), p. 889.
108. See Chapter 1.
109. Jeffrey B. Morris, "Chief Justice Edward Douglass White and President Taft's Court," in *Supreme Court Historical Society Yearbook 1982*, p. 39.
110. John E. Semonche, *Charting the Future: The Supreme Court Responds to a Changing Society, 1890–1920*, Westport, Conn.: Greenwood Press (1978), p. 397.
111. Ibid., p. 412.
112. Morris, op. cit., p. 41. See also Umbreit, op. cit., p. 384.
113. Alpheus T. Mason, *The Supreme Court from Taft to Warren*, Baton Rouge: Louisiana State Univ. Press (1968), p. 61.
114. Lash, *From the Diaries of Felix Frankfurter*, op. cit., p. 313.
115. 94 U.S. 113 (1877).
116. 101 U.S. 814 (1880).
117. *Pollock v. Farmers Loan and Trust Co.*, 157 U.S. 429 and 158 U.S. 601 (1895).
118. Felix Frankfurter, *The Commerce Clause*, Chicago: Quadrangle Books (1964), p. 96.
119. 109 U.S. 3 (1883).
120. 94 U.S. 113 (1877).
121. Frankfurter, *The Commerce Clause*, p. 87.
122. *Railroad Commission Cases*, 116 U.S. 307 (1886).
123. 99 U.S. 700 (1879).
124. 118 U.S. 557 (1886).
125. 101 U.S. 814 (1880).
126. 21 Wallace 162 (1875).
127. 16 Wallace 36 (1873).
128. *Walker v. Sauvinet*, 92 U.S. 90 (1875).
129. 92 U.S. 542 (1876).
130. 92 U.S. 214 (1876).
131. 92 U.S. 542 (1876), 554–55.
132. 92 U.S. 214 (1876), 217.
133. 109 U.S. 3 (1883).
134. 95 U.S. 485 (1878).
135. Magrath, op. cit., p. 153. Magrath devotes an entire chapter (9) to "The Chief Justice and the Negro." See also Trimble, op. cit., pp. 158–74.
136. A fund established by millionaire George Peabody of Massachusetts used to subsidize Negro education in the South. Waite served as a trustee of the fund and lobbied for federal money for the education of blacks.
137. Umbreit, op. cit., p. 317.
138. King, op. cit., p. 332.
139. Semonche, op. cit., p. 125.
140. 157 U.S. 429 (1895) and 158 U.S. 601 (1895).

Chief Justice

141. Principally *Hylton* v. *United States*, 3 Dallas 171 (1796); *Pacific Insurance Company* v. *Soule*, 7 Wallace 433 (1869); *Springer* v. *United States* 102 U.S. 586 (1881).
142. 156 U.S. 1 (1895).
143. 163 U.S. 537 (1896).
144. 198 U.S. 45 (1905).
145. *Chicago, Milwaukee and St. Paul Railway Co.* v. *Minnesota*, 134 U.S. 418 (1890); *Smyth* v. *Ames*, 169 U.S. 466 (1898).
146. 188 U.S. 321 (1903).
147. 169 U.S. 649 (1898).
148. 149 U.S. 698 (1893).
149. 163 U.S. 228 (1896).
150. *Downes* v. *Bidwell*, 182 U.S. 244 (1901); *DeLima* v. *Bidwell*, 182 U.S. 1 (1901); *Dooley* v. *United States*, 183 U.S. 151 (1901).
151. 182 U.S. 244 (1901).
152. Umbreit, op. cit., p. 354.
153. Ibid., p. 346.
154. Ibid., p. 345.
155. King, op. cit., p. 336.
156. See Sister Marie Klinkhamer, "The Legal Philosophy of Edward Douglass White," 3 *University of Detroit Law Journal* 174–99 (1957) for a carefully documented discussion of the natural law views of Chief Justice White.
157. *Downes* v. *Bidwell*, supra, 290–1.
158. *Hawaii* v. *Mankichi*, 190 U.S. 217 (1903).
159. *Rasmussen* v. *United States*, 197 U.S. 516 (1905).
160. *American Insurance Company* v. *Cantor*, 1 Peters 511 (1828).
161. 166 U.S. 290 (1897).
162. Ibid. at 351.
163. *Standard Oil Company* v. *United States*, 221 U.S. 1 (1911); *United States* v. *American Tobacco Co.*, 221 U.S. 106 (1911).
164. Highsaw, op. cit., p. 96.
165. 240 U.S. 1 (1916).
166. *Guinn* v. *United States*, 238 U.S. 347 (1915).
167. *Myers* v. *Anderson*, 238 U.S. 368 (1915).
168. 245 U.S. 60 (1917).
169. Highsaw, op. cit., p. 163.
170. *Adams Express Co.* v. *Ohio State Auditor*, 165 U.S. 194 (1897), at 240.
171. Letter to President McKinley, Fuller Papers, Library of Congress, as quoted in King, op. cit., p. 247.
172. As quoted in Magrath, op. cit., p. 284.

Chapter 4

LEADERSHIP THROUGH
POLITICAL AND
EXTRA-COURT ACTIVITIES

ONLY THREE CHIEF JUSTICES, Fred Vinson, William Howard Taft and Warren Earl Burger, had served at some length on lower appellate courts before each was appointed to the Supreme Court. Taft had the unique distinction of having been president of the United States, but before his election to the presidency he had spent three years as a judge of the Ohio superior court in Cincinnati and eight years on the federal Court of Appeals for the Sixth Circuit. He made it clear to all who knew him that his service as a judge was the most satisfying of all the public offices he had held, including the presidency. Burger served for thirteen years on the Court of Appeals for the District of Columbia, the post from which he was elevated to the Supreme Court.

Both Taft and Burger were conservative midwestern Republicans selected by conservative Republican presidents. Warren Harding and Richard Nixon were to be remembered primarily for their failures, monuments to the hazards of democratically choosing political leaders; yet, in spite of the flawed character of Harding and Nixon, each appointed a competent, incorruptible chief who, on the basis of his previous record, was expected to bring a conservative bias to the high court. Neither president was disappointed, although neither could have predicted that Taft and Burger, very different in temperament, having grown up in disparate worlds and educated in dissimilar institutions, would similarly use the office of chief justice as a spearhead for judicial reform. Each engaged in extrajudicial activities in order to improve not only the Supreme Court but the entire American legal system, state and federal, and no chief prior to Taft and none who followed him had expended so much energy on such activities until Burger assumed office in 1969.

This is not to suggest that Taft and Burger neglected their main duties as head of the Supreme Court, but given the enormity of the job of managing the Court's business, only a person of extraordinary energy and talent can maintain a smooth, efficient Court while attending meetings, giving speeches and lobbying for new legislation that will affect the judicial function positively. The fact is that Taft in his nine years as chief and Burger in his sixteen (as of 1985) were more successful as judicial reformers than as leaders of the Supreme Court, but had they spent less time on the former and more with the latter there is no evidence that either would have led a Court that was externally less controversial, internally more cohesive, or productive of a more consistent and effective jurisprudence. Thus, we cannot say that the Taft and Burger periods were golden ages of constitutional law, but as chiefs they gave the judicial branch a leadership of a special kind, perhaps the only kind they were capable of giving. As a result of Taft's efforts the duties of the office were given a new administrative coherence, enabling those who followed to manage the Court and to direct the judiciary with less frustration and with greater efficiency than ever before. The results of Burger's efforts are not yet wholly visible, but his work, too, may make the job of future chiefs less enervating and more amenable to constructive leadership.

BACKGROUND, TEMPERAMENT, AND TRAINING

William Howard Taft was born in the year that Chief Justice Taney wrote the *Dred Scott* decision, and in 1921, 64 years later at an age when most men are thinking about calling their careers to a halt or at least slowing them down, Taft became the nation's tenth chief justice. He had already had an illustrious public career and would have had little interest in taking on the duties of any other such demanding job, but the chief justiceship had been a persistent goal not only for him[1] but for his father before him, and he was not about to let his age interfere with the consummation of a lifelong ambition, of a familial destiny.

Taft's father had moved to Cincinnati from Vermont; his mother, Louise Torrey, had been born and raised in Massachusetts. Alphonso Taft was a successful attorney who had attained some distinction as minister to Vienna and St. Petersburg and as a member of Grant's cabinet, but Willie, the "round . . . fat . . . cherubic" child[2] who was his father's favorite and who in turn had great affection and respect for his father, became far more famous in spite of the fact that, with the exception of the chief justiceship, he never coveted public office. He was, for example, a very reluctant candidate for president who "wriggled and squirmed and suggested other men almost up to the day that the Republican National Convention assembled in June 1908."[3]

In the Taft family it had been assumed that Willie would follow in his father's footsteps and go to Yale and become a lawyer. In 1878 he was graduated from Yale, second in a class of 132. Twenty years later he was to be offered the presidency of Yale which he turned down, primarily for the reason that he did not subscribe to orthodox Christian principles.[4] As a Unitarian who did not believe in the divinity of Christ, he feared that as Yale's president he would alienate some of the university's most influential supporters. He was also uncertain about his qualifications in that he had no experience in the field of education and entertained some doubts about the wisdom of a public, political figure leading a university rather than a professional educator.

Life at Yale for Taft was not appreciably different in the mid-1870s than it had been for Morrison Waite forty years earlier. He followed a rigorous schedule with classes beginning at five in the morning—six in the winter months—with daily compulsory religious services.[5] The teachers whom Taft remembered as having the greatest influence on his life were Cyrus Northrup who taught rhetoric; Thomas Thatcher, Latin; Henry Beers, literature; and most important, the famous political economist, William Graham Sumner, of whom Taft would write a half century later "that he had more to do with stimulating my mental activities than anyone under whom I studied during my entire course."[6]

Sumner was a towering intellectual figure in nineteenth-century America whose influence not only on Taft but on several generations of Yale students and on the American political leadership of his day cannot be underestimated. He was not only a vigorous teacher but a prolific scholar who wrote scores of books and essays between 1883 and 1910 in which he publicized the theory of economic individualism or social Darwinism, originally propounded by Herbert Spencer in *Social Statics*, published in 1850.[7] The thrust of social Darwinism was the survival of the fittest, a concept of a natural order of things in society in which those with merit and talent will rise to positions of responsibility and those of lesser competence will be sifted out at lower levels. According to Sumner many of the ills of his day were the products of unnatural intervention of the state, of government "tinkering" and "meddling" with the vital conflict arising from the natural inequality of human beings. All the government's attempts to foster equality of conditions, in Sumner's view, simply make matters worse. Prior to his encounters with Sumner, Taft's propensities were conservative with a strong anti-government, pro-individual freedom bias but Sumner undoubtedly helped to confirm his suspicions and harden them into formidable principles. During his entire life Taft was a critic of government regulation, always concerned with safeguarding private property which he considered the bulwark of civilization. His spirit was, according to one biographer, one "of unyielding resistance to the social service state."[8]

Rather than pursue the study of law at a prestigious eastern law school like Yale or Harvard, Taft preferred to return to his native Ohio where he entered the Cincinnati Law School in the fall of 1878. Two years later he passed the Ohio bar and embarked on a public career which, except for the hiatus between 1913 and 1921 when he served as professor of law at Yale, he was to pursue until one month before his death in 1930. Even during those nine years in private life after being defeated in his bid for a second term for the presidency, he served as an officer of several quasi-public organizations—president of the American Bar Association, president of the American Academy of Jurisprudence, co-chairman of the National War Labor Conference Board during World War I, and president of the postwar League to Enforce Peace. He seemed incapable of settling down to a quiet, private existence.

Leadership Through Political and Extra-Court Activities

Taft's early entry into the public realm was in no small measure due to his father's political influence. Within a year of his admission to the Ohio bar, he was appointed assistant prosecuting attorney for Hamilton County and prior to his appointment to the superior court of Cincinnati in 1887, he served for a year as district collector of internal revenue (his first federal post) and for over two years as assistant county solicitor. When not yet thirty Taft became a judge after Governor Foraker offered the position to Mrs. Helen Taft's father, Ohio state senator John Williamson Herron, who was not interested and urged that his son-in-law be the recipient of the honor. There was no question of Taft's ability or his temperament, but in the end the determining factors in his early success were his sound political connections. As Taft himself was to admit modestly many years later: "Like every well-trained Ohio man I always had my plate the right side up when offices were falling. . . . I got my political pull first, through father's prominence; then through the fact that I was hail-fellow-well-met with all of the political people of the city convention going type. I also worked my ward. . . ."[9]

Taft's appointment to the superior court was for the remaining fourteen months of a five-year term, and when completed he had to run for the office to which he was elected. This and the presidency were the only elective offices he ever sought. Taft resigned before the end of his term to accept President Harrison's offer in 1890 to be solicitor general of the United States, a post which he held for two years. In 1892 President Harrison appointed him to the United States Circuit Court of Appeals for the Sixth Circuit where he was to remain for eight years, the happiest eight years of his life, although his handling of labor cases came to plague him in his bid for the presidency. "To be known as the inventor of government by injunction," he said "is not a valuable political asset."[10]

Although labor leaders branded him as anti-labor, it was not a fair accusation since the rules governing labor disputes were in their formative stages, and like other judges of his day Taft was attempting to formulate some equitable regulations. Balanced against his bitter hostility toward the Pullman strike, his sending of Frank M. Phelan, a Eugene Debs lieutenant, to jail for six months on a contempt charge, and his enjoining of illegal strikes and secondary boycotts were his decisions upholding railway safety laws, workmen's compensation and railway liability. Taft also wrote the first opinion justifying the dissolution of a business combination under the Sherman Act.[11] Taft deplored labor strife which resulted in violence and in the destruction of property, but he certainly accepted the principle of labor unions, of the right to strike, and the legitimacy of seeking better wages and working conditions. Always in the forefront of Taft's thinking was the necessity of preserving private property, the true mark of civilization, a boon to all, to capitalist and workingman alike, and the courts, he contended, must be willing to stop any inroads that might be made upon it.

In an address at the University of Michigan in 1894 when he was only thirty-seven, Taft expounded upon those principles that he was to espouse his entire life, whether on the bench, in the presidency, or in private endeavor:

> While we inherited from our English ancestors the deep seated conviction that security of property and contract and liberty of the individual are indissolubly linked, as the main props of higher and progressive civilization, we have by our complicated form of government, with its many checks and balances, been able to give substantial guaranties of those rights, much further removed from the gusty and unthinking passions of temporary majorities, than has our mother country.[12]

Constitutional guarantees enforced by courts have protected and must continue to protect private property against encroachments by overbearing, transient majorities. In Taft's view it was a "principle of natural justice that one should enjoy what his labor produced,"[13] and the "advantage to be derived from the security of private property in our civilization is that it turns the natural selfishness and desire for gain into the strongest motive for doing that without which the upward development of mankind would cease and retrogression would begin."[14]

Aware that some men of great wealth had driven corrupt bargains with public officials, Taft contended that "the remedy for the evil of corruption is to put men in political control not susceptible to corrupt influences, rather than to take away from everybody that, which, while it is a means of corruption, is also a means of securing every material good."[15] Once the right to "lawful accretion" of property is conceded, argued Taft, "and inequalities of wealth are to be remedied by legislation, there is no logical stopping place between that and practical socialism."[16] The former student of William Graham Sumner had learned well but he was also attuned to James Madison's concept of the American union as an extended commercial republic and to Tocqueville's principle of self-interest rightly understood.

If Taft's father and Sumner had had a profound influence on Taft's thinking, it was his wife, the former Helen Herron, who had the greatest influence on the direction of his career. She had had strong misgivings when he resigned as solicitor general to accept the appointment to a federal circuit court and enthusiastically supported his leaving the bench when President McKinley and Secretary of War Elihu Root asked him to head a commission to establish civil rule in the newly acquired Philippine Islands. It was not without a promise from the president that he would later receive another judicial appointment—possibly to the Supreme Court—that Taft left his beloved judgeship and took on this sensitive and difficult task in 1900. As in everything he did, Taft tackled the new job with energy and enthusiasm and within a year he had established a civil service, improved educational facilities, revised the tax structure, formed municipal governments in many areas, and instituted improvement of public facilities. He was in a sense too successful, for McKinley decided that Taft would make the ideal first civilian governor of the islands, and he took over from the returning military governor, General Douglas MacArthur, on July 4, 1901. He was to remain in office until December 1903 when President Theodore Roosevelt virtually ordered him to report to Washington as his secretary of war. Twice during that period as governor general he could have had the job he had always desired, Supreme Court justice, but on being offered the appointment, he refused each time out of loyalty and devotion to the people of the Philippines, a loyalty and devotion that was reciprocal. As secretary of war, Taft continued to control the policies and destiny of the Philippines until June 1908 when he was nominated for president of the United States.

Taft's work in the Philippines was a huge success, perhaps the most successful of his career, and President Roosevelt was quick to recognize that Taft was a skillful administrator whose talents could be used to the president's and the nation's advantage. Although formally secretary of war in Roosevelt's cabinet, he became the president's troubleshooter, the indispensable handy man, extinguishing political fires and doing those tough jobs that all presidents must delegate to others with the assurance that they will be done right. Traveling thousands of miles both in and outside the United States, Taft was able to calm political storms of potential hurricane proportions in the Philippines, in Cuba, in Japan, and in Panama where he supervised the building of the canal. Working well with Secretary of State Elihu Root and with Roosevelt, Taft and they referred to themselves as the Three Musketeers, sometimes signing their letters as D'Artagnan (Roosevelt), Athos (Root), and Porthos (Taft).[17] During this period the portly Taft was able, through self-discipline, to reduce his weight from 320 pounds to 250, but the public image of Taft as a "jovial fat man" was always to remain.

It has been suggested that Taft the president was in an untenable position from the beginning since there "is no place for a crown prince who succeeds to the throne while the old king is still alive,"[18] particularly when the old king perceives his successor as reversing his pet policies. The perception was incorrect; nevertheless Roosevelt, Taft's mentor and old friend, was to attack him relentlessly, eventually splitting the Republican party and ensuring Taft's defeat when he ran for a second term in 1912. Taft was not happy as president, however, primarily because he was temperamentally unsuited to the political tasks that the office required. He was too sensitive to ignore the personal attacks made upon him, he hated the time-consuming job of dealing with patronage, and resented the necessity of planning for reelection, so much so in fact that he advocated a single presidential term of six years,[19] a proposal that remains alive today.

Despite his lack of enthusiasm for the presidential life, Taft's term as chief executive was reasonably successful and his public reputation as the benefactor of the rich with a callous disregard of the poor was undeserved. He used the Sherman Act more effectively than Roosevelt to restrain business monopoly;

Leadership Through Political and Extra-Court Activities

he worked vigorously and successfully at tariff reform; he urged upon Congress progressive measures such as postal savings, limits on the issuing of injunctions, and setting aside public lands for conservation purposes. And as always he was concerned with judicial matters. He was a consistent advocate of streamlining the entire judicial system and of revitalizing the Supreme Court. Like Warren Burger, Taft was enamored of the British system and used it as a model which American courts might emulate and, like Burger, he deplored the proliferation of procedural safeguards surrounding criminal prosecutions, suggesting that even some of the constitutional guarantees might be of "doubtful utility."[20]

In particular he believed that the rules against self-incrimination, unreasonable searches and seizures, and the necessity of confrontation by witnesses often proved to be effective obstacles to putting criminals behind bars. Furthermore, juries had too much power and should, as in English practice, be subjected to greater supervision by judges. In his presidential campaign and in his annual messages to Congress as president he continued to advocate reform of the judicial system, contending that one of the gravest defects in our government was "our failure to secure expedition and thoroughness in the enforcement of public and private rights in our courts."[21] The Supreme Court, he argued, should take the lead in reforming procedural rules for the system generally, including limiting its own docket to "typical" cases. Only after Taft's intensive lobbying as chief justice was the latter reform to come to fruition with the passage of the famous Judiciary Act of 1925 which gave the Supreme Court almost complete discretion over the caseload. For Taft the judiciary was to be the buffer against the excesses of democracy and only if it were "more efficient, less costly, and less time consuming. . . . would [it] remove a major source of popular dissatisfaction, thereby dissipating the Populist drive to abolish private property."[22]

During Taft's four years as president six vacancies occurred on the Supreme Court, giving him the opportunity to appoint more justices than any president since George Washington and more than any one-term president ever. The appointment of Charles Evans Hughes and the elevation of Edward Douglass White suggest that Taft could on occasion be a wily, Machiavellian politician. When Chief Justice Fuller died in 1910, President Taft had the personally self-torturing task of choosing someone to fill a post that he had always coveted. As he wrote Justice Moody, "It seems strange that the one place in government which I would have liked to fill myself I am forced to give to another."[23]

In March 1910 Justice David Brewer died, and it was at this point that Taft had turned to Charles Evans Hughes, a potential political rival—a strong presidential possibility—and in a sense a rival for the chief justiceship. In offering him the position of associate justice, Taft sent his now famous letter of calculated ambiguity. He wrote:

> The Chief Justiceship is soon likely to be vacant and I should never regard the practice of not promoting Associate Justices as one to be followed. Though, of course, this suggestion is only that by accepting the present position you do not bar yourself from the other, should it fall vacant in my term.

Then in a postscript Taft appeared to strengthen the offer of the chief justiceship with one hand and to withdraw it with the other:

> Don't misunderstand me as to the Chief Justiceship, I mean that if the office were now open I should offer it to you and it is probable that if it were to become vacant during my term, I should promote you to it; but of course conditions change, so that it would not be right for me to say by way of promise what I would do in the future. Nor, on the other hand, would I have you think that your declination now would prevent my offering you the higher place, should conditions remain as they are.[24]

Always the gracious gentlemen, Hughes in his letter of acceptance agreed that Taft should "properly reserve entire freedom" with respect to the future chief and that he did not wish Taft to "feel committed in the slightest degree."[25]

On July 4, 1910, just two months after Hughes had been confirmed as an associate, Chief Justice Fuller died, but Taft did not immediately promote Hughes. After a seven-month delay Taft finally turned to Edward Douglass White, a popular, capable member of the Court and the preferred choice of the sitting brethren. Although there were good visible reasons for appoint-

ing White including the compatibility of his views on constitutional issues with those of the president, Taft's willingness to
break with precedent and to choose the 66-year-old White in
preference to the 48-year-old Hughes had led to the conjecture
that Taft had cleverly played the odds and won.

As it turned out, events for Taft could not have unfolded more
perfectly. When White died in 1921 a Republican was in the
White House, and who was better qualified for the chief justiceship than a former federal judge and a former Republican
president? Yet by no means was Taft's appointment a foregone
conclusion. After Harding's election, Taft, still in his professo-
rial chair at the Yale law school where he had settled after his
defeat by Woodrow Wilson in 1912, met with the president-
elect in Marion, Ohio, and was informed that if he would accept
a position on the Court, Harding would put him there. Taft
pointed out, however, that since he had appointed three of the
present associate justices as well as three others, had himself
declined appointments twice, and had protested against the
Brandeis nomination, he could not accept any place but the
chief justiceship.[26] However, Taft's old appointee Edward Douglass White, had, figuratively speaking, posted a NO VACANCY
sign, in spite of the fact that he had once said he was holding the
job for Taft. In ailing health for some time White died on March
19, 1921, more than seven months after Harding had spoken
with Taft, but the president made no move to appoint Taft, in
part because Senator George Sutherland, Harding's campaign
adviser, also had court ambitions, and Harding had hoped for a
resignation or retirement from the Court which would then permit him to nominate Taft and Sutherland simultaneously.
Meanwhile Taft's friends, particularly Gus Karger, his old campaign manager, and Attorney General Harry M. Daugherty,
were pressing the president to name Taft. He finally did so on
June 30, and Senate confirmation came quickly with only four
dissenting votes by Progressives Hiram Johnson, William E.
Borah and Robert M. LaFollette and the radical populist Tom
Watson. Taft had finally made it "after more than thirty years of
dreaming, pining, skillful planning—and a dash of luck."[27]

On May 21, 1969, Warren Earl Burger at the age of 61 was
nominated by President Richard Nixon to be the nation's fifteenth chief justice. In announcing his choice, the president

said that he had known Judge Burger for 21 years and that he "would evaluate him as being qualified intellectually, qualified from the standpoint of judicial temperament, qualified from the standpoint of his legal philosophy and, above all, qualified because of his unquestioned integrity throughout his public and private life."[28] The new chief, who was to be quickly and easily confirmed by the Senate, expressed his gratitude to the president and said that he hoped his performance on the Court would "earn and deserve [Nixon's] gracious expressions of confidence."[29] Within five years the president's appointee would speak for a unanimous bench, upholding federal district court Judge John Sirica's subpoena directing Nixon to produce tape recordings and documents that contained possible evidence for use at the Watergate trial of six former aides to the president. It was not long afterwards that Richard Nixon resigned, the first president ever to do so, in order to avoid virtually certain impeachment proceedings. Ironically, he was absolutely correct when he had earlier emphasized Burger's "unquestioned integrity."

Warren Burger, one of seven children in a family that never had much money, was born in St. Paul, Minnesota, in 1909. Unlike Taft he had no paternal influence, no family name, no Yale degree to smooth his entrance into public life. He was, however, a self-starter with a driving energy that more often than not separates the successful from the rest of mankind. He, far more than Taft, tends to fit the "survival of the fittest" theories of Sumner and Spencer, although he has never made any public espousal of what are today considered heartless doctrines by enlightened conservatives and liberals alike. Burger obtained his academic credentials the hard way, working days and attending classes at night, eventually attaining his undergraduate degree from the University of Minnesota and his law degree from the St. Paul College of Law (now the Mitchell College of Law), the latter *magna cum laude.* Burger practiced law in St. Paul, taught courses at his alma mater, and eventually became a partner in the firm of Faricy, Burger, Moore and Costello where he handled a variety of criminal and civil litigation. He argued many cases before state and federal tribunals including some twenty before the Supreme Court and began to dabble in Republican politics.

At age 54 he was a successful attorney, comparable to earlier midwestern chiefs Waite and Fuller and, like them, little known outside his home state. He had been an early supporter of Harold Stassen, his fellow Minnesotan, for president, but Stassen's coattails were never long enough to bring any political favors to Burger. His life changed radically, however, after the Republican convention of 1952. He had backed Eisenhower in the Minnesota primary which Ike won and had helped him capture the Texas delegation, a crucial turning point in Ike's struggle with Ohio Republican Robert Taft for the presidential nomination. It was at this time that he came to know Herbert Brownell who as attorney general in Eisenhower's administration brought Burger into the justice department as one of his assistants. Three years later Brownell recommended him to President Eisenhower when a vacancy occurred on the Court of Appeals for the District of Columbia, a court second in power and prestige only to the Supreme Court itself. For a few Supreme Court justices of the past, service on a federal court of appeals has been a stepping-stone to the high bench, but if a blue ribbon panel of legal scholars, politicians, leaders of the bar and sitting judges in 1968 had been asked to name the most likely candidates to succeed Earl Warren, it is very doubtful that Warren Burger's name would have been among them.

Assuming his seat on the court of appeals in 1956 just three years after Earl Warren became chief justice, Burger worked in the shadow of the Supreme Court for thirteen years, and during that time both in his opinions from the bench and in his public speeches and writings he quite openly disagreed with the Warren Court's activism, particularly with its broad interpretation of the rights of suspects and defendants in criminal trials. On the surface at least he appeared to fit the "law and order" orientation that the Nixon administration espoused and by which it hoped to transform the Supreme Court. Once again but for a strange quirk of fate Richard Nixon would have had no chance to appoint a chief justice and although Warren Burger might have made it to the Supreme Court, it would have been as an associate.

Shortly after Chief Justice Warren wrote to President Lyndon Johnson in June of 1968 that he intended to retire as soon as a successor could be confirmed, the president nominated Associate Justice Abe Fortas to succeed Warren and at the same time chose an old Texas crony, William Homer Thornberry, a federal appellate judge, to fill the Fortas seat. Normally an astute politician, Lyndon Johnson in this instance failed to gauge the political climate accurately and lost both nominations. It was a presidential election year in which the Democratic incumbent was virtually without authority and prestige as a result of his unpopular policies on the Viet Nam War, and the Republicans, certain of capturing the presidency, were not about to give two seats on the Court to the Democrats. Although Fortas was a talented jurist by any standard, his support of Warren on key constitutional issues, his active advising of the president while on the Court, and the fact that he had accepted a fee of $15,000 to conduct a series of university seminars in 1968 furnished the opposition with adequate ammunition to block the appointment. Although the nomination managed to obtain a favorable report from the Judiciary Committee of the Senate, it ran into a buzz saw on the floor in the form of a strong filibuster that could not be terminated by an attempted closure vote. Fortas then asked the President to withdraw his name which he did without offering another nomination. That, of course, was the end of Thornberry as well, and Earl Warren continued as chief for another year, this time firmly announcing that he would retire at the close of the 1968–69 term.

During the presidential campaign Nixon had promised to name to the Court a man "who recognizes that it is the role of the court to interpret the law and to leave to Congress that of writing the law."[30] Like most presidents Nixon had not found his ideal appointment. Certainly the new chief was to view his and the Court's role somewhat differently than his predecessor; nevertheless, no radical changes in the Court's procedures or its orientation would be immediately evident, for as always eight associate justices were in place when the new chief arrived, and some of them would probably be there after he had gone.

Among those who knew Warren Burger the reaction to his appointment was mixed. Two of his associates on the Court of Appeals, J. Skelly Wright and David Bazelon, with whom he had often been in sharp disagreement, personally disliked him, and Wright, who was present at the presidential announcement, was "visibly shaken."[31] One law professor is reputed to have uttered the damning remark: "Warren Burger looks like a chief justice in about the same way that Warren Harding looked like a president."[32] Yet Dean Robert McKay of the New York University Law School, having known Burger as a colleague who taught a short summer seminar for appellate judges, said Burger would be much like Earl Warren, describing him as "a great, hearty, kind of big bear of a man with a jovial demeanor quite like Justice Warren. He was a tough prosecutor, but so was Earl Warren."[33] After three years as chief Burger was to be described by another professor of law, Arthur S. Miller of George Washington University, as closely resembling the man who chose him:

> Both in ideology and in methods of operation President Nixon and Burger are, if not twins, at least intellectual siblings. Each is hard driving, shrewd, tenacious, organized, in tight control of himself, far from intellectual and ruthless. And each is a believer in the old-fashioned virtues of work and piety, politically cunning, who will and, not infrequently, does bend when he perceives defeat to make the best of situations that had theretofore been intolerable. Admirers call that flexibility and a pragmatic approach to problem solving; others label it opportunistic, even unprincipled.[34]

Burger's official life was not to be made any easier nor his public image any brighter when the attorney general who backed him was sent to prison and the president who named him avoided a criminal prosecution only by a presidential pardon. The chief, totally removed from the Watergate scandal, had in fact written the opinion upholding the order to the president which brought forth incriminating evidence. Nevertheless the affair was an embarrassment to the public official who more than any other is perceived as morally responsible for maintaining the nation's constitutional order. After more than a dozen years in office Warren Burger was still seen as an enigma, even by close observers of the Supreme Court, but perhaps Everette E. Dennis of the University of Minnesota's school of journalism had it right when he wrote in 1980: "It is damnably difficult . . . to get a fix on this man because he continues to defy stereotypes that others have conjured up for him."[35]

MANAGING THE COURT

During William Howard Taft's chief justiceship from 1921 to 1930, twelve associates served on the Court, but three, Mahlon Pitney, William R. Day, and John H. Clarke, were to be gone

within a year, and another, Joseph McKenna, within four years.
Effectively, the Court that Taft led consisted of Willis Van Devanter, Oliver Wendell Holmes, Jr., Louis Brandeis, James
McReynolds, George Sutherland, Pierce Butler, Edward Sanford, and Harlan Fiske Stone, the latter to become chief himself
in 1941 upon the resignation of Hughes. Viewing the Taft Court
one is immediately struck by the fact that there are almost as
many stars as satellites, and none among the nine could be easily
manipulated by the most talented of chiefs. Of the group only
Van Devanter had been appointed by Taft when president, but
as chief Taft was not without influence upon Harding's choices
of Sutherland, Butler and Sanford, and Coolidge's appointment
of Stone.

Primarily though, Taft when chief was successful in discour-
aging appointments rather than in obtaining his first choices.
At the time of Butler's appointment, for example, he had favored
Wall Street lawyer John W. Davis, and his voice was strongly
felt in keeping appellate judges Benjamin Cardozo, Learned
Hand, and Cuthbert Pound off the Supreme Court.[36] Taft always spoke of staffing the federal courts and particularly the
Supreme Court, with men of "sound" views, meaning "constitutional conservatism of his own brand . . . the only safeguard
against 'radicals,' 'progressives,' 'bolshevists' and 'social-
ists.' "[37] Thus, he not only deplored the views of Holmes and
Brandeis, but was not overly happy with the extreme reactionary posture of McReynolds. With the latter, however, he could
at least count on his voting "correctly" on constitutional issues.

As head of the Court Taft was energetic, efficient, passionately
concerned with teamwork and clearly in charge, his vivacious
personality usually furnishing the lubrication for easy personal
relationships on a smooth-running, extremely hard-working
bench. Personal interactions had never been friendlier on the
Court than during Taft's tenure and the pleasant, compatible atmosphere had a salutary effect on the justices' work as compromises were made with little or no rancor. Even McReynolds, at
least after the resignation of John H. Clarke, was generally cooperative with everyone including Brandeis whom he personally
detested.

Taft's closest friends were Van Devanter, Butler and Sutherland but he had congenial relationships with all of the brethren

including Brandeis whose nomination he had opposed, and with Holmes whose ideas were often at a polar extremity from those of the chief. After serving several months under Taft, Holmes wrote to Pollock that he and his colleagues were "very happy with the present chief,"[38] and upon Taft's retirement in 1930 Holmes composed the farewell letter signed by the Court in which he wrote of the Chief's "humor" and "golden heart" that "smoothed over the rough places" and brought him "love from every side, and, most of all, from your brethren whose tasks you have made happy and light. . . ."[39] Yet as Taft's private correspondence indicates, harnessing his eight colleagues into a team, his ever constant goal, was never easy and at times he was close to despair.

There was, in fact, a considerable disharmony between the jovial, kind public face and the inner private thoughts of the very human Taft. Of McKenna he once wrote that he was an Irishman who "makes up his mind on impressionistic principle. . . . a Cubist on the bench, and Cubists are not safe on the bench."[40] Taft wrote bitterly at one point that "McReynolds and Brandeis belong to a class of people that have no loyalty to the court and sacrifice almost everything to the gratification of their own publicity and wish to stir up dissatisfaction with the decision of the Court, if they don't happen to agree with it."[41] And in an insulting tone, he once wrote of Holmes that he was "so completely under the control of Brother Brandeis that it gives Brandeis two votes instead of one" and that he had "more interest in, and gives more attention to, his dissents than he does to the opinions that he writes for the Court, which are very short, and not very helpful."[42] Yet Taft had the grace to admit his own shortcomings. As he wrote in 1926: "I am old enough to know that the best way to get along with people is to restrain your impatience and consider that, doubtless, you have your own peculiarities that try other people."[43]

Appearances were also deceiving in that Taft's easygoing nature did not manifest itself in sloppy administration. He was a master at organization and displayed a keen interest in every administrative detail of the chief's job including such matters as increasing the salary of the clerk, revising and strictly enforcing the Court's rules, cutting the cost of printing records and reducing the time from fifteen months to less than a year between the filing and the hearing of a case. He also used particular skills of the associate justices for administrative purposes by appointing committees. Brandeis, for example, headed the committee on accounts, Van Devanter the committee on rules.[44] The results of Taft's efforts were immediate as the Court disposed of more cases in his first year as chief than it ever had in a single term.

At the conference an unusual but nevertheless successful situation existed as Taft relied on his close friend and appointee, Willis Van Devanter, to carry the ball intellectually. It was a leadership coalition, "one of the strongest and most effective . . . in the Court's history."[45] At one time or another all the great minds on the Court with Taft—Holmes, Brandeis, Stone, Hughes, Sutherland and Butler—attested to Van Devanter's outstanding legal ability and to his incisive analytical mind. Always there was a deference and a respect for Van Devanter's views of a case even from those justices who radically disagreed with him. Ironically, though, it was sheer torture for Willis Van Devanter to put his thoughts on paper, and during his 26 years on the Court he wrote fewer opinions than any of his colleagues and has one of the worst records for output in the Court's history. Taft, on the other hand, while less talented than Van Devanter in verbal analysis, was a prolific writer. From 1921 to 1930 the Court handed down 1,596 opinions, of which Taft wrote 253 or one-sixth of the total.[46] During his tenure he averaged just under 32 opinions per term, more than any of his associates. Thus Taft's leadership of the Court seems to have been diminished not at all by his deference to Van Devanter at the conference. In part this was due to his administrative skills and his willingness to do more than his equitable share of the Court's work. Contributing heavily to the respect in which he was held was his common decency and that open, likeable, good-humored personality with which he was born.

In his opinion assignments Taft appeared to rely heavily on three factors: his estimate of the justice's ability, his concern for the justice's views, and his understanding of the justice's temperament and knowledge of his physical condition. Thus Van Devanter and to a lesser extent, Sanford, both of whom Taft called "opinion shy" were given lighter assignments than the others. When a justice was not in good health Taft would lighten his load, picking up the extra work himself. In cases involving

noteworthy constitutional issues, Taft's assignments were generally in tune with his assessment of the justice's views and talents, with Butler and Sutherland receiving the largest number—
Van Devanter would have been in this group had he been able to
write with greater alacrity—and McReynolds and Brandeis receiving the least, the former because he was lazy and not always
cooperative, the latter because of his liberal views.[47] It is certainly legitimate for a chief to influence the Court's constitutional posture through his opinion assignments, but he must do
so without alienating a colleague through what may be perceived
as unfair maneuvering. Undoubtedly Brandeis, and possibly
McReynolds, might have made an issue of Taft's discrimination
in assigning them very few significant cases, but they did not,
again because of Taft's warm, personal nature. Always it was
clear to the brethren that Taft's highest value was a harmonious
bench, that he would subordinate all else to this end, including
his own views if forced to make a choice.

Warren Burger, like Taft, is attuned to all the administrative
details of his office and, like Taft, he has been instrumental in
streamlining the Court's operations, very often with the efficient use of modern technology. Likewise similar to Taft, he is a
tireless worker and while he does not have Taft's natural warmth
or his innate affability, he does have a personal charm and a general demeanor that, combined with his energy, have made him
an effective chief justice.

In 1980 Barrett McGurn, the chief of the Supreme Court's
public information office told me this story. "When the Chief
Justice took office eleven years ago he asked his messenger for a
xerox copy of a paper. The messenger said 'yes sir,' not knowing
any other appropriate reply. The correct response would have
been: 'there is no duplicating machine at the Court. When draft
opinions are circulated the junior Justice receives the sometimes barely legible eighth carbon copy!' "[48] It was not long before photocopying machines were available and by the end of
the 1980–81 term the clerk's docket was computerized, furnishing an instant recall by computer screen of the status of the
4,000-plus current cases. Also made available on the computer
was the roster of 100,000 names of attorneys who have been admitted to practice before the Supreme Court. Perhaps most important the old hot-metal print shop which had produced the

opinions of the Court since the thirties was replaced by computer typesetting which is done directly from the nine chambers.[49] The clerk's office which had been scattered through the north and east sides of the ground floor was reorganized on work-flow principles, saving lost steps and allowing for neighboring workers to cover the phones of absentees. All such innovations are typical of the Burger administrative style which, like Taft's, is primarily concerned with efficiency although, also like Taft's, Burger's efforts extend to minutiae or what his critics call trivia. He was able to coax higher budgets out of Congress which were used both for additional help for the justices and for refurbishing the Supreme Court building. Each associate was able to hire an additional clerk and the chief reorganized his own office with a larger staff.

In 1969 when he took office the chief justice had three secretaries, three clerks, and a messenger. In addition to four law clerks he now has an administrative assistant with his own staff to oversee what has now become a minor bureaucracy of over 300 people. Burger has also provided the Court with its first personnel officer who advises him as he sits in judgment on hirings, promotions, raises and firings. Perhaps the tighter bureaucratic management was inevitable, but as a law clerk in an earlier day of a smaller, less rigid organization put it, working at the Supreme Court is "no longer fun."[50] Burger's efforts did not end with personnel changes. He spent $8,000 to remodel the bench, which formerly seated all nine justices in a straight line, into a three-sided arrangement in which all of the justices can see and hear each other as well as the attorneys appearing before them.

In addition to authorizing the expansion of the justices' chambers and the sprucing up of the dining room, Burger had expensive plastic plants installed around the building and ordered the fountain pools painted blue. He created the office of curator who has charge of the artifacts spawned during the Court's history and who supervises revolving exhibits in the building. One of the justices is reported to have said: "The Chief is acting more like a frustrated interior decorator than a Chief Justice."[51] But unquestionably Warren Burger has not only improved the Court's efficiency but has made its home a more attractive place for the 600,000 tourists who visit the headquarters of the judicial branch of the government annually. Another little publicized but significant innovation is the change in the procedure for admitting lawyers to practice before the Supreme Court bar. Formerly, new admittees had to travel to the Court building—even from distant Guam—but now admissions are handled by mail, thus reducing lawyer expenses and saving the Court precious time.

The chief's penchant for efficiency has spilled over to both the conference and the delivering of opinions. In addition to the Friday conference the justices meet on Wednesdays at 3:00 P.M. after the last pleading is completed. The cases heard on Monday are discussed, and the Friday conference is reserved for the Tuesday and Wednesday cases and for drafting orders, mostly *certiorari* denials. Also in the interest of efficient use of time, Burger emphasized the need to read excerpts rather than to deliver opinions fully as written, a procedure used since the 1930s and one that shortens each presentation by fifteen minutes or more.

Although not without inevitable changes, the Court's personnel has been relatively stable during most of Burger's tenure. When he took his seat in 1969, still on the Court were two Roosevelt appointees, Hugo Black and William O. Douglas, three Eisenhower choices, Potter Stewart, John M. Harlan and William Brennan, the single Kennedy appointment, Byron White, Lyndon Johnson's Thurgood Marshall, and another Nixon appointee, Harry Blackmun. The latter had replaced Abe Fortas after *Life* magazine published a story revealing that he had accepted—and later returned—a fee of $20,000 from the Wolfson Foundation. Fortas was to receive $20,000 annually as an advisor to the Foundation prior to his canceling the agreement after Louis Wolfson was sent to prison for stock manipulations. Although Fortas maintained that he was innocent of any wrong doing, and in a literal sense he was, even so much as a hint of personal corruption is damaging to the Court, and the perceptive Fortas simply stepped down rather than place the Court's reputation in jeopardy.

By 1971 Black and Harlan, both in very poor health, had resigned and were replaced by Lewis Powell and William Rehnquist. In deteriorating health for some months after suffering a stroke Douglas resigned in 1975 and was replaced by President Gerald Ford's only appointee, John Paul Stevens. The first woman and newest member of the Court, Sandra Day O'Connor, was appointed by President Ronald Reagan in 1981 when Potter Stewart decided that he would prefer to spend his remaining years in retirement. Thus, sitting with Burger virtually from the beginning were Brennan, Stewart, White, Marshall, Blackmun, Powell and Rehnquist with Stevens having served for ten of Burger's fifteen years as of the end of the 1984–85 term.

Internal leadership of the Supreme Court by the chief justice depends not only on his personal characteristics and his intellectual powers but, like all else in life, upon fortuitous circumstances. If the chief is to lead the Court along a path of ideological unity, the associates, at least four of them, must share his views, or less likely and less plausible, simply accept his leadership out of a lack of conviction of their own. Viewing Burger's voting record for thirteen terms beginning with his first in 1969, it is notable that with the exception of the 1969 and 1981 terms he voted with the majority over 80 percent of the time, and in eight terms, close to 90 percent.[52] This, of course, means that Burger controlled the opinion assignments in all but a very few cases each term. Although the record indicates that Burger spent large amounts of time on tasks other than opinion writing, he consistently wrote as many opinions as any of the associates and occasionally wrote the largest number for the term. Raw numbers indicate that no justice could complain that the chief either did less than his share of the work or that the workload was distributed unevenly.

As important as an equitable division of labor may be, however, it tells us very little about the substance of a chief's leadership. For example, in any given year, one-half to two-thirds of the cases decided by full opinion are routine—Justice Harlan called them "pee-wees"—and how the chief assigns the remaining noteworthy (those receiving attention in law reviews) or the truly landmark cases is of greater significance in assessing his fairness. Have all of the justices had a chance to write the Court's opinion in cases that might be of lasting significance? The answer is a qualified yes. A detailed analysis of opinion assignments during Burger's first seven terms in which the author casts his generalizations in the framework of liberal-conservative voting patterns—the liberal or conservative designations denoting the justice's view of civil rights claims—suggests that

although a voting bloc theme pervades Burger's opinion assignments, all the associates (with the possible exception of Marshall) were asked to write a fair share of the Court's opinions in
significant cases.[53]

While all chief justices have been on the receiving end of
some adverse criticism either from the press, from legal scholars, or from vituperative know-nothings, Warren Burger had to
suffer through an ordeal greater than any faced by a previous sitting chief justice excepting Taney following his *Dred Scott*
opinion. In 1979 two of the modern breed of investigative reporters, Bob Woodward and Scott Armstrong, published *The
Brethren* in which they purported to give the American people
an intimate view of how the Supreme Court functioned under
the leadership—or lack of it—of Warren Burger during his first
seven years in office.[54] While claiming that the information in
the book was "based on interviews with more than two hundred
people, including several justices, more than 170 former law
clerks, and several dozen former employees of the Court"[55]
whose confidence was protected in order to obtain their cooperation, documentation was elusive and obscure, and attributed
to all of the Court's members were quotations which the reader
was asked to take on faith. What the authors portrayed was a
Court of eight contentious, horse-trading, squabbling politicians who had little or no interest in arriving at a just result for
the litigants. The justices appeared to be concerned primarily
with writing their personal views of public policy into the law
and were led in this endeavor by an ignorant, arrogant, abrasive,
intellectually dishonest "product of Richard Nixon's tasteless
White House."[56] Some of the justices were quoted as referring
to the chief in contemptuous terms, Stewart reputedly calling
him a "show captain"[57] and Brennan calling him "dummy"[58]
and "that bastard."[59] Throughout the book there is more of the
same, including unflattering references by the justices to each
other, the use of obscene gestures and the kind of language that
one does not expect of the nation's most important, if not always most esteemed, jurists.

Although reviews of *The Brethren* were mixed, the preponderant reaction to the book was negative, the most frequently
voiced criticisms being that it was based on gossip and hearsay,[60]
was full of "cheap shots, slanted assessment and innuendo,"[61]

and painted a picture of the Supreme Court as "populated by a gaggle of talented clerks—plus nine meddlesome interlopers."[62] The book did not, of course, tell us anything new about how the Supreme Court conducts its business, and although the authors seem to have intended to shock the American people by intimating that the Burger Court is somehow different from those of the past, that it is more rancorous and politically motivated than previous Courts, historians and constitutional lawyers know better. There always has been and must be a full and open exchange of ideas among the justices as they attempt to arrive at a consensus that must finally be distilled into coherent language, conform to constitutional and legal norms, and not alienate too many segments of the Court's constituency. It should have come as no surprise that these nine normal human beings are at times arrogant, petty, profane, intractable, and concerned about their own reputations as judges.

The key question, however, is: Did this "exposé" based on a betrayal of confidence on a massive scale in any way alter or impair the Court's ability to function and the chief's ability to lead? There is no evidence that the Court acted any differently after the 1979 term than it had before the advent of this unflattering public portrait. Any small group working in close proximity on a daily basis on issues of exceptional moment will inevitably engender friction. Individual habits will become irritating, sometimes reaching a flashpoint at which unkind remarks will be made, and only a person of extreme insensitivity would not be aware of what his colleagues think of him. Thus, the justices could not have been shocked to read of the intemperate remarks made in moments of frayed tempers, nor did they suddenly realize that trusted friends were really mortal enemies. If nothing else, the book makes a solid case for keeping the conference secret.

Perhaps the most serious criticism leveled at Burger by some of his colleagues, according to Woodward and Armstrong, was that he lacked conviction in that he frequently executed all sorts of maneuvers in order to retain the opinion assignment power. The authors charged that he would withhold, reserve or switch his vote with the purpose of ending up in the majority, seemingly having little interest in the outcome of, or any consistent position on, the issues.[63] There is nothing wrong or unusual in a chief justice changing his vote or in attempting to give the Court an appearance of greater unity. At one time or another, most chiefs, including the greats like Marshall, Hughes and Warren, have changed their votes and have voted with the majority with whom they disagreed. Taft, of course, was noted for his attempts to keep dissent at a minimum.

As with others it is possible that Burger may, in the words of Professor Alschuler of the University of Colorado law school, "simply want to preserve credibility with his fellow justices and to be an architect of consensus on the Supreme Court. People who bend with the majority and who strive to 'work from within' usually think of themselves as realists and as team players. They are usually surprised that their hidden agendas are perceived, that their lack of 'straight shooting' is resented, and that they frequently incur the enmity of all factions."[64] And yet, figures indicate that Burger from 1969 through 1972 was dissenting as much as anyone on the Court and more than most as he averaged just over 13 dissents per term.[65] A decade later in the 1981 term he cast a dissenting vote in 37 cases out of 141 handed down by full opinion. His dissenting posture does not differ greatly from his predecessor, Earl Warren, a fact that tends to refute charges that he has no intellectual integrity and lacks conviction. On the other hand a chief who is frequently in dissent is not a leader on the substantive issues and is not able to build a coalition to support his views on some of the crucial problems of the day.

EXTRA-COURT ACTIVITIES

By utilizing the prestige of the office to promote judicial reform both Chief Justices Taft and Burger provoked critics into comparing them to the English lord chancellor and accusing them of desiring to make the chief justiceship a "political" rather than a judicial office.[66] Although the chief justice and the lord chancellor head their nation's respective judiciaries, constitutionally the powers of the offices are very different. The lord chancellor is both a political and a judicial officer and among his prerogatives are the authority to determine the number of judges that are needed and the power to appoint or be consulted in the appointment of all judges, high and low, in the British system.[67]

Chief Justice

It is inconceivable that the Congress or the president would ever relinquish their respective powers to fix the size of the federal judiciary and to appoint the judges, by supporting the requisite constitutional amendment, and even to suggest, as did Taft, that eighteen new judges be appointed as district judges at large to be assigned where needed by the chief, raised a storm of protest.[68] Several other recommendations of Taft, however, did become law. The first, the Act of September 14, 1922, was enacted after a concerted effort by the chief justice, including speeches before regional and national bar associations (American and Canadian) and testimony before the House and Senate judiciary committees. While not agreeing to Taft's request for judges at large, Congress did approve twenty-four additional district judges.

The law also provided that the chief might, with the approval of the senior circuit judge in each area, shift judges temporarily from underworked to overworked districts, and it embodied Taft's suggestion that judicial statistics be kept and reported annually. Perhaps the most important feature of the Act, however, was the creation of the Conference of Senior Circuit Judges, consisting of the chief and the (then) nine senior circuit judges, which would meet annually to discuss the problems and needs of the federal judiciary and recommend measures to Congress. Taft called the first meeting on December 27, 1922, and from that time on this new adjunct to the chief became extremely influential in setting judicial policy. It was also to increase the power dimensions of the office of chief justice.

Next Taft turned his attention to the logjam of cases before the Court. In spite of Taft's continuing pressure on his colleagues to dispose of more cases, the brethren could not decongest the docket. As a result of regulatory legislation enacted under Progressive leadership, the federal courts were inundated with litigation. Laws such as those dealing with safety appliances, food and drugs, meat inspection, narcotics, white slavery, packers and stockyards, automobile theft and grain futures inevitably spawned legal controversies. Also adding to the load were lawsuits involving legislation passed in pursuance of two constitutional amendments, the first authorized an income tax, and the second, the prohibition amendment, outlawed the manufacture and sale of alcoholic beverages. Analyzing the problem in a

Leadership Through Political and Extra-Court Activities

speech delivered in February 1922, Taft called for congressional action that would reserve "to the discretion of the Supreme Court to say whether the issue . . . is of sufficient importance to justify a hearing of it in the Supreme Court."[69]

Taft was referring to what became the enlarged *certiorari* jurisdiction in which the Court would have discretion over roughly 90 percent of its caseload, and although he was successful eventually, the project took a great deal of his time and energy as he enlisted the support of the press, the American Bar Association, and friends in Congress. After publicly recommending the reform and writing to Senator Albert Cummins of Iowa, chairman of the Senate Judiciary Committee, that the Court was preparing a bill which they hoped to bring before the committee, Taft received a green light from Cummins, the result of which was Taft's appointment of a committee consisting of Associate Justices Day, Van Devanter and McReynolds—to be aided by Sutherland and Taft himself—to complete the proposal for congressional consideration.

After a three-year struggle, including intense lobbying by Taft in the halls of Congress, the "Judges' Bill" as it was called became law in February 1925. Now the only obligatory appeals to the Supreme Court came in those cases in which a lower court, state or federal, had declared a federal law or treaty unconstitutional or in which a state court had upheld a state law against a challenge of unconstitutionality. The Act of 1925 thus took its place with the Judiciary Act of 1789 and the Circuit Court of Appeals Act of 1891 as one of the three most important pieces of legislation in the Court's history. The docket was finally manageable.

Another vision of Taft's, however, the cutting of the cost of litigation by simplifying judicial procedure and expediting final judgment, was not to be realized in his lifetime. There were in existence about one hundred different systems of procedure in American courts in Taft's day, and the best of lawyers had to sift through a "miasma of writs, pleadings, forms of process, motions, and procedures in civil actions at law," compounded in difficulty by the historic separation of law and equity.[70] For years Taft had been urging a rewriting of the procedural rules, and as a consequence of his consistent pressuring including testimony before the Senate Judiciary Committee, in 1926 the committee reported out a procedure bill embodying Taft's views. This time, however, the opposition, including several members of the Court and particularly Senator Thomas Walsh of Montana who persuaded a number of his colleagues that the reform would concentrate too much power in the federal courts at the expense of the states, was able to consign the bill to oblivion. Four years after Taft's death Congress changed its mind and enacted into law the rules he had advocated.[71]

Unlike the often esoteric and arcane minutiae of legal procedure with which only the initiated have a familiarity, a more visible legacy of Taft's is that monument in granite and marble, the Supreme Court building. He was instrumental in convincing key members of Congress that the Court needed, as he put it, "breathing space," and once again his success depended upon vigorous lobbying with House and Senate appropriations committees as well as with the conference committee.[72] Even after President Coolidge had signed the measure Taft continued to work his way with congressional leaders, obtaining places for Justice Van Devanter and himself on the building commission, giving them a voice in the selection of Cass Gilbert as the architect. Taft did not live to see the magnificent edifice but at the laying of the cornerstone in October 1932 Chief Justice Hughes extended appropriate recognition, declaring that "we are indebted to the late Chief Justice William Howard Taft more than to anyone else. . . . this building is the result of his intelligent persistence."[73]

No chief justice prior to Taft had expended so much time and effort on activities not connected with the actual deciding of cases. He loved being a judge and making difficult choices in hard controversies, but he was also a politician, a mover and shaker, and he held tenaciously to the view that his office called for leadership across a broad spectrum of activities, and he did not hesitate to use his prestige, his influence and his powers to achieve a more efficient judicial system. Always Taft remembered that successful lobbying requires strong personal involvement, attending committee hearings and keeping in touch with sympathetic souls in high places who could wield influence over others. Moreover, Taft never forgot that all of his eight associates did not necessarily share his point of view, and he took great care not to alienate those justices who disagreed with him. Whether or not one agrees with Taft's conception of the role of chief justice, it is certain that the office was never quite the same after he left it. For those who followed, it would be impossible to assume a passive posture, to be simply chief justice of the Supreme Court. Yet the degree of energy expended on extra-case activity by the chiefs who followed Taft varied with the interests of the incumbent, and of the five—Hughes, Stone, Vinson, Warren, and Burger—only Burger will be remembered less for his leadership in fashioning the law and more for his zeal for judicial reform.

In response to a question from the Senate Judiciary Committee holding hearings on his nomination Burger, while conceding that his main duty would be to decide cases, suggested that the chief justice should use whatever tools were available to make the system work better. "I would," he concluded, "expect to devote every energy and every moment of the rest of my life to that end should I be confirmed."[74] There is no question that after sixteen years in office Warren Burger has consistently lived up to that commitment. He has used the prestige and power of his office to pressure all components of the judicial-legal-political community to initiate institutional reforms in areas ranging from legal education to court management to judicial procedures to prison administration. Burger's style has been less the lobbyist with Congress or with the executive branch and more the catalyst and speech-giver at opportune times and places.

Particularly significant have been his annual addresses to the American Bar Association beginning in 1969 in which he has, in the manner of a presidential state of the union message, outlined his proposals with the goal of enlisting the support of the most prestigious organization of lawyers in the nation. But also used as a forum for propounding his ideas have been such disparate groups as the American Law Institutes, the National Conference of Christians and Jews, the Seminar on Legal History, the American Society of Newspaper Editors, along with university law schools and various conferences dealing with legal reform. Very effective in disseminating his suggestions were several exclusive interviews granted to the editors of *U.S. News and World Report* beginning in 1970. In a sense, however, it may be that in supporting so many causes, all of them good, he has had fewer successes than if he had concentrated on those matters more directly affecting the Supreme Court's work.

Chief Justice

In his initial speech to the American Bar Association in August 1969 Burger made three proposals, all of which were sympathetically received and given the association's backing for serious study and consequent action. First, Burger emphasized the need for introducing modern methods of administration into the courts and proposed the creation of an institute to train court manager-executives. Within six months the Institute for Court Management was in operation at the University of Denver, and the first class of 31 people graduated in December of 1970. By mid-1980 some 350 people had gone through the institute and were serving as court executives in the federal circuit courts[75] and in courts in all states except Mississippi. In 1980 Burger announced to the bar association that he was asking Congress to expand the program to the 15 largest metropolitan district courts,[76] indicating his pleasure with the success of his project.

In his second proposal Burger urged the ABA to reexamine the penal system at all levels of government in response to which the association created a commission composed of laymen, judges, law professors, and penologists to see what might be done. In Burger's view the terrible shortcoming in the system, particularly at the state level, was the "lack of any meaningful educational system for inmates, many of whom can't even read or write, and then the lack of vocational training and the lack of what we vaguely call 'rehabilitation' in terms of psychological testing and counseling to get them ready to make a living on an honest basis."[77] It would be the objective of the committee, according to Burger, "to persuade the States and Congress to do what is necessary: the rebuilding of plants; hiring of training personnel, psychologists, teachers; putting in the personnel and equipment for training people to do a great variety of useful things when the inmate is released."[78]

Prison reform is not a high priority in federal or state budgets, and the chief justice, while continuing to press for changes over the years, declared in 1980: "I would like to be able to report great progress in the administration of our criminal justice system. In all candor I cannot do so."[79] Following an earlier suggestion Congress created a National Institute of Corrections to train prison and correctional personnel and the ABA Commission on Correctional Facilities and Services developed a program aimed at modifying laws that foreclose areas of employment to persons with criminal records. The commission also advocated a system of accreditation for penal institutions similar to that used for hospitals and universities and has proposed the establishment of grievance procedures for prisoner complaints, and community programs that would direct youthful first offenders away from the criminal process entirely.[80] Changes are being wrought slowly but the Chief's active support has at least provided the incentive for some forward momentum in an area that most of us wish would just go away.

In his third major proposal Burger contended that the law schools were not doing an adequate job in training lawyers for "the realities of litigation," that while not deficient in their knowledge of law, up to half of today's practicing attorneys are not qualified to render competent representation to a client. He suggested that before a lawyer engage in practice he should be given specialized training in trial advocacy.[81] Once again the ABA responded by creating a Task Force on Trial Advocacy and by joining with the American College of Trial Lawyers and the Association of Trial Lawyers in America to sponsor a National Institute for Trial Advocacy.[82] The result has been a greater emphasis on training for trial work in the law schools which is expected to raise the quality of representation for litigants all over the country.

Like Taft a half century earlier, Burger has been concerned with the growing caseload, and in 1971 he appointed a committee chaired by Paul Freund of the Harvard Law School to study the problem and suggest some remedies. On December 19, 1972, the Freund committee submitted a report with four recommendations,[83] a majority of which Congress has enacted into law.[84] Spawning the most controversy in the report was the proposal that a national court of appeals be created to screen *certiorari* petitions and jurisdictional statements for the Supreme Court. Reaction among the justices was divided as some, notably Brennan and Douglas, voiced opposition to this intermediate appellate court which would be sandwiched between the courts of appeals and the Supreme Court. Burger gave the scheme qualified approval, maintaining that if Congress did not cease to add burdens to the Supreme Court, then "it must create an additional appellate court."[85]

Chief Justice

Although Congress did not move on the new appellate court idea, by the end of 1983 it had enacted more than 40 laws aimed at improving the federal courts, a large percentage of which were the direct result of the promotional activities of the chief justice.[86] At Burger's urging Congress created 152 new federal judgeships in 1978. In order to cope with the ever-increasing load on the courts, Congress must add new judges periodically, but generally it simply reacts to pressure instead of facing the problem systematically. The chief justice has recommended that Congress authorize the Judicial Conference to determine the need for additional judges and establish new positions subject to congressional veto,[87] a very sensible idea surely, but as we have pointed out, his opinion in the *Chadha* case in 1983 would appear to repudiate the concept.

Another of the chief's pet ideas is the establishment of a permanent tri-partite body consisting of appointees from each of the three branches of the national government to report to the president and Congress on the problems and needs of the judiciary. Although there is as yet no permanent body, Congress created a commission (called the Hruska commission) chaired by Senator Roman Hruska of Nebraska and consisting of appointees by the chief justice along with those from the legislative and executive branches. Following the commission's recommendations Congress authorized any court of appeals having more than 15 judges to divide itself into separate administrative units,[88] and one of the circuits with the greatest work load, the Ninth, promptly divided itself into three parts for administrative purposes. In a second statute[89] Congress added a new circuit to the existing ten by dividing the Fifth containing 26 judges into two, the Fifth (Louisiana, Mississippi, Texas and the Canal Zone with 14 judges) and the Eleventh (Alabama, Florida and Georgia with 12 judges). While these measures have improved the system somewhat, the chief contends that the entire structure of all the circuits needs reexamination.

Warren Burger's efforts at improving the efficiency of American courts have encompassed the entire national court structure, not simply the federal judiciary, and again his initiatives have borne fruit. Over 30 states have created state-federal judicial councils consisting of judges from both jurisdictions who reduce friction and hostility between the state and federal courts

by conferring on mutual problems. They have cooperated in fixing the calendar, in the use of joint jury rolls, in the use of court-
houses, in coordinating diversity of jurisdiction cases and in
effecting cooperation among probation offices. In some cases
federal and state judges have sat simultaneously to hear pretrial
motions in multiple disaster cases.[90] Furnishing technical assistance to state courts and acting as an information and training
center is another brainchild of Burger's, the National Center for
State Courts, with headquarters in Williamsburg, Virginia. The
chief first proposed the establishment of such an institution in
1970, continued to reiterate his support for it in public speeches,
and finally dedicated its new building in 1978.

On October 25, 1978, Chief Justice Burger received the
Fordham-Stein award which is given annually to a member of
the legal community whose work in the law exemplifies outstanding contributions to the advancement of justice and brings
credit to the legal profession by emphasizing in the public mind
the positive contribution of lawyers to society and the American system of government. In accepting the award he appeared
to be defensive about his role as judicial reformer as he declared:

> If the judges, whose lives are devoted to these problems,
> are not qualified to advise on such matters, one may well
> ask, "who is?" This takes nothing away from the preroga-
> tives of Congress or the executive. . . .
> The problems of the Courts do not have high visibility.
> They reach the attention of other branches and the public
> only if they are pressed forward by someone—and often not
> even then. . . . Someone must make these problems of the
> courts known to the public and Congress, if intelligent
> choices are to be made. . . .
> This is very clearly one of the obligations of the office I
> occupy. . . . If a Chief Justice, as spokesman for the Judicial
> Conference, failed to participate in the process, he would
> be shirking his obligations.[91]

Inevitably Warren Burger has received mixed reviews for his
activities in behalf of judicial reforms. On the one hand he is
seen by his critics, including some members of the Court, as
spreading himself too thin with the result that intra-Court management and his own primary role as a judge are not as well executed as they might be in spite of his fourteen-hour working

days. However, as one lawyer sees it: "Those of us who have toiled long in the vineyards of judicial reform feel we could never have gotten many of our projects off the ground without Burger's help. I'm sure some Justices find this offensive. The Chief is so rushed by outside things that he takes short cuts in other things inside the Court. But you can't be activist without arousing opposition."[92]

Probably his strongest support has come from the American Bar Association which he early enlisted in his crusade. In 1974 ABA President Chesterfield Smith wrote glowingly that "Burger has been the single-most effective, innovative, and significant figure in this country in the area of judicial improvement in recent times. . . . The practicing bar as a whole has welcomed this magnificent leadership by the Chief Justice. . . ."[93] Yet, as the legal profession well knows there are limits to the time and energy a chief can devote to projects, worthy as they are, outside the primary realm of guiding the Supreme Court in its role of deciding cases without impairing his own and the Court's effectiveness.[94] It is the chief, however, who makes the choices on how he spends his time, and as I have suggested earlier, it seems doubtful that the judicial function or the final outcome in individual cases of the present court would be any different were Warren Burger to curtail or even to eliminate his advocacy role. He apparently feels comfortable with his division of labor and its results or he would alter it. We can only conjecture on how history will judge his incumbency.

PHILOSOPHY AND LEGACY

In reading the judicial opinions of Taft and Burger, we see a strong congruence in their views of the Constitution, of the Bill of Rights and of the American system generally. The times, of course—the decade of the 1920s for Taft and the 1970s and 1980s for Burger—were very different, with litigants before the Court raising dissimilar questions, but if we cut through the issues to the legal and constitutional concepts, we note a reasonably close similarity of view.

During Taft's tenure the Supreme Court delivered just short of 1,600 opinions of which Taft wrote 253. Although he wrote several opinions that dealt with some crucial constitutional issues, he tended to assign himself the technical, legal cases, particularly those involving patents and trademarks. As a judge, he seemed to enjoy wrestling with the intricacies of the law as much as dealing with broad questions of policy, but in all areas Taft's propensity was to stick with precedent. Thus in his writing on constitutional questions, there is, with a few exceptions, little innovation or creativity.

Taft's most liberal opinions, in the sense of upholding national regulatory powers, were in the area of interstate commerce where his ideas were compatible with John Marshall's as well as with late twentieth-century judicial thinking. Giving the commerce clause an expansive quality was his notable opinion in *Stafford* v. *Wallace*[95] in which he emphatically approved an act of Congress which sought to regulate the meat packing industry. In answer to the contention that meat packing was a local business and not subject to federal control, Taft spoke of the stockyards not as a place of final destination but as "a throat through which the current flows, and the transactions which occur therein are only incident to this current from the West to the East, and from one state to another." Fortunately the chief was not forced to choose between precedent and personal principle, for Holmes had written in *Swift and Co.* v. *United States*[96] in 1905 that the Sherman Act was applicable to meat packers, so now Taft was able to rely on the language in *Swift* and to emphasize the "stream of commerce" doctrine or "flow theory." Following a similar line of reasoning in *Board of Trade* v. *Olsen*[97] Taft wrote for the Court, sustaining an act of Congress forbidding trading in grain futures except under supervision of the secretary of agriculture. Although the regulation in both instances was of a local transaction, each was clearly a part of interstate movement, and Taft could accept with equanimity both the legislative judgment of the matter and previous judicial holdings.

Speaking for a unanimous Court in *Dayton–Goose Creek Railway Co.* v. *United States*[98] Taft again approved congressional regulation even to the extent of limiting corporate profits. Under the Transportation Act of 1920 the Interstate Commerce Commission was empowered to divert earnings of a railroad in excess of 6 percent to other roads whose earnings were less. In upholding the Commission's ruling against the

Dayton–Goose Railway Company of Texas, Taft distinguished between profits earned from investment in an ordinary business as opposed to the profits of one dedicated to public service. In the latter, he maintained, one cannot expect either high or speculative dividends but only a fair and reasonable return.

Taft also wrote for a unanimous Court in *Brooks* v. *United States*[99] in which he sustained the Motor Vehicle Theft Act of 1919. It was a legitimate regulation of commerce for Congress to make it a crime to drive a stolen automobile across state lines even though the theft occurred locally. Again the chief was able to rely on a line of cases beginning with *Champion* v. *Ames*[100] in 1903 in which the Court had given a green light to federal prohibition of articles or transactions from commerce which might have a harmful effect, not on the commerce, but on society at large. Illustrative of Taft's view of commerce in the face of a clash between state and national interests were his opinions in two cases in which the Interstate Commerce Commission overrode state laws that permitted lower than interstate passenger rates on local runs. Upholding the commission Taft maintained that national authority must prevail over intrastate rates on those railroads that are tied in to interstate commerce.[101]

In stark contrast to Taft's organic and progressive approach to commerce was his reactionary and activist opinion in *Bailey* v. *Drexel Furniture Co.*[102] in which he violated the old and respected canon of judicial restraint established by John Marshall that legislative motives may not be the basis for invalidating a law. In 1918 the Court had struck down Congress' attempt to prohibit child labor under the commerce power in a narrow 5 to 4 decision,[103] and now Congress through another route tried once again. This time the statute provided for a special tax of 10 percent to be levied upon the net profits of all firms that employed children. Taft wrote that the law was unconstitutional for two reasons: first, it was an attempt to regulate a matter reserved to the states; second, the tax on its face was a penalty rather than a revenue raising measure. As Taft saw it:

> The good sought in unconstitutional legislation is an insidious feature because it leads citizens and legislators of good purpose to promote it without thought of the serious breach it will make in the ark of our covenant, or the harm that will come from breaking down recognized standards.

... But in the act before us, the presumption of validity cannot prevail, because the proof of the contrary is found in the
very face of its provisions. ... To give such magic to the
word "tax" would be to break down all constitutional limitation of the powers of Congress and completely wipe out
the sovereignty of the states.[104]

In support of his opinion Taft relied upon *Hammer* v. *Dagen-
hart* in which the Court had invalidated the first child labor law
but this was rather farfetched since the reasoning in *Dagenhart*
had dealt with commerce and not taxation. Furthermore, a leading precedent was the case of *McCray* v. *United States*[105] in
which the Court had upheld a tax on oleomargarine colored to
look like butter that was forty times the levy on white oleomargarine and was clearly coercive, but in that case Chief Justice
White relied on the Marshall dictum that it was not the province of the courts to question the motive of the legislature. Taft
weakly distinguished between a tax which on its face was a revenue raising measure and the child labor tax which was a penalty
in order to make his point that Congress had transgressed constitutional limits and entered the domain of state authority. To
support his position he purported to rely on his hero John Marshall, by quoting a passage from *McCulloch* v. *Maryland* which
appeared to permit judicial probing of legislative motive, but as
Alpheus Mason points out, Taft quoted Marshall out of context,
neglecting to include his qualifying language disclaiming "all
pretensions to such a power."[106] It was not one of Taft's finer
moments.

On the matter of economic due process Taft seemed unable to
make up his mind as he vacillated between reliance on precedents that had moved the Court away from the old "liberty of
contract" rule of *Lochner*[107] (that a state might not regulate conditions of employment) and remaining with the line of cases in
which the Court had invalidated regulatory measures on the
ground that the subjects were not businesses "affected with a
public interest," the latter being more in tune with his innate
conservatism. In one of his rare dissents, for example, Taft
wrote a vehement criticism of Sutherland's opinion in *Adkins*
v. *Children's Hospital*.[108] Striking down a minimum wage law
for the District of Columbia in which a board was empowered
to fix minimum wages for women and children, Sutherland,

while admitting that freedom of a person to contract in matters of wages and hours was not absolute, maintained that freedom was the general rule and restraint the exception. Engaging in interesting judicial gymnastics Sutherland argued first, that the *Lochner* case in which the Court had invalidated New York's attempt to limit hours of labor in bake shops was controlling; second, that *Bunting* v. *Oregon*[109] and *Muller* v. *Oregon*,[110] both of which had upheld the state's limiting of hours, were inapposite since they dealt with hours not wages and, besides, *Muller* differed from *Lochner* in that the former involved only women. Thus Sutherland fashioned the curious rule: all regulation of wages is bad; regulation of hours for men is bad, but may be permissible for women since there is a connection between a woman's health and the number of hours she works. Barely conceding the last point, Sutherland suggested that the differences between men and women "have come now almost, if not quite, to the vanishing point."

Taft, of all people, condemned the majority for invalidating a law not on sound constitutional grounds but because it was "passed to carry out economic views which the Court believes to be unwise or unsound." The chief saw no valid distinction between fixing minimum wages or regulating maximum hours, and in any event the most recent precedent was *Bunting* which in Taft's view had *sub silentio* overruled *Lochner*.

In the same year Taft executed an abrupt about face when in *Wolff Packing Company* v. *Court of Industrial Relations*[111] he spoke for the Court which invalidated a Kansas law providing for compulsory arbitration of wage disputes. Calling the scheme a deprivation of property and liberty of contract, Taft relied for support on the very opinion in *Adkins* which he had so recently condemned. Another interesting aspect of the case was Taft's response to the state's assertion that it might determine what businesses were affected with a public interest and then regulate them. Taft suggested that businesses clothed with a public interest were of three types: those carried on under a public grant such as railroads and public utilities, exceptional occupations such as keepers of inns, cabs, and gristmills, and those that may have become so affected through special circumstances. Since Kansas was not dealing with the first two categories, the third was at issue. It was not enough for the legislature to make the judgment that a business is affected with a public interest, said Taft, since the "circumstances of its alleged change from the status of a private business and its freedom from regulation into one in which the public have come to have an interest are always the subject of judicial inquiry." Thus Taft reserved to the courts the final judgment on whether a business is to be included in the third category, and although he suggested a standard—"the indispensable nature of the service and the exorbitant charges and arbitrary control to which the public might be subjected without regulation"—its subjectivity precluded any legislative determination which the courts would be bound to accept. Within a dozen years the Court was to discard Taft's dictum when Justice Owen Roberts declared for a majority: "The phrase 'affected with a public interest' can, in the nature of things, mean no more than that an industry, for adequate reason, is subject to control for the public good."[112]

Taft's most lasting contributions to public law came in the area of presidential power, an area in which quite naturally a past president would consider himself peculiarly qualified to render judgment. In *Ex parte Grossman*[113] the chief had no difficulty carrying the entire Court with him, but in *Myers* v. *United States*[114] he provoked unalloyed opposition from the extremes of the judicial spectrum including Holmes, Brandeis and McReynolds. At issue in *Grossman* was the meaning of the language in the Constitution authorizing the president to grant pardons "for offenses against the United States." Ignoring a court injunction ordering him to stop selling liquor, Philip Grossman was fined and sentenced to a year in prison. Subsequently, President Coolidge commuted the penalty to the fine, but the district court judge recommitted Grossman to prison. In order to reach a decision on whether to grant Grossman a writ of *habeas corpus*, Taft had to answer the contention that offenses against the United States included only crimes triable by jury and did not extend to contempts of federal courts. He had no difficulty in concluding that offenses against the United States embraced any offense whatsoever, that the authorizing language was intended to distinguish offenses against the states and not to limit the executive prerogative. In a sweeping dictum, Taft declared: "The executive can reprieve or pardon all offenses after their commission, either before trial, during trial or

after trial, by individuals, or by classes, conditionally or absolutely, and this without modification or regulation by Congress."

In *Myers* the issue could not be disposed of so cleanly. Myers,
a first class postmaster in Portland, Oregon, had been fired by
President Wilson in violation of an act of Congress that required
senatorial consent to such removals from office. Unlike *Grossman* in which constitutional language needed judicial construction, there was no language to be interpreted. The Constitution
is absolutely silent on the president's removal power and constitutional silence, although it invites the judges to weave new
cloth, also requires extraordinary hard work. Taft spent more
time on the case—over a year—than he had on any other, believed it to be his most important opinion in its effect, and with
it ran into the bitterest opposition during his tenure. He was so
upset over the dissents that he wrote to his brother Horace
questioning McReynolds' and Brandeis' loyalty to the Court.[115]

Taft's opinion is a curious mixture of his personal view of the
need for a strong executive and a distortion of history. Relying
on debates in the first Congress, he concluded that the members
intended the president to have full authority to remove his appointees. He then argued that the framers intended to create a
strong executive and that the executive could not be strong unless he had full control over his subordinates. Without such
control he could not, in fact, carry out his constitutional duty of
executing the laws. In a sweeping declaration he attributed to
the president the power to remove any executive officer at any
level. Holmes, Brandeis and McReynolds wrote separate dissents, but each believed Taft's reading of history to be wrong
and that nowhere in the Constitution was there any removal
authority granted to the president, nor was there any limit on
the right of Congress to restrict the removal of inferior officers.
The debates in the first Congress dealt only with cabinet-level
appointees and, according to McReynolds' reading, the framers
had rejected every proposal to confer unlimited powers of removal. Nevertheless, *Myers* has never been overruled, although
it was clearly limited in its scope by the *Humphrey's* case in
1935.[116]

In the relatively few civil liberties cases heard by the Taft
court, the chief consistently expressed his concern for fairness
but was reluctant to handcuff the police or to strike out in any

new directions. Yet in several instances a majority, which included Taft's silent concurrence, began to create new rights which it found inherent in the substance of due process, a concept which had towering consequences for constitutional liberty in the latter half of the twentieth century. Most important was the case of *Gitlow* v. *New York*[117] in which the Court took the initial step which was to result in the incorporation of most of the Bill of Rights into the Fourteenth Amendment. It seems unlikely that Taft had any idea what a train of Court activism would be set in motion when Justice Sanford wrote in *Gitlow*, "For present purposes we may and do assume that freedom of speech and of the press—which are protected by the First Amendment from abridgment by Congress—are among the personal rights and 'liberties' protected by the due process clause of the Fourteenth Amendment from impairment by the States."

Within a decade and a half all of the First Amendment guarantees would be incorporated into the Fourteenth as protections against state abridgment, and by 1970 all of the major components of the Bill of Rights would become a part of due process of law. Also laying the groundwork for the concept that some rights are fundamental—again within the due process umbrella— were the opinions in *Meyer* v. *Nebraska*[118] and *Pierce* v. *Society of Sisters*.[119] In the former the Court invalidated a Nebraska statute which made it unlawful to teach German to pupils who had not finished the eighth grade. Here it was the reactionary McReynolds who, with Taft's blessing, wrote that the liberty guaranteed by the Fourteenth Amendment included the right of parents to educate their children, within reason, according to their own conscience. And in *Pierce*, again with McReynolds as spokesman and with the chief's concurrence, the Court struck down an Oregon statute that required children between the ages of eight and sixteen to attend public schools. Parents, ran the logic, had the right to raise children as they saw fit, but in addition the law destroyed property rights in private schools. Both *Meyers* and *Pierce* were cited as precedents by Justice Blackmun in 1973 in the controversial decision which "created" the constitutional right to abortion embraced by those magic words, due process of law.[120]

Two enduring precedents, one written by Taft, the other receiving his concurrence, support strong protections for persons accused of a crime. In *Tumey* v. *Ohio*,[121] Taft spoke for the

Court in declaring unconstitutional an Ohio law that permitted magistrates in lower courts to share in fines paid by violators of the prohibition laws. Any judge, said Taft, who profited financially from a conviction might not be impartial. In *Moore* v. *Dempsey*,[122] a mob-dominated trial was held to violate due process and equally important, the Court asserted that a federal court might determine independently the facts of a state criminal trial.

The chief justice, however, was not about to permit criminals to go free on technicalities nor let the federal system stand in the way of punishment by either or both jurisdictions. When Vito Lanza and his cohorts had been indicted and convicted by the state of Washington and then indicted by the federal government, in both cases for violating prohibition laws, Taft wrote that no double jeopardy existed since there are "two sovereignties, deriving power from different sources, capable of dealing with the same subject matter within the same territory. . . . an act denounced as a crime by both national and state sovereignties is an offense against the peace and dignity of both, and may be punished by each."[123] This has never been overruled. Nor has *Carroll* v. *United States*[124] in which Taft formulated the rule that the Fourth Amendment does not bar the search of a moving automobile without a warrant so long as the police have probable cause to believe that the vehicle contains contraband or that the occupants are engaged in illegal activity.

Lasting for some forty years but finally discarded in 1967 was the famous *Olmstead* case[125] in which Taft, able to muster only a bare majority of five, declared that wiretapping was not a search within the meaning of the Fourth Amendment. As he characterized the procedure used to obtain evidence from a wire tap: "There was no searching, there was no seizure." Although this decision was handed down in 1928, fourteen years after the enunciation of the *Weeks* rule which stated that evidence seized in disregard of Fourth Amendment standards was to be inadmissible in court,[126] Taft happily alluded to the common law rule that "the admissibility of evidence is not affected by the illegality of the means by which it was obtained." Of course, since Taft had maintained that this was not a Fourth Amendment issue, there was technically no inconsistency with *Weeks*.

Leadership Through Political and Extra-Court Activities

By the time that Warren Burger became chief justice, Taft's worst fears about the evils of popular rule had been realized. As he lay dying in March 1930, the Roosevelt revolution was already in the making and within a few short years would be in full swing. Those conservative brethren with whom he had been allied—Van Devanter, McReynolds and Butler—would, with help from Hughes and Roberts, be able to stop the expansion of federal power and its encroachment on private property only briefly, and within a decade the Court itself would be staffed with men of the New Deal. Then, as the new jurisprudence gave approval to a broad construction of congressional powers, particularly over commerce, the Court's agenda began to change as the bulk of its work involved civil liberties litigation rather than economic questions. Ironically, one of the reasons for the shift was the increased number of appeals brought under the Fourteenth Amendment after the Supreme Court had made the due process clause a repository for the guarantee of the Bill of Rights, a movement begun by the Taft Court.

It will be recalled that Burger was appointed by President Nixon as a counterweight to the Warren policies of expanding judicial power, and in some cases the chief has undeniably assumed the expected posture. In others, however, like Earl Warren, Burger has either written or approved judicial amending of the Constitution by attributing to the fundamental law various rights that are nowhere in evidence and can be derived only by tortuous rationalization. Foremost in this respect are the abortion decisions[127] in which Burger apparently agreed with Blackmun's assertion that the right of privacy was founded in the "Fourteenth Amendment's concept of personal liberty" and was "broad enough to encompass a woman's decision whether or not to terminate her pregnancy." In his concurrence he attempted to soften his support for the majority opinion with this qualification: "Plainly, the Court today rejects any claim that the Constitution requires abortion on demand." The fact is, however, that like all constitutional guarantees, the right to an abortion as articulated in the decision is not a positive requirement but a negative restraint on government intervention. Any woman in the first trimester of pregnancy, if she can find a physician to perform it and can pay for it, may have an abortion. Thus, "on demand" is qualified very slightly if at all since most physicians will perform the surgery and will even do it without a fee in some instances as a contribution to charity.

In 1983, a decade after the initial abortion decision, Burger again joined the majority in striking down several provisions of an Akron, Ohio, city ordinance which the majority believed inhibited a woman's right to an abortion.[128] By elevating the right of a woman to terminate her pregnancy to constitutional status, the Court foreclosed the compromises that can be made legislatively and thus polarized the pro-choice and anti-abortion people into armed camps. Ironically, it would have been relatively simple to leave the entire issue up to the discretion of electorally responsible bodies. Some chiefs might have been able to persuade the Court to do just that rather than trigger another "self-inflicted wound."

Certainly of lasting significance was the politically painful opinion written by Burger in *United States* v. *Nixon*[129] in which he ruled against the president who appointed him, but nevertheless gave broad constitutional sanction to the principle of executive privilege, a principle that he admitted was nowhere stated in the Constitution. Balancing the "President's need for complete candor and objectivity from advisers against a defendant's right to the production of all evidence at a criminal trial" Burger concluded that the latter outweighed the former. He ordered Nixon to produce tape recordings of conversations made in the president's office for viewing by Judge John J. Sirica, the presiding district court judge over a trial of some of the president's former aides and associates. In his opinion, however, Burger took great pains to give the broadest possible scope to what he called "this presumptive privilege." "Absent a claim of need to protect military, diplomatic, or sensitive national security secrets," he wrote, "we find it difficult to accept the argument that even the very important interest in confidentiality of Presidential communications is significantly diminished by production of such material for in camera inspection with all the protections that a district court will be obliged to provide." This statement appears to authorize the president to withhold any information from a court if he decides it is in the interest of national security. Even John Marshall in his opinion at the trial of Aaron Burr, while recognizing executive privilege, did not go this far. Marshall maintained that the courts should make a final judgment on whether to respect the president's wishes to keep material secret, that the president should be given the benefit of the doubt but that he was not above the law. Given his view of executive power, one suspects that Chief Justice Taft, in spite of his reverence for John Marshall, would have written an opinion similar to Burger's.

When Burger first became chief, he tended to write for the Court in the tough, controversial cases arising out of the Bill of Rights and the equal protection and due process clauses of the Fourteenth Amendment,[130] but in his later years, excepting the First Amendment issues of religious freedom and obscenity, he was more likely to assign the hard cases to others, or on occasion to dissent from a liberal majority. During Earl Warren's final year as chief a unanimous Court in an opinion reflecting exasperation and frustration over the failure of the "all deliberate speed" formula to produce racially integrated schools, dealt with freedom of choice plans in which no white child chose to attend predominantly black schools. Justice Brennan declared that states formerly operating dual school systems had the "affirmative duty to take whatever steps might be necessary to convert to a unitary system in which racial discrimination would be eliminated root and branch" and that school boards must "fashion steps which promise realistically to convert promptly to a system without a 'white' school and a 'Negro' school, but just schools."[131]

Foot dragging continued, however, in spite of that forceful, incontrovertible order, and the Court in 1969, now under Burger's leadership, faced another petition seeking to terminate a dual school system. Continuing a unanimous response in a *per curiam* opinion, the Court said that the time of procrastination was over and that "every school district is to terminate dual school systems at once and to operate now and hereafter only unitary schools."[132] Despite the judicial rhetoric, racial imbalance in the schools continued, and the chief in 1971, again the spokesman for a unanimous Court, put his imprimatur on the desegregation controversy.[133] Dealing with what he called "four problem areas" the chief justice declared that a district court in fashioning remedies (1) might make limited use of racial quotas; (2) should make every effort to eliminate one-race schools including the transfer of those in a majority racial group of a particular school to other schools; (3) might pair and group noncontiguous zones; and (4) might order children transported by bus to schools outside their neighborhoods. When the North Carolina legislature prohibited busing and the assignment of students to schools for the purpose of achieving racial balance, Burger again for a unanimous Court declared the law unconstitutional, observing that "if a state-imposed limitation on a school authority's discretion operates to inhibit or obstruct the operation of a unitary school system or impede the disestablishing of a dual school system, it must fall. . . ."[134]

As the segregation controversy moved to northern cities where segregation had never been statutorily mandated, Burger no longer exclusively spoke for the Court. Nor were the justices unanimous as they became embroiled in disagreement over remedial measures, particularly busing in school systems that had never intended to segregate but were nevertheless racially segregated as a result of housing patterns. It was perhaps inevitable that the question of coercing racial mixing rather than simply requiring racial neutrality would require the Court's attention and, like some of his associates, the chief seemed ambivalent about the role of the judiciary. What we can say is that Burger and his Court have been more liberal on the issue than the public at large.

On other equal protection questions the chief has generally not written for the Court. When minority groups pressed the claim that disparities in public school financing between rich and poor districts violated equal protection, he joined the opinion of Justice Powell rejecting the contention that education is a fundamental right. Women's rights and claims of gender discrimination along with the rights of aliens and illegitimate children have had a positive response by the Burger court but for the most part the opinions have not been the chief's. He did write the opinion in Reed v. Reed,[135] the first case in which the Court held sex discrimination violative of equal protection, the statute in this instance preferring males to females when two persons were otherwise equally entitled to be the administrator of an estate, but he did not suggest as did Justice Brennan in a later decision[136] that classifications based upon sex were inherently suspect. He relied instead on the traditional equal protection test that a classification must be reasonable and rest upon a ground of difference having a fair and substantial relation to the object of the law.

It was in the area of criminal procedure that many observers believed Warren Burger might exert a special influence, that he would persuade the Court to reverse some of the decisions of the Warren era such as *Miranda* v. *Arizona*[137] which in the public mind contributed to the increase in crime because of its overzealous concern for protecting the rights of suspects by guaranteeing them the right to a lawyer and the right to remain silent at the police interrogation level. After twenty years, however, *Miranda* though slightly bruised is still healthy, and Burger, while dissenting in some cases involving the *Miranda* doctrine, has never said that it should be overruled. He spoke for a bare majority in *Harris* v. *New York*[138] in 1971 in deciding that a statement made to the police by an unwarned suspect, while not admissible as evidence, might be used to impeach his credibility at the trial should he elect to testify in his own behalf. Burger also joined the majority in several additional cases that narrowed the scope of *Miranda*[139] and registered a strong dissent in *Brewer* v. *Williams*[140] when the Court reversed the conviction of a man who had been adjudged guilty of raping and murdering a ten-year-old girl. In this instance the defendant, on the advice of counsel, had surrendered to the police in Davenport, Iowa, who were to transport him to Des Moines with the agreement that he would not be questioned enroute, but he acceded to an appeal by a detective to locate the body of the victim and subsequently made incriminating statements. It was Burger's contention that the defendant had waived his rights and that his disclosures were voluntary. Thus, Burger implicitly accepted the *Miranda* principles but interpreted them narrowly and in assessing disputed facts tended to support the police.

Certainly the most important issue relating to the punishment of criminals addressed by the Burger Court was that of the death penalty. In *Furman* v. *Georgia*,[141] the first in a line of cases, the Court in a brief *per curiam* opinion declared that the death penalty under the current arbitrary and randomly administered system constituted "cruel and unusual punishment" in violation of the Eighth and Fourteenth Amendments. This was not, however, a neat judicial guide for the forty states that had death penalty statutes; nor was it instructive for the lower federal and state courts. Nine separate opinions were written, including four dissents, covering 230 pages in the official reports. The decision put on hold the execution of some 600 persons waiting on "death rows" throughout the country and was a nightmare of conflicting views. In dissent the chief contended that the death penalty was not "cruel and unusual" in the constitutional sense and that the "decisive grievance" of the majority opinions was "that the present system of discretionary sentencing in capital cases has failed to produce evenhanded justice . . . that the selection process has followed no rational pattern." Such a claim, he continued, "is not only lacking in empirical support, but it manifestly fails to establish that the death penalty is 'cruel and unusual' punishment." Then, chastising his colleagues for their inability to reach a coherent position, Burger observed that the future of capital punishment was "left in uncertain limbo" as a result of the Court's inability to provide "a final and unambiguous answer on the basic constitutional question."

In the decade following the *Furman* case the Court continued to speak with many voices, usually rendering plurality decisions, as it faced revised death penalty statutes, although a majority finally agreed that the death penalty is not cruel and unusual punishment under all circumstances,[142] and that a mandatory death penalty is unconstitutional[143] as is the death penalty for rape.[144] Burger dissented in the latter case, arguing that the Court was substituting its views on the wisdom and desirability of the death penalty in rape cases in place of interpreting the Eighth Amendment and was not showing sufficient respect for the diversity and flexibility of the federal system. This respect for state experimentation and diversity was not evident in the chief's support for the abortion decisions, but on that issue at least, the states have reliable guidance and clear standards.

Burger has been an outspoken critic of the "exclusionary rule" promulgated by the Court in 1914[145] when it held that illegally seized evidence in search and seizure cases is inadmissible in federal court, a rule extended to state courts in 1961.[146] His first official attack on the doctrine came in 1971[147] when he dissented in a damage suit against federal narcotics agents in which a majority held that a person was entitled to recover money damages for any injuries suffered as a result of a federal agent's violation of the Fourth Amendment. After writing a long critique of the rule which he maintained did not do what it was supposed to do, namely, to act as a deterrent to unlawful police conduct, Burger contended that the Court "should be faulted for clinging to an unworkable and irrational concept of law . . .," that the Court "should be prepared to discontinue what the experience of over half a century has shown neither deters errant officers nor affords a remedy to the totally innocent victims of official misconduct." He then suggested that Congress should statutorily provide a new remedy which would permit lawsuits against overzealous law enforcement officials and simultaneously prohibit the exclusion of evidence obtained in violation of the Fourth Amendment.

Although not permitting the use of illegally seized evidence, Congress responded by amending the Federal Tort Claims Act of 1946 to cover assault, battery, false imprisonment, false arrest, abuse of powers and malicious prosecution by officials empowered to make searches, seizures and arrests, and Burger was able to convince a majority of the brethren to curb the scope of the rule. For example, the Court has held that the Fourth Amendment does not preclude the use of illegally seized evidence by a grand jury,[148] or bar its use in civil cases.[149] It also held that where a state has provided for full and fair litigation of a Fourth Amendment claim, a state prisoner may not obtain federal *habeas corpus* relief on the ground that evidence obtained from an illegal search was introduced at his trial.[150]

Constitutional areas where Warren Burger has written with conviction and has frequently brought a majority with him are the creation of a new obscenity standard, church-state relations, and matters of religious conscience. In two cases handed down on the same day[151] Burger was able to muster a majority of five to reexamine the old obscenity standard formulated by Justice Brennan[152] and to promulgate a new rule that would permit state and local officials greater flexibility in coping with what Justice Harlan had called "the intractable obscenity problem." Initially in 1957 a majority of the Warren Court had concurred in Brennan's formulation of a tripartite constitutional test: "whether to the average person, applying contemporary community standards, the dominant theme of the whole appeals to prurient interest," but in the decade and a half that followed, the Court floundered and vacillated, producing mainly plurality opinions in case after case as the nation witnessed a veritable flood of sexually explicit books, magazines and movies that local officials attempted to curtail through prosecutions under what they alleged were overt anti-obscenity statutes.

In Burger's opinions two alterations were made in the standard. First, to merit First Amendment protection "prurient, patently offensive depiction or description of sexual conduct must have serious literary, artistic, political, or scientific value" and second, the "community standards" which had been interpreted to be national now became local. In the chief's words, "our nation is simply too big and too diverse for this Court to reasonably expect that such standards could be articulated for all 50 States in a single formulation, even assuming the prerequisite consensus exists." Justice Brennan, supported by Marshall, Stewart and Douglas, sounded the alarm of repression. While admitting that the states' interests in protecting community morality were not trivial, they could not "justify the substantial damage to constitutional rights and to this Nation's judicial machinery that inevitably results from state efforts to bar the distribution even of unprotected material to consenting adults." Burger's answer was traditional and sensible as he maintained that "to equate the free and robust exchange of ideas and political debate with commercial exploitation of obscene materials demeans the grand conception of the First Amendment and its high purposes in the historic struggle for freedom."

At bottom the argument between the conservative chief and the liberal Brennan was over the right of the popularly governed local community to have some say in setting public moral standards, as Burger contended that the First Amendment does not inhibit majority rule in this respect simply because something is being communicated on paper or through films to consenting adults. Both Brennan and Burger agreed that the First Amendment is not absolute and that obscenity is not protected speech but in their disagreement over where and how the line should be drawn, there was a deep philosophical cleavage over both the meaning of the Constitution and the kind of society it is supposed to foster.

In cases involving the religion clauses of the First Amendment, Burger has written the majority opinions with some fre-

quency, but has not been able, for the most part, to take all of the
brethren with him. In 1970 not long after he joined the Court
Burger expressed this view of church-state relationships: "The
general principle deducible from the First Amendment and all
that has been said by the Court is this: that we will not tolerate
either governmentally established religion or governmental interference with religion. Short of those expressly proscribed
governmental acts there is room for play in the joints productive of a benevolent neutrality which will permit religious exercise to exist without sponsorship and without interference."[153]
He went on to uphold a property tax exemption for churches as
"only a minimal and remote involvement between church and
state and far less than taxation of churches." In a lone dissent
the venerable Douglas disagreed, contending that a "tax exemption is a subsidy" for religion.

   In a group of cases in 1971 the chief spoke only for a plurality
as he attempted to formulate principles covering state aid to religious schools.[154] Held unconstitutional were statutes providing financial support to church-related primary and secondary
schools, including payment of teachers' salaries, textbooks and
instructional materials, but upheld was an act of Congress
which granted funds to colleges and universities, whether or
not religiously affiliated, for the construction of buildings and
facilities used solely for secular educational purposes. In cases
such as these the chief said that four questions must be considered: Does the law have a secular legislative purpose? Is the primary effect of the law to advance or inhibit religion? Does the
administration of the law foster an excessive government en-
tanglement with religion? Does the implementation of the law
inhibit the free exercise of religion?

   The problem with tests of this nature is the inability to apply
them objectively, for any two justices viewing identical circumstances may, and often do, come to diametrically opposed conclusions. In case after case in the 1970s and 1980s in which the
establishment clause was at issue, the Court was always split,
but the chief was in dissent in only three of eight cases and in
each of them he would have upheld the government.[155] In the
remaining five he voted against the government in two, object-
ing in one instance to the National Labor Relations Board's cer-
tifying unions for teachers in church-operated schools, and in
the other, to a state university's denial of its facilities to student

religious groups which were open to all other student organizations.

In four significant cases in which the free exercise of religion was the issue Burger was the Court's spokesman, but in none was there unanimity, and in one Burger wrote only for a plurality. Coming ten years apart were two controversies involving members of the Amish faith. At issue in the first, *Wisconsin* v. *Yoder*,[156] in 1972 was the refusal of members of the Amish church to conform to a Wisconsin law that required school attendance of all children up to the age of sixteen. In order to preserve the Amish way of life the religious orders would not permit their children to attend school after the eighth grade, asserting that the statute violated their First and Fourteenth Amendment rights. Taking the position that enforcement of the state's "requirement of compulsory formal education after the eighth grade would gravely endanger if not destroy the free exercise of respondent's religious belief," Burger, in effect, gave the Amish an exemption from state laws.

Ten years later, however, when an Amish employer failed on religious grounds to withhold social security taxes from employees' wages or to contribute the employer's share to the social security system, the chief justice retreated from his earlier position.[157] Justifying the distinction for practical reasons, he observed that unlike the situation in *Yoder*, "it would be difficult to accommodate the comprehensive social security system with myriad exceptions flowing from a wide variety of religious beliefs." Yet, the chief seems to have opened the door to precisely what he condemns when he delivered the Court's opinion approving the right of a Jehovah's Witness to receive unemployment benefits, who, as a matter of religious conscience, quit his job with a company that was engaged in the manufacture of turrets for military tanks.[158] There were precedents leading to that result but Justice Rehnquist in dissent bluntly charged that the decision "adds much to the already muddied waters of First Amendment jurisprudence" and accused Burger of interpreting the Free Exercise clause in total disregard of his construction of the Establishment clause, and of exacerbating the "tension" between the two. If a state were to legislate in conformity with this decision—granting unemployment compensation to persons who quit their jobs for religious reasons—the statute would be in contravention of the chief's own language in those cases alleging a violation of the principle of separation of church and state since, charged Rehnquist, it would serve a religious and not a secular purpose and would "advance" religion by facilitating the exercise of a religious belief. Here, of course, is a clear example of the subjectivity of the standard, as Burger apparently saw no incompatibility in his opinions in the two cases. He willingly let them stand publicly beside Rehnquist's sharply critical rejoinder.

William Howard Taft and Warren Earl Burger were not creative jurists in spite of the fact that they wrote scores of opinions, a selective number of which we have analyzed. Neither is a luminous figure in American constitutional law in that had either been an associate justice rather than chief his opinions would not have accorded him a reputation as one of the "great" judges to sit on the Supreme Court. Yet neither is a failure as a judge by any standard. Each wrote with conviction in behalf of human liberty and each, despite his views that American legal and constitutional procedures are overly protective of accused criminals, wrote to overturn convictions when they saw clear examples of unfairness. Taft was able to transcend his personal biases in behalf of unfettered private enterprise and to uphold federal regulations only by broadening his own horizons on interstate commerce. Burger has been able to soften his midwestern, traditional values enough to support women's rights, abortion and affirmative action, all of which were antipathetic to his values of self-reliance, family integrity and traditional roles for men and women. Both he and Taft were aware that as judges they had to make some accommodation with their times and with their colleagues, thus sacrificing principle to expediency.

Both have been accused of being inconsistent in their judicial pronouncements, which they were, and both have been criticized for not producing a coherent jurisprudence—Burger more than Taft in this regard—of not giving the lower federal and state courts reliable guidance, which is true. There is a certain unfairness in judging chief justices as judges since always they must be concerned not only with what they say but with what the Court says as a collective entity. In order to create a united front, to control the opinion assignments or even to make a personal accommodation, a chief's view of the law may often be somewhat different than the opinion he writes or of the one in which he joins, thus leaving him open to the charge of inconsistency, hypocrisy and incoherence. There can be no doubt, however, that while Taft and Burger may not have been brilliant jurists, they were competent judges.

Differing in personality and style, Taft led and Burger leads the Supreme Court internally under conditions largely of their own making. The external face of the Court under Taft was one of a hardworking group of cohesive comrades who settled their differences amicably and were led by a jovial, cheerful chief whose headship was respected and accepted. Internally we know that this was not always the case, that Taft was at times bitterly critical of some of his colleagues when he wrote or spoke to friends and relatives, particularly of Holmes and Brandeis, and that the successful conferences were as much due to the intellectual leadership of Van Devanter as to Taft.

Publicly the Burger court has not displayed any open ruptures, but if credence can be given to the reporters of the Washington scene or even to the authors of *The Brethren*, the calm within the Court is superficial since some personal animosities toward the chief reside just below the surface. This view tends to be supported by the unusually large number of plurality opinions in which the chief cannot muster five votes in support of a clear majority opinion and by the sharp, almost insulting remarks found all too frequently in the dissenters' opinions themselves. Nevertheless, the Burger Court has worked as hard as any Court ever, has grappled with some of the toughest issues ever, and has resolved them, if not to everyone's satisfaction, at least without inciting a major constitutional crisis.

For Taft and Burger, however, the greatest successes came in their extra-court activities, in their broad roles as chief justices of the United States where they consistently worked for improvements in the entire judicial establishment, including greater efficiency in the procedures of the Supreme Court. No doubt some of the decisions of both the Taft and Burger courts will remain as landmarks in American constitutional law and a few of the opinions which they wrote will also be a part of the significant gloss on the Constitution. However, William Howard Taft and Warren Earl Burger will more likely have lasting

213

Leadership Through Political and Extra-Court Activities

reputations as judicial reformers, as catalysts for systematic improvements of all procedures and institutions connected with courts and judges. They were extremely able chiefs but do not quite fit into that special mold called greatness.

NOTES

1. Alpheus Thomas Mason, *William Howard Taft: Chief Justice*, New York: Simon and Schuster (1964), p. 87.
2. Henry F. Pringle, *The Life and Times of William Howard Taft*, 2 vols., New York: Farrar and Rinehart (1939), Vol. 1, p. 1.
3. Ibid., p. 318.
4. Ibid., pp. 44–45.
5. Ibid., p. 31.
6. Ibid., p. 34.
7. See particularly Sumner's *What Social Classes Owe to Each Other*, New York: Arno Press (1972), Reprint of 1883 ed.
8. Mason, op. cit., p. 15.
9. As quoted in Pringle, op. cit., pp. 57–58.
10. As quoted in Kenneth Bernard Umbreit, *Our Eleven Chief Justices*, 2nd ed., New York: Harper & Bros, 1938, Vol. 2, p. 414.
11. *United States* v. *Addyson Pipe and Steel Co.*, 85 Fed. 271 (C.C.A. 6th, 1898).
12. William H. Taft, "The Right of Private Property," 3 *Michigan Law Journal* 215 (Aug, 1894) p. 218.
13. Ibid., p. 220.
14. Ibid., p. 224.
15. Ibid., p. 226.
16. Ibid., p. 231.
17. Pringle, op. cit., p. 275.
18. Umbreit, op. cit., p. 427.
19. Ibid., p. 432.
20. Address to the graduating class of the Yale law school, June 26, 1905, in William Howard Taft, *Present Day Problems: A Collection of Addresses Delivered on Various Occasions*, Freeport, N.Y.: Books for Libraries Press, (1908), p. 343.
21. Address to the Civic Forum, New York City, April 28, 1908, as quoted in Mason, op. cit., p. 51.
22. Mason, ibid., p. 64.
23. Ibid., p. 34.
24. David J. Danelski and Joseph S. Tulchin, *The Autobiographical Notes of Charles Evans Hughes*, Cambridge: Harvard Univ. Press (1973), pp. 159–60.
25. Ibid., p. 160.
26. Mason, op. cit., p. 78.
27. Ibid., p. 87.
28. *New York Times*, May 22, 1969, p. 36.

29. Ibid.
30. Ibid.
31. Monrad G. Paulsen, "Some Insights Into the Burger Court," 27 *Oklahoma Law Review* 677 (1974), p. 678.
32. Quoted in Arthur S. Miller, "Lord Chancellor Warren Earl Burger," *Society*, March/April 1973, p. 18.
33. *New York Times*, op. cit., p. 36.
34. Miller, op. cit., p. 19.
35. Everette E. Dennis, "Overcoming Occupational Heredity at the Supreme Court," 66 *American Bar Association Journal* 4, (1980), p. 43.
36. Mason, op. cit., pp. 171–72.
37. Ibid., p. 164.
38. Mark DeWolfe Howe (ed.), *Holmes-Pollock Letters*, Cambridge: Harvard Univ. Press (1941), Vol. 2, p. 96.
39. Letter from the Court to Taft, Feb. 10, 1930, Taft Papers. Quoted in Mason, op. cit., p. 235.
40. Letter to Helen Taft Manning as quoted in Pringle, op. cit., Vol. 2, p. 969.
41. Letter to H. O. Taft, Oct. 27, 1926, ibid., p. 1025.
42. Letter to H. L. Stimson, May 13, 1928, ibid., pp. 969–70.
43. Letter to R. A. Taft, Jan. 10, 1926, as quoted in Mason, op. cit., p. 226.
44. Mason, ibid., pp. 192–97.
45. David J. Danelski, "The Chief Justice and the Supreme Court," doctoral dissertation, Univ. of Chicago, 1961, p. 77.
46. Mason, op. cit., p. 231.
47. Danelski, op. cit., pp. 82, 149–50.
48. Conversation subsequently confirmed in a letter from Barrett McGurn dated January 8, 1981.
49. Ibid.
50. Miller, op. cit., p. 23.
51. Nina Totenberg, "Supreme Court Seethes," *National Observer*, June 17, 1972, p. 3.
52. Statistics for the 1969–1975 terms are taken from Dennis Haines, "Rolling Back the Tax on Chief Justice Burger's Opinion Assignment Desk," 38 *University of Pittsburgh Law Review* 631 (1977), p. 677. For the 1976 through the 1981 terms the statistics were compiled by Carl Will, a law student at Boston College.
53. Haines, ibid., pp. 672–76.
54. Bob Woodward and Scott Armstrong, *The Brethren: Inside the Supreme Court*, New York: Simon and Shuster (1979).
55. Ibid., p. 3.
56. Ibid., p. 315.
57. Ibid.
58. Ibid., p. 359.
59. Ibid., p. 419.
60. See William Safire, "Our Brethren's Keepers," *New York Times*, Dec. 10, 1979, p. 7; C. Robert Zelnick, *Christian Science Monitor*, January 14, 1980; Anthony Lewis, "Supreme Court Confidential," *New York Review of Books*, Feb. 7, 1980, p. 31, "A Tale of Rancor on the Burger Court," *U.S.*

News and World Report, Dec. 17, 1979, p. 33; "Sharp Blows at the High Bench," *Time,* March 10, 1980, p. 48.

61. Martin Shapiro, "Character Assassination by Attribution," *Wall Street Journal,* December 12, 1979, p. 22.

62. Floyd Abrams, "Trivializing the Supreme Court," *Fortune,* March 10, 1980, p. 129.

63. Woodward and Armstrong, ibid., pp. 417–20.

64. Albert W. Alschuler, "Burger's Failure: Trying Too Much to Lead," *National Law Journal,* Feb. 18, 1980, p. 19.

65. Blaustein and Mersky, ibid., pp. 146, 149.

66. See for example the Congressional Record, Vol. 62, 67th Congress, pp. 4853–855; Miller, "Lord Chancellor Warren Earl Burger," *supra,* note 31.

67. See Robert J. Steamer, "Judicial Leadership: English and American Experience," in John Schmidhauser, ed., *Comparative Judicial Systems,* Santa Barbara, Calif.: Sage-IPSA Publications (1986).

68. Mason, *Taft,* op. cit., p. 100.

69. "Three Needed Steps of Progress" 8 *American Bar Association Journal,* 1922, p. 36.

70. Mason, *Taft,* op. cit., p. 114.

71. Act of June 19, 1934, 48 Stat., 1064. See Mason, ibid., p. 120.

72. See Mason, *Taft,* op. cit., pp. 133–37 for a detailed discussion of Taft's persistent lobbying.

73. "Corner Stone of New Home of Supreme Court of the United States Is Laid," 18 *American Bar Association Journal* 723 (Nov., 1932), p. 728.

74. *Nomination of Warren E. Burger: Hearing Before the Senate Committee on the Judiciary,* 91st Congress, 1st Session (1969), p. 5.

75. Authorized by Congress in the Circuit Court Executive Act of Jan. 5, 1971, 84 Stat. 1907.

76. Warren E. Burger, "Annual Report on the State of the Judiciary," *Mid-Year Meeting of the American Bar Association,* Chicago, Feb. 3, 1980. Congress appropriated funds for 5 district court executives in 1981.

77. "Interview with Chief Justice Warren E. Burger," *U.S. News and World Report,* Dec. 14, 1970, p. 33.

78. Ibid.

79. Warren E. Burger, "Annual Report on the State of the Judiciary," 1980, op. cit., p. 11.

80. Warren E. Burger, "We Refuse to Be Responsible for the People We Imprison," Address at 1972 *Annual Dinner, National Conference of Christians and Jews.*

81. Warren E. Burger, "The Special Skills of Advocacy," 42 *Fordham Law Review* 227 (1973), p. 234.

82. Edward A. Tamm and Paul C. Reardon, "Warren E. Burger and the Administration of Justice," 1981 *Brigham Young University Law Review* 447, p. 500.

83. The proposals were: (1) the elimination by statute of three-judge district courts and direct review of their decisions in the Supreme Court; the elimination of direct appeals in Interstate Commerce Commission and

antitrust cases; and the substitution of *certiorari* for appeal in all cases where appeal is now the prescribed procedure in the Supreme Court; (2) the establishment of a nonjudicial body to investigate and report on prisoners' complaints. Recourse to this tribunal would be available to prisoners filing petitions and to federal judges with whom petitions were filed; (3) Promote greater staff support to the justices, their law clerks, the Supreme Court library and the clerk's office; (4) Establish by statute a National Court of Appeals, to screen *certiorari* petitions and jurisdictional statements for the Supreme Court.

84. In 1975 Congress abolished direct appeals to the Supreme Court from three-judge district courts in ICC cases (88 Stat. 1917) and in 1976 three-judge courts were abolished in all cases except those challenging federal or state reapportionment and cases arising under the Civil Rights Act of 1965. Congress has also authorized increased staff for the justices, the library and the clerk's office.
85. Warren Burger as quoted in Tamm and Reardon, op. cit., pp. 510–11.
86. Tamm and Reardon, ibid., list 44 laws enacted between 1969 and 1981, pp. 481–82.
87. Warren E. Burger, "Annual Report on the State of the Judiciary," *Mid-Year Meeting of the American Bar Association*, Feb. 3, 1980, p. 7.
88. Omnibus Judgeship Act, 92 Stat. 1629 (1978).
89. The Fifth Circuit Reorganization Act of 1980, 94 Stat. 1994.
90. Tamm and Reardon, op. cit., p. 499.
91. Unpublished speech of Warren E. Burger, Oct. 25, 1978.
92. Totenberg, op. cit., p. 2.
93. Letter to *New York Times*, January 30, 1974, as quoted in Tamm and Reardon, op. cit., p. 518.
94. See Arthur R. Landever, "Chief Justice Burger and Extra Judicial Activism," 22 *Journal of Public Law* 524 (1971), for a balanced discussion of the problem and his endorsement of the chief's activities.
95. 258 U.S. 495 (1922).
96. 196 U.S. 375 (1905).
97. 262 U.S. 1 (1923).
98. 263 U.S. 456 (1924).
99. 267 U.S. 432 (1925).
100. 188 U.S. 321 (1903).
101. *Railroad Commission of Wisconsin* v. *Chicago, Burlington and Quincy R.R. Co.* 257 U.S. 563 (1922) and *New York* v. *United States*, 257 U.S. 591 (1922).
102. 259 U.S. 20 (1922).
103. *Hammer* v. *Dagenhart*, 247 U.S. 251 (1918).
104. *Bailey* v. *Drexel Furniture Co.*, op. cit., pp. 37–38.
105. 195 U.S. 27 (1904).
106. Mason, op. cit., p. 261.
107. *Lochner* v. *New York*, 198 U.S. 45 (1905).
108. 261 U.S. 525 (1923).
109. 243 U.S. 426 (1917).
110. 208 U.S. 412 (1908).
111. 262 U.S. 522 (1923).

112. *Nebbia* v. *New York*, 291 U.S. 502 (1934).

113. 267 U.S. 87 (1925).

114. 272 U.S. 52 (1926).

115. As quoted in Pringle, op. cit., p. 1025.

116. *Humphrey's Executor* v. *United States*, 295 U.S. 602 (1935).

117. 268 U.S. 652 (1925).

118. 262 U.S. 390 (1923).

119. 268 U.S. 510 (1925).

120. *Roe* v. *Wade*, 410 U.S. 113 (1973).

121. 273 U.S. 510 (1927).

122. 261 U.S. 86 (1923).

123. *United States* v. *Lanza*, 260 U.S. 377 (1922).

124. 267 U.S. 132 (1925).

125. 277 U.S. 438 (1928).

126. *Weeks* v. *United States*, 232 U.S. 383 (1914).

127. *Roe* v. *Wade*, 410 U.S. 113 (1973); *Doe* v. *Bolton*, 410 U.S. 179 (1973).

128. *City of Akron* v. *Akron Center for Reproductive Health*, 462 U.S. 416 (1983), the court held unconstitutional provisions that required: (1) physicians to tell women seeking abortions that "the unborn child is a human life from the moment of conception" and that abortion is "a major surgical procedure" that can produce "serious complications"; (2) all pregnant unmarried minors under 15 to obtain the consent of one parent or a court prior to an abortion; (3) all second-trimester abortions to be performed in a hospital but not in an outpatient clinic; all women to wait at least 24 hours after signing a consent form before obtaining an abortion; and (4) a fetus to be "disposed of in a humane and sanitary manner."

129. 418 U.S. 683 (1974).

130. In the 1969 term he spoke for a unanimous court in *Rowan* v. *United States Post Office*, 397 U.S. 728 (1970); *Price* v. *Georgia*, 398 U.S. 323 (1970); and *Alexander* v. *Holmes County Board*, 396 U.S. 19 (1969). In the 1970 term he wrote the opinions in *Organization for a Better Austin* v. *Keefe*, 402 U.S. 415 (1971); *Lemon* v. *Kurzman*, 403 U.S. 602 (1971); *Tilton* v. *Richardson*, 403 U.S. 672 (1971); *Harris* v. *New York*, 401 U.S. 222 (1971) and *Swann* v. *Charlotte-Mecklenburg*, 402 U.S. 1 (1971).

131. *Green* v. *County School Board*, 391 U.S. 430 (1968).

132. *Alexander* v. *Holmes County Board* of Education, 396 U.S. 19 (1969).

133. *Swann* v. *Charlotte-Mecklenburg Board of Education*, 402 U.S. 1 (1971).

134. *North Carolina State Board of Education* v. *Swann*, 402 U.S. 43 (1971).

135. 404 U.S. 71 (1971).

136. *Frontiero* v. *Richardson*, 411 U.S. 677 (1973).

137. 384 U.S. 436 (1966).

138. 401 U.S. 222 (1971).

139. *Oregon* v. *Hass*, 420 U.S. 714 (1975); *Michigan* v. *Mosley*, 423 U.S. 96 (1975); *Oregon* v. *Mathiason*, 429 U.S. 492 (1977).

140. 430 U.S. 387 (1977).

141. 408 U.S. 238 (1972).

142. *Gregg* v. *Georgia*, 428 U.S. 153 (1976).

143. *Woodson* v. *North Carolina*, 428 U.S. 280 (1976).

144. *Coker* v. *Georgia*, 433 U.S. 584 (1977).

145. *Weeks* v. *United States,* 232 U.S. 383 (1914).

146. *Mapp* v. *Ohio,* 367 U.S. 643 (1961).

147. *Bivens* v. *Six Unknown Agents of the Federal Bureau of Narcotics,* 403 U.S. 388 (1971).

148. *United States* v. *Calandra,* 414 U.S. 338 (1974).

149. *United States* v. *Janis,* 428 U.S. 433 (1976).

150. *Stone* v. *Powell,* 428 U.S. 465 (1976).

151. *Miller* v. *California,* 413 U.S. 15 (1973); *Paris Adult Theater I* v. *Slayton,* 413 U.S. 49 (1973).

152. *Roth* v. *United States,* 354 U.S. 476 (1957) and *A Book Named "John Cleland's Memoirs of a Woman of Pleasure"* v. *Attorney General of Massachusetts,* 383 U.S. 413 (1966).

153. *Walz* v. *Tax Commission,* 397 U.S. 664 (1970).

154. *Lemon* v. *Kurtzman, Early* v. *Di Censo, Robinson* v. *Di Censo,* 403 U.S. 602 (1971); *Tilton* v. *Richardson,* 403 U.S. 672 (1971).

155. Burger dissented in *Committee for Public Education and Religious Liberty* v. *Nyquist,* 413 U.S. 756 (1973); *Stone* v. *Graham,* 449 U.S. 39 (1980); *Larson* v. *Valente,* 456 U.S. 228 (1981). Burger was in the majority in *Meek* v. *Pittenger,* 421 U.S. 349 (1975); *Wolman* v. *Walter,* 433 U.S. 229 (1977); *Committee for Public Education and Religious Liberty* v. *Regan,* 444 U.S. 646 (1980); *National Labor Relations Board* v. *Catholic Bishops of Chicago,* 440 U.S. 490 (1979); *Widmar* v. *Vincent,* 454 U.S. 263 (1981).

156. 406 U.S. 205 (1972).

157. *United States* v. *Lee,* 455 U.S. 252 (1982).

158. *Thomas* v. *Indiana Employment Security Division,* 450 U.S. 707 (1981).

Chapter 5

LEADERSHIP MINIMIZED IN THE SHORT-TERM CHIEFS

IN THIS FINAL GROUPING of chief justices I have admittedly arbitrarily placed those chiefs who, compared to the others, served for relatively brief periods ranging from six months for John Rutledge to seven years for Salmon P. Chase. (Chase was actually Chief for eight years but after suffering a stroke, he did not sit during the 1870–71 term.) What they have in common is a collective record of adequate to moderately successful leadership, a fact which may be, although not necessarily is, related to their short terms of office. It is interesting that all but Vinson were chosen by the nation's strongest and greatest presidents, Washington, Lincoln, and Franklin Roosevelt; Truman who chose Vinson, while not in the same league as the "greats" was nevertheless among our strong presidents. Paradoxically, the chiefs whom I have suggested were the Court's greatest leaders—Marshall, Hughes and Warren—were appointed by some of our less successful presidents—John Adams, Herbert Hoover, and Dwight Eisenhower. For purposes of analysis the remaining six chief justices are divided into two groups: Jay, Rutledge, and Ellsworth who fit a similar pattern and Chase, Stone, and Vinson whose service years were either during or immediately following America's most critical and devastating wars and whose Courts dealt with special problems growing out of those wars.

Chief Justice

JOHN JAY, JOHN RUTLEDGE, AND OLIVER ELLSWORTH

For the twelve years prior to the appointment of John Marshall in 1801, the Supreme Court under the headship of John Jay, John Rutledge, and Oliver Ellsworth, while not rudderless, was not led with real conviction by any of the first three chiefs. It was a time in which the Supreme Court was searching for a role under the new Constitution which had defined its duties only in scant outline and those of the chief justice not at all, but none of the first three occupants was temperamentally able, as was Marshall a few years later, to initiate boldly a pattern for managing the Court's business and to assert that in interpreting the Constitution the Court was to be the final authority. As contributors to the building of the American nation Jay, Rutledge, and Ellsworth are remembered and respected not for their work on the Supreme Court but for their endeavors in other areas. Nevertheless, the Court under President Washington's chief justices was by no means a total failure as it established some important, lasting ground rules and made several significant pronouncements in constitutional law.

John Jay, born the eighth child of a family of ten in 1745, was educated at Columbia (then King's) College from which he graduated in 1764 as salutatorian of his class. Studying law while simultaneously clerking in a New York law office, Jay acquired a master's degree from King's in 1767 and was admitted to the bar in the colony of New York the following year. He was to practice law for less than six years as he allied himself with the revolutionary forces then gathering momentum, serving first with the Committee of 51, then in both the First and Second Continental Congresses, as president of the latter. Jay was congenitally conservative and initially believed in conciliation with England. In the words of one biographer, he was the "embodiment of the paradoxes by which the American Revolution is especially characterized: he was a prudent revolutionary,"[1] and he was described by another as having "none of the fire or passion that animated the thought and gesture of a Henry, an Adams, or a Hooper; but he had habits of reflection and solidity of judgment which, in the practical affairs of mankind, are admirable substitutes for more brilliant qualities."[2]

Like most of the patriots of the Revolutionary period Jay served both his new independent state of New York and the emerging nation. After the adoption of the Declaration of Independence, Jay was appointed to a committee to draft a constitution for New York and much of the final document was his handiwork. It has been suggested that his most original contribution to political science was the Council of Revision,[3] a provision in the New York constitution that empowered the chief judicial officers of the state to sit jointly with the governor and exercise a veto over acts of the legislature which the council deemed unconstitutional.

Later as New York's chief justice Jay was to serve on the council and to author several opinions. Possessing deep religious convictions growing out of a Huguenot background, he was suspicious of Roman Catholicism and would have excepted Catholics from the New York constitution's "free exercise of religion" clause, but his view was not acceptable to his colleagues. He was able to gain assent for the incorporation of clauses barring ministers and priests from holding civil or military posts, to require that all naturalized persons renounce allegiance to foreign princes and states in matters "ecclesiastical as well as civil," and to qualify liberty of conscience with the language that it "shall not be construed to encourage licentiousness, nor be used in such a manner as to disturb or endanger the nature of the state." Jay failed, however, to obtain the adoption of a clause requiring the abolition of slavery, a project which he later pursued for the state as governor and continued to support actively for the nation in retirement.

For just a few months short of five years beginning in 1779 Jay served the collective interests of the new states abroad, first as minister to Spain and then in Paris as one of the commissioners to negotiate a peace treaty with Britain. Except for the wine, and the cigars then unknown in America, both of which he continued to enjoy the rest of his life, he equally hated Spain and his mission to raise money at which he was only moderately successful. Thus, he was pleased to receive the assignment to Paris where an amiable agreement was reached with the British who were as eager as the Americans to end the war.

Returning to New York with the intention of entering private life, Jay found that Congress had elected him secretary of foreign affairs, a post which he held until the new government came into being in 1789 and in which he saw almost daily the inherent weaknesses in a confederation—a system with no

Chief Justice

strong, central authority and no power to work its will in foreign affairs. Unfortunately Jay was not a delegate to the Convention of 1787 because of his opposition to New York's Governor George Clinton, but his influence was clearly felt by his author- ship of five of the *Federalist* papers (he might have written more except for illness which interrupted his participation) and his election to the New York ratifying convention where 46 of the 57 delegates initially opposed the adoption of the Constitution. He continued at his post of secretary of foreign affairs through- out the Constitution-making and Constitution-adopting period, and in the words of one biographer: "He buried the old govern- ment and supervised the birth of the new."[4] A close friend and trusted confidant of George Washington, he probably could have had any post he wished in the new administration, so he must have been pleased to receive the president's letter on Oc- tober 5, 1789, beginning: "It is with singular pleasure that I ad- dress you as Chief Justice of the Supreme Court of the United States, for which office your Commission is enclosed."

The pleasure of being chief justice was, however, relatively short-lived, for he attended no session of the Supreme Court after 1793. George Washington persuaded him to accept an ap- pointment in 1794 as emissary to Great Britain to settle the unresolved differences between England and America, the ulti- mate result being the Jay Treaty, a not universally popular agree- ment although it may have been the best attainable between a weak new nation and a powerful colonial empire. Upon his re- turn from England in 1795 Jay found that his supporters in New York had secured his election as governor. While sitting on the Court in 1792 he had been persuaded to run for governor, stipu- lating that he would not campaign for the job, but he was defeated by the incumbent, George Clinton. Now he had the choice: re- main as chief justice or resign and take up the governorship. He chose the latter in part because of the debilitating job of circuit riding, in part because he was not convinced that the Supreme Court would ever become an important cog in the wheels of the national government. As he wrote to John Adams in 1800 after learning that the president had nominated him again for chief justice:

I left the bench perfectly convinced that under a system so defective, it would not obtain the energy, weight, and dignity which was essential to its affording due support to the National Government; nor acquire the public confidence and respect which, as the last resort of the justice of the nation, it should possess. Hence, I am induced to doubt both the propriety and the expediency of returning to the Bench under the present system. . . . Independent of other considerations, the state of my health removes every doubt. . . .[5]

Jay lived until 1829 and thus was able to witness the extraordinary developments in American constitutional law as well as the emergence of the judiciary as a prestigious, independent, and powerful third branch of government under John Marshall. Jay was the only chief to live a substantial number of years after retiring or resigning from office. Most died while serving; only three, Ellsworth, Hughes and Warren, lived a few years after retirement, seven, five and seven respectively. Living out his years on an 800-acre farm in Bedford in Westchester county, Jay was the New York counterpart of Thomas Jefferson as he experimented in agriculture and devoted much of his time to his major interests, the abolition of slavery and the advancement of religious faith.

It cannot be said in any sense that John Rutledge who presided over the Supreme Court for only one month ever gave it leadership of any consequence. Described as "one of the most shadowy of that rather statuesque group of patricians who fathered the world's greatest democracy,"[6] Rutledge has the dubious distinction of being the only chief justice—the only justice, in fact—to serve under a recess appointment who was not subsequently confirmed by the Senate. Although he had hoped to be the nation's first chief justice, Rutledge was instead appointed to the Court by President Washington as an associate justice, in which capacity he attended no meetings of the Court and wrote no opinions. In 1790 he sat with Justices Wilson and Blair on the federal circuit court in North Carolina, but again he wrote no opinions.

Born in 1739 in Charleston of a wealthy family, Rutledge was destined from birth to become one of the political leaders of the colony and state. He studied law with his uncle, Andrew Rutledge, who was speaker of the royal colonial assembly, and in England at Middle Temple. Admitted to the English bar in 1760, he returned to South Carolina in 1761 where he entered upon a legal and political career which saw him attain undisputed leadership in the councils of his colony and later his state as well as in national affairs as the movement for independence grew in spirit and intensity. Rutledge was a delegate to all the major unifying and nationalizing meetings from the Stamp Act Congress, to every Continental Congress, to the Convention of 1787. Throughout these turbulent years Rutledge vacillated between loyal Englishman and fervent South Carolinian and, finally, like many others, became a reluctant unionist. At the Convention he was a prominent participant and his ideas were a significant contribution to the shaping of the final document.

First and foremost Rutledge was an elitist, concerned with the protection of private property and with the preservation of upper-class interests, giving only grudging assent to any mass participation in the new government. Rutledge served on the committee that proposed one of the major compromises of the Convention, the legislative package including equal representation of the states in the Senate, representation by population in the House with three-fifths of the slaves counted for both representation and taxation and the requirement that all revenue raising measures originate in the lower house. He also proposed the supremacy clause which was incorporated into the final document (Article VI) without substantial change, and he served as chairman of the Committee on Detail which wrote the first draft of the Constitution. Although he consented to the clause that would permit Congress to end the slave trade in 1808, he made it clear that the Carolinas and Georgia would never join the union if the new government were to have any immediate power to interfere with slavery.

Certainly the convention's presiding officer did not fail to notice that Rutledge along with Madison, Hamilton, Wilson, Randolph, Paterson, and Ellsworth was one of the convention's leaders and as president, George Washington quite naturally wished to bring this talent into the new government. He considered Rutledge along with Jay and James Wilson for the role of chief justice, but after deciding upon Jay, appointed both Rutledge and Wilson as associates. During its first four terms—the Court then met for two six-week sessions each year—from February 1790 until August 1791 Rutledge never sat with the Court, but he did participate briefly in circuit riding, swearing in lawyers as members of the new federal bar and sitting on a single case in North Carolina.[7] Resigning in 1791 to accept the more prestigious position of chief justice of the South Carolina court of common pleas, he served competently until 1795 when he accepted Washington's offer of chief justice of the Supreme Court. Although Rutledge, upon learning of Jay's resignation in June had written Washington indicating that he was "available" for the vacancy, said in fact that his qualifications were somewhat better than Jay's, the president might well have turned to him without the entreaty. Since Congress was not in session when the August term of the Court opened, Rutledge began his service as a recess appointment awaiting confirmation by the Senate, confirmation which never came.

The Jay Treaty with Britain, signed on November 19, 1794, was far from perfect in that it permitted the British to deal as they wished with American ships including the humiliating impressment of American seamen and contained no provisions for compensating slave owners for blacks taken by the British when they evacuated the colonies. There was an outburst of public anger around the country, including a meeting in Charleston where John Rutledge, according to newspaper reports, denounced the treaty in damning language, "insinuating that Mr. Jay and the Senate were fools or knaves, duped by British sophistry or bribed by British gold . . . prostituting the dearest rights of free men and laying them at the feet of royalty."[8] Loyal Federalists were not happy with one of their own leaders criticising official policies with such invective and hyperbole, and opposition to Rutledge quickly began to build. It is possible that this one impetuous act might not, by itself, have been enough to condemn the appointment, but a second factor also militated against confirmation.

There had been suggestions in private correspondence that Rutledge had become mentally unstable, particularly after 1792, the year in which both his wife and mother died, and later events indicate that the imputations of recurrent periods of insanity were not simply malicious gossip. On December 15, 1795, the Senate failed to confirm Rutledge by a vote of 14 to 10, the first rejection of a major appointment of the first president. A week later, after hearing the news of the Senate's decision, Rutledge in what appeared to be a suicide attempt jumped off a wharf into Charleston Harbor but was saved by two slaves. He died five years later at the age of 61. The capable John Rutledge that Washington knew at the Convention of 1787 was not the same man he appointed in 1795, and those senators who voted against him, whatever their motives, had sound reasons for doing so. Had Rutledge been confirmed and served for five years, it is improbable that Marshall would have been his successor in 1801. Thus, in the view of Supreme Court historian Charles Warren, "upon the event of one chance speech regarding a British treaty hinged the future course of American constitutional law."[9] In the context of Rutledge's later years, however, the speech seemed less an isolated "chance" and more in keeping with his neurotic disposition.

Unlike the appointments of Jay and Rutledge, that of Ellsworth was not Washington's first choice. He turned first to Patrick Henry who declined and then without consulting him sent the name of the eldest sitting associate justice, William Cushing, to the Senate where it was confirmed without dissent. After a week's consideration Cushing decided to continue as an associate where he served until 1810, the last surviving appointee of President Washington's original Supreme Court. Technically he was chief justice for one week, but the only function he performed was to attend a dinner party given by the president at which he was accorded a seat appropriate to his position.[10]

Commissioned as chief justice on March 4, 1796, Oliver Ellsworth served until the fall of 1799 when John Adams persuaded him to head a mission to Paris to negotiate a modus vivendi with Napoleon which he did with only moderate success. Returning to the United States in poor health he resigned from the Court in November 1800 at the relatively young age of 55, having actually sat as chief for a brief three and one-half years.

Oliver Ellsworth was born on a farm in Windsor, Connecticut, on April 29, 1745, and his family, certainly not poor by the standards of the day, did not begin to approach the patrician status of Ellsworth's predecessors. Oliver's father wished him to become a minister of the gospel and sent him to Yale which he left after two years, the record being uncertain whether he quit voluntarily. Under parental pressure he then entered Princeton where he graduated in 1766, thereafter studied theology for a year but finally decided to pursue a career in law, being ad-

Leadership Minimized in the Short-Term Chiefs

mitted to the bar in 1771. Married in 1772 and barely eking out a living for the next three years, Ellsworth lived on a small farm leased to him by his father, cutting and selling wood and attempting to build a law practice at which initially he earned three pounds per annum Connecticut money. This was a hard transition period through which Ellsworth changed from a frivolous, easy-going, not especially serious student to a respectable and respected attorney. As he put it himself, "Sir, after I left college I took a deliberate survey of my understanding. I felt that it was weak—that I had no imagination and but little knowledge or culture. I then resolved on this course of study: to take up but a single subject at a time, and to cling to that with an attention so undivided that if a cannon were fired in my ears I should still cling to my subject. That, sir, is all my secret."[11]

After 1775 personal and financial success came rapidly to Ellsworth as he built a substantial practice of upwards of a thousand cases and moved into public service. He served in the Connecticut assembly, as state's attorney for Hartford County and during the war years represented his state in the Continental Congress. Although he served on a number of congressional committees, among the most interesting was his membership on the Committee of Appeals which was in effect the first national judiciary as it disposed of prizes captured by ships sailing under American authority. This along with his service on the supreme court of errors in Connecticut gave him an opportunity for judicial experience which may have been helpful in light of his future position as chief justice.

Undoubtedly of greatest significance to the developing American nation were Ellsworth's contributions at the Convention of 1787 and his leadership in the first Senate of the new government. At the Convention Ellsworth understood the concept of a federal system, a new theory of governmental organization that seemed implausible and unworkable to many of his fellow delegates. In one of his speeches he went to the heart of the problem, arguing that the "general government" must be built "on the strength and vigor of the state governments. . . . The only chance we have to support a general government is to graft it on the state governments." His insistence on retaining strong state governments within the new system won him the support of John Rutledge and other delegates from the slaveholding and nonslaveholding states alike as they supported the famous Connecticut Compromise of which he and Roger Sherman were the architects. A bicameral system in which representation would be based upon population in one house and equality of the states in the other along with the three-fifths role on slavery and noninterference with the slave trade by the new government for twenty years was the only way to obtain delegate concurrence for a federal union. Ellsworth never forgot that the delegates were there to establish a *government* and not to make social reforms, as desirable as such reforms might be. It is also noteworthy that Ellsworth went on record at the Connecticut ratifying convention as assuming that the federal judiciary would have the power to declare national laws unconstitutional. Had he been chief justice for a longer time, it is likely that he rather than John Marshall would have written the first opinion invalidating a federal law.

In the Senate Ellsworth became a tireless worker for Federalist policies as he supported Hamilton's financial plan and served on committees to organize an army, a post office, the taking of a census, and he chaired the committee that established the rules for the Senate. Ellsworth's lasting contribution to the new nation, however, was the Judiciary Act of 1789 which "had far more influence on the development of the Supreme Court than any judicial decision he every rendered."[12] His work as chairman of the committee responsible for drafting the measure was in a sense a continuation of constitution writing since unlike Articles I and II which clearly specified the qualifications for holding office in the Congress and the presidency and both enumerated and limited powers, Article III left to the discretion of Congress such crucial questions as the size of the Supreme Court, qualifications of federal judges and whether there should be any lower federal courts at all. Under Ellsworth's guidance the first judiciary act passed the Senate and House and was signed into law by President Washington on September 24, 1789.

According to James Madison, Ellsworth's original draft of the bill "was not materially changed in its passage into law."[13] Consisting of thirty-five sections it not only established a Supreme Court to be staffed by five associates and a chief justice, but created a complete judicial department consisting of thirteen districts covering the United States and three circuits (eastern, middle and southern), each with appropriate courts to handle federal litigation. The circuit courts were to be staffed by two Supreme Court justices and a district court judge and would hear appeals from the district courts. They would also have original jurisdiction in controversies between foreigners and citizens and between citizens of different states in cases involving more than two thousand dollars. Controversial for some time was the 25th section which essentially gave the Supreme Court the power to invalidate state laws as it provided for appeals to the Supreme Court in cases in which a state court had upheld a state law against a charge of unconstitutionality under the federal Constitution. When the Marshall Court began to invalidate state laws with some regularity, recurrent movements surfaced in Congress to repeal the 25th section, but to this day Ellsworth's language remains intact.

John Adams, like George Washington, perceived the chief justice as an officer to be used for special tasks at the discretion of the president, and in 1799 he sent Ellsworth to France to conclude a protocol with Napoleon which would ease the tensions between France and the United States. When Ellsworth sent the results of his negotiations to Adams in 1800 he included his resignation from the Supreme Court. He spent the remaining seven years of his life at Elmwood, his farm in Connecticut, where he died in 1807 at the age of 62.

LEGACY OF THE EARLY CHIEF JUSTICES

During the twelve years between the establishment of the Supreme Court in 1789 and the appointment of John Marshall in 1801 the record of the first three chiefs is indeed a modest one. The Supreme Court disposed of 79 cases, 53 on the merits, but published full-scale opinions construing the Constitution in only three cases, *Chisholm* v. *Georgia*,[14] which held that a state might be sued in a federal court without its consent; *Hylton* v. *United States*[15] in which a federal tax on carriages was held not to be a direct tax and thus was not required to be apportioned among the states according to the population; and *Calder* v. *Bull*[16] holding that the *ex post facto* prohibition in the Constitution applied only to criminal and not civil statutes. In none of the three did the chief justice play a prominent part. John Jay wrote only three opinions during his tenure, John Rutledge wrote one, Oliver Ellsworth, eleven, and in just a few instances did the views of the first three chiefs have any permanent effect on American constitutional development.

John Jay wrote one of the four opinions for the majority in *Chisholm* in which he detailed his views of the suability of a state, contending that suability was not incompatible with state sovereignty. In a concluding statement he declared that the extension of federal judicial power to suits between a state and citizens of another state "appears to me to be wise, because it is honest, and because it is useful." Leadership in the states thought differently, however, and overruled the *Chisholm* case by ratifying the Eleventh Amendment in 1797. Thus Jay's major constitutional opinion attained no permanence. Of greater importance was his brief opinion in *Glass* v. *The Sloop Betsey*[17] in which he reversed a federal district court on a question of admiralty jurisdiction. At issue was whether the United States district court in Maryland had admiralty jurisdiction over a French prize captured and brought into port at Baltimore. In clear and unequivocal language Jay wrote that "every district court possesses all the powers of admiralty" and is competent to decide questions of restitution "consistently with the law of nations and the treaties and laws of the United States." Furthermore, he continued, "no foreign power can of right institute, or erect, any court of judicature of any kind, within the jurisdiction of the United States." The decision, in support of Washington's neutrality policy, increased respect for American sovereignty among other nations and "spared it dangerous foreign involvements."[18]

Given the paucity of business in the Supreme Court during John Jay's incumbency, his—and the associate justices'—circuit riding was of paramount importance to the new government. Supreme Court justices were, in effect, national ambassadors to the proud, suspicious and emotionally independent state populations, and how they conducted themselves, what they said, could make the difference between hostility and amicable relations. Jay was well suited to this task. Modest and unassuming, he nevertheless conveyed a moral authority in his bearing and in his judicial conduct. In his charge to the grand jury as he held the first meeting of the circuit court in New York, a charge repeated in all the federal districts of the eastern circuit, his language could not have been better calculated to attain respect for federal authority:

> It cannot be too strongly impressed on the minds of all how greatly our individual prosperity, and how greatly our National prosperity depends on a well-organized, vigorous Government, ruling by wise and equal laws faithfully executed. Nor is such a government unfriendly to liberty—to that liberty which is really estimable. On the contrary, nothing but a strong government of laws irresistibly bearing down arbitrary power and licentiousness, can defend it against these two formidable enemies. Let it be remembered that civil liberty consists, not in the right to every man to do just as he pleases, but it consists in the equal right to all the citizens to have, enjoy, and do, in peace, security, and without molestation, whatever the equal and constitutional laws of the country admit to be consistent with the public good.[19]

John Jay, sitting on circuit along with Justice Cushing and district judge Henry Marchant, set the stage for some of the later Marshall opinions when he and his colleagues unanimously held that Rhode Island might not permit a debtor to extend his obligations for three years and grant him immunity from arrest and penalties during the extension.[20] Such an action, in Jay's view, was an unconstitutional violation of the contract clause of Article I, Section 10. This was a clear affirmation of national supremacy and of federal judicial authority.

In another circuit opinion Jay and his associates asserted the unequivocal independence of the federal judiciary, again setting a precedent for the emergence of full-blown judicial review. Jay expressed the view that Congress had no authority to assign to the courts nonjudicial functions, in this instance the duty to pass on applications for military pensions, subject to suspension by the secretary of war and revision by Congress. He declared that "by the Constitution, neither the Secretary of War, nor any other executive officer, nor even the Legislature, are authorized to sit as a court of errors on the judicial acts of opinions of this Court."[21] Perhaps Jay's most enduring contribution to the integrity of the Supreme Court was his insistence that the Court give no legal advice to the executive. When an enraged

Alexander Hamilton wrote to Jay suggesting that the Supreme
Court ought to render an opinion on the resolution passed by
the Virginia House of Representatives declaring that the congressional bill for the assumption of the state debts was unconstitutional, Jay's response was a calm but firm no. Later when
President Washington asked the Chief Justice for advice on
questions arising under Washington's Neutrality Proclamation,
Jay wrote to the President:

> We have considered the previous question stated in a let-
> ter written by your direction to us by the Secretary of State,
> on the 18th of last month regarding the lines of separation,
> drawn by the Constitution between the three departments
> of the government. These being in certain respects checks
> upon each other, and our being Judges of a Court in the last
> resort, are considerations which afford strong arguments
> against the propriety of our extra-judicially deciding the
> questions alluded to, especially as the power given by the
> Constitution to the President, of calling on the heads of de-
> partments for opinions, seems to have been *purposely* as
> well as expressly united to the *Executive* departments. We
> exceedingly regret every event that may cause embarrass-
> ment to your Administration, but we derive consolation
> from the reflection that your judgment will discern what is
> right, and that your usual prudence, decision and firmness
> will surmount every obstacle to the preservation of the
> rights, peace, and dignity of the United States.[22]

Always concerned with propriety Jay wisely maintained the
distinction between official conduct—what would become a
precedent for future chiefs as well as subsequent Supreme
Courts—and private relationships. Thus he did not hesitate to
counsel his friends in the executive and legislative branches, including Washington and Hamilton, in private conversation.
Jay's position was, however, unique in that he was a close personal friend of the president who appointed him and the only
president under whom he served. Despite his lack of judicial
craftsmanship and the brief time in which he might display his
personal talents, Jay was successful in establishing the dignity
of the office and the independence of the Supreme Court. Although he could make no pretensions to genius or even to ex-

ceptional learning,[23] Jay was a man of principle and integrity in whom people willingly placed their trust. He was, in short, very much like the man who appointed him.

It has been said the Oliver Ellsworth had a special gift for the terse phrase and that his brief opinions "suggest the tone and style of Marshall's,"[24] yet he wrote no opinions of lasting importance. In *Hylton* v. *United States* and *Calder* v. *Bull*, he took no part; nor did he write an opinion in *Ware* v. *Hylton*,[25] the only other constitutionally significant case during his tenure, in which his colleagues held that a Virginia law sequestering debts due British subjects was in violation of the peace treaty with Great Britain. If Ellsworth gave little in the way of intellectual leadership, he continued to maintain the dignity and independence of the Court and, of primary importance, began to move toward a small consolidated opinion.

In one of the few cases in which he wrote a detailed discussion of the issue, in this instance whether the Supreme Court could reexamine the facts and the law on a writ of error as well as appeal, Ellsworth spoke of "the opinion of the Court" and only one dissent, that of James Wilson, was recorded.[26] In seven other cases Ellsworth headed his opinion with phrases "of the Court," "By the Court" or "In delivering the opinion of the Court,"[27] thus paving the way for John Marshall to end completely the original *seriatim* method of delivering opinions.

Ellsworth like Jay was not a brilliant theoretician, and he would not, probably could not, expound on a legal point at length but, like Jay, he inspired confidence and compelled respect, personal and human characteristics more desirable in a chief justice perhaps than erudition or genius. Under their leadership it was not a time of boldness or creativity for the Supreme Court, in part because of the novelty of the federal judicial system, in part because both Presidents Washington and Adams saw fit to use the chief in extrajudicial roles. Nevertheless, the Court under John Jay and Oliver Ellsworth "set a pattern of constitutional adjudication that was to endure,"[28] and while lacking in vision perhaps, they were competent, conscientious men of integrity whose contributions to the new nation as chief justices, in spite of being powerfully dwarfed by those of the great Marshall, cannot be dismissed as negligible.

SALMON P. CHASE, HARLAN F. STONE, AND FRED VINSON

Constitutional historians do not differ greatly in their assessments of Chief Justices Chase, Stone, and Vinson in the sense that none can be classified as a great or exceptional leader. Nevertheless each had his strengths, and given the times, the events and the personnel with whom they served, the record for each, although spotty, is not devoid of positive contributions to the Court institutionally or to American constitutional development. Fred Vinson, the least successful of the three, appeared to be the best qualified for personal, although not intellectual, leadership. He was, moreover, the only one of the three, who was a personal friend of the president who appointed him and who had the support of former Chief Justice Hughes, as well as Associate Justice Roberts. He was liked and respected by those who worked with him, and given what was a rancorous and divided Court at the time, Fred Vinson appeared to be an ideal choice to give the kind of personal leadership required to reestablish, if not perfect harmony among the brethren, at least some semblance of professional cooperation. Salmon Chase and Harlan Stone, while not personally close to the presidents who named them, were very well known quantities who, in the judgment of Presidents Lincoln and Roosevelt, held views of public policy compatible with their own. Like several chiefs, Chase and Stone were calculated political appointments and neither was a strong personal preference of the chief executive.

BACKGROUND AND TEMPERAMENT

When Salmon Portland Chase was Senator from Ohio, he once told a friend that he would like to hold two offices: president of the United States and chief justice, and he pursued them both unceasingly until the time of his death. In fact, his unrelenting seeking of the former even after he had attained the latter probably reduced his effectiveness as chief and certainly diminishes his stature as a great statesman which he indisputably was. Although lusting for high office, Chase was not an opportunist but a man of principle and conviction who pursued what he conceived to be righteous causes throughout his life, the most prominent being the defense of runaway slaves during his early days as an attorney when it was not a popular activity in his home city of Cincinnati.

Salmon Chase's early life seemed not to portend the successful career that later matured. Born in the town of Cornish, New Hampshire, in 1808, first schooled locally, then in Windsor, Vermont, Chase began his higher education at Cincinnati College where his uncle, Bishop Philander Chase, was president, but after a year he returned to New Hampshire, entered Dartmouth College as a junior in 1824, graduating two years later with a creditable but undistinguished record. For three years he taught at a boys' school in Washington, D.C., while undertaking the study of law with the renowned William Wirt, although his law studies were without much substance as Chase himself admitted. He wrote that "very seldom had any candidate for admission to the bar presented himself with a slenderer stock of learning,"[29] and later a friend was to observe that "Chase was not a great lawyer, but a great man who had knowledge of the law."[30] Admitted to the bar in 1829 Chase decided to cast his lot with the rapidly expanding West, and he settled in Cincinnati where he believed, and rightly so, that the opportunities were boundless for an intelligent, albeit not very well trained, lawyer.

In an attempt to fulfill his literary ambitions he contributed two articles to the prestigious *North American Review* and discussed with friends the idea of publishing a literary quarterly which never got off the ground. He did, however, undertake and complete a project that involved the consolidation into three volumes, the thirty-one volumes of Ohio laws plus all the public laws for the Northwest Territory, an effort that brought praise from Justice Story and gave him some stature as a legal scholar. But Chase did not possess the temperament of a scholar; he desired power, the kind of power that can be attained only through actual participation in political life, power to be exercised through leadership of men and influence over events. Thus he eventually sought and won public office.

In Chase's life two overriding forces influenced virtually his every public act: his all-consuming hatred of slavery and his relentless, almost psychopathic ambition to be president of the United States, a post for which he considered himself better qualified than any of his contemporaries including Abraham Lincoln. According to one biographer Chase's "desire to govern

ChiefJustice

cannot be described as vanity; it was far deeper than that. It was an intense egotism, a confirmed conviction that there was nobody in the country who was quite his equal as a statesman, a conviction which preyed upon him to such an extent that it made much of his life unhappy. The sad part of it was that his egotism was largely justified."[31] Although Chase's antislavery activities were based on sincere moral principles and were not popular in Cincinnati, in many ways a southern city, it was his crusading zeal that brought him to public prominence and eventually to political success. Chase was not an abolitionist of the Garrison school although he consorted with abolitionists and said that he did not mind being called one. He was a unionist who believed that slavery could be destroyed without war, that it could be done by repealing all laws protecting slavery, by prohibiting slaveholding in all places of exclusive national jurisdiction, by congressional action forbidding slavery in all states carved out of national territories and by electing and appointing public officials dedicated to carrying out these measures.

Chase's initial entry into national politics came in 1832 when he became a delegate to the National Republican convention that nominated Henry Clay. In 1836 and 1840 he supported the Whig nominee for president, William Henry Harrison, but by 1841 he had become disenchanted with the Whigs because of the unwillingness of the party's leadership to take an antislavery stand. He could not join the Democrats since they, too, would not alienate the slaveholders who were a significant part of their electoral base. Thus, Chase joined, eventually becoming its prime mover and leader, the Ohio antislavery Liberty Party which had been initially organized by James G. Birney. Ultimately this move led him to the famous Free Soil convention of 1848 in Buffalo which consisted of the old Liberty people now joined by the New York antislavery defectors from the Democrats—the Barnburners—whose goal was to unite all antislavery people into a party that would hold the balance of power in the 1848 election.[32] An agreement was reached that permitted Chase to be instrumental in drafting the platform with a strong "no more slave states and no more slave territory" plank while giving the New Yorkers the choice of the candidate who became quite predictably former President Martin Van Buren. In the election the Free Soilers caused Lewis Cass, the standard bearer

Leadership Minimized in the Short-Term Chiefs

for the Democrats, to lose New York and helped guarantee the election of the Whig and slaveholder, Zachary Taylor. Cass, a northern "doughface," was hardly different from Taylor on the slavery issue, but for Chase the election determined the direction of his future political career, for the Free Soilers had elected eleven members of the Ohio legislature and would now have a strong voice in choosing the next United States senator.

It was not without a bitter struggle in the legislative forum that Chase became Ohio's junior senator in March 1849. Although he now considered himself a Democrat, elected by Democrats, who hoped to reshape the Democratic Party into an antislavery vehicle, Chase was perceived by his Senate colleagues as a representative of a "small and very disagreeable third party" who would drag "the slavery question into debate when respectable people were tired of it."[33] When the Senate was organized, the Southern Democrats prevented his receiving any committee assignments, although in subsequent years he managed to secure appointments to a few committees. Chase was a good nuts-and-bolts senator, working conscientiously for his constituency and for decent causes, but primarily he was the chief anti-slavery spokesman in the Senate as he tried in vain to defeat the Compromise of 1850 and the Kansas-Nebraska Bill, both of which permitted the extension of slavery to the territories.

When his term in the Senate ended, Chase still called himself an Independent Democrat, but in the turmoil of the late 1850s that witnessed the disintegration of the Whigs, the split in the Democrats between the pro- and antislavery wings, and the intrusion of the National American or Know-Nothing party which also opposed slavery, Chase moved into the emerging Republican Party which nominated him for governor of Ohio in 1855. He defeated the Whig, Medill, and Trimble, the Democrat, served his two-year term and was reelected in 1857. Although a candidate for president at the first Republican National Convention in 1856, he never really had a chance to best John C. Fremont who had widespread support. Returned to the Senate as a Republican in 1860, he was one of the front-runners for the presidential nomination at the convention which as fate would have it, turned to Abraham Lincoln. It was Chase's friends in the Ohio delegation who put Lincoln over the top at the crucial moment when they saw Chase's strength declining, thus giving Chase a favorable political position with the Republican nominee. In spite of his disappointment at losing, Chase campaigned vigorously for Lincoln, and when the votes were counted, Lincoln carried Ohio by a majority of 21,000 votes over the combined total of Douglas, Breckenridge and Bell, the nominees of the three Democratic factions. Chase wrote after the election that "the first of the great wishes of my life is accomplished. The slave power is overthrown."[34]

Somewhat less than tranquil was Chase's relationship with Lincoln as he served as secretary of the treasury in the President's war cabinet. In spite of the friction between the two vigorous contenders for national leadership, there was a mutual respect that prevented the tenuous relationship from disintegrating, and Lincoln was the first to admit that Chase's contributions to the successful prosecution of the war were of monumental proportions.

Financing the war was as crucial to success as winning on the battlefield, and Lincoln, not experienced in matters of high finance, generally gave Chase a free hand in the day-to-day management of the money machine. In 1862 the government was spending at a rate of $2,500,000 a day with an income of $600,000 a day, and it was Lincoln in this instance who had to convince, perhaps order, Chase to relinquish his constitutional scruples and support the issuance of "greenbacks" that would be legal tender for all debts, public and private, except for tariffs and the government's interest on its own debt.[35] As Carl Sandburg relates the story, David Taylor of Ohio had suggested the plan for issuing greenbacks to Lincoln who told him to talk with Chase who in turn said it was unconstitutional. Upon hearing this from Taylor, Lincoln said, "[G]o back to Chase and tell him not to bother himself about the Constitution. Say that I have that sacred instrument here at the White House, and I am guarding it with great care."[36] It was Chase who later said in defense of the government's financial policies that "the war must go on until this rebellion is put down, if we have to put out paper until it takes $1000 to buy a breakfast."[37]

As the administrator of the treasury department Chase was fair and efficient, carefully hiring and promoting on merit the some 10,000 employees whom he supervised. Although Lincoln rarely interfered in Chase's appointments, on one of the few occasions in which he did so, Chase sent a letter of resignation to the president who went directly to Chase's home and persuaded him to withdraw it. Chase was the first department head to open up employment to women in public service, although he never felt very comfortable doing business with them,[38] and he was the prime mover in laying the foundation for a national banking system, successfully pressing Congress for legislation to charter national banks subject to federal supervision.[39]

Relations between Lincoln and Chase became unduly strained in the spring of 1864 when Chase in an undoubted act of personal disloyalty encouraged the organization and expenditure of funds in his behalf in order to secure the Republican nomination for president. Much was done in secret at first, but the movement became public when newspapers all over the country printed the famous "Pomeroy Secret Circular," a letter prepared for private and confidential distribution signed by Senator Samuel C. Pomeroy of Kansas, one of the leaders in the anti-Lincoln, pro-Chase organization. The general thrust of the circular was that Lincoln had been a bad president who should not serve a second term and that Chase was the man who could save the Republic. In a moment of remorse Chase wrote to Lincoln disclaiming any knowledge of the circular and indicating that he did not wish to administer the treasury department without the president's full confidence. Lincoln's response was that he had known of the movement in behalf of Chase, but saw no reason for him to quit the treasury post. On June 7 the Republican convention met in Baltimore and nominated Lincoln although Chase had never halted the activities which he had hoped until the end would make him the Republican standard-bearer. Within the month Chase, for the fourth time, sent Lincoln his resignation, ostensibly over a political squabble with respect to the appointment of the assistant treasurer at New York. His patience at an end, Lincoln accepted the Secretary's resignation, and Chase wrote in his diary: "So my official life closes. . . . I am too earnest, too anti-slavery, and, say, too radical, to make the President willing to have me connected with the Administration, just as my opinion is that he is not earnest enough, not anti-slavery enough, not radical enough."[40]

Chief Justice

On October 12, 1864, Chief Justice Taney died, thus giving Abraham Lincoln the opportunity to choose a chief justice, an opportunity denied to the nine presidents who had preceded him. As is always the case, the position of national chief magistrate did not want for candidates, but Salmon Chase was the front-runner, strongly supported by the press, by influential senators and by some of his former cabinet colleagues. Lincoln had once said that no one in the country would make a better chief justice than Chase and that if he had the opportunity he would appoint him, but he had a serious reservation. "I have only one doubt about his appointment," said Lincoln, "He is a man of unbounded ambition, and has been working all his life to become President. That he can never be; and I fear that if I make him chief-justice, he will simply become more restless and uneasy, and neglect the place, in his strife and intrigue to make himself President."[41] Lincoln sent Chase's name to the Senate on December 6 and the nation's sixth chief justice took his seat on December 15. In 1868 Chase sought the Republican nomination, and after losing to Grant, became a candidate for the Democratic nomination which was also unattainable. After suffering a stroke in 1870 and unable to discharge his duties for a year, he still allowed his name to be put in nomination at the Democratic Convention of 1872. Salmon Chase was the only sitting chief justice ever to seek the presidency actively, the result of which was an impairment of public confidence in him personally and a weakening of the high office to which he had been entrusted. Lincoln's worst fears had been realized.

Harlan Fiske Stone, very much unlike Chase, was a lawyer and legal scholar preeminent who had served for sixteen years as an associate justice of the Supreme Court prior to being elevated to chief. Never having sought an elective office, his only political service was as attorney general of the United States under President Coolidge, a post which gave him the entrée to the Supreme Court. Until he entered government service in 1924, where he would remain until his death in 1946, Stone had been a successful practicing lawyer and law teacher.

Tracing his ancestry back to Simon Stone who, with his wife and children, had emigrated to America in 1635, Harlan Stone grew up on a farm near Amherst, Massachusetts, his family having moved there from his birthplace of Chesterfield, New Hampshire, when Harlan was two years old. Fred and Ann Stone were stern disciplinarians who did not hesitate to use a horsewhip on occasion when the sometimes obstreperous Harlan misbehaved, but they were also loving parents who desired the best for their children including an education at a university. Harlan entered Massachusetts Agricultural College (now the University of Massachusetts) in 1888 to study scientific farming, but two years later was expelled for disorderly conduct culminating in an incident in which he roughed up a professor during a general student fracas in the chapel. Fred Stone was furious as he told his son that his school days were over. "You're through," he said, "From now on, it is the farm for you."[42] Farming was not to be Harlan's destiny, however, as his father, on the importuning of young Stone's cousin Nellie, permitted him to enter Amherst College after Stone had made a direct appeal to the institution's president. His record at Amherst was a distinguished one as he was elected to Phi Beta Kappa and voted the most likely to succeed by the class of 1894.[43]

Earlier in his life Stone had expressed a desire to study medicine and throughout his college years was known as "Doc," but after graduation he spent a year teaching at Newburyport High School where in his spare moments he would attend sessions of the state superior court. He became friendly with district attorney William H. Moody, a future Supreme Court justice, who suggested that Stone study law,[44] and in 1895 he entered Columbia Law School. Stone was exposed to some of the best scholar-teachers in the nation, law school dean William Keener, lawyers George W. Kirchway, William and George W. Canfield, and political scientists John W. Burgess, Monroe Smith, Frank J. Goodnow and John Bassett Moore who taught the legal theory and history courses. He became a lifelong friend of Keener, Moore and Canfield, serving for a time with them on the Columbia law faculty and practicing law for several years with Canfield.[45]

For a half dozen years after commencement Stone divided his time between part-time lecturing at the law school and learning the practical ropes with Canfield's firm which he finally joined full time in 1905. Stone, however, had always enjoyed the academic life, and was to write to a friend in 1941 about his year at Newburyport High School: "I liked it so much that I came near never leaving it."[46] It thus seemed appropriately in character when he accepted the position of professor of law and dean of the law faculty at Columbia on July 1, 1910, a post which he held until 1923 when he returned to private practice once again. His decision to leave academia was not an easy one. His biographer suggests that contributing to the decision were such factors as disgust with the typical petty bickerings that pervade university faculties, boredom with the details of administration, disagreements over policy with Columbia's imperious president, Nicholas Murray Butler, and certainly the fact of an increase in salary from $15,000 to $100,000 per annum,[47] although the latter reason was by no means primary since a year later his salary was reduced to $12,000 when he became attorney general.

Influencing the president's selection to some degree was the old friendship between Stone and Coolidge when they were students at Amherst College, but Stone had a solid reputation as scholar-lawyer and as a man of integrity who had strongly opposed the notorious "red raids" made by former Attorney General A. Mitchell Palmer. He was not simply a college crony. In managing the justice department he gradually discharged many of the holdovers from the "Ohio gang" and demonstrated "that he stood squarely against the malevolence that marked the treatment of civil liberties" under Presidents Wilson and Harding.[48] As he was about to initiate an antitrust suit against the Aluminum Company of America, Justice McKenna announced his retirement and President Coolidge nominated Stone for the vacancy.

During his sixteen years as an associate justice, Stone forged a solid record of achievement that by itself was enough to give him an enduring reputation as one of the nation's better creative jurists, but there were times when he entertained the thought of leaving the bench. In fact, at the height of the Court fight with President Roosevelt in 1936 Stone wrote Frankfurter that he had regrets about not yielding to his "inclination to seek other occupation."[49] He had had both lucrative and prestigious opportunities to leave the Court—an offer to return to his law firm of Sullivan and Cromwell, an appointment as secretary of state in 1929 by President Hoover—and he was tempted, but in the final analysis he was unwilling to give up what was a rewarding, demanding job that gave him the kind of national recognition he appeared to desire. Moreover, there was always the chance that he might become chief. When his friend, John Bassett Moore advised him against taking the position as secretary of state, he said that he hoped Stone would eventually become chief,[50] and a year later when Taft retired and President Hoover consulted him about Taft's successor, Stone hoped that he might be in the running, but it was Hughes, against Stone's advice incidentally, who received the appointment. Eleven years later when President Roosevelt spoke with Hughes about his successor, Hughes strongly recommended Stone.

Upon Hughes' retirement conjecture in the press over the appointment of a new chief centered on two names, Stone and Attorney General Robert H. Jackson. The influential *Washington Post* and *New York Herald Tribune* both suggested that Jackson was the president's first choice,[51] although much of the press supported Stone on the basis of his distinguished service. Stone, a Republican and hardly a New Dealer, had nevertheless frequently voted with Brandeis and Cardozo to uphold some of the controversial pre-1936 Roosevelt programs and had consistently supported the president's legislative program after the Court fight. At the same time Jackson had been a trusted and respected Roosevelt lieutenant who had rendered yeoman service as solicitor general and attorney general and had been told by Roosevelt that he would like to see him in the center chair.[52] Ultimately what seemed to be controlling was the need of the president, with World War II on the horizon, to show unity by appointing a Republican, one who was well qualified and who had strong support in the Court's major constituencies throughout the nation.

On June 12, 1941, President Roosevelt named Harlan Fiske Stone as the twelfth chief justice of the United States and at the same time rewarded Jackson with the appointment to Stone's vacated seat. Everybody was happy. There were rumors of a deal in which Stone, then 68, would retire in two years and Jackson would succeed him, but in an interview with his biographer, Jackson said that there was no such deal, no promise, only that the president would like to make him chief when Stone retired,[53] and that he had told FDR that it was "entirely agreeable to me that Stone be named."[54] No appointment of a chief justice had ever elicited greater national approval as ecstatic voices were raised in behalf of the president's choice by the press, the bench, the bar and by partisan politicans of every stripe. The good natured, intelligent, competent, massive (200-pound) Stone looked every inch a chief, a worthy successor to his immediate predecessors, Taft and Hughes.

Stone's mind is most often described as powerful rather than brilliant, more like Taft's than like Hughes'. He also resembled Taft in personality, a big bear of a man who wished to have friendly relations with everyone around him, sometimes to the point of fault as he would go to great lengths to avoid personal conflict or acrimony.[55] This meant that he was usually on good terms with his colleagues but at a price, as he would withhold his own views to avoid confrontation and then suffer inwardly. This inability to engage forthrightly in debate because of his dread of conflict tended to weaken his leadership as did another characteristic, his vanity. His desire for approval by the brethren, by legal scholars and even by newspapers and laymen bordered on the pathological, a flaw that could not be overcome by his warm personality. As one commentator suggests: "Dread of conflict militates against effectual leadership in the decision of cases; vanity militates against group action and makes for individuality."[56] Stone might have been a great chief even during those five short years but the flaws in his personality stacked the deck against him.

Fred M. Vinson, Stone's successor in 1946 appeared to possess all of Stone's good personal qualities—friendliness, warmth, relaxed demeanor—and none of the bad. He was not vain, not fearful of conflict and was known for his ability to conciliate the views of warring factions. Lacking Stone's intellectual power, Vinson nevertheless came to the Court with an innate common sense and broad political experience in national affairs going back to 1924 when he was elected to the House of Representatives from Kentucky.

Fred Vinson's career is in the mold of the American dream. He was a small-town boy born to parents of modest cicumstances who, through perseverance and application moved into the highest circles of the national government, serving with competence in all three branches. As with all chiefs a certain amount of luck was involved in his being named to the top judicial post.

Leadership Minimized in the Short-Term Chiefs

In this instance being the president's closest confidant was a great help, but Vinson did not want for qualifications. He received his pre-college education in the public schools of the town where he was born, Louisa, Kentucky, and he acquired both his bachelor's and law degree from Center College. Practicing law in Louisa, he began to dabble in Democratic politics, serving successively as city attorney and commonwealth attorney before winning a seat in the House of Representatives in 1924.

With the exception of 1928–30 when Herbert Hoover carried a Republican on his coattails from Vinson's congressional district, he served in the House until 1937 when President Roosevelt named him to the court of appeals for the District of Columbia. In the House Vinson quickly rose to a position of leadership on the powerful Ways and Means Committee which he chaired for several years. Although possessing the outlook of a conservative southern Democrat on fiscal policy, he was basically a pragmatist who saw the need to use federal power to cope with the depression. Thus he supported Roosevelt not only on tax measures but also backed his attempt to curb the Supreme Court which Vinson thought was appropriate medicine for the justices who had not exercised reasonable restraint. Vinson's support for the president's policies was not automatic, however, as he occasionally fought him on major issues such as the soldier bonus bill for which he voted and the president subsequently vetoed. Described as "an instinctive budget balancer" and a "borderline New Dealer, as strongly anti-Socialist as he is anti-reaction,"[57] he nevertheless was helpful enough to the president to be rewarded with the appointment to the nation's most prestigious circuit court.

After serving on the federal bench for six years Fred Vinson resigned to become President Roosevelt's chief troubleshooter during the difficult war years of 1943 and 1944 or, as described by Senator Claude Pepper of Florida, "the general utility man of the Government."[58] He was successively director of Economic Stabilization, a job that required him to withstand pressures from all components of the economy in order to hold prices down; Federal Loan administrator and head of the Reconstruction Finance Corporation, a $40,000,000 operation; and director of War Mobilization and Reconversion. Success in these roles required not only wise managerial sense and financial acumen but an ability to exact settlements among warring factions who did not accept compromise without a fight. Although he ran these agencies for relatively short periods, the president seemingly moving him where he was needed most, there was no doubt among close observers that Vinson had a special talent for dealing with abrasive people in tense and antagonistic situations and for conciliating their interests to serve a national purpose. He was, like Salmon Chase, one of the president's key aides in a supreme effort to mobilize the nation for a victory in war. In personality Vinson and Chase were virtually exact opposites. Stone possessed the affable, easy-going manner of Vinson, and in spite of his vanity did not approach the supreme egotism of Chase. All three had in common, however, an inner toughness that enabled them to stand on principle and to retain the respect of their associates even when in total disagreement.

In the inevitable shuffling of the personnel in positions of leadership in a new administration, Harry S. Truman upon acceding to the Presidency in April 1945 named Vinson to succeed Henry Morgenthau, Jr., as secretary of the treasury. A strong bond had developed very quickly between Harry Truman and Fred Vinson as the latter became a dominant, perhaps the dominant, figure in the new administration as well as a close personal friend of the president. There was a natural affinity between these border state Democrats who, while conservative in tendency, had become a part of the New Deal construct and of the war machine, each in his own way having contributed to the Roosevelt successes. Somewhat bewildered at suddenly being thrust into a job which he never expected to hold and for which he entertained some doubts of his qualifications, Truman wisely relied on known quantities, particularly those with whom he felt comfortable, for major appointments, and Fred Vinson was a perfect fit for the treasury. As in his previous executive posts, however, Vinson served only a short time, just one month less than a year.

On April 13, 1946, Chief Justice Stone appeared vigorous and healthy as he attended the annual dinner of the Gridiron Club, but in less than a fortnight he suffered a massive cerebral hemorrhage and died within a few hours. Now President Truman, still cautious and somewhat uncertain in his role as chief executive after only one year, had to make the most significant appointment of his career, a chief justice of the United States. Although the president spent several weeks in consultation about the appointment, one gets the impression that Truman had very early made up his mind to choose Vinson and was seeking support for his decision. Controversial to this day was a conference between Truman and Charles Evans Hughes after which Truman claimed that Hughes had recommended the appointment of Vinson. In a memorandum approved by Hughes and recorded by his official biographer, Merlo Pusey, Hughes made no mention of Vinson but instead recommended that Associate Justice Robert Jackson be elevated to the post.[59] After meeting with former Associate Justice Owen Roberts, the president said that he too had recommended Fred Vinson, a statement that Roberts neither denied nor confirmed, claiming that the conversation was private and should remain so.

On June 6 President Truman nominated Fred M. Vinson, 56-year-old son of a Kentucky county jailer to head the nation's high court. It was a *New York Times* editorial that best summed up the nation's reaction to the Vinson appointment when it suggested that it was "likely to arouse neither strong opposition nor great enthusiasm." Vinson, the editorial continued "has been an able public servant. He has sometimes acted with unusual political courage. He has spent many years in Congress as a practical legislator and he has had experience on the bench. . . . But he is hardly the ideal appointment to the highest judicial office in the land, and he can hardly be said to measure up to the stature of his most recent predecessors . . . Chief Justice Hughes and the late Chief Justice Stone."[60]

Within a week Justice Jackson, on leave from the Court to serve as chief American prosecutor of the war crimes in Nuremburg, publicly attacked his colleague Hugo Black, in a statement issued at a news conference and cabled to the House and Senate judiciary committees. In an intemperate outburst Jackson said that a long-standing feud had existed between him and Black, that Black had wrongly participated in decisions affecting a former law partner and that Black had threatened him (Jackson) with "war" unless he covered up facts in a case in which Black's law partner had been involved. Rumors of dissension among the brethren had been rife for some time and now there appeared to be open warfare. The new chief had his work cut out for him.

MANAGING THE COURT'S BUSINESS

From the standpoint of experience and temperament Chase, Stone, and Vinson appeared to be well qualified for the job of chief administrator of the Supreme Court. All had shown a talent for managerial knowhow, Chase and Vinson in Congress and in the president's cabinet, Stone as a law school dean and attorney general. Yet none of them lived up to expectations in this respect, and only Stone would go down in history as an exceptionally able jurist, but even that reputation had been established during his years as an associate justice. In part the inability of each to lead the Court along a path of unity and doctrinal coherence was the result of the individualistic bent of some of the brethren who adhered to their own views of the law whether or not they conformed to the chief's. In part it was a personal flaw in the leader: Chase's ego and his unwillingness to try to persuade his colleagues to accept his point of view; Stone's vanity and his abhorrence of conflict; Vinson's lack of intellectual vigor and a tendency to leave the hard work to others.

By the time of Chase's appointment in 1864, Abraham Lincoln had effectively remade the Supreme Court by naming five new members to the bench, the largest number chosen by a single president since Andrew Jackson was able to name six. Of the justices who had participated in the *Dred Scott* decision, only four, Samuel Nelson, Robert C. Grier, James M. Wayne, and John Catron were on the Court when Chase joined it in 1864, and although Nelson, Grier and Catron were technically in the majority in that they agreed that it was up to the courts of Missouri to decide Dred Scott's status after his return to the state's jurisdiction, only Wayne had concurred in Taney's extravagant pronouncement that a Negro could not be a citizen of the United States under the Constitution. A fifth justice, Nathan Clifford of Maine, was a Buchanan appointee, a staunch Democrat named in 1858 to replace Benjamin Curtis who resigned in protest after the *Dred Scott* decision and who would serve well beyond Chase until 1881.

Very early in his administration Lincoln had four vacancies to fill, but he held off naming anyone in the hope that peace would come quickly and that a Southerner could be among the new appointees. In 1862, however, he chose three in quick succession: Noah H. Swayne, Virginia-born but adopted Ohioan and strongly

Leadership Minimized in the Short-Term Chiefs

opposed to slavery; Samuel F. Miller, a leader of the Iowa bar who had originally been a physician and who was to be one of Lincoln's best appointments and one of the Court's greatest figures; and David Davis, Lincoln's manager at the Chicago convention of 1860 who preferred politics to judging and resigned in 1877 to become a United States senator. When Congress created a tenth circuit and a tenth seat on the Supreme Court, Lincoln appointed Stephen J. Field, then the chief justice of the California supreme court and an antislavery, pro-war Democrat. Catron died in 1865 and Wayne in 1867 but no new appointments were made until 1870 as the Congress in 1866 in its bitter struggle with Andrew Johnson reduced the size of the Court to seven as vacancies should occur. Thus, serving with Chase up to the time of his stroke in August 1870 was a stable group consisting of Lincoln's appointees and Nelson, Grier and Clifford plus Wayne until 1867.

Despite the fact that the Supreme Court under Chase declared eight acts of Congress unconstitutional and decided several crucial questions growing out of Reconstruction, the bulk of litigation before the Court was dull, boring and of little significance for future national policy. In fact Chase wrote in 1865: "Working from morning till midnight, and no result, except that John Smith owned this parcel of land or other property instead of Jacob Robinson; I care nothing, and nobody caring much more, about the matter."[61] Chase appears to have had less interest in crafting opinions or in obtaining a consensus on the Court than any chief before or since. This is not to suggest that he was not a hard worker. He was. He averaged just under 17 opinions per term excluding dissents of which he wrote very few. Only Miller and Swayne spoke for the Court more often than Chase.

In terms of sheer volume, it was a productive Court under Chase, the average number of cases decided each year by full opinion running over 120 with a high during the 1869 term of 169. This was virtually double the annual number decided during Taney's final four years which indicates a change in the public respect for the Court when the author of the *Dred Scott* case was replaced by a chief whose antislavery activities had been at the core of his public life. Renewed respect for the Court was not in itself reason enough for doubling the Court's workload; the territorial expansion of the country, additional legislation, and issues arising out of the war and Reconstruction helped to swell the docket. Since more and more cases were being held over for decision, the Court convened in special sessions in October preceding the statutory term that began in December. In 1873 Congress confirmed this practice by enacting a statute setting the opening of the Court's term on the second Monday in October, a regulation that endures to this day.

Internally the Court was neither especially efficient nor thorough in a corporate sense, a fault that must be laid at Chase's door for giving only minimal direction at the conference. At the Saturday conference, in addition to the discussion and voting on cases, each justice who had been assigned the writing of an opinion would bring his manuscript and simply read it, the others usually hearing it for the first time.[62] There might be a suggestion here and there, but for the most part the opinion remained the opinion of the author and less the collegial affair it became under future chiefs when opinions were circulated among the brethren for comment well in advance of any final draft. In addition to his lack of interest in forging the Court into some semblance of a team, Chase failed to consult the brethren on matters of vital interest to the Court as an institution. This is best exemplified by his activities in 1866 in which he lobbied for judicial reorganization.

Two bills had been introduced in Congress, both of crucial importance to the Court. One would have created a system of intermediate appellate courts; the other proposed to return the Court to a membership of nine. In 1869 both were enacted into law although the justices of the Supreme Court continued to act as circuit judges until 1891. Chase, on his own, working through friends in the House and in the Senate attempted to obtain amendments to the bills embodying ideas which he had never shared with the justices except for a letter he had written to Miller, unsuccessfully asking for support.[63] First, Chase proposed that the size of the Court be reduced permanently to seven, reasoning that the judges' salaries might then be increased substantially, from $6,000 to $10,000 for the associates and from $6,500 to $12,000 for the chief. Second, he suggested that the chief be empowered to appoint a marshal, a departure from the principle established by the Judiciary Act of 1789 which had authorized the appointment of a clerk by the entire Supreme Court and not simply by the chief justice.

Congress eventually enacted statutes in 1866 and 1867. In the first the Court's size was reduced, an ill-considered move given the Court's increasing business, but the salaries remained unchanged. While the law reorganized the circuits for which the justices would be responsible, it made no provision for assigning them to a specific circuit. Congress remedied this in 1867 by enacting a statute granting to the Court the responsibility for making the allotments to the circuits. Also in the law was the authorization to appoint a marshal but the chief was given no more say in the matter than his brethren. It was not long before Congress realized that a Supreme Court of seven members was inadequate for handling the nation's judicial business, and the size was restored to nine in 1869. In 1871 the salaries of the justices were raised—$8,000 for the associates and $8,500 for the chief—considerably below the level Chase had suggested earlier. In 1873, two months before Chase's death, another increase brought the annual compensation to $10,000 with the usual extra $500 for the chief.

INTERPRETING THE CONSTITUTION

Amidst the routine cases before the Supreme Court during Chase's tenure were the very complex and significant issues growing out of the Civil War and Reconstruction. Initially the Chase Court had before it some of the tangled property issues and particularly during the 1865 and 1866 terms, a large number of prize cases, a majority of which Chase assigned to himself. They involved intricate questions of international law such as rights of neutrals, powers of belligerents and in some instances, appeals against condemnation under laws to suppress the slave trade.[64] In a dozen memorable cases between *Ex parte Milligan*[65] (1866) and the *Slaughter House Cases*[66] decided just before Chase's death in 1873, in only two, *Mississippi* v. *Johnson*[67] and *Ex parte McCardle*[68] did the chief speak for a unanimous Court. Several were decided by one vote, and two, the test oath and legal tender cases, saw Chase in dissent.

One of the earliest and most emphatic pronouncements in behalf of constitutional liberty made by the Supreme Court was the opinion of Justice Davis in *Milligan*, a case in which Chase chose to concur in the result but disagreed with the broad sweep of Davis's language. L. P. Milligan, arrested in 1864 under an

1863 Act of Congress authorizing the suspension of *habeas corpus*, was tried by a military commission and sentenced to be hanged. Milligan was a Peace Democrat who would have stopped the fighting and recognized the Confederacy as an independent state, but he and others went much further than simply proclaiming their beliefs. They organized a secret society called the Sons of Liberty and actually planned military style operations to release Confederate prisoners held in Indiana and Ohio.

They were convicted of conspiracy against the government, giving aid to the rebels, inciting insurrection, disloyal practices and violating the laws of war. Before the Supreme Court were three questions: (1) ought a writ of *habeas corpus* be issued; (2) should Milligan be released; and (3) did the military commission have jurisdiction to try and sentence Milligan. All nine justices agreed that the commission that tried Milligan was without jurisdiction under the terms of the 1863 statute and ordered that he be discharged. All nine also agreed that Congress had not intended to authorize military tribunals in regions where civil courts were open but only five took the position that constitutionally Congress *could not* authorize such proceedings. In Justice Davis's memorable words: "The Constitution of the United States is a law for rulers and people, equally in war and in peace, and covers with the shield of its protection all classes of men, at all times, and under all circumstances. No doctrine, involving more pernicious consequences, was ever invented by the wit of man than that constitutional rights can be suspended because of war."[69] Thus, he concluded, "Martial law cannot arise from a threatened invasion" and "can never exist when the courts are open, and in the proper and unobstructed exercise of their jurisdiction."[70]

Davis also carefully delineated the meaning of a "suspension" of the writ of *habeas corpus*. The suspension, he correctly maintained, is of the *privilege,* not of the writ itself which issues as a matter of course, and the courts must determine whether the party applying for the writ may proceed any further. Chief Justice Chase speaking for a minority of four contended that the inquiry should end with the Act of 1863 which clearly contemplated a civil and not a military trial under the circumstances. This was not simply a matter of self-restraint, however, since he went on to maintain that it is within the power of Congress to determine that a public danger is of such magnitude that it "justifies the authorization of military tribunals for the trial of crimes and offenses against the discipline or security of the army or against the public safety."[71]

Soon after the *Milligan* case the Court faced challenges to the test oaths, one enacted by the state of Missouri, the other by Congress, and in both cases Chase was in dissent with a minority of four. At issue in *Cummings* v. *Missouri*[72] was a retroactive oath of loyalty required by the new Missouri constitution of 1864 under which anyone "by act or word" who had sympathized with the rebellion was prohibited from voting, holding public or corporate office and from practicing any profession. The *Garland* case[73] challenged an Act of Congress that imposed a similar oath for attorneys to practice before the Supreme Court. In *Cummings* the law had prevented a Catholic priest from practicing his profession and Garland, although admitted to practice before the Supreme Court prior to the war and now pardoned by the president was not exempted from the oath. In both cases Chase was not able to carry a majority with him as he and three other Lincoln appointees, Miller, Swayne and Davis dissented. Justice Field, the remaining Lincoln appointee, joined the prewar Justices Grier, Nelson, Clifford and Wayne to strike down both measures as bills of attainder and *ex post facto* laws. Attacks on the Court by the radical Republicans in Congress and by much of the press had become commonplace after the *Milligan* case, but following the decision in *Cummings* and *Garland*, they began to build to a crescendo as newspapers accused the Court of attempting to reverse the results of the war, and some members of Congress introduced legislation that would have had the effect of nullifying the Court's decisions.[74]

It was also a time of continuing crisis as the Court, in the midst of all the hyperbole, now had to face the issue of the constitutionality of the Reconstruction program providing for military occupation of the former Confederacy, a program that Congress had passed over a presidential veto based on constitutional scruples. In form the case came down to the question of the Court's jurisdiction, as counsel for the state of Mississippi asked leave to file an injunction restraining the president from enforcing the laws on the ground of unconstitutionality. For a unanimous Court Chase denied the request to file the bill, declaring that the judiciary could not and would not issue an injunction ordering the president to refrain from enforcing a law and from performing his official and, in this instance, discretionary duties. In the main Chase's reasoning relied on the absurdity of the president refusing to obey an injunction and the Court being powerless to do anything about it, or conversely the president obeying the injunction and then being impeached by the Senate for not enforcing the law.[75] Not to be outdone, the states of Mississippi and Georgia then tried to obtain the same result by requesting injunctions to restrain Secretary of War Edwin M. Stanton and General Grant from executing the Reconstruction Acts.[76] Once again the Court dismissed the suit, this time for a divided Court, on the ground that it called for the adjudication of political rights, of sovereignty, of the corporate existence of a state, matters over which the Court has no jurisdiction. Justice Nelson authored the opinion in which the chief justice joined, but apparently Chase had problems with Nelson's reasoning, for he wrote: "Without being able to yield my assent to the grounds stated in the opinion I concur fully in the conclusion. . . ."[77] Unfortunately Chase did not give his reasons, but apparently he could not persuade a majority to concur in them, whatever they may have been.[78]

In one of the few cases growing out of the bitter conflicts of the post-Civil War turmoil in which Chase was to obtain unanimous agreement, the ruling remains controversial to this day. Ostensibly the case was similar to *Milligan* in that it involved a trial of a civilian by a military commission, but other crucial issues overshadowed that simple point. The *McCardle*[79] case has in fact been characterized as "a memorable test of nerve between Congress and the Court."[80] In February 1868 the Court placed on the docket the case of William H. McCardle, a Mississippi editor who had been charged with seditious activity for publishing libels about the military governors and for impeding Reconstuction in the South. After an unsuccessful petition for a writ of *habeas corpus* in the federal circuit court, counsel for McCardle appealed to the Supreme Court under the Habeas Corpus Act of 1867 which Congress had passed in order to protect federal officials and other loyal unionists from adverse action by courts of the former Confederate states. Under its terms federal courts might grant writs of *habeas corpus* in all cases in which a person was restrained of his liberty in violation of the Constitution, a treaty, or a law of the United States, and McCardle had cleverly maneuvered the Court into a position where it would have to rule on the validity of the Reconstruction program.

When Congress became aware, however, that the Court had docketed McCardle's case, it moved to forestall judicial scrutiny by tacking on to a bill extending the Supreme Court's jurisdiction in cases involving customs and revenue officers an amendment repealing the Habeas Corpus Act of 1867 and prohibiting the Court from hearing cases of this kind that had already been docketed. President Johnson vetoed the bill, noting that he could not assent to a measure that proposed to deprive persons restrained of liberty in violation of the Constitution from the right of appeal to the nation's highest judicial authority. Moreover, he observed, the retroactive provision would operate most harshly on those persons who allegedly had been denied justice in the lower courts. Both the Senate and House overwhelmingly overrode the veto, and now the Court which had already heard several days of arguments in the case, chose, over the protests of Justices Field and Grier, to hold it over for decision until the following term. Then, of course, the justices had to face the question of the new law withdrawing jurisdiction.

Upholding the law and dismissing McCardle's case, Chase spoke for a unanimous Court in declaring that judicial duty "is not less fitly performed by declining ungranted jurisdiction than in exercising that which the Constitution and laws confer." Pointing to the language of Article III which permits Congress to make regulations and exceptions to the Court's appellate jurisdiction, Chase observed that Congress had made a specific exception, that the judiciary was not at liberty to inquire into legislative motives and that the Court's only recourse was to dismiss the case. Chase was on firm constitutional footing when he agreed that Congress might deny appellate jurisdiction or repeal jurisdiction once given, but for Congress to snatch away a case already docketed and on which arguments had been heard is another question. When the Supreme Court, usually by circumstances beyond its control, is forced from the periphery of the political scene to its center, it must itself weigh political considerations, and such was the case in this instance.

Under attack by the Radicals in Congress, particularly after the *Milligan* decision, Chase and his brethren were uncomfortably aware that they would be the losers if they wished to engage in unlimited battle with a Congress that had the votes and the will to render the Court powerless. Having neutralized the president, the Congress was in no mood to brook interference with its policies by the Supreme Court. The problem for Chase was that of assessing the circumstances under which the Court would apply the pressures of power and those under which it would acquiesce in the will of Congress. In hindsight it seems unlikely that a judicial rebuke to Congress in 1868 would have been tolerated, given the legislative mood, and that the Court more likely would have suffered a severe, perhaps fatal, blow had it in its political discretion miscalculated a calculated risk. For all the lack of cohesion on Chase's Court, the chief did manage to obtain unanimity on this politically sensitive decision.

In the fall of 1869 the Court again appeared to be flirting with its own demise when it docketed the case of *Ex parte Yerger*[81] in which another Mississippi editor had petitioned for a writ of *habeas corpus*, this time under the original Judiciary Act of 1789. With renewed vigor Congress threatened the Court with extreme measures, forbidding it to hear political questions—their nature to be determined by Congress—and prohibiting the exercise of judicial review altogether, but neither came to a vote since Yerger's attorney reached an agreement with the government by which he would be protected from military harassment, thereby rendering the case moot.

In the 1869 term Chief Justice Chase wrote the opinion for a divided Court in *Texas v. White*,[82] an opinion which the chief considered his finest and one with memorable rhetoric but one which left the immediate issue in a state of confusion. In fairness to Chase the opinion needs to be divided into two parts, the jurisdictional question which Chase used to enunciate a theory of permanance in the American union and the holding on the merits which was later overruled. Through its governor Texas brought suit to enjoin the payment of a group of bonds owned by Texas prior to the war and negotiated by the state while a member of the Confederacy. Originally Texas had acquired the bonds—$10,000,000 worth at 5 percent—from the federal government in payment of certain boundary claims, and the legislature provided that the bonds might not be transferred to another party without the endorsement of the governor. In 1862 after Texas had joined the Confederacy the legislature repealed the provision requiring gubernatorial endorsement and empowered a military board to use the bonds for purchasing supplies. Subsequently the board contracted with White and others to buy war materials in exchange for some of the bonds but when the war ended, Texas sought to reclaim the bonds on the ground that they had been illegally transferred without the governor's endorsement.

Prior to reaching the substantive issue the Court had to decide whether Texas had standing to sue which in turn required a clear statement on the meaning of secession and the nature of the union. On this point Chase was firm, clear, thorough. Under the Articles of Confederation the colonies had formed a union which they declared to be "perpetual" which in turn became "a more perfect union" in the language of the Constitution, a progression that contemplated permanency. In Chase's eloquent declaration: "The Constitution, in all of its provisions, looks to an indestructible Union, composed of indestructible states." Thus, Chase concluded, "Texas continued to be a state, and a state of the Union" in spite of her acts of rebellion under which she temporarily gave up the rights and privileges of membership. "These new relations imposed new duties upon the United States. The first was that of suppressing the Rebellion. The next was that of reestablishing the broken relations of the state with the Union. . . ." Texas was entitled to sue and the case fell within the original jurisdiction of the Court.

In this, the significant part of his opinion for American constitutional law, Chase accomplished three things. First, he wrote into the law the results of the Civil War as well as Lincoln's theory of the union as opposed to the state suicide theory which he had earlier espoused. Second, he essentially approved of the principles of Reconstruction, presumably even their constitutionality although this was not technically before the Court; and third, he recognized as legitimate the provisional government of Texas that was in existence before the state had been permitted to send representatives to Congress. Unfortunately there were three dissenters, Grier, Swayne and Miller, on the matter of jurisdiction but only Grier maintained that Texas had been constitutionally out of the Union. Swayne and Miller simply contended that Congress must make the decision as to the status of a state whose rights had temporarily been suspended. On the merits of the case Chase declared that Texas was entitled to recover the bonds since the statute repealing the requirement of the governor's endorsement was intended to aid the rebellion and was therefore of no legal effect. Furthermore, anyone who accepted the bonds should have satisfied himself that the legislature had placed illegal restrictions on their transfer. In 1885 the Court declared that the latter proposition "must be regarded as overruled."[83]

Undoubtedly the issue which most clearly exemplifies Chase's inability to lead intellectually and one which severely taxed him personally—to the point of being one of the causes of his breakdown in health—was the Court's handling of the legal tender question. As secretary of the treasury, Chase had reluctantly supported the issuance of "greenbacks"—millions of dollars worth of paper money—to circulate as legal payment for debts. Overcoming his constitutional scruples, he became "convinced that, as a temporary measure, it (was) indispensably necessary" to the war effort. Now as chief justice he faced the uncomfortable task of repudiating his own policies or giving them constitutional support, and in choosing the former he diminished not only his own stature but that of the Supreme Court as well.

Originating in Kentucky the case of *Hepburn* v. *Griswold*[84] was first argued at the December term in 1863, reargued in 1868 and finally decided in 1870. Amidst unusual external political shenanigans along with sharp internal divisions, four members of the Court, speaking through the chief, held the Legal Tender Act of 1862 unconstitutional as it applied to any debts contracted prior to its passage, thus confining the decision without coming to grips with the key issue whether Congress might permit the use of legal tender notes at all. That issue was settled, however, in 1872 just two years after the *Hepburn* decision when the Court in an unprecedentedly brief time reversed itself and held the Legal Tender Acts valid as to preexisting or *post facto* contracts, the chief now writing for four dissenters.[85] Speaking for the majority was President Grant's recent appointee, William

Strong, who was expected to take the position he did although, despite conjecture, there is no evidence that Grant had exacted a promise or that Strong had agreed to any bargain. Strong maintained that if Congress might constitutionally give treasury notes the character and quality of money there was no distinction between their applicability to debts made before or after the law's enactment. He then argued that the Legal Tender Acts had been deemed necessary to the preservation of the union, that under its enumerated powers Congress had a wide choice of means for their execution and that nothing in the Constitution prohibited what Congress had done.

Chase in dissent disagreed. Reiterating what he had written in *Hepburn* Chase contended that the measures were not "a means appropriate, plainly adapted, really calculated to carry into effect any express power vested in Congress." There was, he said, no connection between the power to coin money and the "inference that the government may, in any contingency, make its securities perform the functions of coined money, as a legal tender in payment of debts."[86]

This was not an easy time for the chief justice. When the *Hepburn* case was discussed in conference, it will be recalled that the Court consisted of eight members and the original vote was 4 to 4 which would not have established any firm holding. Justice Grier, old and infirm, originally voted with Swayne, Miller and Davis to declare the Legal Tender Act unconstitutional. Then, when making some remarks inconsistent with his original position and so informed by a colleague, he changed his vote.[87] It appeared that in his enfeebled state he was not quite certain what his vote meant. Meanwhile Congress provided that any federal judge who had attained the age of 70 and had served at least ten years might retire and receive his current salary for life. Upon the unanimous urging of his brethren with Justice Field as spokesman Grier was persuaded to quit, which he did effective January 31, 1870, just prior to the handing down of the *Hepburn* opinions. Charles Fairman in his detailed analysis of the Chase years suggests that the Court was in no condition to settle the legal tender question.[88] It had now become a 4 to 3 decision, although Chase wrote at the end of his opinion that in conference Grier had agreed with the majority. Chase, it seems, was determined to press his view into constitutional law, but given external events he should have known it would not be permanent.

Congress had increased the size of the Court to nine members, and given Grier's resignation, President Grant now had two appointments to the high bench. In spite of his usual bumbling Grant managed to choose two justices who would join the three dissenters in *Hepburn* to make up the majority of five to reverse Chase and his three supporters, Clifford, Nelson and Field. Grant first nominated Secretary of War Ebenezer R. Hoar, an able, independent man who had incurred the wrath of enough senators to bring about his rejection. For Grier's vacated seat Grant chose Edwin M. Stanton, who was approved by the Senate immediately but who died within a few days of his confirmation. Upon the recommendation of Hoar, Grant then appointed William Strong, a distinguished state judge from Pennsylvania and Joseph P. Bradley, a successful and skillful attorney from New Jersey. Grant was accused in some quarters of "packing the Court" in order to obtain a favorable ruling on the legal tender question, but Grant did what every president before and after him had done, choose people whose views were compatible with his own with no commitment on the part of the appointees that they would vote in a certain way on a specific case.

It was at the very end of Chase's life and at the time of his impaired health that the Court construed the newly adopted Fourteenth Amendment,[89] the text of which had in part been authored by Chase himself. He was, however, incapable of doing more than joining Field's dissent without writing an opinion, but he was on record as giving the amendment's clauses a much broader application than that granted by Miller and the majority.

IMPEACHMENT OF A PRESIDENT

At the height of one of the Court's most difficult moments, the consideration of the *McCardle* litigation, Chief Justice Chase had to spend the better part of two months presiding over the impeachment trial of President Andrew Johnson. Characterized as "[t]enacious, scrupulously honest, courageous" but lacking Lincoln's "subtlety, his irresistible chuckle, and his miraculous understanding of the human heart,"[90] Andrew Johnson, very soon after acceding to the presidency, moved on to a collision course with Congress. Interested primarily in restoring the status quo and thus bringing the Southern states quickly back into the Union, Johnson was at odds with the Radicals in Congress who, with an overwhelming majority after the election of 1866, sidetracked the president's program of reconciliation and instituted a punitive scheme of their own. Ignoring the new state governments Congress divided the former Confederacy into five military districts administered by the army and headed by a general whose orders could not be countermanded by the president. Moreover, in addition to refusing to recognize the president's amnesty and pardoning powers, Congress passed the Tenure of Office Act which prohibited the president from removing his own appointees, including those of cabinet level, without the consent of the Senate. For Johnson it was a matter of fighting back or accepting total immobilization of executive authority.

While there had been open talk of impeachment in Congress the catalyst was not furnished until Johnson moved against Secretary of War Edwin M. Stanton who was in league with the Radicals, helping them whenever possible to undermine the president. In August 1867, Johnson demanded Stanton's resignation and upon his refusal, suspended him and placed General Grant in charge of the War Department. This was followed by a bizarre series of events in which: (1) the Senate refused to concur in the president's action; (2) Grant left and Stanton returned; (3) Stanton was dismissed but refused to leave; and (4) Johnson nominated Thomas Ewing as secretary of war, a nomination ignored by the Senate. Ewing had been named on February 22, 1868, and within a week the House voted 128 to 47 to impeach the president. Although the eleven articles of impeachment attributed various improprieties to the president such as the attempt to bring "disgrace, ridicule, hatred" upon the Congress, the only charge with any basis was that he had violated the Tenure of Office Act in removing Stanton. To convict the president 36 votes were necessary, there being 54 Senators. In support of Johnson were 9 Democrats and 3 Johnson Republicans thus leaving the magic number of 7 additional votes needed for acquittal. The trial opened at 1:00 P.M. on

March 5, 1868, and closed on May 26 with the voting on the first ten articles, but practically speaking Johnson was acquitted on May 16 when the vote was taken on the eleventh article, so moved by the Senate since its generalized charges seemed the most likely to succeed. Johnson's acquittal by one vote was a dramatic ending to a constitutional crisis second in importance only to the Civil War itself.

As umpire for the proceedings conducted in such a highly charged political atmosphere, Chase's performance was dignified, fair and discreet. It has in fact been characterized as "the most respectable and admirable action of his entire career,"[91] and given the totality of the circumstances that judgment certainly cannot be faulted. Chase still wished to be the nominee of the Republican Party in 1868 and any show of sympathy toward Andrew Johnson or even neutrality in the proceedings would ruin his chances. Perhaps his standing with the radical Republicans had been ruined in any event. He had after all taken a position against military rule in the *Milligan* case; he had refused to hold court in his circuit that included Maryland, Virginia and North Carolina until the president had proclaimed that the judiciary was not subordinate to the military; and he had avoided sitting on the trial of Jefferson Davis, had in fact postponed it to the point that Davis was ultimately included in President Johnson's general amnesty of December 25, 1868. Furthermore, although unhappy with Johnson's unwillingness to press for full equality for the Negro, Chase nevertheless entertained constitutional scruples against the impeachment and the Radicals knew it. As he confided to a friend during the trial; "to me the whole business seems wrong, and if I had any opinion under the Constitution, I would not take part in it. . . . How can the President fulfill his oath to preserve, protect and defend the Constitution, if he has no *right* to *defend* it against an act of Congress, sincerely believed by him to have been passed in violation of it?"[92]

From the very beginning Chase made it clear that as chief justice he would conduct the trial in a spirit of fairness and impartiality. When the Senate drew up the rules governing the proceedings prior to the commencing of the trial itself, Chase insisted that the rules be adopted by the Senate sitting as a court under his supervision, and at the trial when the Senate argued that it would not be bound by strict legal procedures, Chase again asserted his right as a presiding judge to rule on the admissibility of evidence subject to Senate revision if a vote were called for. He also insisted upon his right to vote in case of a tie. For his attempts at impartiality he drew only scorn from the Radicals who considered him a traitor to their cause and accused him of appeasing the Democrats in order to obtain that party's nomination. But Chase the politician was not without high motives, and always in tension with his ambition was a strong adherence to Christian principles ever so evident in his lifelong battle for the rights of black people. This was a time when Chase's second nature won out over his baser instincts and one of his biographers, although inclined to be overly flattering to Chase, was on the mark when he concluded: "At no time in his life did he show more calmness, good judgment, and foresight than in the impeachment trial; and for his efforts to raise the proceedings above a partisan investigation, and to hold them to their proper character of a judicial process, he deserves the credit of averting a great public danger."[93] One might add that Chase's conduct not only enhanced the integrity and authority of the chief justiceship but also contributed in no small measure to the independence of the presidency and to the preservation of executive authority.

While Harlan Stone's years as chief were in some ways as controversial as Chase's, the reasons for the lack of high marks for leadership in both instances differ in many respects, and yet the Court's internal dysfunctions under both chiefs have some origins in common. First, each presided over a Court on which several justices' intellectual equipment and strength of character were such that they could not be easily persuaded by any chief justice to reconsider their ideas or modify their positions. Such was the case with Miller, Field and Davis under Chase and with Black, Frankfurter, Jackson and Douglas under Stone. Second, both Chase and Stone were reluctant to pressure colleagues to change their views, Chase out of an invincible ego that told him that his was the correct view and what others did was not of great import, and Stone out of humility and an abhorrence of

personal conflict. In a sense both acted more like associate justices than chiefs, but the circumstances in which they served
undoubtedly were strong contributing factors to the inability of
each to orchestrate a smoothly functioning Court.

Harlan Stone's elevation to the chief justiceship in 1941 after
having served on the Court for fifteen years was met with universal approval. Lawyers, judges, politicians and laymen lauded
the appointment and the Senate confirmed it without dissent,
but there had been some discordant voices. Back in 1929 when
Stone was being mentioned as Taft's successor, Taft had written
to his son Charles, that "Stone is not a leader,"[94] and even
Stone's friend, Judge Augustus N. Hand, had voiced doubts
about his leadership "because of a certain inability to express
himself orally and to maintain a position in a discussion."[95]
How prescient they were. For the second time in the Supreme
Court's history an outstanding associate justice elevated to
chief would turn out to be, not a failure certainly, but less than a
great success as the man in charge.

During Stone's five years as chief the Court's personnel
changed only slightly. Owen Roberts, the only holdover from
the Hughes Court of the 1930s, remained on the Court bench
until 1945 when, just a year before Stone's death, he resigned
and was replaced by Harold Burton, Harry Truman's first appointment. Joining the Court at the time of Stone's promotion
was James F. Byrnes who resigned after one year of service and
was replaced by FDR's final appointee, Wiley Rutledge. Except
for the single years of Byrnes and Burton, the Court under Stone
consisted of Roosevelt appointees, Hugo Black, Stanley Reed,
Felix Frankfurter, William O. Douglas, Frank Murphy, Robert
Jackson, and Wiley Rutledge plus Owen Roberts. New Dealers
all, except for Roberts, once on the Court they varied significantly in their views of constitutional interpretation, and as
fairly young men—from Douglas at 40 to Frankfurter at 56—they
were vigorous, ambitious and while not ideologically immov-
able, were nevertheless relatively consistent in outlook. Excepting Frankfurter, the prominent legal scholar with a mental rigor
second to none, all had been successful politicians. Predictions
that Stone would "find no sharp divergence of opinion among
his colleagues" and that there would be "virtual unanimity" on
the tribunal could not have been more wrong as the group early
began to divide, often bitterly, over the emerging issues.

Leadership Minimized in the Short-Term Chiefs

Within a few months of Stone's first term the Japanese had bombed Pearl Harbor and all but his final term saw him in charge during the years of World War II. Naturally much of the significant litigation to reach the Court grew out of the war itself, and to complicate matters, FDR was inclined to use the justices for special assignments that the war had spawned. Roberts was on the committee investigating Pearl Harbor; Byrnes was being consulted on economic planning; later, Jackson was America's special prosecutor at the Nuremberg trials. All of this meant that the Court was frequently operating at less than full strength and although it may have been a contributing factor, it was not the major reason for the weaknesses in Stone's leadership. He had had the good fortune to be able to observe two models of court management first-hand, Taft for five years and Hughes for ten, but for reasons deep in his psychological makeup he was incapable of emulating either, and very soon the Court became a fragmented body with individual justices exercising more influence on their colleagues than the chief.

In part this was the result of Stone's style of managing the weekly conference which was seen not as a chief-directed meeting, but as a chief-moderated "university seminar"[96] in which the permissive quality of participation may have been interesting and enlightening but was inappropriate to the Court's role. Unlike a university seminar in which no agreement on the issues need be reached, the Supreme Court must seek a majority vote and a decision, and if the chief justice does not exert pressure to that end, one or more of his colleagues will fill the void. Nevertheless, Stone stuck to the principle of free and open debate, partly because he had not always been happy over the Hughes' method of moving expeditiously, even to the point of cutting off discussion. Hughes opened the conference on Saturday at noon and adjourned promptly at four-thirty; Stone began at eleven in the morning and adjournment often came as late as six o'clock, and even then additional conferences would be scheduled for Monday, Tuesday or even Wednesday of the following week.

Although Justice Douglas wrote that "Stone's tolerance of full and free discussion produced a most healthy environment for judicial work,"[97] and Alpheus Mason, Stone's biographer, contends that: "Emphasis on deliberation, the disposition to encourage free-wheeling discussion, to magnify the role of the conference, are to Stone's credit,"[98] the fact remains that on balance Stone's leadership in this respect was wanting. Frankfurter said it well when he suggested that good work could not be done after long conferences. In his view after four hours the law of diminishing returns sets in as the justices are mentally fatigued.[99]

Given Stone's temperament, as a result of which he always remained the participant rather than the leader, he was not able to calm the charged atmosphere, to act as a moderating force, to restore harmony in the midst of bitter debate and frayed tempers. Thus, seemingly free debates often became endless bickering and escalated into personal animosities, all of which might have been controlled had Stone been of a different persuasion. Despite the lack of social cohesion on Stone's Court he was well liked by his colleagues, and with a little firmness and a posture of intellectual neutrality rather than partisanship he might have kept personal discord out of the conference room.

Although an inordinate amount of time was spent debating the merits of the controversies before it, the Court's annual average of cases decided by full opinion—with a low of 127 in 1943 and a high of 154 in 1946—did not differ greatly from the Hughes years. Stone wrote 145 opinions during his five years as chief (more per term than any of his colleagues), 96 of which were as spokesman for the majority, but he was in dissent more often than any chief before or since his incumbency. This is a reflection of the fierce intellectual independence not only of Stone but of the other members of the Court as well. A spirit of compromise was only minimally present as each justice insisted on maintaining his own position, and the chief was equally adamant as he refused to alter his views in order to remain in the majority as other chiefs had done in the past. As admirable as this intellectual integrity may be, it does not produce a cohesive court nor a chief who is in control of the opinion assignments in the overwhelming majority of cases.[100]

In a number of the significant cases a majority led by Justice Black determined the outcome and Black as the senior associate either wrote or assigned the writing of the opinion. In his own opinion assignments, Stone favored the justices whom he respected the most—Douglas, Frankfurter or Roberts—with a greater share of the important cases and he assigned fewer to Murphy and Rutledge whom he considered "weak sisters."[101]

Leadership Minimized in the Short-Term Chiefs

Like all chiefs, Stone took on his share of the more controversial and difficult cases, and some were so politically sensitive and constitutionally unprecedented that even Stone's valiant attempts to justify the results were not always convincing. Among these were the notorious cases of the German saboteurs, the trial for war crimes of Japanese General Yamashita, and the exclusion of Japanese-Americans from the west coast, all of which found Stone upholding the government. In another emotionally charged case, however, he spoke for the majority in reversing the conviction of Nazi propagandist George Sylvester Viereck on the ground that the prosecution had misconstrued the foreign agent registration statute. In twelve war-related civil liberties cases Stone wrote the Court's opinion in only four, although he was in the majority in all but two, thus generally controlling the opinion assignments.[102]

Controversial to this day are the cases upholding executive and subsequently congressional power to single out American citizens of Japanese ancestry for treatment that can be justified, if at all, only under conditions of extreme emergency. At issue were military proclamations made pursuant to a presidential order and later approved by Congress, that first established a curfew for all persons of Japanese ancestry, alien and citizen alike, and second, ordered the removal from their homes and the resettling of 112,000 Japanese Americans in "relocation centers in the interior of the country." In *Hirabayashi* v. *United States* Stone spoke for six members of the Court upholding the curfew and giving the war powers of the government a broad construction. In his view the Constitution gives the president and Congress "wide scope for the exercise of judgment and discretion in determining the nature and extent of the threatened injury or danger and in the selection of the means for resisting it."[103] Although the entire Court agreed to uphold the curfew, Murphy, Rutledge and Douglas wrote separate concurrences dissociating themselves from Stone's sweeping language. When the Court was asked to judge the constitutionality of the entire military program of curfew, exclusion from designated military areas and removal from the west coast, the Court managed to confine its decision to the exclusion order only and avoided ruling on the legality of the relocation centers. This time Stone assigned the opinion to Justice Black who spoke only for four;

Frankfurter wrote a separate concurrence; Roberts, Murphy and Jackson protested bitterly against permitting the military to abridge constitutional rights.[104]

In *Ex parte Endo*[105] the Court considered the validity of a relocation and detention order and unanimously held, through Justice Douglas, that Mitsuye Endo was entitled to be released by the War Relocation Authority, not on constitutional grounds but because the language authorizing the evacuation program had nowhere used the word "detention." It seems doubtful that in these cases involving the appropriate use of military authority over civilians in wartime that Stone and the majority would have incurred congressional wrath had they overturned the military orders as well as the executive and legislative authorization. It was not the hostile confrontational-type situation faced by Chase and his Court as they grappled with military rule under Reconstruction.

Stone, however, was unwilling to substitute a judicial judgment for that of the military and it may be that it is too great a risk for a judge to decide that the commander-in chief cannot temporarily suspend rights during a war in which the nation's very existence is at stake. Stone may also have remembered that when Chief Justice Taney said that the president could not suspend the writ of *habeas corpus*, Abraham Lincoln ignored the judicial command. Stone was consistent when he wrote a concurrence to Black's opinion holding that the phrase "martial law" in the organic act establishing government for Hawaii did not intend the supplanting of civilian courts by military tribunals. Agreeing with that principle, Stone, however, could not support Black's broad view that except for military government over occupied territory military tribunals could never be substituted for civilian courts. Contending that in an unusual emergency martial law may be necessary for protecting the public safety,[106] Stone wrote a concurrence virtually identical to that written by Chase in the *Milligan* case; neither would lay an unqualified restriction on Congress during conditions of an extreme national emergency.

In two unusual cases, one at the beginning and one at the end of the war, Stone chose to speak for the Court as it wrestled with unprecedented appeals. In late June 1942 German submarines landed eight members of the German marine infantry, four at

Leadership Minimized in the Short-Term Chiefs

Amagansett Beach, Long Island, and four at Ponte Verde Beach, Florida, all of whom discarded their uniforms. Dressed as civilians and armed with explosives, they moved to various parts of the country intent on committing sabotage. Within two weeks they were apprehended by the FBI and on July 8 were being tried by a military commission of eight army generals appointed by President Roosevelt. The president's proclamation establishing the tribunal declared that enemy saboteurs were subject to the laws of war and would have no access to the regular American courts. Very quickly defense counsel moved for Supreme Court review of the legality of the military commission, and for the first time in twenty-two years the Court met in a special summer session to hear the case. In a brief *per curiam* opinion it upheld the jurisdiction of the military tribunal which adjudged the Nazi saboteurs guilty.[107] Six were executed, one was given a life sentence and one, thirty years at hard labor. When the Court met in the fall of 1942 in its regular session, Stone wrote a detailed opinion for a unanimous Court in which he maintained that the president and Congress, acting under the war powers in the Constitution, had adequate authority to create the commission. This he buttressed with the argument that the commission was an appropriate vehicle for trying unlawful combatants under the Articles of War adopted by Congress. Dealing with the *Milligan* precedent Stone observed correctly that it was inappropriate since Milligan was a civilian and the German saboteurs were not. More significant than the ruling was Stone's insistence that even in total war the Supreme Court will determine the legality of the government's actions against the enemy.

After the surrender of the Japanese a military commission was established by General MacArthur to try Japanese General Yamashita for crimes committed during the occupation of the Philippines. Yamashita was found guilty of violating the laws of war by permitting his troops to commit brutal atrocities and was sentenced to death. Once again the legality of the commission was questioned. Unable to obtain unanimity Stone wrote a rather weak opinion upholding the right of Congress to create such tribunals, declaring that the Supreme Court was concerned only with "the lawful power of the commission to try the petitioner for the offense charged"[108] and not with the question of guilt or innocence. It was important for Stone and the majority to assert the Court's authority to review the powers of Congress and the president to create such ad hoc tribunals, but implicit in the dissenting opinions of Rutledge and Murphy was the charge that the Court will not really clamp down on the use of arbitrary power against the enemy during and immediately following wartime conditions.

The one other war-related civil liberties case in which Stone was able to obtain unanimity was *Baumgartner* v. *United States*.[109] In this instance the Court set aside the denaturalization of a German-American citizen accused of allegiance to the German Reich. Totally split, however, was the Court in *Schneiderman* v. *United States*[110] in which the majority held that the citizenship of Communists cannot be revoked on the ground that they favor the overthrow of the government by force and violence (Stone in dissent). Nor could the chief obtain agreement in *Hartzel* v. *United States*[111] in which the majority including Stone upheld the right of a person to attack the war, the president, England and the Jews in vicious invective or in *Cramer* v. *United States*[112] in which Cramer's conviction for treason (he had befriended one of the Nazi saboteurs) was overturned by a majority (Stone in dissent).

The justices also split in *Girouard* v. *United States*[113] (Stone again in dissent) in which the majority held that the oath of citizenship provision under the Naturalization Act of 1940 requiring one to support and defend the Constitution did not bar a person who refused to bear arms. This case was particularly difficult for Stone since he had earlier dissented in cases in which the Court had upheld statutes denying citizenship to pacifists.[114] Now he was in dissent from a majority that had espoused his earlier position, but he maintained that consistency required him to support a law which Congress had revised in order to conform to the Supreme Court's earlier judgment.

Also decided during the war years were several significant civil liberties cases involving, first, the rights of blacks and, second, crucial problems of religious liberty, and as was generally the case under Stone the Court was split into warring camps. Clearly a landmark case was that of *Smith* v. *Allwright*[115] in which the Court overruled an earlier decision and declared unconstitutional the notorious "white primary," a device by which blacks had been kept out of the Democratic primary and thus had been effectively disenfranchised. Since the nominee of the Democratic party had little or no opposition in the general election, victory in the primary was the key to success, and if blacks could not vote in the primary they were politically neutralized. Beginning in the 1920s a series of cases had reached the Court, culminating in 1935 in the ruling that the Democratic Party of Texas was a private organization and thus not subject to the constitutional restraints of the Fourteenth Amendment which applied only to government or state action.[116] Logically Stone should have written the opinion in the *Allwright* case since just prior to his promotion to chief justice, he had laid the groundwork for what the majority now agreed upon.

In the case of *United States* v. *Classic*[117] he had declared for the Court that several election commissioners in Louisiana who had falsified election returns in a contest for Representative to Congress in a Democratic primary were properly indicted under the federal criminal code. In order to reach that conclusion Stone first had to make the point that the right to vote in a primary is a right secured by the Constitution and within the reach of Congress to protect. He did so by contending that the primary was an integral part of the election process and that the right to choose in every aspect of that process was a right protected by Article I, Section 2 of the Constitution. Exclusion of black voters from party primaries was not at issue in *Classic,* but it seemed strange indeed that primaries were now elections in which federal law could protect the integrity of the vote but were at the same time the preserve of private clubs whose membership might be restricted to white voters.

Stone assigned the opinion in *Smith* v. *Allwright* to Justice Reed who was joined by all but Justice Roberts in invalidating the white primary, a move that not only emphasized judicial consistency but moral necessity as well. Yet, discarding precedents of such late vintage always raises the question of stability in the law and of the fickleness of the judges who are saying: we made a mistake, let's undo it. Judges are not supposed to make mistakes of that magnitude. As Roberts said in his terse dissent: "The instant decision . . . tends to bring adjudication of this tribunal into the same class as a restricted railroad ticket, good for this day and train only."[118]

Another example of the justices' change of mind is seen in the notorious Jehovah's Witnesses cases in which one precedent was overruled in less than a year and another in less than three.

In 1940 the Court had sustained the constitutionality of a school's flag salute requirement over the protests of Jehovah's Witnesses who contended that their religious liberty had been curtailed.[119] Frankfurter had written for a majority of eight, with then Associate Justice Stone, alone in dissent, insisting that this was coercion by the state as it compelled children to profess a belief that violated their deepest religious convictions. It was, said Stone, a clear suppression of free speech and of the free exercise of religion.

In 1942 the Court decided another case brought by Jehovah's Witnesses, *Jones* v. *City of Opelika*,[120] in which the majority held that the Witnesses were subject to a municipal ordinance imposing a license tax on the privilege of selling books or pamphlets either on the streets or house to house. To the Witnesses' contention that it was a tax on religion and therefore a violation of the First Amendment as applied to the states through the Fourteenth, Justice Reed answered that the sales were more commercial than religious. As might be expected, Stone dissented, but in an act of contrition never before seen on the Supreme Court, Justices Black, Douglas and Murphy appended a note to the Stone dissent stating that they believed the flag salute case had been wrongly decided. Taking this as an invitation to try again, the Witnesses initiated litigation challenging the flag salute. Meanwhile Justice Byrnes who had been a part of the majority in *Opelika* resigned and was replaced by Wiley Rutledge, a turn of fate for the Witnesses, for on the docket was a group of cases growing out of their activities.

First was the renewed attack on the compulsory flag salute, *West Virginia State Board of Education* v. *Barnette*;[121] second, was a reargument scheduled in *Opelika* and two companion cases; and the third involved a local tax that had been applied to the Witnesses' proselytizing.[122] Rutledge joined a majority which decided all five cases in favor of the Jehovah's Witnesses, thus overruling both the original flag salute decision and the first *Opelika* case. In one sense Stone might deserve congratulations for bringing a majority around to his libertarian point of view, but on the other hand a Supreme Court that changes its mind before the fallout has settled from its previous pronouncement is hardly providing the kind of guidance that is needed by the hundreds of judges around the nation.

Leadership Minimized in the Short-Term Chiefs

With one major exception the Court under Stone was able to agree much more readily in commerce clause litigation than on civil liberties issues. In three landmark cases *Edwards* v. *California*,[123] *Wickard* v. *Filburn*[124] and *Parker* v. *Brown*[125] the Court was unanimous although in *Edwards* it split into two distinct groups when it came to providing reasons for the decision. For the majority Byrnes, following Stone's advice,[126] invalidated the California law making it a crime to transport indigent migrants into the state on the ground that the law was an unconstitutional burden on interstate commerce. Writing separate concurrences in which Black and Murphy joined, Justices Douglas and Jackson would have resurrected the privileges and immunities clause of the Fourteenth Amendment as they argued that the right of free movement from state to state is an attribute of national citizenship. It was Stone's view of the issue that prevailed, however, as he was able to swing a majority of his colleagues away from placing a construction on the privileges and immunities clause that had been rejected for a half a century.

In *Wickard* the justices had no problem in upholding the marketing quotas of the Agriculture Adjustment Act of 1938 as a legitimate regulation of interstate commerce even when applied to a farmer who grew wheat only for his own use. "Home grown wheat," said Justice Jackson to whom Stone had assigned the opinion, "in this sense competes with wheat in commerce." Stone wrote the opinion in *Parker* v. *Brown* which upheld California's state monopoly for controlling the marketing of raisins. This was not a burden on commerce, Stone argued, since the regulation took place before interstate shipment and was thus a local activity.

These cases were in Stone's early years as chief when unanimity was attainable, but in 1944 in the very difficult case of *United States* v. *Southeastern Underwriters Association*[127] the squabbling among the brethren was clearly in evidence. At issue was whether the Sherman Act could be used to prosecute fire insurance companies engaged in rate-fixing schemes. This was not so tough a question on its face, but back in 1869 the Court had held that insurance was not interstate commerce and could be regulated by the states without running afoul of the commerce clause.[128] In order to permit the application of the Sherman Act the Court would now have to overrule a long-standing precedent and raise havoc with the network of state laws in existence. Adding to the confusion was the fact that only 7 justices had participated in the case and had divided 4 to 3 which meant that no clear majority of 5 was in agreement. Stone tried but failed to persuade the Court to issue a *per curiam* opinion stating that a constitutional issue of such gravity involving the overruling of a long-standing precedent should not be decided by less than a full Court.[129] Ultimately Black wrote for the majority of 4 holding that the insurance business was interstate and that the Sherman Act was applicable. Stone, Frankfurter and Jackson wrote separate dissents.

In his analysis of Chief Justice Stone, David Danelski suggests that under Stone the old tradition of loyalty to the Court's opinion was gone as the justices refused to acquiesce in silence in order to obtain unanimity.[130] In part this was Stone's doing as he ran a permissive conference and by his own example would not join majorities with which he disagreed in order to obtain a consensus. At the same time it is doubtful that he or anyone else could have persuaded Black to abandon his position in *Southeastern Underwriters*, or Murphy and Jackson to remain silent in *Korematsu*, or Roberts to join him and the others in overruling *Grovey*. Stone did not run a tight ship, but he did not choose the crew. In spite of the personal antagonism, the intellectual differences, the militancy on holding to doctrinaire positions, the Court was productive and creative, and with all its unpleasant internal bickering, it settled some of the most controversial issues of the day—of any day—and as we shall see, a change of chiefs did not result in cooperation, compromise and accommodation among these fiercely independent, sometimes perversely so, nine very human, human beings appointed for life.

Fred Vinson viewed the Court's role in the American system as a limited one and the chief's role as a managerial executive who must rely heavily on staff assistance which he did, including the hiring of a third law clerk and an administrative assistant. Chiefs before Stone had had only one clerk or, in the early days, none at all. Stone had added a second. In keeping with his concept of a limited judicial function, in which the Court should hear only cases of national importance, Vinson was responsible for reducing the Court's work load by significant proportions. Whereas under Hughes and Stone the Court had been disposing of some 200 cases each term by full opinion, the average annual number dropped to half that during the Vinson years, with a high of 142 during his first term and a low of 84 in 1951. Vinson believed that the justices were overworked, a view that was strengthened after the deaths of Rutledge and Murphy in 1949 at the relatively early ages of 59 and 55. Of course Vinson himself was to die at age 63 after only seven years of this lightened workload. In any event the Court was soon accused of denying *certiorari* in cases that ought to be heard,[131] and one commentator charged that the number of cases decided had "plummeted to a new and scandalous low" due in part to "sheer laziness,"[132] and even in Vinson's final term the number had only inched upward to a meager 104.

Vinson had to work with those same determined justices that had not made life easy for Stone—Black, Douglas, Frankfurter and Jackson—and although the public feuding of the past had faded, the deep divisions continued to surface in the large numbers of concurrences and dissents. Also remaining on the bench from the Stone years were Reed and Burton who, after the deaths of Murphy and Rutledge, generally joined the chief and President Truman's new appointees, Tom C. Clark and Sherman Minton, to make up a conservative majority that more often than not supported the government against the individual in civil liberties cases.

In viewing the cold statistics of the Court's work under Vinson, one can conclude first, that the chief bent every effort to align himself with the majority and thus to control the opinion assignments. He did so in over 86 percent of the cases, never falling below 80 percent in a given term, and in 1949 he voted with the majority in 82 out of 86 decisions, or more than 95 percent of the time. Prior to Stone's tenure chiefs had registered very few dissents—less than 6 per term—but Stone broke all records with an average annual number of 18. Vinson, while not matching the low number of the pre-Stone years, averaged just over 9 per term. A somewhat different picture of Vinson's leadership emerges, however, when one views the number of cases decided unanimously. Prior to the 1930s the Court fairly consistently decided over 80 percent of their cases unanimously, a situation that began to change under Hughes and became markedly different thereafter. During Vinson's first term, the Court decided only 36 percent of its cases unanimously; in 1948 the number had dropped to 26 percent[133] and in 1952 to 22;[134] in 1950 it rose to 39 percent,[135] but then dipped to 27 in 1951.[135] All of which indicates that the chief, while able to control opinion assignments most of the time, faced intractable dissenters in an extraordinarily large number of cases. Unlike Stone, however, he seldom joined them.

Initially there was considerable disparity in the workload division although there does not appear to have been any dissatisfaction with the chief's allocation. In Vinson's first term, for example, he assigned 27 opinions to Justice Black, 24 to Justice Douglas and only 7 and 6 to Justices Rutledge and Burton respectively. This pattern remained for two terms but then began to abate and in his final three terms the assignments ranged from a high of 10 to 12 for some to a low of 6 to 9 for the others.[137] Contributing to satisfaction among the brethren with the workload was the fact that Vinson rarely reserved the landmark cases for himself, but generously spread them among the justices. As a result, however, the number of opinions of lasting consequence authored by Vinson can be counted on the fingers of one hand,[138] or with magnanimity, on two.

Without doubt Vinson's greatest permanent success was in the area of racial segregation in which he not only spoke for a unanimous Court in two major cases, but also boldly cleared the path for the momentous decisions later orchestrated by Earl Warren. In the first, *Shelley* v. *Kraemer*,[139] the pernicious "restrictive covenant" whereby successive property owners were bound to resell or lease their property only to members of their own race was given an overdue burial.[140] Since the Fourteenth Amendment had after 1888 been held consistently to bar action only by the state governments and not by private persons the Court had earlier upheld restrictive covenants as private agreements and thus untouchable by constitutional limitations.[141] In a carefully reasoned opinion Vinson first reiterated the old rule that private parties might enter into racially restrictive covenants, but second, such agreements were unenforceable in the state courts. Heretofore, the term "state action" was held to encompass legislation and executive or administrative rules;

now it embraced the courts as well. In Vinson's words: "state action as that phrase is understood for the purposes of the Fourteenth Amendment, refers to exertions of state power in all forms." It was a neat way of dealing with the issue in that no precedent was overruled, but the inclusion of courts as a part of "the full panoply of state power" rendered the racially restrictive covenant useless.

Obtaining unanimity once again Vinson wrote for the Court in *Sweatt* v. *Painter*,[142] the practical effect of which was to end racial segregation in universities and to invite an attack on it at all levels of education. *Sweatt* involved the validity of a dual law school system in Texas in which under the "separate but equal" doctrine Texas had built a separate law school for blacks. In ordering a black student admitted to the previously all white University of Texas law school, Vinson's opinion emphasized the unequal aspects of the black and white law schools. Not only were the physical facilities unequal, but so were countless intangibles such as reputation and size of the faculty, volumes in the library, and lack of any alumni support. Most important, Vinson pointed out, some 85 percent of the population of the state, including "most of the lawyers, witnesses, jurors, judges and other officials" with whom a black graduate would be dealing as a practicing lawyer were excluded from the black law school. Once again as in *Shelley* Vinson avoided overruling any precedents, but in taking intangible factors into account in the "separate but equal" equation he set the stage for the doctrine's inevitable demise and, equally significant, he spoke for a unanimous Court.

In other areas of constitutional liberty the Vinson record is spotty. His personal tendency was to uphold the government and the majority of civil liberties cases saw a preponderence of concurrences and dissents which frequently left the rules in a state of uncertainty. A major exception to Vinson's pro-government stand were those cases in which the right to hold meetings in public places were subject to the unrestrained discretion of an administrative official. He wrote for a unanimous Court reversing the conviction of two Jehovah's Witnesses who had been arrested for conducting a meeting in a public park in Havre de Grace, Maryland.[143] Such a denial, said Vinson, "in the absence of narrowly drawn, reasonable and definite standards for the officials to follow" amounted to prior restraint on freedom of speech. And for a near unanimous Court—only Justice Jackson dissented—he set aside a conviction of a Baptist minister who had been denied a permit to hold religious meetings on the streets of New York after he had made contemptuous and demeaning remarks about other religions. In Vinson's view the issue was suppression, not punishment.[144]

In both cases Vinson wrote in the libertarian tradition of Hughes and Stone, but his reputation tends to rest on his allegedly illiberal position taken in other cases, particularly in *Dennis* v. *United States*[145] in which the Court upheld the conviction of the top Communist Party officials in the country and in *American Communications Association* v. *Dowds*[146] which sustained the validity of the anti-Communist oath required of labor union officers under the Taft–Hartley Act. In both cases Vinson spoke only for a plurality of four as the Court was badly divided between the majority, the concurrences, and the dissents, divided in part over the chief's narrow interpretation of the "clear and present danger" doctrine. Maintaining that speech may be punished or prevented "only when force is very likely to follow an utterance before there is a chance for counter argument," he concluded in *Dowds* that Congress, in requiring union officials to take an anti-Communist oath, was dealing with the possibility of a political strike that could be called by Communist bosses, an evil which Congress might anticipate and prevent. As to the abridgment of speech Vinson declared that under certain circumstances free speech had to give way to a greater value: "When the effect of a statute or ordinance upon the exercise of the First Amendment Freedoms is relatively small and the public interest to be protected is substantial, it is obvious that a rigid test requiring a showing of imminent danger to the security of the Nation is an absurdity." This modification of Justice Holmes original idea that the danger or evil triggered by speech must be imminent presaged Vinson's opinion in the *Dennis* case a year later.

In September 1949 the eleven top-ranking leaders of the Communist Party of the United States were convicted of conspiracy to organize the party as a vehicle to teach and advocate the overthrow of the government by force and violence and of advocating such overthrow. Again speaking for only four justices

(Clark did not participate, Jackson and Frankfurter filed separate concurrences and Black and Douglas wrote dissents), Vinson once more defended what he considered a valid restriction on speech. This time, however, he was able to rely on the highly respected Judge Learned Hand who had written the opinion upholding the Communist convictions in the Federal Court of Appeals for the Second Circuit. As in *Dowds* the thrust of Vinson's opinion was that the danger posed by speech need not be "imminent" in the Holmesian sense. Preserving the government, said Vinson, was the "ultimate value" and overthrow "by force and violence is certainly a substantial enough interest for the Government to limit speech." Adopting Judge Hand's formulation that in each case courts must ask "whether the gravity of the 'evil,' discounted by its improbability, justifies such invasion of free speech as is necessary to avoid the danger," Vinson contended that the government need not wait until a conspiratorial group attempted its overthrow but could punish them for advocating the duty and necessity of doing so. Since the evil was very grave and the danger substantial, the "improbability" of success must be discounted.

Vinson's novel construction of "clear and present danger" was not to attain any permanence, for in 1957 just six years later the Court, in distinguishing carefully between advocacy of abstract doctrine and incitement to unlawful action made it virtually impossible to send a member of the Communist Party to jail for violating the Smith Act,[147] and in 1969 the Court declared emphatically that the advocacy of any idea is protected as long as it does not call for immediate illegal action.[148]

A great deal of confusion was added to the law of searches and seizures by Chief Justice Vinson as he circumvented some long-standing rules in order to support the government. It was in his first term as chief that he wrote the opinion for the majority in *Harris* v. *United States*,[149] an opinion clearly at odds with previous search and seizure doctrine which had held that a search incident to a valid arrest permitted an officer to search a suspected person for weapons and to search the "immediate area" of arrest and no more. In *Harris*, however, FBI agents armed with an arrest warrant for forgery but no search warrant ransacked the suspect's four-room apartment for five hours. Although they found nothing to support the alleged forgery, they discovered a sealed envelope containing Selective Service documents. Convicted for illegal possession of the documents, Harris contended that the evidence used to send him to jail was the result of an invalid search, but Vinson saw the matter differently, insisting that given the circumstances the police acted properly. In a harshly critical dissent Frankfurter suggested that such a view of the Fourth Amendment "considers it on the whole a kind of nuisance, a serious impediment to the war on crime."

A year later Vinson was not able to forge a majority in a similar case[150] when the Court ruled in favor of the defendant, but he reemphasized his position in dissent as he wrote: "To insist upon the use of a search warrant in situations where the issuance of such a warrant can contribute nothing to the preservation of the rights which the Fourth Amendment was intended to protect, serves only to open an avenue of escape for those guilty of crime and to menace the effective operation of government which is an essential precondition to the existence of all civil liberties."

Following the replacement of Justices Murphy and Rutledge by Clark and Minton, however, the chief justice once again commanded a majority support for his point of view. In 1950 he assigned the opinion to Justice Minton in *United States* v. *Rabinowitz*[151] which also involved an extended search incident to lawful arrest but without a search warrant. Once again Frankfurter lashed out at the majority, calling the reasoning unjustified by previous decisions of the Court and characterizing the opinion as "progressive distortion" and "an uncritical confusion" of what is and what is not permitted under the Fourth Amendment.

Merits of the argument aside, the search and seizure cases during Vinson's tenure indicate how a shift in personnel is often the crucial factor in determining whether the chief's views or those in opposition will prevail. This supports my thesis that a chief justice can exert leadership in the sense of converting those who disagree with him only in extraordinary circumstances. Furthermore, if changes in personnel mean changes in the law, and clearly this has been the case, life tenure for the judges makes good sense. If the law of the land is to remain stable and predictable, changes must come slowly and incrementally and judicial life tenure, admittedly not without its faults, is a strong structural support for continuity in the fundamental rules by which the nation is governed.

Two remaining cases deserve mention since they lend emphasis to the generalization that Fred Vinson's instincts were to support the government and to avoid placing restraints on public officials. Both involved the public seizure of private property as a means of consummating a settlement in a typical labor-management quarrel. In one, the *United Mine Workers* case,[152] Vinson wrote the Court's opinion in which he brushed aside all precedents in order to uphold President Truman's seizure of the nation's coal mines as the means to break a strike. It was a struggle between titans as the powerful leader of the United Mine Workers, John L. Lewis, defied the president, as well as a temporary lower court injunction, but Lewis lost. He and his union had to pay heavy fines when Vinson declared that the Norris–LaGuardia Act which restricted the issuance of injunctions in labor disputes was not applicable to government-seized properties. Disruption of government processes was anathema to Vinson, and he was determined to find a rationale for punishing the disrupters. In this telling phrase in his opinion, the chief's view of the matter is manifestly apparent: "the course taken by the union carried with it such a serious threat to orderly constitutional government, and to the economic and social welfare of the nation that a fine of substantial size is required in order to emphasize the gravity of the offense." This opinion has been called "brutal" because it ignored opposing precedents and reached the result from "the necessities of the situation rather than from the doctrine of the cases."[153]

A few years later when President Truman used his power to attempt to avert a strike through seizure of an industry, Vinson could persuade only two of his colleagues to support his position in upholding the president. Climaxing a long dispute between the steel companies and the United Steelworkers of America over terms of a new collective bargaining agreement was President Truman's seizure of the steel mills through an order issued to his secretary of commerce, William Sawyer. The order was not based on any statutory authority but simply on an executive judgment that a strike would be detrimental to national defense at a time when American troops were engaged in combat in Korea. Every member of the majority of six wrote his own concurring opinion, but the upshot was that the president had no inherent constitutional power to seize private property.[154] As Vinson saw matters, speaking for the three dissenters, the president had acted "in full conformity with his duties under the Constitution." Vinson wrote of the "Genius of the Founding Fathers, who created a Government subject to law but not left subject to inertia when vigor and initiative are required" and of their concern for the danger in "Executive weakness." Within that context the chief justice argued that "extraordinary times" called for "extraordinary powers," that given the threat of "terrifying global conflict" it was not "a time for timorous executive action." As in the *Mine Workers* opinion Vinson based his case on "necessity" and he spoke with conviction if not with caution or concern for power expanded beyond prudent limit.

These views, however, conformed quite logically to Fred Vinson's fundamental judicial philosophy, namely, that the Court should be a passive agent, intervening to restrain the other branches only as a last resort and under exceptional circumstances and, for the most part, this was the posture of the Supreme Court under his chief justiceship. He was able to orchestrate a unified approach to public law in only one area, but one of the utmost importance in American life, that of the legal status of black Americans; otherwise the Court tended to be as rancorous and divided as it was under Stone. Yet unlike Stone, Vinson, whether by loose conviction, by gentle persuasion or simply fortuitous circumstances was able to identify with the majority most of the time and thus to retain control of opinion assignments.

LEGACY

In assessing the impact of Chief Justices Chase, Stone and Vinson on the Supreme Court and on American public law, we must conclude first that none can be ranked among the best of the fifteen. Of the three only Stone deserves a seat in the hall of fame for judicial craftsmanship, and the bulk of his reputation was made during his sixteen years as an associate justice rather than in his five as chief. As managers of the Court's business these short-term chiefs were not incompetent, but neither were they in control of the Court in the manner of Marshall, Hughes

or Warren, or even of the more passive chiefs like Fuller and
Waite. We know that in part flaws in their leadership can be attributed to the colleagues with whom they worked, in part to
their brief terms in office, but always ingredients in the mix—
precisely how much we can never know—are those subtle, elusive, dimly perceived individual factors bound up in personality
and temperament.

Of the three chiefs only Chase was consumed with ambition
to be president, and his almost pathological pursuit of this unattainable goal overshadowed his public successes including the
chief justiceship. It was a common witticism among official
Washington that as Chase readied for his daily shave he addressed his mirror with the words: "Good morning, Mr. President,"[155] and Carl Sandburg, while paying tribute to Chase's
ability, called Chase's "growing ambition" a "chronic personal
ailment beyond remedy or softening."[156] Two of the justices
who served with him similarly acknowledged his greatness but
could not refrain from alluding to his unending quest. Justice
Miller wrote after Chase's death that he "was a great man and a
better man than public life generally leaves one, after forty
years of service,"[157] that he was "endowed by nature with a
warm heart and vigorous intellect, but all these warped, per-
verted, shrivelled by the selfishness generated by ambition. I
doubt if for years before his death, his first thought in meeting
any man of force, was not invariably how can I utilize him for
my presidentical aspirations."[158]

Writing in 1870 after Chase had suffered the paralytic stroke,
Justice Davis called him "the most ambitious man, except
Douglas, that I ever knew personally. As long as the Presidency
is not reached, everything else that he has obtained is as dust
and ashes."[159] For Chase the chief justiceship was simply a way
station on the road to the presidency, and yet Chase could never
do a job half-heartedly or haphazardly. He was an energetic chief
and judge. There is, however, very little in the way of permanence in his opinions, and his record as Court manager is adequate if mediocre, in both instances because his concentration
on the job was never quite full. Only in his opinion in *Texas* v.
White do we find memorable rhetoric worth repeating—an indestructible union of indestructible states—a fitting and re-
sounding epitaph to the Civil War.

Chief Justice

His presiding over President Johnson's impeachment trial was a high point of personal integrity, judicial propriety and sound constitutional practice and his performance in this regard may be his greatest contribution to the nation's highest judicial office. Chase, however, could not lead the Supreme Court even though he carried the necessary intellectual baggage. His lack of warmth and his inability to see humor in the human condition militated against his establishing those vital relationships that form the basis of personal leadership. Although Chase, in Sandburg's words, "filled the eye as an imposing figure, the pathos ran over his life and letters of a man trying to be a hero to himself, not knowing when he was hero, marplot or simple snob."[160] A sympathetic biographer suggests that Chase's defects in character were a lack of a sense of proportion and a lack of imagination,[161] that he "had a certain Roman aggressive virtue about him" that repelled others and made personal relations difficult.[162] Thus, had Salmon Chase been able to serve as chief without the shadow of the presidency playing about his head, it still seems doubtful that his talents, great and varied as they were, would have enabled him to manage a small group with any more than moderate success.

Stone's talents lay in another direction, that of the scholar-judge, and while not wanting in personal warmth, humor and imagination, he, like Chase, was unable to direct the tiny judicial oligarchy with the degree of success attained by other chiefs. Stone, however, has left a rich personal legacy to American constitutional law, forged primarily, although not exclusively, during his sixteen years as an associate justice. It has been suggested, in fact, that Stone's philosophy of judging "was more fully and carefully developed than that of any Chief Justice since Marshall."[163] Judge Learned Hand called Stone "a thorough craftsman as a judge" who "had the right—absolutely right—measure of the Court's limitation on constitutional questions. . . . but he was not an originator and, to be frank, had not an original mind."[164] Not original perhaps, but as a result of his constant searching for objectivity in his opinions he was unquestionably creative. Along with Holmes, Brandeis and Cardozo whom he often joined in dissent, Stone believed in deferring to the legislative judgment, but he was aware that legislatures do transgress constitutional boundaries on occasion and that the Supreme

Leadership Minimized in the Short-Term Chiefs

Court is duty bound to call a halt. He thus formulated his now famous dictum in a footnote to an opinion in a traditional due process case: "There may be a narrower scope for operation of the presumption of constitutionality when legislation appears on its face to be within a specific prohibition of the Constitution such as those of the first ten Amendments, which are deemed equally specific when held to be embraced within the Fourteenth."[165]

Essentially Stone proposed two standards of judicial review: deference to the legislative judgment when normal political forces can act as a check on the lawmakers, but strict scrutiny of any interference with individual liberties, with the burden of proof of constitutionality in such circumstances resting with the government. Later Stone refined the principle into what he called the "preferred position" of First Amendment guarantees, and out of Stone's original concept has grown an entire framework of standards for adjudication of constitutional rights, including not only those specifically written into the Constitution but derivative rights, such as the right of a woman to an abortion, now deemed "fundamental" by the Court. The standard is also used in "equal protection" litigation which involves allegations of unfair discrimination or unreasonable classification on the basis of race, alienage, age, illegitimacy or gender.

During Stone's years as associate justice the burning issues before the Court were first, the powers of state legislatures to regulate the economy and to raise revenues for new functions; second, the extent to which the federal government might use its authority over interstate commerce and taxation to develop a national "police power"; and third, the emerging civil liberties questions. In many of the cases involving state or national regulation Stone was in dissent when the conservative majority on the Hughes Court would strike down state laws under the due process clause of the Fourteenth Amendment using the "liberty of contract" or "business affected with a public interest" rationale or would negate national laws as outside the delegated powers of Congress. Stone's dissents later became the law as the Court, during his lifetime, discarded one by one the old doctrinal props that had prevented both state and federal regulation of the economy. He must have taken great personal satisfaction in speaking for the Court in 1939 and in 1941 when it buried two old landmark cases, *Collector* v. *Day*[166] and *Hammer* v. *Dagen-hart.*[167] In the first he brought to a close the "reciprocal immunity" system whereby the salaries of state and federal employees could not be taxed by the opposite government;[168] in the second, he conceded that the commerce clause authorized Congress to outlaw child labor and establish minimum wages and maximum hours.[169]

Stone "attempted to accommodate personal flexibility with institutional constraint,"[170] which in practice permits judges to change the meaning of the Constitution, but they must always give sound and compelling reasons for doing so. In a column entitled, "Stone, a Gifted Judge," written shortly after the chief's death, Arthur Krock declared that Stone's opinions, and principally his dissents "make up a noble and important literature",[171] and he chose to quote from Stone's dissent in *United States* v. *Butler*[172] in which the majority had declared the first Agriculture Adjustment Act unconstitutional. Strung together, these quotes sum up succinctly Stone's judicial philosophy and his legacy. The power of courts to declare a statute unconstitutional should be subject to two judicial guides, he suggested: "One is that courts are concerned only with the power to enact statutes, not with their wisdom"; the other is that judges should remember that "the only check upon our own exercise of power is our own sense of self restraint. . . . Courts are not the only agency of government that must be assumed to have capacity to govern." This admonition together with Stone's view of the exceptional judicial role in civil liberties cases produce a balanced model that any Supreme Court judge would be wise to adopt.

More successful as an internal manager of the Court's business than either Chase or Stone, Vinson the judge was severely limited by his profound belief that the vitality of the American system depended upon a strong and effective government that should not be hampered by judicial controls even when individual liberties were at stake. Thus, his record shows an absolute unwillingness to curb executive authority or to invalidate acts of Congress. However, he placed state laws and administrative acts of state officials in a different category. Presiding over and writing for a unanimous Court in civil rights cases, he deserves eternal credit for advancing the cause of black Americans by creating the judicial foundation for a construct that terminated constitutionally sanctioned racial discrimination. One critic charged that for "all his undoubted patriotism, chauvinist style, Vinson, less than any other man who headed the Court . . . understood the real meaning of Democracy,"[173] but this is a narrow view of a statesman who may have erred on the side of authority in that eternal conflict with liberty, but he did so out of a sincere concern for national safety and not in a mean spirit of suppressing dissent. Vinson, like Chase, had a relatively minor impact on American law, but neither can be adjudged a failure as a chief, for they were men of substance, who, while not precisely tailored for the role of chief justice, never demeaned the office and in some measure contributed to its sustenance and growth.

NOTES

1. Richard B. Morris, *John Jay, the Nation and the Court*, Boston: Boston Univ. Press (1962), p. 3.
2. Henry Flanders, *Life and Times of the Chief Justices of the Supreme Court of the United States*, Vol. 1, Philadelphia: J. B. Lippincott (1858), p. 88.
3. Kenneth B. Umbreit, *Our Eleven Chief Justices*, New York: Harper and Brothers (1938), p. 25.
4. Ibid., p. 40.
5. As quoted in Charles Warren, *The Supreme Court in U.S. History*, Vol. 1, Boston: Little, Brown (1922), p. 173.
6. Umbreit, op. cit., p. 55.
7. See Leon Friedman, "John Rutledge" in Leon Friedman and Fred L. Israel, eds., *The Justices of the United States Supreme Court 1789–1969: Their Lives and Major Opinions*, New York: Chelsea House (1969), pp. 33–49, for a detailed discussion of John Rutledge and his brief stay on the Court.
8. As quoted in Warren, op. cit., p. 130.
9. Ibid., p. 139.
10. Herbert Alan Johnson, "William Cushing," in Friedman and Israel, op. cit., p. 66.
11. William Garrott Brown, *The Life of Oliver Ellsworth*, New York: Macmillan (1905), p. 26.
12. Umbreit, op. cit., p. 101.
13. As quoted in Brown, op. cit., p. 185.
14. 2 Dallas 419 (1793).
15. 3 Dallas 171 (1796).
16. 3 Dallas 386 (1798).
17. 3 Dallas 6 (1794).
18. Irving Dilliard, "John Jay," in Friedman and Israel, op. cit., p. 29.
19. As quoted in Flanders, op. cit., p. 384.

20. *Champion and Dickason* v. *Casey*, U.S. District Court for the District of Rhode Island, June 2, 1792.
21. *Hayburn's Case*, 2 Dallas 409 (1792).
22. Warren, op. cit., v. 1, pp. 110–11.
23. Flanders, op. cit., p. 429.
24. Michael Kraus, "Oliver Ellsworth," in Friedman and Israel, op. cit., p. 233.
25. 3 Dallas 199 (1796).
26. *Wiscart* v. *D'Auchy*, 3 Dallas 321 (1796).
27. *Hills* v. *Ross*, 3 Dallas 184 (1797); *Brown* v. *Von Braam*, 3 Dallas 344 (1797); *Clerke* v. *Harwood*, 3 Dallas 342 (1797); *Brown* v. *Barry*, 3 Dallas 365 (1797); *Hollingsworth* v. *Virginia*, 3 Dallas 378 (1798); *Bingham* v. *Cabot*, 3 Dallas 382 (1798); *Wilson* v. *Daniel*, 3 Dallas 401 (1798).
28. David P. Currie, "The Constitution in the Supreme Court: 1789–1801," 48 *University of Chicago Law Review* 819 (Fall 1981), p. 885.
29. As quoted in Albert Bushnell Hart, *Salmon Portland Chase*, New York: Haskell House (1969) p. 11.
30. Ibid., p. 23.
31. Umbreit, op. cit., p. 249.
32. Hart, op. cit., p. 96.
33. Ibid., pp. 112–13.
34. Ibid., p. 196.
35. Carl Sandburg, *Abraham Lincoln: The War Years*, New York: Harcourt, Brace & Co. (1936), Vol. 1, pp. 651–52.
36. Ibid., p. 652.
37. Hart, op. cit., p. 223.
38. Ibid., p. 220.
39. Ibid., pp. 274–89.
40. Sandburg, op. cit., v. 3, p. 112.
41. Ibid., p. 592.
42. Alpheus Mason, *Harlan Fiske Stone: Pillar of the Law*, New York: Viking Press (1956), p. 40.
43. Ibid., p. 64.
44. Ibid., p. 67.
45. Ibid., p. 72.
46. Letter to The Reverend Frederick D. Hayward, as quoted in Mason, ibid., p. 65.
47. Ibid., pp. 137–38.
48. Charles Beard in a prefatory note to Samuel J. Konefsky, *Chief Justice Stone and the Supreme Court*, New York: Macmillan (1945), p. xviii.
49. Mason, op. cit., p. 445.
50. Ibid., p. 268.
51. See Eugene C. Gerhart, *America's Advocate: Robert H. Jackson*, New York: Bobbs-Merrill (1958), pp. 229–33 for an account of the Stone and Jackson appointments.
52. Mason, op. cit., p. 567.
53. Gerhart, op. cit., p. 231.
54. Ibid., p. 230.

Leadership Minimized in the Short-Term Chiefs

55. David J. Danelski, "The Chief Justice and the Supreme Court," unpublished dissertation, University of Chicago (1961), p. 69.
56. Ibid., p. 71.
57. *New York Times*, June 7, 1946, p. 4.
58. Ibid.
59. See Gerhart, op. cit., pp. 277–88 for a complete analysis of the Truman-Hughes-Pusey accounts, including copies of letter and memoranda.
60. *New York Times*, June 7, 1946, p. 18.
61. Quoted in Charles Fairman, *History of the Supreme Court of the United States*, Vol. 6, part I, New York: Macmillan (1971), p. 34.
62. Ibid., p. 70.
63. Ibid. See pp. 160–74 for an analysis of the judiciary bills and subsequent Judiciary Acts of 1866 and 1867 and Chase's involvement in their passage.
64. Ibid., pp. 36–44.
65. 4 Wallace 2 (1866).
66. 16 Wallace 36 (1873).
67. 4 Wallace 475 (1867).
68. 6 Wallace 318 (1868).
69. *Ex parte Milligan*, p. 120.
70. Ibid., p. 127.
71. Ibid., p. 140.
72. 4 Wallace 277 (1867).
73. 4 Wallace 333 (1867).
74. Warren, op. cit., v. 3, pp. 173–76.
75. *Mississippi* v. *Johnson*, 4 Wallace 475 (1867).
76. *Georgia* v. *Stanton*, 6 Wallace 50 (1867).
77. Ibid., p. 77.
78. Charles Fairman suggests that Chase may have wished to make the ground for dismissal the fact that Georgia did not admit that the new freedmen were a part of the state's political society. As counsel for Georgia, Charles O'Conor, had argued that the state of Georgia stood before the Court as a state composed "exclusively . . . of white male citizens," Fairman, op. cit., p. 393.
79. 6 Wallace 318 (1868).
80. Fairman, op. cit., p. 437.
81. 8 Wallace 85 (1869).
82. 7 Wallace 700 (1869).
83. *Morgan* v. *United States*, 113 U.S. 476 (1885).
84. 8 Wallace 603 (1870).
85. *Legal Tender Cases* (*Knox* v. *Lee* and *Parker* v. *Davis*), 12 Wallace 457 (1871).
86. Ibid., p. 574.
87. Fairman, op. cit., p. 716.
88. Ibid., p. 719.
89. *Slaughter House Cases*, 16 Wallace 36 (1873).
90. Thomas Graham Belden and Marva Robins Belden, *So Fell the Angels*, Boston: Little, Brown (1956), p. 175.

91. Ibid., p. 186.
92. Ibid., p. 185.
93. Hart, op. cit., p. 360.
94. Taft Papers as quoted in Danelski, op. cit., p. 94.
95. Hand letter to Hughes as quoted in Danelski, ibid.
96. Alpheus Mason's phrase in *Stone*, op. cit., p. 589.
97. Justice Douglas as quoted in Mason, ibid., p. 791.
98. Ibid., p. 794.
99. Danelski, op. cit., p. 99.
100. The lack of cohesion was seen immediately at the end of Stone's first term when statistics indicated that 16 of the Court's decisions were split 5–4 and that 36% of the total were nonunanimous. Stone had disagreed with the majority 22 times. The number of dissents gradually increased from 158 during the 1941 term to 165 in 1942, 186 in 1943 and 231 in 1944. See Mason, ibid., pp. 582, 591, 639. See also C. Herman Pritchett, *The Roosevelt Court: A Study in Judicial Politics and Values*, New York: Macmillan (1947), p. 25.
101. Mason, op. cit., p. 793.
102. Stone wrote the opinion of the Court in Ex parte *Quirin*, 317 U.S. 1 (1942); *Viereck* v. *United States*, 318 U.S. 236 (1943); *Hirabayashi* v. *United States*, 320 U.S. 81 (1943); and *In re Yamashita*, 327 U.S. 1 (1946). He joined the majority in *Korematsu* v. *United States*, 323 U.S. 214 (1944); *Ex parte Endo*, 323 U.S. 283 (1944); *Baumgartner* v. *United States*, 322 U.S. 665 (1944); *Duncan* v. *Kahanamoku*, 327 U.S. 304 (1946); *Hartzel* v. *United States*, 322 U.S. 680 (1944). Stone registered dissents in *Schneiderman* v. *United States*, 320 U.S. 118 (1943); *Girouard* v. *United States*, 328 U.S. 61 (1946); and *Cramer* v. *United States*, 325 U.S. 1 (1945).
103. 320 U.S. 81 (1943) at 93.
104. *Korematsu* v. *United States, supra*, note 102.
105. 323 U.S. 283 (1944).
106. *Duncan* v. *Kahanamoku, supra*, note 102.
107. *Ex parte Quirin, supra*, note 102.
108. *In re Yamashita, supra*, note 102.
109. *Supra*, note 102.
110. *Supra*, note 102.
111. *Supra*, note 102.
112. *Supra*, note 102.
113. *Supra*, note 102.
114. *United States* v. *Macintosh*, 283 U.S. 605 (1931); *United States* v. *Bland*, 283 U.S. 636 (1931).
115. 321 U.S. 649 (1944).
116. *Grovey* v. *Townsend*, 295 U.S. 45 (1935).
117. 313 U.S. 299 (1941).
118. *Smith* v. *Allwright, supra*, at 670.
119. *Minersville School District* v. *Gobitis*, 310 U.S. 586 (1940).
120. 316 U.S. 584 (1942). Also decided in the same way were two companion cases, *Martin* v. *Struthers* and *Douglas* v. *City of Jeanette*.

121. 319 U.S. 674 (1943).
122. *Murdock* v. *Pennsylvania*, 319 U.S. 105 (1943).
123. 314 U.S. 160 (1941).
124. 317 U.S. 111 (1942).
125. 317 U.S. 341 (1943).
126. See Mason, op. cit., p. 579 for a discussion of Stone's position as stated in a memorandum to Justice Byrnes.
127. 322 U.S. 533 (1944).
128. *Paul* v. *Virginia*, 8 Wallace 168 (1869).
129. Mason, op. cit., p. 619.
130. Danelski, op. cit., pp. 212–13.
131. Fowler V. Harper and A. S. Rosenthal, "What the Supreme Court Did Not Do in the 1949 Term—An Appraisal of Certiorari," 99 *University of Pennsylvania Law Review* 293 (1950).
132. Fred Rodell, "Our Not So Supreme Court." *Look*, July 31, 1951, p. 60.
133. Richard Kirkendall, "Fred M. Vinson," in Friedman and Israel, *The Justices of the United States Supreme Court*, Vol. 4, op. cit., p. 2642.
134. David Fellman, "Constitutional Law in 1952–53," 48 *American Political Science Review*, March 1954, p. 64.
135. David Fellman, "Constitutional Law in 1950–51," 46 *APSR*, March 1952, p. 159.
136. David Fellman, "Constitutional Law in 1951–52," 47 *APSR*, March 1953, p. 127.
137. Statistics were compiled by Tamami Ushiki.
138. John P. Frank, "Fred Vinson and the Chief Justiceship," 21 *University of Chicago Law Review* 212 (Winter 1954), p. 213.
139. 334 U.S. 1 (1948).
140. In *Hurd* v. *Hodge*, 334 U.S. 24 (1948), with the restrictive covenant at issue for the District of Columbia, the Court ruled similarly to *Shelley*, relying on the due process clause of the Fifth Amendment since the equal protection clause of the Fourteenth was applicable only to "states." Chief Justice Vinson again spoke for a unanimous court.
141. *Corrigan* v. *Buckley*, 271 U.S. 323 (1926).
142. 339 U.S. 629 (1950).
143. *Niemotko* v. *Maryland*, 340 U.S. 268 (1951).
144. *Kunz* v. *New York*, 340 U.S. 290 (1951).
145. 341 U.S. 494 (1951).
146. 339 U.S. 382 (1950).
147. *Yates* v. *United States*, 354 U.S. 298 (1957).
148. *Brandenburg* v. *Ohio*, 395 U.S. 444 (1969).
149. 331 U.S. 145 (1947).
150. *Trupiano* v. *United States*, 334 U.S. 699 (1948).
151. 339 U.S. 56 (1950).
152. *United States* v. *United Mine Workers*, 330 U.S. 258 (1947).
153. Frank, op. cit., p. 217.
154. *Youngstown Sheet and Tube Co.* v. *Sawyer*, 343 U.S. 579 (1952).

155. Milton Lomask, *Andrew Johnson, President on Trial*, New York: Octagon Books (1973), p. 277.
156. Sandburg, op. cit., v. 1, p. 147.
157. Charles Fairman, *Mr. Justice Miller and the Supreme Court, 1862–1890*, Cambridge: Harvard University Press (1939), p. 252.
158. Ibid., p. 251.
159. As quoted in Fairman, *History of the Supreme Court*, op. cit., p. 1465.
160. Sandburg, op. cit., p. 146.
161. Hart, op. cit., p. 432.
162. Ibid., p. 423.
163. G. Edward White, op. cit., p. 217.
164. Letter to Alpheus Mason, as quoted in Mason, op. cit., p. 777.
165. *United States* v. *Carolene Products Co.*, 304 U.S. 144 (1938).
166. 11 Wallace 113 (1871).
167. 274 U.S. 251 (1918).
168. *Graves* v. *New York* ex rel. *O'Keefe*, 306 U.S. 466 (1939).
169. *United States* v. *Darby*, 312 U.S. 100 (1941).
170. White, op. cit., p. 219.
171. *New York Times*, April 24, 1946, p. 28.
172. 297 U.S. 1 (1936).
173. Rodell, op. cit., p. 309.

Chapter 6

JUDICIAL LEADERSHIP

IN A FEW INSTANCES the presidential choice of a chief justice has been the president's most enduring contribution to the nation's political culture. This is true of John Adams with his fortuitous choice of John Marshall, of Herbert Hoover with his naming of Charles Evans Hughes, and of Dwight Eisenhower with his appointment of Earl Warren; and one need not press the point very far to include Grant's choice of Morrison Waite and Harding's nomination of William Howard Taft. Although the record of the remaining ten chiefs in no way diminished the reputation of the presidents who appointed them, other positive contributions of most chief executives overshadowed that particular aspect of their stewardship.

In assessing the performance of the men who have occupied the head chair of the nation's highest tribunal, it is evident that the leadership they provided—social, intellectual and managerial—has been qualitatively uneven, that the reasons for exceptional leadership are complex, enigmatic, and in large measure dependent upon imprecise, intrinsic qualities. It has been possible to appraise the impact of the chief on alterations in the Court's internal procedures, to note his influence as a judicial architect, that is, his success in effecting improvements in various aspects of the legal system from court structures to law practice or even prison reform, and to evaluate him as a judge, to analyze his judicial philosophy and his written opinions.

293

Chief Justice

I have not attempted to rank chief justices on any performance scale—with the possible exception of denoting Marshall, Hughes, and Warren as "great"—but considerable variation is evident in both style and result among the fifteen occupants of the office. What accounts for the disparity? There are several underlying causes. First is that vague term, personality, upon which social leadership depends; yet even this is elusive since good leaders do not possess any one type of personality. Some of the chiefs had better rapport with the associate justices than others, but none could be deemed a total failure in this respect. Over half—Marshall, Taney, Waite, Fuller, White, Taft, Vinson, and Warren—had a natural affability that made them easy to like, principally because they instinctively liked others. Some, like Hughes with his reserve, Stone with his vanity, Chase with his ego, were disadvantaged but by no means disabled in their personal relationships. None was abrasive, testy or irritable like McReynolds, and only in the case of Chase was leadership impaired by arrogance and apparent lack of warmth.

We know, however, that being warm, friendly and likable is not in and of itself enough to gain the requisite loyalty and support that is needed to ensure a socially cohesive court. Necessary in addition are firmness, fairness and consistency without which respect for the leader begins to erode, and no amount of pleasantry can compensate for what is lost when there is uncertainty over the rules or when they are administered haphazardly, arbitrarily or in a spirit of favoritism. A lack of firmness in managing the conference was present in varying degrees in Taney, White, and Stone and detracted from the respect in which they were held, and Vinson with his permissive administrative style was unable to stabilize what had already been a rudderless Court under his predecessor.

Personality, which encompasses a host of characteristics, is a major determinant of effective leadership, but the fact that a chief justice must work his will with eight independent souls not chosen by him is a formidable barrier to his success. Thus, it can be argued that the better leaders among the chiefs were simply lucky, that they happened to be placed in charge of a group largely in agreement with their views. This argument is not without merit but it has only limited application. It may be true that John Marshall's influence was at its height when only Federalists sat on the bench, but the Federalist monopoly ended with Jefferson's appointment of William Johnson in 1804. By 1811 all of the original Federalist appointees excepting Marshall and Bushrod Washington had been replaced and yet some of the Marshall Court's greatest decisions were yet to come including *Gibbons*, *McCulloch*, and *Dartmouth College*. And as we know, Joseph Story, who eventually became Marshall's most consistent and ardent champion, was a Jeffersonian appointed by James Madison. Thus Marshall's ability to mass the Court in support of his position depended upon something other than receptive minds.

Charles Evans Hughes faced a strong willed and strongly divided bench during most of his eleven-year tenure and under conditions of a political and constitutional crisis of a magnitude only surpassed by the Civil War. A man of lesser talents might not have been able to maintain the institutional integrity of the Court nor the respect of the nation. Once again, those whom he led were anything but putty in his hands.

During Earl Warren's fifteen years shifting majorities that shared his views did exist and this was undoubtedly a factor in his ability to exorcise from American politics some shabby and malevolent practices. As we have pointed out, however, Fred Vinson had the opportunity but not the inclination or perhaps the will to grapple aggressively with the same issues that Warren insisted on meeting head on.

If the more successful chiefs were not dependent solely on tractable colleagues, was intransigence and stubbornness on the part of associate justices the major cause of the somewhat flawed performances of the others? I think not. Although there has always been a cantankerous justice or two on every Court, one cannot point to the administration of a single chief in which his associates were deliberately uncooperative and unwilling to accept his direction as the titular head. Only for a brief period was Morrison Waite in the embarrassing position of a rejected leader, but by sheer force of character he was able to assume his rightful place very quickly. With Stone and White there was some frustration with the way in which they handled the conference, but never was there any open rebellion, probably because each had a formidable intellect and was an adept legal scholar. William Howard Taft is somewhat of a puzzle since he maintained a strong position of respect while relinquishing the leadership of the conference to Van Devanter, a move that normally would impair a chief's influence and authority. Apparently his consummate social leadership was able to overcome whatever disabilities resulted from his deference to an associate better able to orchestrate the conference.

INTELLECTUAL LEADERSHIP

Of the fifteen chief justices only White and Stone could be called legal philosophers, men truly learned in the law and temperamentally more scholar than politician. They were unquestionably respected for their ideas but their lasting contributions to the law had been formulated when they sat as associate justices, they—along with Hughes—having had this opportunity not available to the remaining twelve incumbents. Compared to other chiefs the record of Stone and White as internal leaders of the Court is relatively weak. They seemed more comfortable in the study or the seminar rather than in the administrator's chair. By contrast those chiefs with minimal legal learning, probably with the capacity for deep analytical thought but without the inclination to pursue it, were, while not the most creative jurists, the Court's most efficient managers. Those persuasive administrative skills attributed to Waite and Fuller, however, while not to be discounted, were not qualitatively as significant to American constitutional development as the doctrinal concepts propounded by Stone and White.

POLITICAL LEADERSHIP

How does one answer the question: which were the better leaders, the legal philosophers or the adroit managers? Unfortunately the answer is elusive. Those chiefs whom I have designated the best in overall performance—Marshall, Hughes, and Warren—had neither the most imaginative minds nor were they necessarily the most deft managers; they were first and foremost very skillful politicians. On the Supreme Court as in any other unit of government political success must be measured both internally and externally. Internally the political dimension cannot be overemphasized. Involving more than smooth

Judicial Leadership

personal relationships, internal politics pervades the entire range of the chief's duties at every stage of the judicial process from organizing and running the conference to assigning opinions to presiding over hearings. In Justice Frankfurter's words, this "deployment of judicial force by the Chief Justice is his single most influential function." "Judicial force" must be deployed in such a manner that the chief's point of view will be reflected in the final product, the Court's opinions, if the chief can be said to have given his colleagues a sense of purpose and direction. Although no chief has been without notable successes, there has been as we have suggested, considerable variation in the performance of the incumbents.

External politics encompasses a plethora of activities, some of which are initiated by the chief. Others are thrust upon him. Ideas for legislation which have improved the Court's efficiency have frequently originated with the chief, or at least the chief has been instrumental in motivating congressional leadership to act. This is certainly true of two of the most important judicial statutes ever passed by Congress, the Acts of 1891 and 1925, both of which were the direct result of lobbying by Fuller and Taft. Extra-Court activities, whether in behalf of reforms in the lower federal and state courts, in law school curricula, in prisons or in judicial administration, have received an impetus by pressures strategically applied by the chief justice. Particularly successful were Taft and Burger and today no chief justice can ignore this component of his office.

External politics of a different nature surfaces when the Court is subjected to a hostile attack by the president, by Congress, or both. How the chief reacts may be crucial in maintaining the institutional integrity of the Court as well as in affecting the direction of national public policy. Always there has been some dissatisfaction with the Court's work on the part of the executive and legislative branches but only occasionally has it reached crisis proportions. When this happens the chief has very limited options since in a public confrontation with the other branches he must rely almost entirely on the prestige of the office. He has no votes and only a small constituency of legal practitioners, academic philosophers and journalists who rarely are unanimous in support of the Court. For the most part in explosive situations in which judicial authority and power was at stake, chiefs have been passive, retreating graciously where possible. John Marshall stood by quietly when Jefferson and his followers initiated the impeachment of Samuel Chase, although he emerged the victor in the battle with Jefferson when in a subtle mixture of censure and withdrawal he wrote the opinion in *Marbury*.

After *Dred Scott* Taney was a powerless, pathetic figure unable to recapture his and to a certain degree the Court's authority. In the *McCardle* fracas Chief Justice Chase refused to invalidate a constitutionally doubtful act of Congress but had he not acquiesced, whatever political capital he possessed would have been inadequate to best Congress in a showdown. Like John Marshall's quarrel with Thomas Jefferson, Hughes' struggle was also with the president and like Marshall, Hughes in a combination of censure and retreat was able to defeat the president's frontal assault on the Court's integrity.

Earl Warren's travails were only secondarily the result of congressional antagonism and primarily with the states in the federal system. Although some of the Warren Court's decisions affected Congress directly—particularly those dealing with investigations—most involved curtailment of state power, desegregation, reapportionment, criminal procedure, and civil liberties generally, and the states' representatives in Congress attempted to curb the Court with scores of proposals for limiting its powers. In this instance the chief's attitude was for the most part one of dignified silence as powerful friends of the Court carried the ball in defeating anti-Court measures. However, in 1963 when, in response to *Baker* v. *Carr* the Council of State Governments had begun a campaign to amend the Constitution including the creation of a "Court of the Union" consisting of fifty state chief justices which might review and overrule Supreme Court decisions, Warren spoke out boldly against it in a speech at Duke University. During the years of his incumbency Warren never faced a president bent on limiting institutional power as did Marshall with Jefferson or Hughes with Roosevelt. Nor were the Warren Court's decisions ever without considerable support throughout the country. The buckshot approach taken by Congress, while harassing and not to be discounted, was never as formidable a political threat as the big cannon aimed by President Roosevelt.

Judicial Leadership

Currently, presidential and congressional disagreement with the Burger Court is concentrated on sniping primarily in two areas—the decisions invalidating anti-abortion laws and those prohibiting any religious exercises in the public schools. Constitutional amendments have been introduced which would overrule the Court, but they have not had the necessary support for passage. Given the lack of presidential follow-through, one surmises that the issues seem more deserving of lip service than of any determined action to reverse the Court. Proposals to limit the Court's jurisdiction in selected areas were introduced in Congress after Ronald Reagan's victory in 1980 but these too are destined for oblivion. Early in his tenure Burger made public responses to criticism of the Court's rulings on desegregation and individual rights, but for the most part he has squandered very little political capital to protect the Court from external attacks. He has instead chosen to concentrate on lobbying for institutional reforms that would streamline judicial procedures and ensure a manageable workload for the Supreme Court.

JUDICIAL POWER: INDEPENDENT, PERSONAL, FLEXIBLE, LIMITED

Only in the judicial branch of the American tripartite system are the personnel, including the leader, appointed rather than elected. Since the chief justice serves for life with the only stricture being the remote possibility of impeachment, he is neither electorally accountable nor obligated in any way to the president who nominated him or to the Senate that concurred in the president's choice. Leadership of the judiciary and of the executive branch is unitary rather than collective or shared as in Congress, but with that the similarity of the chief justiceship to the presidency ends. Presidents choose their own cabinet members, assistants and advisors; a chief justice must work with eight colleagues who are already in place, some of whom resent his leadership even before it begins.

In any system of government that has attained a level of maturity and stability, all of its officials will be confined to a great extent by tradition and custom, forces as significant as any in moderating the official conduct of those in power, and the chief justice is no exception. Not only is he inhibited by the internal procedures that were established by his predecessors, he must also function within the Anglo-American legal framework, a limiting dimension of some magnitude. As formidable as these constraints are, the office of chief justice possesses enough plasticity to permit the incumbent considerable latitude and, excepting John Rutledge, all have left a personal imprint on the Court's work and in greater or less degree on American constitutional development.

Until after the Civil War the role of the chief justice was almost exclusively internal. Primarily the chief managed the Court's caseload which included presiding over the conference, assigning opinions and holding open court sessions along with the onerous task of traveling to and from and sitting on the circuit court. Eventually, the external roles of lobbyist for legislation to improve the judicial branch, national spokesman for law reform and general administrator of the federal court system have come to command a greater share of the chief's time. Modern chiefs have, like presidents, been able to cope because they have persuaded Congress to appropriate funds for additional help. Clearly, however, the more tasks that a chief takes on and the more he must rely on others for advice and information, the less personalized and the more bureaucratic the Court environment becomes.

In spite of the increase in duties of the office over the years, the chief justiceship still requires, as it always has, that the incumbent be a judge whose views of the Constitution and of the law must be thoughtfully formulated and expounded in a written opinion, and no matter how efficient a manager in the manner of a Hughes, or how successful a social leader in the mold of a Taft, his role as a jurist cannot be discounted. He need not be the greatest mind on the Court but he must carry his intellectual weight to retain the respect of his colleagues and of the Court's constituencies in the nation's universities, on the bench, at the bar and in the responsible press. He must also be able to recognize the diverse talents on the bench and use them both to his own advantage and to that of the Court and the nation, for in the final analysis a chief's place in history will be determined by the caliber of the product for which he is responsible. The decisions and the opinions with justifying reasons, though bearing an in-

dividual justice's name, are fundamentally a collegial effort, reflecting the chief's leadership or lack of it.

After the inauspicious beginning under John Jay, John Rutledge, and Oliver Ellsworth, the American chief justiceship became an office in power, prestige and authority second only to
the presidency. Some chiefs may well have made good presidents, although Taft—the only one to hold both positions—was
less successful as president, but the two offices require persons
of different temperaments, for the day-to-day tasks bear little re-
semblance. The chief justice, while obliged to undertake some
roles of a public nature, works primarily outside the spotlights
of the media. He does not hold nationally televised press conferences, address roaring crowds, negotiate with heads of state or
hold leadership of a political party. As chief justice of the United
States he is responsible for the smooth functioning of one of
three independent, yet subtly interdependent, branches of government and within the constraints of time, he oversees the nation's judicial machinery. More important, however, as chief
justice of the Supreme Court he manages a very small group and
he must do so with a deft and subtle mixture of personal leadership and technical know-how, but he must also be a scholar, attuned to the teachings of history.

The chief must be sensitive to institutional limits: the language of the Constitution, the judicial gloss created by his predecessors and the discipline of Anglo-American law, and he
must always be alert to the political and social needs of the
times. When he does face the public, he must act with restraint
and dignity and without political or personal rancor against his
critics. To excel in the multiple roles of chief justice requires extraordinary talent and although none of the incumbents has performed perfectly, a few have been brilliant; several have been
distinguished; all have been competent. Despite the partisan
politics frequently surrounding the appointment of chief justices, the record of their service has been uncommonly free of
petty partisanship, and not so much as a hint of personal or public corruption has ever tainted the office. It is a record to which
the nation can point with justifiable pride.

SELECTED BIBLIOGRAPHY

BOOKS

Abraham, Henry. *The Judicial Process.* 4th ed. New York: Oxford Univ. Press, 1980.

———. *Justices and Presidents.* New York: Oxford Univ. Press, 1974.

Baker, Leonard. *John Marshall: A Life in Law.* New York: Macmillan, 1974.

Baum, Lawrence. *The Supreme Court.* Washington, D.C.: Congressional Quarterly Press, 1981.

Belden, Thomas Graham, and Marva Robins Belden. *So Fell the Angels.* Boston: Little, Brown & Company, 1956.

Beveridge, Albert. *The Life of John Marshall.* 4 vols. Boston: Houghton Mifflin Co., 1916–1919.

Blaustein, Albert P., and Roy M. Mersky. *The First Hundred Justices.* Hamden, Conn.: Archon Books, 1978.

Brown, William Garrott. *The Life of Oliver Ellsworth.* New York: Macmillan, 1905.

Carp, Robert A., and Ronald Stidham. *The Federal Courts.* Washington, D.C.: Congressional Quarterly Press, 1985.

Corwin, Edward S. *John Marshall and the Constitution.* New Haven: Yale Univ. Press, 1919.

Cox, Archibald. *The Warren Court.* Cambridge: Harvard Univ. Press, 1968.

Curtis, Benjamin R. *A Memoir of Benjamin Robbins Curtis.* 2 vols. Boston: Little Brown, 1879.

Danelski, David J. "The Chief Justice and the Supreme Court." Diss. Univ. of Chicago 1961.

Bibliography

————, and Joseph S. Tulchin, eds. *The Autobiographical Notes of Charles Evans Hughes*. Cambridge: Harvard Univ. Press, 1973.

Douglas, William O. *The Court Years 1939–1975*. New York: Random House, 1981.

Dunham, Allison, and Philip B. Kurland, eds. *Mr. Justice*. Chicago: Univ. of Chicago Press, 1956.

Elman, Philip, ed. *Of Law and Men: Papers and Addresses of Felix Frankfurter 1939–56*. Hamden, Conn.: Archon Books, 1965.

Fairman, Charles. *History of the Supreme Court of the United States*. Vol. 4, part 1. New York: Macmillan, 1971.

————. *Mr. Justice Miller and the Supreme Court, 1862–1890*. Cambridge: Harvard Univ. Press, 1939.

Faulkner, Robert. *The Jurisprudence of John Marshall*. Princeton: Princeton Univ. Press, 1962.

Fehrenbacher, Don E. *The Dred Scott Case*. New York: Oxford Univ. Press, 1978.

Fish, Peter Graham. *The Politics of Federal Judicial Administration*. Princeton: Princeton Univ. Press, 1973.

————. *The Office of Chief Justice*. Charlottesville: White Burkett Miller Center, Univ. of Virginia, 1984.

Flanders, Henry. *Life and Times of the Chief Justices of the Supreme Court of the United States*. Vol. 1. Philadelphia: Lippincott, 1858.

Frank, John P. *Justice Daniel Dissenting*. Cambridge: Harvard Univ. Press, 1964.

————. *Marble Palace*. New York: Knopf, 1968.

Frankfurter, Felix. *The Commerce Clause Under Marshall, Taney and Waite*. Chapel Hill: Univ. of North Carolina Press, 1937.

————, and James Landis. *The Business of the Supreme Court* New York: Macmillan, 1928.

Friedman, Leon, and Fred L. Israel, eds. *The Justices of the United States Supreme Court 1789–1969: Their Lives and Major Opinions*. New York: Chelsea House, 1969.

Gerhart, Eugene C. *America's Advocate: Robert H. Jackson*. Indianapolis: Bobbs-Merrill Co., 1958.

Glad, Betty. *Charles Evans Hughes and the Illusion of Innocence*. Urbana: Univ. of Illinois Press. 1966.

Halpern, Stephen, and Charles Lamb, eds. *Supreme Court Activism and Restraint*. Lexington, Mass.: Heath, 1982.

Hart, Albert Bushnell. *Salmon Portland Chase*. New York: Haskell House, 1969.

Hendel, Samuel. *Charles Evans Hughes and the Supreme Court*. New York: Russell, 1951.

Highsaw, Robert B. *Edward Douglass White: Defender of the Conservative Faith*. Baton Rouge: Louisiana State Univ. Press, 1981.

Howe, Mark DeWolfe, ed. *Holmes–Pollock Letters.* Cambridge: Harvard Univ. Press, 1941.

Hughes, Charles Evans. *Addresses.* 2nd ed. New York: Harper, 1916.

———. *The Supreme Court of the United States.* New York: Columbia Univ. Press, 1928.

Jackson, Robert H. *The Struggle for Judicial Supremacy.* New York: Knopf, 1941.

Katcher, Leo. *Earl Warren: A Political Biography.* New York: McGraw-Hill, 1967.

King, Willard L. *Melville Weston Fuller, Chief Justice of the United States, 1888–1910.* New York: Macmillan, 1950.

Kluger, Richard. *Simple Justice.* New York: Knopf, 1975.

Lash, Joseph P. *From the Diaries of Felix Frankfurter.* New York: Norton, 1975.

Levy, Leonard. *The Supreme Court Under Earl Warren.* New York: N.Y. Times Book Co., 1972.

Lewis, Walker. *Without Fear or Favor.* Boston: Houghton Mifflin, 1965.

Lomask, Milton. *Andrew Johnson, President on Trial.* New York: Octagon Books, 1973.

Magrath, C. Peter. *Morrison R. Waite: The Triumph of Character.* New York: Macmillan, 1963.

Mason, Alpheus T. *Harlan Fiske Stone: Pillar of the Law.* New York: Viking Press, 1956.

———. *The Supreme Court from Taft to Warren.* New York: Norton, 1964.

———. *William Howard Taft: Chief Justice.* New York: Simon and Schuster, 1964.

McElroy, Robert. *Grover Cleveland: The Man and the Statesman.* 2 vols. New York: Harper, 1923.

Morgan, Donald. *Justice William Johnson.* Columbia: Univ. of South Carolina Press, 1954.

Morris, Richard B. *John Jay, the Nation and the Court.* Boston: Boston Univ. Press, 1962.

Murphy, Walter. *Elements of Judicial Strategy.* Chicago: Univ. of Chicago Press, 1964.

Murray, Charles Augustus. *Travels in North America.* Vol. 1. London: R. Bentley, 1839.

Nevins, Allan. *Grover Cleveland: A Study in Courage.* New York: Dodd Mead, 1932.

Newmyer, Kent. *The Supreme Court Under Marshall and Taney.* Arlington Heights: AHM Publishing, 1968.

Palmer, Ben W. *Marshall and Taney: Statesmen of the Law.* New York: Russell and Russell, 1966.

Bibliography

Pfeffer, Leo. *This Honorable Court.* Boston: Beacon Press, 1965.

Pollock, Jack Harrison. *Earl Warren, The Judge Who Changed America.* Englewood Cliffs, N.J.: Prentice-Hall, 1979.

Pringle, Henry F. *The Life and Times of William Howard Taft.* 2 vols. New York: Farrar and Rinehart, 1939.

Pritchett, C. Herman. *The Roosevelt Court: A Study in Judicial Politics and Values.* New York: Macmillan, 1947.

Pusey, Merle J. *Charles Evans Hughes.* New York: Macmillan, 1951.

Sandburg, Carl. *Abraham Lincoln: The War Years.* Vol. 1. New York: Harcourt, Brace and Co., 1936.

Schmidhauser, John, ed., *Constitutional Law in American Politics.* Monterey, Calif.: Brooks Cole, 1984.

Scigliano, Robert. *The Supreme Court and the Presidency.* New York: Free Press, 1971.

Semonche, John E. *Charting the Future: The Supreme Court Responds to a Changing Society, 1890–1920.* Westport, Conn.: Greenwood Press, 1978.

Smith, Charles W. *Roger B. Taney: Jacksonian Jurist.* New York: Da Capo Press, 1973.

Steamer, Robert J. *The Supreme Court in Crisis.* Amherst: Univ. of Massachusetts Press, 1971.

Story, William W., ed. *The Miscellaneous Writings of Joseph Story.* Boston: Little Brown, 1852.

Sumner, William Graham. *What Social Classes Owe to Each Other.* New York: Arno Press, 1972. (Reprint of 1883 ed.)

Swisher, Carl Brent. *Roger B. Taney.* Hamden, Conn.: Archon Books, 1961.

Trimble, Bruce R. *Chief Justice Waite: Defender of the Public Interest.* New York: Russell and Russell, 1970.

Tyler, Samuel. *Memoir of Roger Brooke Taney.* New York: Da Capo Press, 1970.

Umbreit, Kenneth B. *Our Eleven Chief Justices.* New York: Harper & Bros., 1938.

Warren, Charles. *The Supreme Court in United States History.* Boston: Little Brown, 1923.

Warren, Earl. *The Memoirs of Earl Warren.* New York: Doubleday, 1977.

White, G. Edward. *The American Judicial Tradition.* New York: Oxford Univ. Press, 1976.

———. *Earl Warren: A Public Life.* New York: Oxford Univ. Press, 1982.

Woodward, Bob, and Scott Armstrong. *The Brethren: Inside the Supreme Court.* New York: Simon and Schuster, 1979.

ARTICLES

Alschuler, Albert W. "Burger's Failure: Trying Too Much to Lead." *National Law Journal* (Feb. 18, 1980), p. 19.

Atkinson, David N. "Minor Supreme Court Justices: Their Characteristics and Importance." 3 *Florida State Law Review* 348 (1975).

Bales, Robert F. "Task Roles and Social Roles in Problem Solving Groups." *Readings in Social Psychology,* eds., Maccoby, Newcomb and Harley. New York: Holt. (1958), pp. 437–47.

Bickel, Alexander M. "The Overworked Court." *New Republic* (Feb. 10, 1973), p. 17.

Brant, Irving. "How Liberal Is Justice Hughes." *The New Republic* (July 21, 1937, and July 28, 1937).

Burger, Warren E. "The Special Skills of Advocacy." 42 *Fordham Law Review* 227 (1973).

Currie, David P. "The Constitution in the Supreme Court: 1789–1901." 48 *Univ. of Chicago Law Review* 819 (Fall 1981).

Danelski, David J. "The Influence of the Chief Justice in the Decisional Process." *Courts, Judges and Politics,* eds. W. F. Murphy and C. H. Pritchett. New York: Random House, 1979.

Dennis, Everette E. "Overcoming Occupational Heredity at the Supreme Court." 66 *American Bar Assoc. Journal* 4 (1980).

Ely, John Hart, "The Chief." 88 *Harvard Law Review* 11 (1974).

Fellman, David. "Constitutional Law in 1952–53." 48 *American Political Science Review,* March 1954, p. 64.

Fortas, Abe. "Chief Justice Warren: The Enigma of Leadership." 84 *Yale Law Journal* 405 (Jan. 1975).

Frank, John P. "Fred Vinson and the Chief Justiceship." 21 *Univ. of Chicago Law Review* 212 (Winter 1954).

Frankfurter, Felix. "Chief Justices I Have Known." 39 *Virginia Law Review* 884 (Nov. 1953).

Freund, Paul. "Charles Evans Hughes as Chief Justice." 81 *Harvard Law Review* 4 (1967).

Garraty, J. A. "The Case of the Missing Commissions." *American Heritage* (June 1963), p. 7.

Gossett, William T. "Chief Justice Hughes—A Recollection." *Yearbook 1981.* Washington: The Supreme Court Historical Society, 1981, p. 76.

Haines, Dennis. "Rolling Back the Top on Chief Justice Burger's Opinion Assignment Desk." 38 *Univ. of Pittsburgh Law Review* 63 (1977).

Bibliography

Harper, Fowler V., and A. S. Rosenthal, "What the Supreme Court Did Not Do in the 1949 Term—An Appraisal of Certiorari." 99 *Univ. of Pennsylvania Law Review* 293 (1950).

Hughes, Charles Evans. "Roger Brooke Taney" 17 *American Bar Assoc. Journal* 785–90 (1931).

Hutchinson, Dennis J. "Unanimity and Desegregation: Decisionmaking in the Supreme Court, 1948–1958." 68 *Georgetown Law Journal* 1 (1979).

Klinkhamer, Sister Marie Carolyn. "The Legal Philosophy of Edward Douglas White." 3 *Univ. of Detroit Law Journal* 174 (1957).

Landever, Arthur R. "Chief Justice Burger and Extrajudicial Activism." 22 *Journal of Public Law* 524 (1971).

Mason, Alpheus Thomas. "The Chief Justice of the United States: Primus Inter Pares." 17 *Journal of Public Law* 23 (1968).

McElwain, Edwin. "The Business of the Supreme Court as Conducted by Chief Justice Hughes." 63 *Harvard Law Review* 5 (1949).

Miller, Arthur S. "Lord Chancellor Warren Earl Burger." *Society* (March/April 1973), p. 18.

Moody, Graham B., Jr. "Chief Justice Earl Warren: A Tribute." 2 *Hastings Constitutional Law Quarterly* 15 (Winter 1975).

Morgan, Donald. "Marshall, the Marshall Court and the Constitution." *Chief Justice John Marshall: A Reappraisal*, ed., W. M. Jones. Ithaca: Cornell Univ. Press, 1971.

Morris, Jeffrey B. "The Era of Melville Weston Fuller." *Yearbook 1981*. Washington: Supreme Court Historical Society, 1981, p. 37.

———. "Chief Justice Edward Douglas White and President Taft's Court." *Yearbook 1982*. Washington: Supreme Court Historical Society, 1982, p. 27.

Murphy, Walter. "Marshalling the Court: Leadership Bargaining and the Judicial Process." 29 *Univ. of Chicago Law Review* 640 (1962).

———. "Courts as Small Groups." 79 *Harvard Law Review* 1556 (1966).

Novak, Linda. "The Precedential Value of Supreme Court Plurality Decisions." 80 *Columbia Law Review* 756 (May 1980).

Paulsen, Monrad G. "Some Insights Into the Burger Court." 27 *Oklahoma Law Review* 677 (1974).

Rehnquist, William. "Chief Justices I Never Knew." 3 *Hastings Law Quarterly* 637 (Summer 1976).

Richardson, William A. "Chief Justice of the United States or Chief Justice of the Supreme Court of the United States." *N.E. Historical and Genealogical Register* (July 1895).

Rossett, Arthur. "Chief Justice Earl Warren: A Tribute." 2 *Hastings Constitutional Law Quarterly* 1 (Winter 1975).

Seddig, Robert G. "John Marshall and the Origins of Supreme Court Leadership." 36 *Univ. of Pittsburgh Law Review* 785 (Summer 1975).

Steamer, Robert J. "Judicial Leadership: English and American Experience." *Comparative Judicial Systems: Conceptual and Empirical Analysis,* ed. John Schmidhauser. Santa Barbara: Sage-IPSA Publications, 1986.

Stephenson, D. Grier, Jr. "The Chief Justice as Leader: The Case of Morrison Remick Waite." 14 *William and Mary Law Review* 899 (1973).

Taft, William H. "The Right of Private Property." 3 *Michigan Law Journal* 215 (Aug. 1894).

Tamm, Edward A., and Paul C. Reardon. "Warren E. Burger and the Administration of Justice." 1981 *Brigham Young University Law Review* 447.

Totenberg, Nina. "Supreme Court Seethes." *The National Observer* (June 17, 1972), p. 3.

Ulmer, S. Sidney. "The Use of Power in the Supreme Court: The Opinion Assignments of Earl Warren, 1953–1960." 19 *Journal of Public Law* 49 (1970).

Wheeler, Russell. "Extrajudicial Activities of the Early Supreme Court." *The Supreme Court Review* (1979), pp. 123–58.

Table of Cases

Table of Cases

Table of Cases

Table of Cases

INDEX

Abortion, 201–202, 217n
Abraham, Henry, 33n, 89n, 153n, 154n
Abrams, Floyd, 215n
Adams, John: 39–41, 229; on Marshall, 40
Administrative Office of U.S. Courts, 13
Alien and Sedition Acts, 73
Aliens, 76, 146–147
Alschuler, Albert W., 215n
Armstrong, Scott, 214n, 215n
Atkinson, David N., 93n

Baker, Leonard, 40, 89n, 90n, 91n
Bancroft, George, 132
Beard, Charles, 288n
Belden, Thomas G. and Marva R., 289n
Beveridge, Albert, 34n, 89n, 91n
Bickel, Alexander M., 35n
Bill of Rights. *See* First Amendment; Searches and seizures; Exclusionary rule; Self-incrimination; Double jeopardy; Right to counsel
Black, Hugo: 61, 87; feud with Jackson, 247
Blaustein, Albert P., 33n, 154n, 156n, 215n
Brandeis, Louis: 174–175; on White, 136
Brant, Irving, 92n
Brennan, William, 87, 207–208
Brethren, The, 181–182, 214n
Brown, William G., 287n
Brownell, Herbert, 171
Burger, Warren Earl: 8; biography, 18, 169–173; circuit judge, 171; Court manager, 177–183; the conference, 179–180; opinion assignments, 180–181; extra-Court activities, 186–192, 215n, 216n; on judicial reform, 22, 187–188, 189–192; on prison reform, 188–189; judicial philosophy, 171, 201–211; on abortion, 201–202; on executive privilege, 202–203; on desegregation, 203–204; on sex

discrimination, 204; on self-incrimination, 205; on right to counsel, 205; on Miranda rule, 205; on death penalty, 205–206; on exclusionary rule, 206–207; on searches and seizures, 206–207; on obscenity, 207–208; on freedom of religion, 208–211
Burr, Aaron: trial, 51, 72–73
Business affected with a public interest, 138–139, 195–197

Catron, John, 104
Certiorari, 25–26, 185
Chase, Salmon P.: on office of Chief Justice, 10–11; biography, 234–240; U.S. senator, 237; secretary of treasury, 238–239; Court manager, 248–251; the conference, 250; on judicial reform, 250–251; judicial philosophy, 251–260; on habeas corpus, 251–252, 254–255; on ex post facto laws, 253; on congressional control of Supreme Court jurisdiction, 23, 254–255; on nature of Union, 257–258; on legal tender question, 258–260; on impeachment of Andrew Johnson, 260–263; and Radical Congress, 251–257
Chase, Samuel, 23–24
Chief Justice of the United States, Office of: duties, ix–x, 3–4; salary, 1789, 4; 1985, 4. *See also* individual chief justices
Circuit Court of Appeals Act of 1891, 134–135; 185
Circuit duty, 104–105
Civil Rights Act of 1875, 141
Clay, Henry, 113
Clear and present danger doctrine, 278–279
Cleveland, Grover 122, 125–126
Commerce clause: 71–72, 107–108, 137–139, 144–145, 146, 193–194, 273–274; "flow theory," 193
Communist Party (USA), 79, 278–279
Conference of Senior Circuit Judges, 184

Index

319

Index

Kirkendall, Richard, 291n
Klinkhamer, Sister Marie, 158n
Kluger, Richard, 93n
Konefsky, Samuel, 288n
Kraus, Michael, 288n
Kurland, Philip, 35n, 96n

Landever, Arthur R., 216n
Landis, James, 33n, 156n
Lash, Joseph P., 91n, 157n
Levy, Leonard W., 96n
Lewis, Anthony: 90n, 214n; on
  Warren, 49
Lewis, Walker, 153n, 154n
Liberty of contract. *See* Due process
  of law
Lincoln, Abraham: 237–240, 248–
  249; on Chase, 240
Lomask, Milton, 292n
Loyalty oaths, 253

Magrath, C. Peter, 155n, 156n, 158n
Marshall, John: 7,8; biography, 38–43;
  secretary of state, 40; Court
  manager, 50–53; the conference, 52;
  reaction to Jefferson attack, 23–24;
  judicial philosophy, 69–74; on
  judicial review, 70; on implied
  powers, 70–71; on national
  supremacy, 71; on interstate
  commerce, 71–72; on contract
  clause, 72; on bankruptcy, 72; on
  corporations, 72; on treason, 72–73;
  on Alien and Sedition Acts, 73
Mason, Alpheus T., 265, 33n, 157n,
  213n, 214n, 215n, 216n, 288n,
  290n, 291n, 292n,
McElroy, Robert, 156n
McElwain, Edwin, 34n, 91n, 92n
McGurn, Barrett, 33n, 177–178
McKenna, Joseph, 175
McLean, John: on Taney, 108
McReynolds, James C., 174, 175, 177
Mersky, Roy M., 33n, 154n, 156n,
  215n
Miller, Arthur S., 173, 214n, 215n
Miller, Samuel F.: on Waite, 129; on
  Chase, 283
Miranda rule, 83, 84–86, 205
Moody, Graham B., Jr., 93n
Morgan, Donald, 91n, 94n
Morris, Jeffrey, ix, 156n, 157n
Morris, Richard B., 287n
Morrow, Lance, 33n

Murphy, Walter, xiiin, 33n, 35n
Murray, Charles A., 90n

National Center for State Courts, 191
National Court of Appeals, 189–190
National Labor Relations Act, 58–60
Naturalization Act of 1940, 270
Nevins, Allan, 156n
New Deal, 58–60
Newmyer, Kent, 94n
Nisbet, Charles, 99
Nixon, Richard M., 169–173, 202
Novak, Linda, 32n

Opinion assignments, 29. *See also*
  individual chief justices

Palmer, Ben W., 94n, 153n
Paterson, William, 40, 41
Paulsen, Monrad, 214n
Pfeffer, Leo, 94n
Pinckney, William: on Taney, 99
"Political questions," 112
Pollock, Jack H., 96n
Pomeroy, Samuel C., 239
Powell, Lewis, 26
Pringle, Henry F., 33n, 213n, 217n
Pritchett, C. H., xiiin, 35n, 290n
Privileges and immunities, 140, 273
Public Utility Holding Company Act,
  58
Pusey, Merlo J.: 35n, 156n; on
  Hughes, 247

Racial discrimination: in education,
  65–66, 77–78, 203–204, 277; on
  common carriers, 76, 78, 141, 145;
  in voting, 140–141, 152, 270–271;
  in housing, 152, 276–277, 291n
Radical Congress, 251–257
Randolph, John: on Marshall, 41–42,
  68
Reapportionment, 83–84
Reardon, Paul C., 215n, 216n
Rehnquist, William, 27, 35n, 208–209
Richardson, William A., 32n
Right to counsel, 85–86, 205
Roberts, Owen J.: 247, 91n; on
  Hughes, 55
Rodell, Fred, 291n, 292n
Roosevelt, Franklin D., 23, 58–60,
  243, 245–246
Roosevelt, Theodore, 165–166
Rosenthal, A. S., 291n

Index